AI Prompts for Productivity

A Practical Guide to Automating Tasks and Boosting Your Career

Disclaimer:

This book provides educational guidance on using artificial intelligence (AI) for workplace productivity and career development. The information is based on the state of the field at the time of writing. The world of AI, including the capabilities of specific models and platforms, evolves at an extremely rapid pace, and the information and techniques herein are subject to change.

While every effort has been made to ensure the accuracy and effectiveness of the guidance provided, the author and publisher make no warranty, express or implied, regarding the content. The strategies and prompts described in this book do not guarantee specific career outcomes, promotions, or levels of productivity. The reader assumes full responsibility for the use of this information and for their own application of AI tools.

It is the reader's sole responsibility to adhere to their employer's policies regarding the use of AI, to ensure the security of confidential or proprietary information, and to verify the factual accuracy of all AI-generated content. This book is not a substitute for professional legal advice, financial counsel, or individualized career coaching.

Table of Contents

Introduction: The Prompt Revolution

Imagine it's Monday morning. You arrive at your desk, virtual or physical, and are greeted by a familiar sight: a flood of emails, a list of pending reports, and the looming deadline for a major project proposal. Your calendar is a colorful mosaic of meetings, each demanding preparation. For many of us, this isn't imagination, it's just Monday. The bulk of our week is spent not on the strategic, creative, or deeply analytical work we were hired to do, but on the administrative tasks that keep the wheels of business turning. We draft routine emails, summarize long documents, format presentations, and chase information. This is the work that consumes our time but rarely moves the needle on our careers or contributes to our professional fulfillment.

Now, imagine a different Monday. You still have the emails, the reports, and the proposal. But this time, you have a partner. A tireless, knowledgeable, and exceptionally fast assistant who can help you clear your inbox in a fraction of the time, draft that entire project proposal based on a few key points, summarize hours of meeting transcripts into actionable takeaways, and even help you generate a strategic framework for your next big project. This isn't a human assistant, but an Artificial Intelligence tool, and your ability to communicate with it effectively is the key that unlocks this new level of productivity.

Welcome to the prompt revolution.

The conversation you have with an AI is called a "prompt." It is the single most important component in leveraging the immense power of modern AI. The quality of what you get out of an AI is directly, and unchangeably, tied to the quality of what you put in. A vague, lazy prompt will get you a generic, unhelpful response. A clear, specific, and well-structured prompt will get you a detailed, insightful, and immediately useful result.

This is why learning to prompt is not just another technical skill. It is rapidly becoming the most valuable professional skill of the decade. It is the modern equivalent of learning how to type in the 1980s, how to use the internet for research in the 1990s, or how to master a spreadsheet in the 2000s. Each of these was a fundamental shift that separated those who could leverage new technology from those who were left behind. AI prompting is the next great leap. It is a form of digital literacy that redefines what one person can accomplish in a day.

This book is your practical, hands-on guide to mastering this essential skill. It's not about the complex theory behind AI or how these large language models are built. It's about communication. It's about learning a new language to collaborate with a powerful new kind of professional partner. It's about turning your ideas and needs into precise instructions that an AI can understand and execute, saving you time, elevating the quality of your work, and freeing you up to focus on what truly matters.

Why AI Prompting is the Most Valuable Skill of the Decade

In any profession, your value is determined by the results you produce. Whether you are a project manager delivering a project on time, a marketer creating a successful campaign, an entrepreneur building a business, or a student writing a research paper, the quality and efficiency of your output are paramount.

For decades, the primary tools for increasing this output were time management techniques and software applications like word processors and spreadsheets. These tools helped us organize our work, but they didn't do the work for us.

AI changes this equation entirely. For the first time, we have a tool that can actively participate in the creation, analysis, and execution of our tasks. It can write, summarize, analyze, code, plan, and brainstorm alongside us. But this powerful engine doesn't have a complicated dashboard with hundreds of buttons and menus. Its user interface is simply language. Your words are the controls.

This makes the act of prompting, of crafting the right instructions, both the bottleneck and the amplifier. Your ability to prompt well determines how effectively you can leverage this technology. Here's why this skill is so critical:

- **It creates a productivity advantage.** The professional who can use AI to draft a comprehensive report in thirty minutes has a massive advantage over a colleague who spends four hours on the same task. The time saved is not just about efficiency, it is about opportunity. That reclaimed time can be reinvested into strategic thinking, client relationships, creative problem-solving, or learning new skills, the very activities that lead to promotions and career growth.
- **It improves the quality of your work.** AI can serve as an expert consultant available on demand. You can ask it to review your writing for clarity, challenge your assumptions in a business strategy, or generate alternative approaches to a problem you're stuck on. Using AI effectively is like having a team of tireless junior analysts, editors, and researchers at your disposal. It helps you catch errors, refine your ideas,

and explore possibilities you might have missed, leading to a more polished and thoughtful final product.

- **It accelerates learning and skill development.** Need to get up to speed on a new industry for a project? Want to understand the basics of a programming language or a complex financial model? Instead of spending hours searching for articles and tutorials, you can ask an AI to explain these concepts to you in simple terms, provide examples, and even quiz you on your understanding. A well-crafted prompt can create a personalized learning path, making continuous professional development faster and more accessible than ever before.
- **It future-proofs your career.** As AI becomes more integrated into business operations, companies will not just value, but expect, employees to be proficient in using these tools. Demonstrating your ability to leverage AI to drive results will become a key differentiator in the job market. It signals that you are adaptable, efficient, and technologically fluent. Those who wait to develop this skill risk being outpaced by those who embrace it today.

Mastering AI prompting is not about becoming a programmer or a data scientist. It is about becoming a more effective communicator, a more strategic thinker, and a more productive professional. It's about shifting your focus from "doing the work" to "designing the work" and letting your AI partner handle the execution.

What This Book Will Teach You (And What It Won't)

My goal is to provide you with a clear, practical, and immediately applicable guide to using AI in your professional life. This book is designed to be a bridge, taking you from a basic awareness of AI to a state of confident, daily use.

Here is what this book will teach you:

- **The Foundations of Effective Prompting:** You will learn the core components of a great prompt. We will break down the anatomy of an instruction, exploring why specificity, context, and format are crucial for getting high-quality results.
- **A Practical Framework for Crafting Prompts:** You will get a simple, repeatable method for building powerful prompts for any task. We will move beyond guesswork and give you a structured approach to follow, ensuring your prompts are clear, concise, and effective.
- **How to Automate Your Most Repetitive Tasks:** We will cover real-world, career-specific use cases. You will learn how to write prompts to manage your email, prepare for meetings, create presentations, write reports, generate marketing copy, and much more. This book is filled with ready-to-use templates you can adapt immediately.
- **Advanced Techniques for Complex Projects:** You will learn how to break down large, multi-step projects into a sequence of prompts, essentially managing the AI to produce a complex deliverable like a business plan or a detailed research summary.
- **How to Integrate AI into Your Daily Workflow:** This isn't just about using AI for one-off tasks. We will explore how to build AI-powered routines and systems that create consistent time savings and productivity gains day after day.
- **How to Think Like a Prompt Engineer:** You will learn to diagnose why a prompt isn't working and how to refine it iteratively. You'll move from simply using templates to understanding the principles behind them, allowing you to

create your own custom prompts for any challenge you face.

Equally important is what this book will not teach you:

- **It will not teach you to be an AI developer.** We will not be diving into Python code, neural networks, or the deep technical workings of AI models. This book is for the user, not the builder. The explanations are simple, analogy-driven, and focused only on what you need to know to be an effective prompter.
- **It is not a theoretical academic text.** While based on proven principles, this guide is all about action. Every chapter is designed to give you skills you can apply the same day. There is no fluff, just practical advice and real-world examples.
- **It is not a source of get-rich-quick schemes.** AI is a powerful productivity tool, not a substitute for professional effort, expertise, and ethics. This book will show you how to augment your skills, not replace them. The goal is to make you better at your job, not to suggest you can achieve success without work.
- **It does not claim AI is a perfect, error-free tool.** AI can make mistakes, provide outdated information, and sometimes generate nonsensical output. A critical part of this guide is teaching you how to work around these limitations, how to fact-check the output, and how to maintain quality control. We will treat AI as a powerful but fallible partner.

By the end of this book, you will be able to approach any professional task and ask yourself, "How can I use AI to do this faster and better?" And you will have the skills and confidence to answer that question.

How to Use This Guide Effectively

This book is structured to be your personal coach, guiding you from foundational knowledge to advanced application. To get the most out of it, I encourage you to treat it as an interactive workbook rather than a passive read.

1. **Read with an AI Tool Open.** The best way to learn prompting is by doing. As you read through the chapters, have your preferred AI tool (like ChatGPT, Gemini, Claude, or Copilot) open in another window. When you see an example prompt, don't just read it. Copy it, paste it into the tool, and see the result for yourself.
2. **Experiment with the Examples.** Don't stop at just running the examples. Tweak them. Change a word, add a constraint, or ask for a different format. See how small changes in the prompt can lead to big differences in the output. This hands-on experimentation is the fastest way to build your intuition.
3. **Complete the Exercises.** Many chapters include small exercises and scenarios. These are designed to help you apply what you've learned to realistic professional situations. Take a few minutes to complete them. The practice will solidify your understanding and prepare you for using these skills in your own work.
4. **Build Your Personal Prompt Library.** As you discover prompts that work well for your specific tasks, save them. Create a dedicated document or note-taking file where you store your most effective prompts. Organize them by category (e.g., "Email Prompts," "Project Planning Prompts"). This library will become your personal productivity arsenal, saving you from having to reinvent the wheel for common tasks.
5. **Follow the Structure.** The book is intentionally designed to

build your skills progressively.

- **Part I: Foundations** will give you the essential mental models for understanding AI and prompts.
- **Part II: Core Skills** will teach you the specific techniques for crafting and refining prompts.
- **Part III: Professional Applications** provides a deep dive into career-specific use cases with extensive templates.
- **Part IV: Workflow Integration** shows you how to make AI a seamless part of your daily routine.
- **Part V: Advanced Applications** explores strategic uses for AI in decision-making and career growth.
- **Part VI: Mastery and Future-Proofing** will help you develop true intuition and stay current in this fast-changing field.

While it may be tempting to jump straight to the chapter most relevant to your job, I strongly encourage you to start with the foundational chapters. Understanding the "why" behind effective prompts will make you much better at applying the "how."

Who This Book Is For

This guide is written for anyone who wants to work smarter in the age of AI. It doesn't matter if you are a tech enthusiast or someone who feels overwhelmed by new technology. The principles are universal, and the language is designed to be accessible and jargon-free. If you recognize yourself in any of the following descriptions, this book is for you.

- **The Busy Professional:** You're a manager, analyst, consultant, or team member in a corporate environment. Your days are filled with meetings, emails, and reports. You feel like you're constantly busy but not always productive. You want to automate the administrative overhead of your job so you can focus on high-impact strategic work that gets you noticed.

- **The Entrepreneur or Small Business Owner:** You are the CEO, head of marketing, sales lead, and customer support specialist all rolled into one. Your most valuable resource is your time. You need to produce professional-quality documents, marketing materials, and business strategies without a large team or budget. You're looking for a force multiplier to help you compete and grow.
- **The Freelancer or Consultant:** You sell your expertise, but a significant portion of your time is spent on non-billable work like writing proposals, managing clients, and marketing your services. You want to streamline your operations, deliver projects faster, and take on more clients without burning out.
- **The Student or Researcher:** You are navigating academic life, which involves absorbing vast amounts of information, writing essays, conducting research, and preparing for exams. You want to learn more efficiently, organize your notes effectively, and improve the quality of your writing and analysis.
- **The Job Seeker or Career-Changer:** You are looking to enter the job market or pivot to a new industry. You want to stand out from the crowd with a polished resume, a compelling cover letter, and excellent interview skills. You want to demonstrate that you possess the modern skills employers are looking for and can add immediate value.

In short, this book is for anyone who is curious, ambitious, and ready to embrace a new way of working. It's for people who believe that technology should serve us, making our work more efficient, our ideas stronger, and our careers more fulfilling.

The Three-Layer Framework: Understanding → Crafting → Applying

To make your journey into AI prompting as clear as possible, I've structured the entire philosophy of this book around a simple, three-layer framework. Mastering each of these layers, in order, is the key to becoming truly proficient.

Layer 1: Understanding (The "Why")
This is your foundation. Before you can give effective instructions, you need a basic mental model of who you're talking to. This doesn't mean you need to know about algorithms or code. It means understanding what an AI language model is at a conceptual level, how it "thinks" in patterns, what its core strengths are (like summarizing, reformatting, and brainstorming), and, just as importantly, what its weaknesses are (like a lack of true understanding, a tendency to invent facts, and an absence of common sense). Understanding this layer prevents frustration. It helps you set realistic expectations and work with the AI's nature, not against it. Part I of this book is dedicated to building this foundational understanding.
Layer 2: Crafting (The "How")
This is the mechanical skill of building a good prompt. Once you understand what the AI is capable of, you need to learn the language it understands best—the language of clear, structured instructions. This layer involves learning the essential components of a powerful prompt: providing context, defining the task, specifying the format, and setting constraints. It's where you learn specific techniques to get the AI to adopt a certain persona, follow a particular style, or reason through a complex problem.

Crafting is the technical core of prompt engineering. Part II is focused entirely on honing these core skills.
Layer 3: Applying (The "What")
This is where the value is created. With a solid understanding and the ability to craft precise prompts, you can now apply these skills to solve real-world professional problems. This layer is about strategy. It's about looking at your daily to-do list and identifying which tasks are best suited for AI automation. It's about building workflows and systems that integrate AI into your routine for maximum benefit. This is where you use your prompting skills to write that marketing plan, analyze that customer feedback, or draft that project update. This is the ultimate goal, and it's the focus of Parts III, IV, and V of this book.
Think of it like learning to cook. First, you need to **understand** your ingredients and your tools (what an oven does, how heat works). Then, you need to learn the techniques of **crafting** a dish (how to chop, how to mix, how to follow a recipe). Finally, you can **apply** those skills to cook specific meals for different occasions (a quick weeknight dinner, a formal presentation).

By moving through these three layers, you will build a complete and durable skill set. You won't just be copying and pasting templates; you will be a confident and creative AI collaborator, ready to tackle any challenge that comes your way.

Your journey to becoming an AI-powered professional starts now. Let's begin.

Part I: Foundations – Understanding AI and Prompts

Chapter 1: AI Demystified – What You Need to Know

Welcome to the foundation. Before we can start building powerful prompts and automating our work, we need to lay a simple, solid groundwork of understanding. The term "Artificial Intelligence" can feel intimidating, conjuring images of complex code and futuristic robots. The reality, at least for our purposes, is much simpler and more practical.

The goal of this chapter is to demystify the technology you're about to use. We are going to strip away the jargon and the hype to give you a clear, functional understanding of what today's AI language models are, how they work, and what that means for you as a user. You do not need a technical background to understand these concepts. In fact, thinking like a user, not an engineer, is the key to becoming a great prompter.

We will explore what is happening behind the screen when you type in a prompt, address some common myths that can hold people back, and establish a realistic set of expectations for what AI can and cannot do. We will also cover the critically important rules of the road regarding privacy, security, and ethics, ensuring you can use these tools safely and responsibly. Finally, we'll take a quick tour of the major AI platforms available today.

Think of this chapter as the essential briefing before you start collaborating with your new AI partner. By the end, you'll have the mental model you need to move from being a passive user to a confident and strategic director of AI.

What AI Language Models Actually Are (Explained Simply)

Let's start with the most fundamental question: what exactly is the tool we are using? When you interact with an AI like ChatGPT, Gemini, or Claude, you are communicating with a Large Language Model, or LLM. That might sound technical, but the concept is surprisingly intuitive.

Imagine the most dedicated, single-minded intern you can think of. This intern has not gone to school in a traditional sense, nor do they have any life experience. Instead, they have been given a single, monumental task: to read a massive portion of the text available on the internet, millions of books, articles, reports, and websites. They have spent all their time absorbing this information, but not in the way a human does. They haven't learned facts or formed opinions. They have only learned one thing: patterns.

This intern has become an unparalleled expert in pattern recognition. They know, with incredible statistical accuracy, which words tend to follow other words. They know how sentences are structured in a business email versus how they are structured in a technical manual. They have analyzed the patterns of a project plan, a marketing brief, and a legal document.

When you give this intern a prompt, you are giving them a starting pattern. For example, if you say, "Write a professional email to a client about a project delay," the intern immediately recognizes this pattern. It scans its vast internal library of text and calculates the most probable sequence of words that should come next to complete this pattern successfully. It might start with "Dear [Client Name]," because its data shows that's a common and appropriate way to begin. It will continue, word by word, predicting the next most likely word to create a coherent and contextually relevant response.

This is, in essence, what an LLM is. It is a sophisticated pattern-matching and prediction engine for human language. It doesn't "know" that a project is delayed or "understand" a client's potential frustration. It simply knows that certain words and phrases are statistically likely to appear in a professional email that discusses a project delay. It is a form of "autocomplete" on an incredibly grand scale, capable of generating paragraphs, pages, and entire documents that are statistically probable and grammatically correct.

This is the first and most important mental model to hold: you are not talking to a thinking entity. You are providing an input pattern to a system that is expertly designed to predict the next part of that pattern. This simple fact is the key to everything that follows.

How AI "Thinks" and Why It Matters for Prompting

Understanding that AI operates on pattern prediction, not true comprehension, is the secret to effective prompting. It changes how you approach your instructions. You are not communicating with a colleague who can infer your meaning and fill in the gaps. You are programming a linguistic machine with words.

Let's use another analogy: a GPS navigation system in a car.

A GPS doesn't "know" the city. It doesn't understand what a traffic jam feels like or appreciate the scenic view on a particular street. It has a map (its training data) and an algorithm. When you give it a starting point and a destination, it calculates the most efficient path based on the patterns and rules in its data. It is predicting the best route.

The quality of its directions depends entirely on the quality of your input.

- **If you give a vague destination ("downtown"), you will get a vague or useless route.** The GPS doesn't know which building you're going to, where you need to park, or what your purpose is.
- **If you provide a precise address (123 Main Street, Suite 400), you will get a precise and useful route.** The system has the specific data it needs to calculate an effective path.

Prompting an AI works in the exact same way. It needs a clear destination from you. Let's see how this plays out in a common workplace scenario.

Professional Scenario: Drafting a Project Update

Imagine you need to draft a quick update for stakeholders on a new software implementation project.

A weak prompt (a vague destination):
"Write a project update."
An AI's response to this will be generic. It might produce a template with placeholders like "[Project Name]" and "[Key Accomplishments]." It's not useful because the AI has no specific pattern to work from. It's like telling your GPS to "just drive."

A strong prompt (a precise destination):
"Act as a project manager. Write a concise, professional project status update for stakeholders. The project is the 'Q4 Enterprise Software Upgrade.' We are currently in Phase 2. The key

accomplishment this week was the successful migration of the user database, completed two days ahead of schedule. The next milestone is to begin user acceptance testing on Monday. The tone should be confident and reassuring."

This prompt gives the AI everything it needs.

- **Role:** "Act as a project manager."
- **Task:** "Write a concise, professional project status update."
- **Context:** The project name, the current phase, a key accomplishment, and the next milestone.
- **Format/Tone:** "Confident and reassuring."

With this level of detail, the AI has a rich starting pattern. It can now predict a sequence of words that perfectly matches the request, producing a draft that is 90% of the way there, saving you significant time and mental energy.

Why this matters for your daily work:

1. **Context is Your Responsibility.** An AI has no awareness of your current projects, your company's goals, or the history of your client relationships. You must provide all the relevant context in the prompt. The more you provide, the better the output will be.
2. **Specificity is a Requirement, Not an Option.** Vague instructions lead to vague results. Every key detail you omit is a gap the AI will have to fill with generic, probabilistic language. Don't make it guess.
3. **The AI Has No Common Sense.** You cannot assume the AI knows unstated industry norms or the subtle politics of your workplace. If something is important, state it explicitly in the prompt. You are the source of all real-world knowledge in this collaboration.

Treating every prompt as a mini-briefing for a very literal-minded assistant is the most effective way to get the results you want.

Common Misconceptions About AI Capabilities

The rapid rise of AI has been accompanied by a whirlwind of hype, excitement, and fear. To use these tools effectively, we need to separate the reality from the myths. Let's address some of the most common misconceptions.

Myth 1: AI truly understands the content it generates.
Reality: As we've discussed, AI is a pattern-matching engine, not a conscious entity. It does not comprehend concepts like a human does. It can generate a brilliant analysis of a financial report because it has processed countless financial reports and knows the patterns of language used in them. It doesn't actually understand what "net profit margin" means for the business. This is why you, the professional with domain expertise, must always be the final judge of the output's quality and accuracy.
Myth 2: The information AI provides is always factual and correct.
Reality: This is perhaps the most dangerous misconception. AI models can and do make things up. This phenomenon is often called "hallucination." Because the AI's primary goal is to generate a plausible-sounding sequence of words, it will sometimes invent facts, sources, or data points if it doesn't have the correct information in its training data. The invented information will often be written in a confident and convincing tone.
Key Takeaway: You must assume that any factual claim, statistic, or specific data point generated by an AI is unverified until you have confirmed it with a reliable source. Never trust, always verify.
Myth 3: AI is going to take over most professional jobs.

Reality: The more likely scenario is that AI will significantly change jobs by automating specific tasks. Just as spreadsheets automated manual calculations but created a new demand for financial analysts, AI will automate routine administrative and creative tasks, freeing up professionals to focus on higher-level strategy, client relationships, and complex problem-solving. The common refrain in the industry is that AI won't replace you, but a person using AI will. This book is about making you that person.
Myth 4: AI can think creatively and strategically on its own.
Reality: AI is an incredibly powerful tool for augmenting human creativity and strategy, but it is not a replacement for them. It can brainstorm a list of 50 marketing slogans in seconds because it can rapidly combine words and concepts in novel ways based on its training data. It cannot, however, have a genuinely original strategic insight based on a deep understanding of your company's unique position in the market. It provides the raw material, the building blocks of ideas. You provide the strategic filter, the creative spark, and the final decision.
By holding a realistic view of AI's capabilities, you can use it as the powerful tool it is, without falling into the common traps of over-trusting its output or underestimating your own critical role in the process.

The Limits of AI: What It Can and Cannot Do

To use any tool effectively, you must know its strengths and weaknesses. You use a hammer for nails and a screwdriver for screws. Using AI is no different. Knowing when to use AI and when to rely on your own skills is crucial for productivity.

What AI Excels At (Its Strengths):

- **Summarizing and Condensing Information:** AI is brilliant at reading a long report, article, or meeting transcript and distilling it into key bullet points or a concise summary.

- **Drafting First Versions:** It is an exceptional "first draft" generator. Use it for emails, proposals, reports, marketing copy, and project plans. It can get you from a blank page to a solid draft in moments.
- **Brainstorming and Ideation:** Stuck for ideas? Ask an AI to generate a list of potential project names, blog post topics, or solutions to a business problem. It can provide a wide range of starting points.
- **Reformatting and Repurposing:** AI can effortlessly turn a paragraph into a bulleted list, a set of notes into a formal email, or a blog post into a series of social media updates.
- **Explaining Complex Topics:** You can ask an AI to explain a difficult concept (like blockchain or a statistical method) in simple terms, using an analogy, as if explaining it to a beginner.
- **Language and Grammar:** It is an excellent tool for proofreading, improving sentence structure, and translating text between languages.

Professional Scenario: Time-Saving Technique
Before your next one-hour meeting, copy and paste the meeting agenda into an AI tool with the following prompt: "Based on this meeting agenda, generate a list of 5-7 critical questions I should be prepared to discuss. For each question, provide three key talking points." This can help you prepare for a meeting in 10 minutes instead of 30.

Where AI Struggles (Its Weaknesses):

- **Real-Time Information:** Standard LLMs have a knowledge cut-off date based on when their training data was collected. They do not know about events that happened yesterday.

(Note: Some AI tools integrate with search engines to mitigate this, but the core model's knowledge is not real-time.)

- **Factual Accuracy and Verification:** As mentioned, AI can hallucinate. It is not a reliable search engine for facts and should not be used as a sole source of truth.
- **Deep Strategic Thinking:** AI lacks the business context, industry experience, and nuanced understanding to make high-stakes strategic decisions. It can provide data and frameworks, but the final judgment must be human.
- **Subjective and Nuanced Opinions:** While you can ask an AI to adopt a persona, it does not have genuine opinions, taste, or ethical judgment.
- **Sensitive or Confidential Information:** For security and privacy reasons, AI should never be used to process proprietary company data, personal employee information, or any other form of confidential material.
- **Complex Mathematical or Logical Reasoning:** While improving, many LLMs can still struggle with multi-step math problems or complex logical reasoning that requires precise, step-by-step accuracy.

The Productivity Rule of Thumb: Use AI for the first 80% of a task. Let it do the heavy lifting of research, brainstorming, and drafting. Then, apply your human expertise for the final 20%—the critical work of verifying, refining, strategizing, and personalizing.

Privacy, Security, and Ethical Considerations When Using AI Tools

Now we arrive at the most important non-negotiable rules of using AI at work. Engaging with these tools without a clear understanding of the risks is a recipe for professional and corporate disaster. Treat this section as a mandatory pre-flight checklist.

Privacy: The Golden Rule

Most public AI tools, especially the free versions, may use your conversations to train their models. This means that whatever you type into the prompt could potentially be seen by developers or become part of the model's future training data. Therefore, the golden rule is absolute:

Never, under any circumstances, input sensitive or confidential information into a public AI tool.

What constitutes sensitive information?

- **Personally Identifiable Information (PII):** Names, addresses, phone numbers, email addresses, or any data about employees, clients, or customers.
- **Company Financial Data:** Revenue figures, profit margins, budgets, or forecasts.
- **Proprietary Information:** Trade secrets, product roadmaps, internal strategies, client lists, or unreleased project details.
- **Login Credentials or Security Information:** Any passwords, API keys, or security protocols.

Workplace Script: What to Do Instead

Let's say you want to summarize a set of performance reviews to identify common themes for a team training program.

Unsafe Action: Copying and pasting entire performance reviews, with names and specific feedback, into an AI. This is a major privacy breach.

Safe and Smart Action: Anonymize and abstract the data first. Go through the reviews and pull out only the generic feedback points.

Your input to the AI should look like this:
"I am developing a training program for a sales team. I have collected the following anonymous feedback points from performance reviews. Please categorize these points into 3-5 key themes and suggest a potential training module for each theme.
Feedback Points:

- 'Needs to improve closing techniques on larger deals.'
- 'Excellent at building initial client rapport but struggles with follow-up communication.'
- 'Could be more proactive in lead generation.'
- 'Has difficulty overcoming price objections.'
- 'Struggles to articulate the technical value proposition of our new software.'"

This gives the AI all the information it needs to help you without exposing any confidential data.

Security: Check Your Company's Policy

Many organizations are now establishing clear policies on the use of external AI tools. Some may have a corporate subscription to a specific, more secure AI platform, while others may block public tools entirely. Before you integrate any AI tool into your workflow, you must:

1. **Consult your IT or Security Department.** Ask them for the official company policy on AI usage.
2. **Ask for Recommended Tools.** They may have a preferred platform that has been vetted for security and has enterprise-

level privacy controls.

3. **Default to Caution.** If there is no clear policy, operate under the assumption that you should not be using public AI tools for any work-related tasks that involve non-public information.

Ethical Considerations: You Are Accountable

Using AI responsibly goes beyond just privacy and security. It requires professional accountability.

- **Transparency:** Do not present AI-generated text as entirely your own, especially in situations where originality is expected. It is a tool for assistance, not a tool for plagiarism. A good practice is to use it for a first draft and then heavily edit it to reflect your own voice and ideas.
- **Accountability for Output:** You are 100% responsible for the work you submit. If an AI-generated report contains a factual error or a biased statement, the fault is yours for not catching it. The AI is your intern, not the one to take the blame.
- **Bias Awareness:** AI models are trained on a snapshot of the internet, which is filled with human biases. As a result, AI output can sometimes contain stereotypes or skewed perspectives. It is your job to review the content critically and edit it to ensure it is fair, objective, and inclusive.

Overview of Major AI Platforms

The AI landscape is evolving at a breathtaking pace, with new tools and updates appearing constantly. Getting attached to one single platform is less important than understanding the general ecosystem. The prompting skills you learn in this book will be transferable across all of them. Here is a brief, non-technical overview of some of the major players as of today.

- **ChatGPT (from OpenAI):** This is the tool that brought LLMs into the mainstream. It is widely known for its strong conversational abilities and its knack for generating creative and human-like text. It's an excellent all-purpose tool for drafting, brainstorming, and explaining concepts. It typically comes in a free version (which is very capable) and a paid subscription version that offers access to more powerful and up-to-date models.
- **Gemini (from Google):** As Google's flagship AI, Gemini's strength lies in its deep integration with the vast knowledge of Google Search, often allowing it to provide more current information than other models. It is designed to be a powerful reasoning engine and is often praised for its ability to handle multi-step logical problems.
- **Claude (from Anthropic):** Claude is a strong competitor often highlighted for two things. First is its large "context window," which means it can process and analyze extremely large documents in a single prompt (think entire research papers or business plans). Second is its emphasis on AI safety and producing more reliable and predictable outputs, guided by a set of principles.
- **Copilot (from Microsoft):** Microsoft's strategy is to embed AI directly into the tools professionals use every day. Copilot is not just a standalone chatbot, it is an AI assistant built into Windows, the Edge browser, and, most importantly, the Microsoft 365 suite (Word, Excel, PowerPoint, Outlook, and Teams). Its primary advantage is its deep integration with your own work documents and data in a secure environment.

Which one should you use?

My advice is to experiment. Most offer free versions or trials. Try the same prompt on two or three different platforms and see which output you prefer. You might find that one is better for creative writing while another is better for technical summaries. The best tool is the one that works best for you and your specific tasks, and that complies with your organization's policies.

The core lesson is this: don't worry about picking the "perfect" tool. Focus on mastering the universal skill of prompting. That is the skill that will endure.

With this foundation in place, you now have a realistic and practical understanding of the tool in your hands. You know what it is, how it "thinks," where its limits lie, and how to use it safely. Now, you're ready to move to the next layer: learning how to craft the perfect prompt.

Chapter 2: The Anatomy of an Effective Prompt

In the last chapter, we established a clear mental model for what an AI language model is: a sophisticated pattern-matching engine that predicts the next word in a sequence. We learned that it doesn't "think" or "understand" in the human sense, which means our instructions need to be incredibly clear and precise. We are not having a conversation with a colleague who can read between the lines. We are providing a blueprint to a builder who will follow our instructions to the letter.

Now, it's time to learn how to draw that blueprint.

This chapter is about moving from theory to practice. We are going to dissect the anatomy of a successful prompt, breaking it down into its essential components. If Chapter 1 was about the "why," this chapter is all about the "how." Think of it like learning the basic grammar and sentence structure of a new language. Once you master these fundamental building blocks, you can combine them in countless ways to express any idea and accomplish any task.

We will introduce a simple yet powerful framework of four essential elements that every great prompt should contain. We'll explore why vague prompts are the single biggest source of frustration and mediocre results, and how to find the perfect level of detail for any situation. We'll also cover how to instruct the AI to match your specific communication style, turning it into a seamless extension of your own professional voice.

By the end of this chapter, you will have a reliable method for constructing prompts that get you better results, faster. You will be able to look at any task on your to-do list and know exactly how to translate it into a set of clear instructions that your AI partner can execute effectively.

The Four Essential Elements: Context, Task, Format, and Constraints

Every effective prompt, regardless of its complexity, is built on a foundation of four key pillars. Forgetting even one of these can be the difference between a brilliant, time-saving result and a generic, useless paragraph. To make them easy to remember, let's think of them as the CTFC framework:

- **C**ontext: The background information. The "Why."
- **T**ask: The specific action you want the AI to perform. The "What."
- **F**ormat: The structure of the desired output. The "How."
- **C**onstraints: The rules and boundaries to follow. The "Don'ts."

Let's break down each one with workplace examples.

1. Context: Providing the Background

Context is the foundation of your prompt. It's the background information the AI needs to understand the bigger picture. Remember, the AI has no knowledge of your job, your project, or your goals. You must provide this crucial information. Good context answers questions like:

- Who is the audience for this output? (e.g., "for an audience of senior executives," "for new interns," "for a technical engineering team")

- What is the overall goal or purpose? (e.g., "The goal is to get budget approval," "The purpose is to create a training document," "We need to persuade a client to upgrade their service")
- What background information is necessary? (e.g., "Our company sells sustainable office furniture," "This project is currently two weeks behind schedule," "The client has complained about our response times in the past")

Professional Scenario: Drafting a Sales Email

Imagine you want the AI to help you write a follow-up email to a potential client.

Without Context: "Write a follow-up email to a potential client."
The AI can only produce a very generic template.
With Context: "I am a sales representative for a company called 'Innovate Solutions' that sells a project management software. I had a 30-minute introductory call yesterday with a potential client, a construction company manager named Ms. Davies. The goal of this email is to thank her for her time and propose a full demo of our software for her team."
With this context, the AI now understands the industry, the product, your role, the client's role, and the specific goal of the email. The resulting draft will be far more relevant and effective.

2. Task: Defining the Action

The task is the specific, actionable instruction you give the AI. It is the verb of your prompt. Vague verbs lead to vague results. Be direct and use precise action words.

Instead of...	Use a stronger verb like...
"Talk about our new software"	"Write a three-paragraph announcement..."
"Help with this report"	"Summarize the key findings of this report..."
"Do something with these notes"	"Organize these meeting notes into a list of action items..."

The task should be a clear command. Think about exactly what you want the AI to *do*.

- **Analyze** this data for trends.
- **Brainstorm** ten potential names for a new product.
- **Compare** the features of these two software systems.
- **Create** an outline for a presentation.
- **Translate** this text into professional German.
- **Rewrite** this paragraph to be more persuasive.

A clear task removes all guesswork for the AI and sets a precise direction for the output.

3. Format: Specifying the Structure

This is one of the most powerful and often overlooked elements of a prompt. How do you want the final output to be structured? If you don't specify the format, the AI will default to a few paragraphs of text, which may not be what you need. Specifying the format saves you immense amounts of time on reformatting and editing.

Be explicit about the structure you want:

- "In a bulleted list..."
- "As a three-column table with the headers: Feature, Benefit, and Use Case..."
- "In the form of a professional email..."
- "As a JSON object..."
- "Create a mind map structure using indentation..."
- "As a step-by-step guide..."

Professional Scenario: Organizing Project Ideas

You have a block of text with raw ideas for a new marketing campaign.

Without Format: "Organize these ideas for a marketing campaign: [paste text]"
The AI might just rewrite them in slightly cleaner paragraphs.
With Format: "Organize the following marketing campaign ideas into a table. The table should have three columns: 'Campaign Idea,' 'Target Audience,' and 'Key Performance Indicator (KPI).' [paste text]"
Now, you will get a perfectly structured table that is immediately ready to be dropped into a report or presentation, requiring zero reformatting on your part.

4. Constraints: Setting the Rules

Constraints are the boundaries you set for the AI. They are the rules of the road that help guide the AI to the precise output you need. Constraints tell the AI what *not* to do, or what specific rules it must follow.

Common constraints include:

- **Length:** "Keep the response under 200 words." "The summary should be exactly three sentences."
- **Tone/Style:** "Do not use technical jargon." "Write in a formal, academic tone." "Avoid using exclamation points."
- **Exclusions:** "Do not mention our competitors by name." "Focus only on the financial aspects and ignore the operational details."
- **Inclusions:** "You must use the phrase 'user-centric design' in your answer." "Ensure the response includes a call to action."

Constraints are like the bumpers in a bowling lane. They keep the AI's output from going in the wrong direction and guide it toward a perfect strike.

The CTFC Framework in Action: A Quick Checklist

Before you hit "Enter" on your next prompt, do a quick mental check:

- **Context:** Have I given the AI enough background to understand the situation?
- **Task:** Is my instruction a clear, specific action?
- **Format:** Have I told the AI exactly how to structure the output?
- **Constraints:** Have I provided the necessary rules and boundaries?

If you can answer "yes" to all four, you are well on your way to crafting an effective prompt.

Why Vague Prompts Produce Mediocre Results

We've all been there. You have a task in mind, you type a quick request into an AI tool, and the response you get back is... underwhelming. It's generic, unhelpful, and feels like a waste of time. The natural tendency is to blame the tool: "This AI isn't very smart." But in 99% of cases, the problem isn't the AI. It's the prompt.

Let's go back to our GPS analogy from Chapter 1. A vague prompt is like telling your navigation system, "Take me to the city." The system has no choice but to make a series of assumptions. Which city? What part of the city? Are we going to a restaurant, an office, a park? What's our final destination? Its response will be a guess, and it will almost certainly be the wrong one.

An AI language model does the exact same thing. When faced with a vague prompt, it is forced to fill in the missing information with the most statistically probable, generic patterns from its training data.

A Side-by-Side Comparison: The Cost of Vagueness

Scenario: You need to create some content for your company's internal blog to encourage employees to use a new expense reporting software.

The Vague Prompt:
"Write a blog post about our new expense software."
Probable AI Output:
"Introducing the Future of Expense Reporting!
Our company is excited to announce the launch of a new, state-of-the-art expense reporting software. This new system is designed to be more efficient and user-friendly, helping to

streamline the process of submitting and approving expenses. With a modern interface and powerful features, managing your business expenses has never been easier. We encourage all employees to start using the new system for their next expense report."

Analysis of the Output:

This is not wrong, but it is completely useless. It's a collection of generic corporate phrases. It contains no specific information, no compelling benefits, and no clear instructions. You would have to rewrite the entire thing from scratch, adding all the important details yourself. You haven't saved any time.

The Powerful Prompt (Using CTFC):

"[Context] Act as an internal communications specialist. Our company is replacing our old, clunky expense system ('OldSystem') with a new, user-friendly software called 'ExpenseEZ.' Employees often complained that the old system was slow and confusing. The goal is to get employees excited about the switch and to clearly guide them on the next steps.

[Task] Write an internal blog post announcing the launch of ExpenseEZ.

[Format] The post should have a catchy headline, a brief introduction, a bulleted list of 3 key benefits for employees, and a final section titled 'How to Get Started' with clear, numbered steps.

[Constraints] The tone should be upbeat, helpful, and concise (around 300 words). Avoid corporate jargon. Focus on how this makes employees' lives easier."

Probable AI Output:

"Headline: Say Goodbye to Expense Headaches: Welcome to ExpenseEZ!

Introduction: Get ready for a much-needed upgrade! We've heard your feedback on our old expense reporting process, and we're thrilled to announce that we're officially launching ExpenseEZ,

our new and incredibly simple expense management tool, starting next Monday.
Key Benefits for You:

- **Save Valuable Time:** Snap a photo of your receipt with your phone, and ExpenseEZ's smart-scan feature will automatically fill in the details. No more manual data entry!
- **Get Reimbursed Faster:** The streamlined approval workflow means your reports get reviewed and approved in days, not weeks.
- Track Everything in One Place: The intuitive dashboard lets you see the status of all your reports at a glance, right from your computer or phone.
  How to Get Started:

1. Look for an email invitation to ExpenseEZ in your inbox on Monday morning.
2. Click the link to set up your account in under two minutes.
3. Download the mobile app to start submitting expenses on the go."

Analysis of the Output:
This is a world apart. It's specific, actionable, and employee-focused. It's ready to be published with minimal editing. The 90 seconds it took to write the detailed prompt saved you at least 30 minutes of writing and editing. This is the core principle of AI productivity: a small upfront investment in a quality prompt pays massive dividends in the output.

The Specificity Spectrum: Finding the Right Level of Detail

It's clear that specificity is key, but it's not an all-or-nothing concept. It's a spectrum. Finding the right point on that spectrum is an art that you will develop with practice. Too little detail leads to generic results, but too much detail can sometimes be counterproductive, leading to awkward or stilted output.

Let's call this the "Goldilocks Principle" of prompting. You want the level of detail to be *just right*.

Level 1: Too Vague (The Underspecified Prompt)
This is the most common mistake. It provides a task but lacks sufficient context, format, and constraints.
Example: "Create a marketing plan."
Problem: The AI has no idea what product you're selling, who your customers are, what your budget is, or what the goals are. It can only provide a generic marketing plan template.
Level 2: Just Right (The Well-Specified Prompt)
This prompt provides all four essential elements (CTFC) with enough detail for the AI to understand the assignment without being excessively constrained. It sets the direction but leaves the AI some room to use its pattern-matching abilities to generate a natural-sounding and useful response.
Example: "Act as a marketing director. Create a high-level marketing plan for the launch of a new product: a premium, insulated water bottle called 'HydroFlow.' Our target audience is active, eco-conscious millennials. The goal is to achieve 10,000 units sold in the first quarter. The plan should be a bulleted list covering three areas: social media strategy, influencer partnerships, and email marketing. The budget is moderate."
Benefit: This gives the AI all the critical variables it needs to produce a relevant, strategic, and well-structured outline that you can then build upon.
Level 3: Too Specific (The Over-Constrained Prompt)
This happens when you try to control every single word and sentence structure. It can be useful for very specific, technical

tasks, but for most professional writing, it stifles the AI and can result in text that sounds robotic and unnatural.
Example: "Write a three-paragraph marketing plan. The first paragraph must be exactly 45 words and start with the phrase 'To successfully launch...' The second paragraph must contain the words 'synergy' and 'leverage' and be a bulleted list of three items. The final paragraph must be a single sentence of 22 words."
Problem: By micromanaging the AI to this degree, you are essentially turning it into a mad-libs-style text filler. You lose the benefit of its sophisticated language modeling. The output will likely be grammatically correct but awkward and poorly written because the constraints are too artificial.

Productivity Checklist: Finding "Just Right"

- **State the Goal, Not Just the Steps:** Instead of telling the AI exactly what to write, tell it what you want to achieve with the writing. (e.g., "Persuade the reader to sign up for a demo" is better than "Write a paragraph with a call to action.").
- **Provide Key Information, Not Every Detail:** Give the AI the critical context (audience, product, background) and let it fill in the connective tissue.
- **Guide the Structure, Don't Dictate the Words:** Ask for a specific format (email, report, list) and tone, but give the AI the freedom to choose the best words to fit those guidelines.
- **Start with "Just Right" and Refine:** It's always a good strategy to start with a Level 2 prompt. If the output isn't quite right, you can use a follow-up prompt to add more constraints. ("That's a good start, but can you make the tone more formal?").

Tone and Voice: Getting AI to Match Your Communication Style

One of the most remarkable abilities of a modern LLM is its capacity to adopt different writing styles. The "Format" element we discussed tells the AI about the structure, but "Tone" and "Voice" tell it about the personality. Mastering this allows you to generate text that aligns perfectly with your company's brand, your team's culture, or your own professional persona.

Tone refers to the attitude or feeling of the writing. It's the emotional color of the words.
Voice refers to the unique personality of the writer or brand. It's the consistent style that makes your writing recognizable.
You can control these by including specific instructions in your prompt, usually as part of the Constraints element.

A Practical List of Tone Words to Use:

- **Professional:** Formal, respectful, and objective.
- **Conversational:** Friendly, informal, and approachable.
- **Persuasive:** Confident, compelling, and benefit-oriented.
- **Supportive:** Empathetic, reassuring, and helpful.
- **Technical:** Precise, data-driven, and jargon-heavy (for the right audience).
- **Inspirational:** Uplifting, optimistic, and motivational.
- **Urgent:** Direct, action-oriented, and time-sensitive.
- **Concise:** To the point, brief, and clear.

Professional Scenario: Communicating a Policy Change

Imagine you are an HR manager who needs to announce a new work-from-home policy. The policy is a positive change, but you need to communicate it clearly to avoid confusion.

Prompt with a "Formal" Tone Constraint:
"...The task is to write an email to all employees announcing this

new policy. The tone should be formal and authoritative."
Probable Output: "This memorandum serves to inform all personnel of a revision to the corporate telecommuting policy... Employees are henceforth permitted to engage in remote work..."
This is technically correct but may feel cold and impersonal.
Prompt with a "Supportive" Tone Constraint:
"...The task is to write an email to all employees announcing this new policy. The tone should be supportive, clear, and positive."
Probable Output: "Hi Team, We're excited to share some great news about our work-from-home policy! Based on your feedback and our commitment to flexibility, we're introducing a new hybrid model... Our goal is to support you in finding a better work-life balance..."
This version feels much more modern and employee-friendly.
The simple act of changing one constraint word completely transforms the output.
Advanced Tip: Teaching the AI Your Voice
If you want the AI to write in your specific voice, you can provide it with an example. This is a technique called "few-shot prompting" which we will cover in more detail later, but the basic concept is simple.
Example Prompt:
"Analyze the following writing sample to understand my professional voice. My voice is direct, uses simple language, and often uses short sentences.
[Paste a sample of your own writing, like a recent email or report]
Now, using that same voice, write a short project update about the successful launch of our new website."
This is a powerful way to get the AI to generate drafts that already sound like you, dramatically reducing your editing time.

Examples: Transforming Weak Prompts into

Powerful Ones

Let's solidify everything we've learned with a few more real-world, side-by-side comparisons. In each example, notice how the weak prompt lacks the core CTFC elements, while the strong prompt includes them all.

Scenario 1: Creating a Job Description

- **The Goal:** You need to write a job description for a new "Junior Project Coordinator" role.
- **Weak Prompt:** "Write a job description for a project coordinator."
- **Analysis of Weakness:** This is a classic "vague destination" prompt. It has a task, but no context, format, or constraints. The AI will produce a generic template that could be for any company in any industry.
- Strong Prompt:
  "[Context] Act as a hiring manager for a mid-sized tech company that creates productivity software. We have a fast-paced, collaborative culture.
  [Task] Write a compelling job description for a 'Junior Project Coordinator' position.
  [Format] The description should include three sections: 'About the Role,' 'Key Responsibilities' (as a bulleted list), and 'Qualifications' (as a bulleted list).
  [Constraints] The tone should be energetic and encouraging, designed to attract ambitious, early-career candidates. Avoid overly formal corporate language. Mention that the role reports to the Senior Project Manager."
- **Analysis of Strength:** The strong prompt provides the persona ("hiring manager"), company context, a clear format, and specific tone constraints. The result will be a job

description that is not only accurate but also reflects the company's culture and attracts the right type of applicant.

Scenario 2: Brainstorming Solutions to a Business Problem

- **The Goal:** Your team is struggling with inefficient meetings. You want ideas to fix it.
- **Weak Prompt:** "How can we have better meetings?"
- **Analysis of Weakness:** This is a question, not a task. The AI will give you a generic list of tips (have an agenda, etc.) that you could find anywhere. It's not tailored to your situation.
- Strong Prompt:
  "[Context] I manage a remote team of 10 software developers. We have a two-hour project sync meeting every week. The feedback from the team is that the meetings often run over, lack clear focus, and don't result in actionable decisions.
  [Task] Brainstorm a list of 5 concrete, actionable strategies we could implement to make our weekly project sync meeting more efficient and productive.
  [Format] Present these strategies as a numbered list. For each strategy, include a one-sentence description of the problem it solves and a two-sentence explanation of how to implement it.
  [Constraints] The solutions should be specifically tailored to a remote software development team."
- **Analysis of Strength:** This prompt gives the AI deep context about the team and the specific problem. It asks for a specific number of actionable strategies and dictates a very useful format for the output, making the ideas easy to understand and implement.

Common Prompting Mistakes and How to Avoid

Them

As you begin your journey with AI, you will inevitably run into some common roadblocks. Being aware of them ahead of time can save you a great deal of frustration. Here are the top five mistakes new users make.

1. The "Vague Conversation" Mistake
This is treating the AI chat window like a search engine or a casual conversation with a person.

- **Example:** "Tell me about project management."
- **The Problem:** The AI doesn't know what you want to *do* with the information. Do you want a definition? A history? A list of methodologies? It has to guess.
- **How to Avoid:** Always frame your request as a **task**. Instead of asking a question, give a command. "Create a study guide explaining the key differences between Agile and Waterfall project management methodologies."

2. The "One-Shot" Mistake
This is the belief that you should get the perfect answer on your very first try.

- **The Problem:** Prompting is a process of refinement. Your first prompt gets you a draft, not a finished product. Getting a mediocre result and giving up is like a sculptor striking a block of marble once and being disappointed it doesn't look like a statue.
- **How to Avoid:** Embrace an **iterative mindset**. Your first prompt is the start of a conversation. Use follow-up prompts to refine the output.
    - "That's a good start. Now make the tone more formal."
    - "Can you expand on the second bullet point?"
    - "Rewrite that last paragraph to be more concise."

- "Remove all references to budget."

3. The "Context Amnesia" Mistake
This is forgetting that each new AI conversation starts with a blank slate.

- **The Problem:** You have a great conversation with an AI, refining a project plan. You close the window. The next day, you open a new chat and say, "Okay, now add the budget details to that plan." The AI has no idea what you're talking about.
- **How to Avoid:** Keep related tasks within the **same conversation thread**. The AI can use the previous parts of the conversation as context. If you must start a new conversation, provide a summary of the necessary context from the old one.

4. The "Implicit Assumption" Mistake
This is assuming the AI understands the unstated norms and definitions of your profession or company.

- **Example:** "Write a standard project proposal."
- **The Problem:** "Standard" means different things in different organizations. Does your standard proposal include a risk analysis? A section on team roles? A detailed budget breakdown? The AI doesn't know.
- **How to Avoid: Be explicit.** Define your terms. "Write a project proposal. For us, a standard proposal includes these five sections: Executive Summary, Project Goals, Timeline, Budget, and Key Stakeholders."

5. The "Trust Without Verifying" Mistake
This is the most dangerous mistake of all. It involves taking the AI's output at face value and using it without a critical review.

- **The Problem:** As we learned in Chapter 1, AI can

"hallucinate" facts, figures, and sources. It can also produce text that is subtly biased or just plain wrong.

- **How to Avoid:** You are always the **final checkpoint for quality and accuracy**. Treat every piece of AI-generated content as a draft from a very fast but sometimes unreliable intern. Your professional reputation depends on it. Fact-check any data. Edit for your own voice. Ensure the message is strategically sound.

Key Takeaways from This Chapter

- An effective prompt is not a simple question, but a well-structured set of instructions.
- Every powerful prompt contains the four essential elements: **Context, Task, Format, and Constraints (CTFC).**
- Vagueness is the enemy of productivity. A small investment of time in a detailed prompt saves a large amount of time in editing and rewriting.
- Find the "Goldilocks" level of specificity: detailed enough to give clear direction, but not so restrictive that it creates awkward, robotic output.
- Use specific words to command the AI's tone and voice to match your exact needs.
- Prompting is an iterative process. Use your first result as a draft and refine it with follow-up instructions.

You now have the fundamental building blocks for effective communication with AI. You understand the grammar and sentence structure of this new language. In the next chapter, we will build on this foundation with a more advanced framework for tackling complex tasks and treating the AI as a true collaborative partner.

Practice Exercise:

Before you move on, take one task from your professional to-do list for this week. It could be writing an email, planning a meeting, or outlining a report. Open a fresh document and, without worrying about writing the perfect prose, draft a prompt for that task using the CTFC framework.

- **Context:** Write down 2-3 sentences of background.
- **Task:** Write one clear command with an action verb.
- **Format:** Specify the exact structure of the output.
- **Constraints:** List 2-3 rules the AI must follow.

This simple exercise will begin to build the habit of structured prompting, a habit that will soon become second nature.

Chapter 3: The Prompt Engineering Framework

In the previous chapter, we dissected the anatomy of an effective prompt. You learned about the four essential pillars: Context, Task, Format, and Constraints (CTFC). Think of these as the raw materials for your instructions. You now know what ingredients you need to give the AI to get a high-quality result.

But knowing the ingredients is different from knowing how to cook. A chef doesn't just have ingredients; they have a process, a series of steps they follow to turn those raw materials into a finished dish. This chapter is about giving you that process. We are moving beyond the "what" of a good prompt and into the "how" of a great prompting workflow.

This is where we introduce the Prompt Engineering Framework. This framework is not a rigid set of rules, but a collection of powerful techniques and mental models that transform your interaction with AI from a simple question-and-answer session into a dynamic, creative partnership. It's how you go from getting simple outputs to producing complex, nuanced, and highly valuable work.

We will start with a simple method for structuring your prompting process. Then, we'll explore the game-changing concept of iterative prompting, which is the true secret to unlocking the AI's potential. We'll dive into advanced techniques like assigning the AI an expert role, teaching it by example, and even instructing it to "think" more logically. Finally, we'll bring it all together by showing you how to create reusable templates that will become the cornerstone of your daily productivity.

By the end of this chapter, you won't just be writing prompts. You'll be designing conversations with AI to achieve specific, professional goals.

The CLEAR Method: Context, Length, Examples, Adjust, Refine

While the CTFC framework from the last chapter describes the *components* of a single great prompt, the CLEAR method describes a five-step *process* for developing a high-quality output. It's a simple workflow you can follow for any significant task, ensuring you cover your bases and build upon your results systematically.

- **C**ontext: Start by clearly defining the background and the persona.
- **L**ength: Specify the desired length and scope of the output.
- **E**xamples: Provide examples to guide the style, tone, and structure.
- **A**djust: Review the first draft and identify what needs to change.
- **R**efine: Use follow-up prompts to iteratively improve the output.

Let's look at this not as a single prompt, but as a sequence of thought.

Step 1: Context
Before you write a single word of your task, ground the AI. This is where you use the "Context" element from our CTFC framework, but with a focus on setting a role for the AI. As we'll discuss later in this chapter, assigning a persona is one of the most effective

ways to focus the AI's response. Your first thought should always be, "Who do I want the AI to be for this task?" A financial analyst? A creative director? A technical writer? You also provide the background information here.

Step 2: Length

Define the scope of the output early. This is a critical constraint. Are you looking for a one-sentence summary or a 500-word report? Specifying the desired length prevents the AI from giving you a response that is too shallow or too dense for your needs. This simple constraint saves a lot of time editing down an overly long response.

Step 3: Examples

If the style or format is important, show, don't just tell. Instead of only describing the tone you want, provide a short example of it. This could be a sentence you wrote or a snippet from another document that captures the desired voice. Providing an example is the single best way to get the AI to match a specific style.

Step 4: Adjust

Your first prompt rarely yields the final product. The fourth step is a critical review of the AI's initial output. Read it carefully and compare it to your goal. Is the tone right? Is the information accurate? Is the format correct? Make a mental or physical list of what needs to be adjusted. Does it need to be more persuasive? More concise? Should it include a specific piece of data you forgot to mention?

Step 5: Refine

This is the heart of the iterative process. Based on your adjustments, you give the AI a series of follow-up commands. This is not about starting over. It's about building on the previous response. "That's a good start, but can you make the second paragraph more data-driven?" or "Please rewrite the introduction to be more engaging for a non-technical audience."

The CLEAR method turns prompting from a single action into a strategic workflow, ensuring a more controlled and higher-quality outcome every time.

Iterative Prompting: Treating AI as a Collaborative Partner

If you take only one lesson from this entire book, let it be this: **prompting is a conversation, not a command.** The single biggest mistake professionals make when using AI is treating it like a vending machine. They put in one prompt (a coin) and expect the perfect product to come out. When it doesn't, they walk away frustrated.

A better mental model is to treat the AI as a very capable, very fast, but very literal-minded junior colleague. You wouldn't give a complex task to a new team member in a single sentence and expect a perfect result. You would give them an initial briefing, review their first draft, provide feedback, ask for revisions, and guide them toward the final product. This back-and-forth process is called iterative prompting, and it is the key to producing sophisticated work with AI.

The goal is not to craft one "perfect" mega-prompt that does everything at once. The goal is to start with a good prompt and then steer the AI's output with a series of simple, targeted follow-up instructions.

Professional Scenario: Refining a Project Proposal Summary

Let's walk through a realistic iterative workflow. Your goal is to create a compelling executive summary for a project proposal about redesigning your company's internal inventory management system.

Iteration 1: The First Draft (Your Initial Prompt)
You start with a solid prompt using the CTFC framework.
"[Context] Act as a senior project manager. I need to write an executive summary for a project proposal. The project is to replace our outdated, manual inventory system ('System A') with a new, automated cloud-based system ('System B'). The audience for this proposal is the senior leadership team, who are focused on ROI and operational efficiency.
[Task] Write a one-paragraph executive summary for this proposal.
[Format] A single, professional paragraph.
[Constraints] The tone should be confident and persuasive. The length should be around 150 words."
AI's First Output (The First Draft):
"This proposal outlines a critical project to replace our legacy inventory management system, System A, with a modern, cloud-based solution, System B. The current system is inefficient, prone to human error, and lacks real-time data, leading to costly overstocking and stock-outs. By transitioning to System B, we will automate key processes, improve inventory accuracy, and provide real-time analytics to stakeholders. This will result in significant operational efficiencies and a clear return on investment. We recommend proceeding with this essential technological upgrade to support the company's growth and profitability."
Analysis: This is a good starting point. It's professional and covers the main points. But it lacks specific data and could be more impactful. Now, the iterative process begins.

Iteration 2: Adding Specific Data (Your First Follow-Up)

Your feedback is targeted and simple.
"That's a good foundation. Now, please revise it to include the following specific data points: the current system causes an estimated 15% inventory error rate, and the new system is projected to reduce operational costs by 20% annually."
AI's Second Output (The Revision):
"This proposal outlines a critical project to replace our legacy inventory management system, System A, which contributes to an estimated 15% inventory error rate, with a modern, cloud-based solution, System B. Our current system is inefficient and lacks real-time data, leading to costly overstocking and stock-outs. By transitioning to System B, we project a 20% annual reduction in operational costs through the automation of key processes, improved inventory accuracy, and real-time analytics. This essential upgrade will provide a significant return on investment and is vital for the company's continued growth and profitability."
Analysis: Much better. The summary is now grounded in specific, compelling numbers that the leadership team will care about. But maybe the tone could be even stronger.

Iteration 3: Adjusting the Tone (Your Second Follow-Up)
Again, a simple, clear instruction.
"Excellent. Now, please make the final sentence more urgent and action-oriented. Frame it as a strategic necessity, not just a recommendation."
AI's Third Output (The Final Polish):
"This proposal outlines a critical project to replace our legacy inventory management system, System A, which contributes to an estimated 15% inventory error rate, with a modern, cloud-based solution, System B. Our current system is inefficient and lacks real-time data, leading to costly overstocking and stock-outs. By transitioning to System B, we project a 20% annual reduction

in operational costs through the automation of key processes, improved inventory accuracy, and real-time analytics. To maintain our competitive edge and ensure scalable growth, moving forward with this strategic investment is an immediate operational imperative."

The Final Result:

In three simple steps, you went from a generic draft to a powerful, data-driven, and persuasive executive summary. Each step took only seconds. This is the power of the iterative mindset. You are the director, and the AI is your creative partner, responding to your guidance at each stage of the process.

Productivity Checklist: The Iterative Workflow

1. **Start Broad:** Begin with a good, clear prompt that defines the overall goal.
2. **Review the Draft:** Assess the first output. Don't expect perfection.
3. **Give Specific Feedback:** Identify one or two things to change at a time. Use simple follow-up prompts.
   - "Add these details..."
   - "Change the tone to be more..."
   - "Expand on this point..."
   - "Rewrite this for a different audience..."
4. **Repeat:** Continue this cycle of review and refinement until the output meets your standards.

Chain-of-Thought Prompting for Complex Reasoning

Sometimes, you need the AI to do more than just retrieve or reformat information. You need it to "reason" through a problem. Because AI doesn't truly reason, it can sometimes jump to conclusions or make logical errors on complex tasks. Chain-of-thought (CoT) prompting is a clever technique to overcome this.

The core idea is simple: you explicitly instruct the AI to "think step-by-step" or "show its work" before giving the final answer.

This does two powerful things:

1. **It forces a more logical process.** By requiring the AI to outline the steps of its reasoning, you constrain it to follow a more logical path, reducing the chance of it making a simplistic error.
2. **It makes the output more transparent.** You can see *how* the AI arrived at its conclusion, which allows you to more easily spot any errors in its logic or assumptions.

When to Use Chain-of-Thought Prompting:

- **Analyzing qualitative data:** When you have customer feedback, survey responses, or interview notes and you want to extract themes.
- **Solving multi-step problems:** For tasks that require several calculations or logical steps in sequence.
- **Strategic decision-making:** When you want the AI to weigh the pros and cons of different options.
- **Debugging or troubleshooting:** When you need the AI to trace a problem back to its source.

Professional Scenario: Analyzing Customer Feedback

Imagine you have a collection of anonymous feedback comments about your company's new software. You want to categorize them and identify the biggest issues.

Standard Prompt (Without CoT):
"Analyze the following customer feedback and identify the main

problems. [paste feedback]"
The AI might give you a decent summary, but it could miss nuances or lump unrelated issues together.
Chain-of-Thought Prompt:
"You are a product manager analyzing customer feedback for a new software. I will provide you with a list of feedback comments. I want you to identify the top 3 most critical problem areas. Before you give me the final list, you must follow these steps:

1. First, read through all the comments and for each one, identify the core user complaint in a single sentence.
2. Second, group the core complaints into broader categories (e.g., 'Usability Issues,' 'Performance,' 'Missing Features').
3. Third, count how many complaints fall into each category to determine their frequency.
4. Finally, based on your step-by-step analysis, present the top 3 problem areas, ranked from most to least frequent.
   Here is the feedback: [paste feedback]"

How this prompt works:
This prompt doesn't just ask for the answer. It provides a clear, logical algorithm for the AI to follow. By forcing the AI to go through the process of summarizing, categorizing, and counting, you are guiding its "thought process" toward a much more accurate and well-reasoned final output. The result will be a more reliable analysis that you can confidently present to your team.

Role-Based Prompting: Making AI an Expert Consultant

Role-based prompting, also known as assigning a persona, is one of the easiest and most effective techniques you can use. As we've touched on, it involves starting your prompt with the phrase "Act as a..." or "You are a..."

Why does this work so well?
Remember, an AI is a pattern-matching engine. When you tell it to "Act as an expert financial analyst," you are priming the pump. You are instructing the AI to filter its vast knowledge base and respond using only the patterns, vocabulary, and frameworks associated with financial analysts. It instantly narrows its focus, leading to a more specialized and higher-quality response. Without a role, the AI responds as a generic "helpful assistant." With a role, it becomes a specialist consultant on demand.

A Practical List of Powerful Professional Personas:

- **For Strategic Thinking:** "Act as a seasoned business strategist," "Act as a skeptical CEO," "Act as a market research analyst."
- **For Marketing and Sales:** "Act as a direct-response copywriter," "Act as a brand strategist," "Act as an experienced sales coach."
- **For Technical Tasks:** "Act as a senior software architect," "Act as a database administrator," "Act as a technical writer creating documentation for developers."
- **For Communication:** "Act as a professional communications coach," "Act as a public relations expert handling a crisis," "Act as an HR manager communicating a new policy."
- **For Learning:** "Act as a university professor explaining a concept to a first-year student," "Act as a tutor creating a study guide."

Professional Scenario: Getting Feedback on an Idea

You have a new idea for a mobile application, but you want to identify potential weaknesses. You can use role-based prompting to get feedback from multiple expert perspectives.

Prompt 1: The Optimistic Product Manager
"Act as an optimistic and forward-thinking product manager. Here is my idea for a new mobile app: [describe your idea]. What are the most exciting opportunities for this app?"
Prompt 2: The Cautious Financial Analyst
"Act as a cautious and detail-oriented financial analyst. Here is my idea for the same app: [describe your idea]. What are the biggest financial risks and potential hidden costs I'm not considering?"
Prompt 3: The Skeptical Chief Technology Officer
"Act as a skeptical but fair Chief Technology Officer. Here is my idea for the same app: [describe your idea]. What are the most significant technical challenges and scalability concerns we would face in building this?"
By asking different personas to analyze the same idea, you can simulate a high-level strategy meeting in a matter of minutes. Each AI "consultant" will provide a different lens, giving you a more holistic and robust view of your idea than you could get from a single, generic prompt.

Few-Shot Learning: Teaching AI Through Examples

Few-shot learning sounds technical, but it's an incredibly simple and practical concept that you briefly saw in the last chapter. It's the process of teaching the AI what you want by showing it a few examples of the desired output directly within your prompt.

- **Zero-Shot Prompt:** You just give the task with no examples. (e.g., "Summarize this article.")
- **One-Shot Prompt:** You give one example of the desired output.

- **Few-Shot Prompt:** You give two or more examples.

The more examples you provide, the better the AI understands the specific pattern you're looking for. This is the ultimate "show, don't just tell" technique.

When to Use Few-Shot Learning:

- When you need a very specific format or structure that is hard to describe with words.
- When you want the AI to match a unique tone or writing style.
- For classification or categorization tasks where you need to define the categories with examples.

Professional Scenario: Standardizing Project Updates

You manage a team where everyone writes their weekly project updates in a different format, making them hard to scan quickly. You want to create a standard format and use AI to help you reformat the old ones.

The Few-Shot Prompt:
"You are an expert project manager. I want you to reformat weekly project updates into a standard template. The template should follow the exact structure of the examples I provide. Here are two examples of the correct format:
Example 1:
Project: Alpha Launch
Status: Green
Last Week's Accomplishments:

- Completed user interface mockups.
- Finalized the database schema.
  Key Goal for Next Week:
- Begin front-end development.

Blockers:

- None.

Example 2:
Project: Bravo Integration
Status: Yellow
Last Week's Accomplishments:

- Initial API tests were successful.
- Drafted the technical documentation.

Key Goal for Next Week:

- Full integration testing with the partner system.

Blockers:

- We are still waiting for final API credentials from the partner's technical team.

Now, please reformat the following project update into this exact template:
[Paste a messy, unstructured update from a team member]"

By providing the AI with clear examples, you have "taught" it the precise pattern you expect. It will now be able to take any unstructured text and reformat it perfectly into your desired template, saving you enormous amounts of time on administrative cleanup.

Template Creation for Repeatable Tasks

The final step in this framework is to operationalize your new skills. As you start using these techniques, you will find that you perform certain tasks over and over again: writing a meeting agenda, summarizing a report, drafting a follow-up email. The goal is to not have to reinvent the prompt every single time.

A prompt template is a pre-written, highly effective prompt for a recurring task that you can save and reuse. It contains all the best practices we've discussed, with placeholders for the specific details of each new instance. Building a personal library of these templates is the ultimate productivity hack.

Step-by-Step Guide to Creating a Prompt Template:

1. **Identify a Recurring Task:** Find a task you do at least once a week. Let's use "Creating a Meeting Agenda."
2. **Deconstruct the Task:** What makes a good meeting agenda? It usually has a clear objective, a list of topics with time allocations, and a list of required attendees.
3. **Build a "Perfect" Prompt:** Using everything you've learned, craft a detailed prompt to generate this agenda. Use role-based prompting, specify the format, and add constraints.
4. **Add Placeholders:** Go through your perfect prompt and replace the specific details with generic placeholders in brackets.

Example: The Meeting Agenda Template

"Act as an expert executive assistant creating a meeting agenda.
Meeting Topic: [Insert Meeting Topic]
Date and Time: [Insert Date and Time]
Objective: The primary goal of this meeting is to [Insert Clear Objective, e.g., 'decide on the Q4 marketing budget'].
Attendees: [List Required Attendees]
Task: Create a detailed meeting agenda based on the information above.
Format: The agenda should be a numbered list of topics. For each topic, include a brief description and the name of the person leading that discussion. Also, assign a specific time allocation for each topic, ensuring the total time does not exceed [Insert Total Meeting Time, e.g., '60 minutes'].

Constraints: The tone should be professional, clear, and efficient."

How to Use Your Template:

Save this text in a notes app or a dedicated document. Now, whenever you need to create an agenda, you simply copy the template, fill in the bracketed information, and paste it into your AI tool. You get a perfectly structured, professional agenda in seconds, every single time.

Key Takeaways from This Chapter

- Move beyond single prompts and adopt a **prompting framework** that treats your interaction with AI as a strategic process.
- Embrace an **iterative mindset**. Your first output is a draft to be improved upon with targeted follow-up prompts.
- Use **chain-of-thought** prompting ("think step-by-step") to guide the AI through complex reasoning tasks for more accurate results.
- Assigning an expert **role or persona** is a powerful way to instantly improve the quality and focus of the AI's output.
- Use **few-shot learning** (providing examples) to teach the AI a specific format or style that is difficult to describe with words.
- The ultimate goal is to build a personal library of **prompt templates** for your most common tasks, creating a system for sustained productivity.

You now have a complete framework for both understanding and crafting effective prompts. You have the individual components (CTFC) and the process (CLEAR, iteration, and advanced techniques). You are ready to move to the next level: applying these skills to a wide range of professional output types.

Part II: Core Skills – Mastering Prompt Techniques

Chapter 4: Writing Prompts for Different Output Types

In the first part of this book, we built our foundation. We demystified AI, established a realistic understanding of what it can do, and learned the fundamental anatomy of a great prompt. You now have the core building blocks (Context, Task, Format, Constraints) and a strategic framework for how to approach your interactions with AI as a collaborative partner.

Now, we move into Part II, where we transition from foundational theory to practical application. This is where the real work of boosting your productivity begins. If the first three chapters were about learning how your tools work, this section is about putting those tools to work on real projects.

This chapter is dedicated to a critical skill: tailoring your prompts to the specific type of output you need. A professional chef knows you don't use a cleaver for delicate slicing, and a skilled project manager knows you don't use a detailed spreadsheet for a high-level vision presentation. In the same way, an effective AI user knows that a prompt designed to generate a persuasive email looks very different from one designed to organize raw data into a table.

We will explore the five most common categories of professional work you will delegate to AI. We will cover the bread and butter of workplace communication: text generation for emails, reports, and summaries. We will then dive into the massive time-saver of data organization, instructing the AI to create perfectly structured tables and lists. From there, we'll move to a more advanced skill:

using AI to analyze information and extract meaningful insights. We will also touch on how to use AI as a creative partner for brainstorming and how to leverage it for technical tasks like writing code and documentation.

For each category, we will provide specific techniques, workplace scenarios, and prompt examples. By the end of this chapter, you will have a versatile toolkit that allows you to confidently match your prompting style to any professional task, ensuring you get the right output, in the right format, every single time.

Text Generation: Emails, Reports, Articles, and Summaries

This is the most frequent and familiar use case for AI in the workplace. From clearing your inbox to drafting a comprehensive report, text generation is at the heart of daily professional communication. Mastering prompts for these tasks can reclaim hours of your week. The key is to provide the AI with the essential ingredients of purpose, audience, and content.

Crafting Effective Emails

Emails are the lifeblood of modern business, and they can also be a significant drain on our time. AI can act as your personal communications assistant, drafting clear, professional emails in a fraction of the time it would take you to write them from scratch.

Key Prompt Elements for Emails:

- **Role/Persona:** "Act as a [Your Role]."
- **Audience/Recipient:** "The email is for [Recipient's Role or Name]."
- **Goal/Purpose:** "The goal of this email is to [Clearly State

Your Objective]."

- **Key Information:** Provide the 3-5 essential points that must be included.
- **Tone:** Specify the desired tone (e.g., "formal," "friendly and conversational," "urgent").

Professional Scenario: Drafting a Client Follow-Up Email

- **The Goal:** You just finished a successful project for a client and want to send a follow-up email to thank them, summarize the outcome, and suggest a future partnership.
- **Weak Prompt:** "Write a follow-up email to a client after a project."
- **Analysis of Weakness:** This prompt lacks all the critical details. The AI has no idea what the project was, what the outcome was, or what you want to happen next. It can only produce a bland, generic template.
- Strong Prompt:
  "Act as a project manager at 'Innovate Solutions.' I need to write a follow-up email to our client, Mr. Smith, at 'Global Corp.'
  The goal of this email is to officially close out the 'Q2 Website Redesign' project, thank him for his partnership, and propose a follow-on project.
  Please include these key points:
  1. The new website successfully launched last Friday.
  2. Mention that initial user engagement metrics are up by 20% in the first week.
  3. Thank him and his team for their excellent collaboration.
  4. Briefly propose a 'Phase 2' project to develop a mobile app version of the new site to further increase engagement.
     The tone should be professional, positive, and forward-

looking."

- **Analysis of Strength:** This prompt provides all the necessary ingredients. The AI knows who you are, who the client is, the context of the project, the specific data to include, and the strategic goal of the communication. The draft it produces will be 95% complete and ready to send after a quick review.

Drafting Reports and Articles

For longer-form content like reports or internal articles, the key is to guide the structure. Don't just ask the AI to write a report; give it the outline and the key building blocks.

Key Prompt Elements for Reports:

- **Role/Persona:** "Act as a market analyst," "Act as a technical writer."
- **Audience:** "The report is for a non-technical executive team," "This article is for new employees."
- **Structure/Outline:** Provide the section headers you want (e.g., "Include an Executive Summary, Key Findings, and Recommendations").
- **Key Data/Sources:** Supply the essential data points, quotes, or information that must be included in the report.

Professional Scenario: Creating a Monthly Social Media Report Summary

- **The Goal:** You need to write a short, high-level summary of your company's social media performance for the past month. The audience is the leadership team, who don't care about vanity metrics but want to know the business impact.
- Strong Prompt:

"Act as a social media manager. Write a two-paragraph summary of our social media performance for last month, intended for the executive leadership team.
The summary must be structured as follows:
Paragraph 1: Briefly state the overall performance and highlight the single biggest win.
Paragraph 2: Explain what this means for the business and state our primary focus for the next month.
Here is the key data:

- Our total reach increased by 15%.
- The campaign for Product X generated 300 qualified leads, which was 50% above our target. This was the biggest win.
- Our engagement on LinkedIn with industry professionals was particularly high.
- Our focus for next month is to convert the leads from the Product X campaign.
  The tone should be concise, professional, and data-driven. Avoid social media jargon like 'likes' or 'shares' and focus on business outcomes like 'leads' and 'engagement'."

- **Benefit:** By providing a clear structure and the specific data, you prevent the AI from generating a generic report filled with irrelevant metrics. You get a targeted, executive-ready summary immediately.

Creating Powerful Summaries

Summarization is a core strength of LLMs. They can ingest large amounts of text and distill them into the key points with incredible speed.

Key Prompt Elements for Summaries:

- **The Source Text:** Paste the article, report, or transcript directly into the prompt.
- **Desired Length:** Be very specific (e.g., "in a single paragraph," "in five bullet points," "in under 100 words").
- **Focus:** Guide the summary's angle (e.g., "Summarize this article with a focus on the implications for the manufacturing industry").
- **Audience:** "Summarize this technical document for a non-technical audience."

Time-Saving Technique: The Meeting Summary
After a virtual meeting, take the automatically generated transcript and paste it into an AI tool with this prompt: "Read the following meeting transcript. Identify all the key decisions made and the specific action items assigned. For each action item, list the task and the person responsible. Format the output as two separate bulleted lists: 'Key Decisions' and 'Action Items'." This can turn a 45-minute transcript into a clear, actionable summary in seconds.

Data Organization: Tables, Lists, and Structured Information

This is where AI transitions from a writing assistant to a powerful data-processing tool. One of the most significant "hidden" time costs in any professional's day is reformatting information. Manually creating tables, organizing notes, or structuring data is tedious work. AI can do it almost instantly, but only if you give it perfectly clear formatting instructions.

Mastering the Art of Tables

Asking an AI to create a table is a productivity game-changer. It can take a messy block of text and transform it into a clean, structured table ready for a presentation or report.

Key Prompt Elements for Tables:

- **The Raw Data:** Provide the unstructured text you want to organize.
- **The Command:** State explicitly, "Organize this information into a table."
- **The Column Headers:** This is the most critical part. You must define the exact headers for each column. "Create a table with the following three columns: 'Task,' 'Owner,' and 'Deadline'."

Professional Scenario: Organizing Brainstorming Notes

- **The Goal:** Your team just had a brainstorming session for a new software feature, and your notes are a jumble of ideas. You want to organize them into a clear table to present to the product manager.
- The Raw, Unstructured Notes:
  "Okay, so we talked about the new dashboard feature. Jane suggested a customizable widget system, maybe for key metrics. Tom said we need real-time notifications, but only for critical alerts to avoid spam. I think the date range filter is the most important thing to get right from the start. Maria brought up that we need an 'export to PDF' function for reporting. Jane also mentioned that the widgets should be drag-and-drop."
- The Powerful Prompt:
  "Act as a project coordinator. I have a set of unstructured notes from a brainstorming session about a new dashboard feature. Please organize these notes into a table.
  The table should have three columns with the following exact headers: 'Feature Idea,' 'Description,' and 'Suggested By.'

Here are the notes: [Paste the unstructured notes from above]"

- **The AI's Structured Output:**

Feature Idea	Description	Suggested By
Customizable Widgets	A system for users to add and arrange widgets for key metrics.	Jane
Drag-and-Drop Widgets	The customizable widgets should have a drag-and-drop interface.	Jane
Real-Time Notifications	The system should provide notifications, but only for critical alerts.	Tom

Date Range Filter	A robust filter to allow users to select specific date ranges.	Me
Export to PDF	A function that allows users to export their dashboard view as a PDF.	Maria

- **Benefit:** In the time it would have taken you to even create the table structure in a document, the AI has done the entire task of parsing, categorizing, and formatting the information.

Using Bulleted and Numbered Lists Effectively

Lists are fundamental to clear communication. Use bullet points for unordered items and numbered lists for sequential steps or ranked priorities.

Key Prompt Elements for Lists:

- **The Command:** "Create a bulleted list of..." or "Create a numbered list of..."
- **The Source Information:** The text or concept you want to list out.
- **Sorting Criteria (for numbered lists):** "Ranked from most to least critical," or "In chronological order."

Workplace Script: Creating an Onboarding Checklist
"Act as an HR manager. Create a detailed, numbered checklist for a new employee's first day. The list should cover all essential tasks in chronological order, from their arrival at the office to the

end of the day. Include items related to workspace setup, IT credentials, team introductions, and initial orientation meetings."

Analysis and Insights: Extracting Meaning from Information

Now we move up the value chain. Beyond generating and organizing, you can use AI to analyze information and surface insights that might not be immediately obvious. This is about asking the AI to act as a junior analyst, finding patterns, themes, and sentiment in the text you provide.

Key Prompt Elements for Analysis:

- **Role/Persona:** "Act as a market research analyst," "Act as a customer experience specialist."
- **The Raw Data:** Provide the text you want analyzed (e.g., customer reviews, survey responses, interview transcripts).
- **The Analytical Task:** Be very specific about what you're looking for.
    - "Identify the top 3 most common themes in this feedback."
    - "Categorize each comment as 'Positive,' 'Negative,' or 'Neutral'."
    - "Extract all mentions of our competitors from this text."
    - "Based on these project updates, what are the biggest risks you see?"

Professional Scenario: Analyzing Survey Feedback

- **The Goal:** You've just received 50 anonymous text responses from a post-event survey and need to quickly understand the main takeaways to share with your team.
- Strong Prompt (Using Chain-of-Thought):
  "Act as a professional research analyst. I will provide you

with a list of anonymous feedback comments from a recent corporate event. I want you to perform a thematic analysis. Before providing the final summary, please follow these steps:

1. First, for each individual comment, identify the core sentiment (Positive, Negative, or Mixed).
2. Second, group the comments into recurring themes (e.g., 'Venue and Logistics,' 'Speaker Quality,' 'Networking Opportunities').
3. Third, count the number of comments associated with each theme.

   Finally, present your analysis in a structured report. The report should have a one-paragraph overall summary, followed by a bulleted list of the top 3 most mentioned themes. For each theme, provide a brief description and one representative (anonymous) quote from the feedback.

   Here is the feedback: [Paste all 50 feedback responses]"

- **Why This Works:** By using the chain-of-thought technique, you guide the AI through a structured analytical process. This prevents it from simply giving you a vague summary and forces it to produce a more rigorous, data-backed analysis that is credible and easy to understand.

Creative Content: Brainstorming, Ideation, and Storytelling

While AI is not truly "creative" in the human sense, it is an exceptional tool for augmenting human creativity. It can generate a vast quantity of ideas, combinations, and starting points, helping you overcome creative blocks and explore new directions.

Using AI for Brainstorming and Ideation

The key to brainstorming with AI is to focus on quantity and variety. Think of it as a creative shotgun, not a sniper rifle.

Key Prompt Elements for Brainstorming:

- **The Core Topic:** The problem or concept you want ideas for.
- **The Number of Ideas:** Ask for a specific quantity (e.g., "Generate 20 ideas..."). This pushes the AI beyond the most obvious answers.
- **Guiding Constraints:** Add rules to focus the creativity.
    - "...for a target audience of small business owners."
    - "...that are low-cost and can be implemented in one month."
    - "...with a focus on sustainability."

Workplace Script: Naming a Project
"Act as a brand strategist. Our team is developing a new internal software tool that helps employees track their professional development goals. We need a project name. Generate a list of 15 potential names for this tool. The names should be short, memorable, and have a positive, growth-oriented feel. Organize the names into three categories: 'Professional & Corporate,' 'Modern & Techy,' and 'Creative & Abstract'."

Using AI for Business Storytelling

A compelling narrative can make a presentation, a marketing campaign, or a case study far more impactful. AI can help you structure these stories.

Key Prompt Elements for Storytelling:

- **The Core Message:** What is the key takeaway you want the audience to remember?
- **The Audience:** Who are you trying to persuade or inform?

- **The Desired Emotion:** "The story should feel inspirational," "It should create a sense of urgency."
- **A Story Framework:** Provide a narrative structure. A simple and effective one is Problem-Agitate-Solve (PAS).
    - **Problem:** Define the initial challenge the customer or company was facing.
    - **Agitate:** Describe the negative consequences of that problem.
    - **Solve:** Introduce your product or solution as the hero that resolves the problem.

Professional Scenario: Opening a Sales Presentation
"Act as a sales presentation coach. I need to create a short, compelling opening story for a presentation about our new logistics software. Use the Problem-Agitate-Solve framework.

- **Problem:** Our potential client, a mid-sized e-commerce company, struggles with late deliveries and inaccurate inventory tracking.
- **Agitate:** This leads to unhappy customers, negative reviews, and wasted staff time chasing down orders.
- Solve: Our software provides real-time tracking and predictive analytics to solve these exact issues.
  Please write a three-paragraph opening story based on this framework."

Code and Technical Documentation

For those in technical roles, AI can be a powerful coding assistant and a tireless documentation writer. The same principles of clarity and context apply, but with a focus on technical precision.

Prompts for Code Generation

Key Prompt Elements for Code:

- **Programming Language:** "Write a Python script..."
- **The Goal:** "...that takes a CSV file of sales data as input..."
- **The Logic:** "...and calculates the total revenue for each product category."
- **Libraries/Frameworks:** "Use the Pandas library for data manipulation."
- **Important Caveat:** AI-generated code is a first draft. It must be reviewed, tested, and secured by a qualified human developer before being used in a production environment.

Prompts for Technical Documentation

This is an incredibly high-leverage activity for AI, as it can automate a tedious but vital task.
Key Prompt Elements for Documentation:

- **The Code Snippet:** Paste the code you want to be documented.
- **The Task:** "Add line-by-line comments to this code explaining what each part does." or "Write a high-level summary paragraph explaining the purpose of this function."
- **The Audience:** "The documentation should be clear for a junior developer."

Matching Prompt Style to Desired Output Quality

By now, you understand that not all tasks require the same level of prompt detail. The final skill in this chapter is learning to match your prompting effort to your desired outcome.

The Three Levels of Prompting Effort:

1. **The Quick Draft Prompt (Low Effort, High Speed):**
   - **When to Use:** When you just need to get started, overcome a blank page, or handle a low-stakes task.

Speed is more important than quality.

- **Structure:** Focus on a clear **Task** and minimal **Context**. (e.g., "Draft a short email to the team reminding them about tomorrow's deadline.")
- **Outcome:** A rough first draft that will require significant editing, but is better than starting from scratch.

2. **The Polished Output Prompt (Medium Effort, High Quality):**
   - **When to Use:** For most professional tasks where the quality of the output matters. You want a near-final draft that requires only minor edits.
   - **Structure:** Uses all four **CTFC** elements. Often includes a **Role/Persona** and may use **Few-Shot Learning** with examples.
   - **Outcome:** A high-quality, well-structured output that is 80-95% complete.
3. **The Analytical/Complex Prompt (High Effort, High Insight):**
   - **When to Use:** When you need the AI to perform multi-step reasoning, analyze data, or tackle a complex problem.
   - **Structure:** Uses all CTFC elements, a strong **Role/Persona**, and a **Chain-of-Thought** framework that breaks the task into logical steps.
   - **Outcome:** A well-reasoned analysis or a solution to a complex problem that would have been difficult for the AI to achieve with a simpler prompt.

Knowing which level of effort to apply is a key productivity skill. Don't spend five minutes writing a perfect prompt for a simple reminder email. Conversely, don't expect a one-sentence prompt to produce a nuanced strategic analysis. Match your effort to the importance of the task.

Key Takeaways from This Chapter

- The most effective prompts are tailored to the specific type of output you need.
- For **text generation**, provide the audience, goal, tone, and key information points.
- For **data organization**, be explicit with your formatting commands, especially when creating tables with specific column headers.
- For **analysis and insights**, assign an expert role and use chain-of-thought prompting to guide the AI's reasoning process.
- For **creative content**, use AI to generate a high quantity of ideas and provide it with frameworks to structure business narratives.
- Match your prompt's level of detail and effort to the desired quality of the output.

You now have a practical guide for applying your prompting skills to the most common categories of professional work. You are equipped to generate text, organize data, and even extract insights. In the next chapter, we will build on this by exploring advanced prompting strategies that will allow you to tackle even more complex, multi-step projects.

Practice Exercise:

1. **Find an email** you need to write this week. Draft a "Polished Output" prompt for it using the CTFC framework.
2. **Find a messy set of notes** or an unstructured block of text from your work. Draft a prompt to organize it into a table with specific column headers.

3. **Identify a problem** or a question you're pondering at work. Draft a brainstorming prompt asking for 10 potential solutions, with at least one guiding constraint.

Chapter 5: Advanced Prompting Strategies

You have officially graduated from the fundamentals. In the previous chapters, we laid the essential groundwork for your journey with AI. You know what a large language model is, you understand the anatomy of an effective prompt, you have a framework for engaging with AI as a partner, and you know how to tailor your instructions for different types of professional outputs. You are already ahead of the curve.

Now, it's time to take the next step. This chapter is where we elevate your skills from crafting individual, high-quality prompts to orchestrating complex, multi-faceted projects with AI. These are the advanced strategies that separate a casual user from a true power user. The techniques we will cover here are what allow you to tackle your most significant and time-consuming work, transforming your AI assistant from a simple tool into a strategic force multiplier.

Don't let the word "advanced" intimidate you. These strategies are not necessarily more difficult to learn, but they do require a more systematic and strategic approach to your conversations with AI. It's the difference between asking for a single brick and providing the blueprint for an entire wall.

We will begin by exploring how to break down your biggest projects into manageable pieces using multi-step prompting and prompt chaining. You will learn how to create sophisticated workflows where the output of one AI task becomes the input for the next, building momentum and saving incredible amounts of time. We will then cover crucial techniques for quality control, including advanced methods to constrain the AI and minimize the risk of errors and factual inventions. You will learn how to use simple formatting tricks like delimiters to bring clarity to complex requests, how to tell the AI what *not* to do, and finally, the ultimate learning hack: how to use the AI to improve your own prompts.

By the end of this chapter, you will have a new set of tools that allow you to manage complex projects, automate sequences of tasks, and produce work of a higher quality and scope than you could with single prompts alone.

Multi-Step Prompting for Complex Projects

Think about the most significant project on your plate right now. Is it developing a business plan? Creating a comprehensive training program? Planning a major marketing campaign? Whatever it is, you know it's far too big to be accomplished with a single instruction. You wouldn't tell a new team member, "Go create the marketing plan," and expect a finished product. A project of that scale requires a series of distinct steps: research, brainstorming, outlining, drafting, and refining.

Multi-step prompting applies this same project management logic to your interactions with AI. Instead of trying to create one massive, all-encompassing prompt, you break the complex project down into its logical phases and use the AI as your dedicated assistant for each individual step. The output from one step becomes the foundation for the next, allowing you to maintain control and inject your own strategic decisions throughout the process.

This approach offers several key advantages:

- **Higher Quality:** By focusing the AI on one specific part of the project at a time, you get a more detailed and relevant output for each phase.
- **Greater Control:** It keeps you in the driver's seat. You can review the output at each stage, make adjustments, and steer the project in the right direction.
- **Reduced Errors:** A huge, complex prompt is more likely to confuse the AI, leading to errors or generic results. Smaller, focused prompts are easier for the AI to execute correctly.

A Step-by-Step Guide to Multi-Step Prompting

1. **Deconstruct the Project:** Before you even open your AI tool, take a few minutes to outline the major phases of your project. What is the logical sequence of tasks? Write it down.
2. **Prompt for Step 1:** Craft a strong, detailed prompt for the very first phase of your project. This is often a research, brainstorming, or outlining task.
3. **Review, Edit, and Select:** Analyze the AI's output from Step 1. This is where your human expertise is crucial. Edit the text, select the best ideas, or organize the information in a way that aligns with your goals.
4. **Use Step 1's Output as Input for Step 2:** Now, craft your next prompt. Critically, you will include the refined output from the previous step as the core context for this new prompt.
5. **Repeat and Build:** Continue this cycle, moving phase by phase through your project outline. Each prompt builds upon the work that came before it, creating a coherent and high-quality final product.

Professional Scenario: Creating a Proposal for a New

Internal Training Program

Let's say your goal is to create a detailed proposal for a new "Project Management Fundamentals" training program for junior employees at your company.

Step 1: Brainstorming Core Modules (The First Prompt)
"Act as an expert in corporate training and development. I am designing a new training program called 'Project Management Fundamentals' for junior employees with 0-2 years of experience. Brainstorm a list of 8-10 potential modules that would be essential for this audience. For each module, provide a one-sentence description of what it would cover."
You review the AI's list, and you decide on the five strongest and most relevant modules for your company.

Step 2: Creating a Detailed Outline (The Second Prompt)
"This is excellent. I have selected the following five modules for the training program:

1. Introduction to Project Lifecycles
2. Effective Stakeholder Communication
3. Task Management and Prioritization
4. Risk Identification and Mitigation
5. Project Reporting and Metrics
   Now, act as an instructional designer. For each of these five modules, create a detailed outline with 3-4 specific learning objectives in a bulleted list. The learning objectives should be action-oriented (e.g., 'Participants will be able to create a basic project timeline')."

The AI generates the detailed outline. You review it and are happy with the structure.

Step 3: Drafting the Proposal Introduction (The Third Prompt)
"Great. Now, act as a senior manager writing a proposal to secure a budget for this new training program. Using the detailed module outline we just created as context, write a compelling two-paragraph introduction for the proposal. The introduction should clearly state the problem (our junior employees lack formal project management training), the proposed solution (the new training program), and the key benefits for the company (improved project outcomes, increased efficiency, and better employee development)."
You would continue this process for each section of the proposal, using the previously generated content as context for the next step. By the end, you have a complete, coherent, and high-quality document that you guided at every stage.

Prompt Chaining: Breaking Big Tasks into Smaller Sequences

Prompt chaining is a close cousin to multi-step prompting, but it operates on a more granular, task-oriented level. If multi-step prompting is like managing the phases of a project, prompt chaining is like creating a mini-assembly line for your content. It's a technique where the output of one prompt becomes the direct, often unedited, input for the next prompt in a rapid sequence.

This is incredibly powerful for tasks that involve transforming a single piece of information into multiple different formats. Think of it as a "one-to-many" content workflow.

Professional Scenario: Repurposing a Single Report into Multiple Communications

Imagine you have just received a dense, 10-page market

research report. You need to communicate the key findings to several different audiences.

Chain Link 1: Distill the Key Findings (The First Prompt)
"I am going to provide you with a market research report. Please read the entire report and extract the top 5 most critical findings. Present these findings as a simple, clear bulleted list."
[Paste the full 10-page report text]
AI's Output:

- Finding 1: Competitor A's market share is declining in the enterprise sector.
- Finding 2: There is a growing demand for subscription-based pricing models.
- Finding 3: Customer satisfaction is strongly correlated with onboarding support.
- Finding 4: The Asia-Pacific market represents the largest growth opportunity.
- Finding 5: Mobile app integration is becoming a standard expectation.

Chain Link 2: Create an Executive Email (The Second Prompt)
"Take the following 5 bullet points and draft a concise email to the senior leadership team. The tone should be professional and strategic. The email should briefly summarize these key findings and state that a full analysis is forthcoming."
[Paste the 5 bullet points from the AI's previous output]
Chain Link 3: Create a Team Briefing (The Third Prompt)
"Now, take the same 5 bullet points and write a more detailed, action-oriented briefing for the product development team. For each finding, add a one-sentence question to prompt discussion (e.g., for Finding 1, 'How can we capitalize on Competitor A's weakness?')."

[Paste the 5 bullet points again]
Chain Link 4: Create a Sales Talking Point (The Fourth Prompt)
"Finally, take only Finding 2 ('There is a growing demand for subscription-based pricing models') and turn it into a persuasive talking point for our sales team to use in client conversations."
In just a few minutes, you have used prompt chaining to transform one large piece of information into three distinct, audience-specific communications. This assembly-line approach can save you hours of rewriting and reformatting each month.

Constraining AI to Avoid Hallucinations and Errors

We know from Chapter 1 that AI models can "hallucinate," which is a polite way of saying they can invent facts, figures, and sources with complete confidence. While this is becoming less frequent as models improve, it remains a critical risk you must manage. Your professional credibility is on the line. Advanced constraints are your primary defense against these errors.

The Golden Rule: Grounding in Provided Text
The single most effective technique to prevent hallucinations is to strictly forbid the AI from using any information outside of a document you provide. You are anchoring its response to a single source of truth: your text.
Workplace Script: The Information Gatekeeper
"Act as a research assistant. Your task is to answer the following questions based only on the information contained within the attached annual report. You must not use any external knowledge or make any assumptions. If the answer to a question cannot be found in the provided document, you must respond with the exact phrase: 'This information is not available in the provided document.'"

This technique is essential when you are working with sensitive, proprietary, or specific data and cannot risk the AI pulling in outside information.

Forcing a Source Check
While you can't always provide the source text, you can prompt the AI to be more rigorous about its own sources. This doesn't eliminate hallucinations, but it makes them less likely.
Workplace Script: The Junior Analyst
"Please identify and summarize the top three emerging trends in the supply chain management industry. For each trend you identify, please cite the source of your information or explain the basis for your conclusion. For example, mention a specific report, a well-known industry publication, or a recent market event."
By asking "how do you know that?", you are applying a chain-of-thought principle that forces the AI to check its own work and discourages it from simply inventing a plausible-sounding trend.

Using Delimiters and Formatting for Clarity

As your prompts become more complex, they will often contain multiple distinct pieces of information. For instance, you might provide a long article to be summarized, a set of specific instructions on how to summarize it, and an example of the desired output format.

To prevent the AI from getting confused about which part is which, we use delimiters. Delimiters are simple, consistent characters or tags that you use to create clear separations between the different components of your prompt. Think of them as file folders for your instructions.

Commonly Used Delimiters:

- Triple hashtags: ###
- Triple quotes: """
- XML-style tags: <text_to_summarize>, </text_to_summarize>
- Simple dashes: ---

The specific delimiter you use doesn't matter as much as using it consistently.

Professional Scenario: A Complex Summarization Task

Imagine you want the AI to summarize a technical article, but you also want it to pull out specific terminology and match a particular style.

A Confusing Prompt (Without Delimiters):
"Summarize the following article in three bullet points. Also, create a list of any technical terms used. The summary should be in a professional but simple tone, like the example I've included. Here's the example: 'The report highlights a new method for data encryption.' The article to summarize is..."
This is a recipe for a confusing output. The AI might mistake your example sentence for part of the article or get confused about the different tasks.

A Clear Prompt (With Delimiters):
"You will be given an article, a set of instructions, and an example.
###INSTRUCTIONS###

1. Summarize the article from the ###ARTICLE### section into exactly three bullet points.
2. Create a separate bulleted list of all the technical terms mentioned in the article.
3. Ensure the tone of your summary matches the tone of the

text in the ###EXAMPLE### section.

###ARTICLE###
[Paste the full technical article here]
###EXAMPLE###
The report highlights a new method for data encryption that could be beneficial for our security protocols.
By using ### to neatly partition each piece of information, you make the task completely unambiguous for the AI. This dramatically increases the probability of getting a perfect result on the first try.

Negative Prompting: Telling AI What NOT to Do

Often, the most efficient way to guide the AI toward the output you want is to tell it what you *don't* want. This is negative prompting. It's a specific type of constraint that carves away the undesirable possibilities, leaving the AI with a much clearer path to the right answer.

This is particularly useful when the AI has a tendency to default to certain clichés, tones, or formats that you want to avoid.

When to Use Negative Prompting:

- To avoid overused jargon or corporate buzzwords.
- To prevent a specific tone (e.g., overly formal, too casual, apologetic).
- To exclude certain topics or information from a response.
- To guide brainstorming away from obvious or unoriginal ideas.

Professional Scenario: Drafting a Job Description

- **The Goal:** You want to write a job description for a software engineer that sounds modern and authentic, avoiding the usual corporate clichés.

- Prompt with Negative Prompting:
  "Act as a tech recruiter. Write a job description for a 'Senior Software Engineer' role at a fast-growing startup. The tone should be engaging and direct.
  Important constraints (what to avoid):
  - Do not use the phrases 'rockstar developer,' 'ninja,' or 'work hard, play hard.'
  - Do not include generic requirements like 'must be a team player' or 'possess strong communication skills.' Focus on tangible, technical skills instead.
  - Avoid an overly formal or corporate tone."

This negative prompt is far more effective than trying to describe the desired tone in only positive terms. By explicitly forbidding the clichés, you force the AI to generate a more original and authentic-sounding description.

Meta-Prompting: Asking AI to Improve Your Prompts

This final technique is perhaps the most powerful for your long-term growth as an AI user. Meta-prompting is the practice of using AI to critique and improve your own prompts. You are, in essence, asking the expert to teach you how to be an expert. It's like having a free, on-demand coach who can help you refine your most important new skill.

The Meta-Prompting Workflow:

1. **Draft Your Prompt:** For any given task, write the best, most detailed prompt you can, using all the principles you've learned.

2. **Craft the Meta-Prompt:** You will now ask the AI to evaluate your prompt.
3. **Review the Suggestions:** The AI will give you feedback on your prompt, explaining where it is vague, what context is missing, or how it could be structured more clearly.
4. **Refine and Execute:** Edit your original prompt based on the AI's feedback, and then use that improved prompt to execute the actual task.

The Universal Meta-Prompt Template:
"Act as an expert in prompt engineering. I am going to provide you with a prompt I have written for an AI language model. Your task is to analyze my prompt and suggest specific ways to improve it. Tell me what information is missing, where I could be more specific, and how I could improve the structure or constraints to get a better-quality output. Explain the reasoning behind each of your suggestions.
Do not answer or execute the prompt itself. Your only job is to critique my prompt and teach me how to make it better.

Here is my prompt:
[Paste your original prompt here]"
Example in Action:

- **Your Original Prompt:** "Write a marketing email for my new product."
- **You feed this into the Meta-Prompt Template.**
- The AI's Probable Critique:
  "This is a good start, but the prompt is too vague to generate a strong result. Here are my suggestions for improvement:
  1. **Add a Persona:** Start with 'Act as a direct-response copywriter.' This will prime the AI to write more persuasive and effective copy.

2. **Specify the Product:** You need to tell the AI what the product is. What does it do? Who is it for?
3. **Define the Audience:** Who is this email being sent to? Are they existing customers or cold leads? This will dramatically change the tone and content.
4. **State the Goal:** What is the single action you want the reader to take? Click a link? Sign up for a demo? Buy now?
5. Provide Key Talking Points: Include 2-3 key benefits of the product that should be highlighted in the email. Reasoning: By adding these elements, you are moving from a generic request to a detailed creative brief, which will allow the AI to draft a much more targeted and effective marketing email."

By using this technique regularly, you will quickly internalize the principles of great prompting. The AI will train you to think more clearly and specifically, making all of your future interactions more efficient.

Key Takeaways from This Chapter

- For large, complex projects, use **multi-step prompting** to break the work into manageable phases, maintaining quality and control.
- Use **prompt chaining** to create content assembly lines, transforming a single piece of information into multiple formats for different audiences.
- Actively constrain the AI to prevent errors by **grounding it in provided text** and telling it explicitly what to avoid with **negative prompting**.
- Use **delimiters** like ### to structure complex prompts and provide clarity to the AI.

- Embrace **meta-prompting** as a learning tool. Regularly ask the AI to critique your prompts to accelerate your own skill development.

You are now equipped with a suite of advanced strategies that will allow you to tackle almost any professional task with confidence. You can manage large projects, create complex workflows, and ensure a higher degree of accuracy and quality in the AI's output. In the next chapter, we will address a crucial part of the process: what to do when things go wrong. We will cover the art and science of debugging and refining your prompts.

Chapter 6: Debugging and Refining Your Prompts

By now, you have a solid arsenal of skills. You understand the core principles of AI, you can construct a well-formed prompt using the CTFC framework, and you have a collection of advanced strategies for tackling complex projects. You are well on your way to becoming a proficient AI user. But even with the best preparation and the most carefully crafted prompts, there will be times when the output you get is not what you expected.

The AI might misunderstand your request, produce a generic or off-topic response, make a factual error, or generate text in the wrong format. This is a normal, and frankly, essential part of the process. It is not a sign of failure on your part or a fundamental flaw in the technology. It is simply a signal that your instructions need clarification.

Think of yourself as a director working with a new actor. The actor is incredibly talented and can perform any role you give them, but they are also very literal. If your direction is ambiguous, their performance will be confusing. The solution isn't to fire the actor. The solution is to refine your direction.

This chapter is your director's handbook. It's a practical guide to the art and science of troubleshooting your prompts. Debugging, a term borrowed from the world of software development, simply means the process of finding and fixing errors. For our purposes, it's the systematic process of figuring out why your prompt didn't work and how to fix it.

We will start by creating a simple diagnostic framework to help you quickly identify the root cause of a poor output. We will then dive deep into the iterative refinement process, showing you how to make small, targeted changes to steer the AI toward the perfect result. You will learn how to A/B test different prompting approaches for your most important tasks, and we'll provide a clear guide on a crucial decision: when to refine a prompt versus when it's more efficient to start over from scratch.

Finally, we will transition from fixing prompts to operationalizing them. You will learn how to build and manage a personal library of your best, battle-tested prompts, creating a powerful, reusable asset that will be the cornerstone of your long-term productivity.

Diagnosing Why a Prompt Isn't Working

When an AI gives you a subpar response, the first step is to avoid frustration and get analytical. Don't just see the output as "bad." Instead, ask yourself, "What specific type of bad is this?" By categorizing the error, you can quickly diagnose the likely flaw in your original prompt. Most issues can be traced back to one of the four CTFC elements we covered in Chapter 2.

Let's create a simple diagnostic checklist. When you get a result you don't like, run through these common problems.

The Prompt Debugging Checklist

1. The Problem: The output is too generic, vague, or superficial.

- **Description:** The AI gives you a bland, high-level response that sounds like a generic encyclopedia entry. It lacks any specific detail relevant to your situation.

- **Likely Cause:** Missing or insufficient **Context**.
- **Diagnosis:** You probably didn't give the AI enough background information. It doesn't know your role, your audience, your company, or your strategic goal. Faced with a lack of information, it defaulted to the most general, statistically probable answer.
- **The Fix:** Rerun the prompt, but this time, add a rich contextual paragraph at the beginning. Use a persona. Define your audience. Explain the "why" behind your request.

2. The Problem: The output is in the wrong structure.

- **Description:** You wanted a bulleted list, but you got a dense paragraph. You wanted a table, but you got a simple list.
- **Likely Cause:** Missing or unclear **Format** instructions.
- **Diagnosis:** You either forgot to specify the format, or your instruction was not explicit enough. "Discuss these points" is not the same as "Present these points in a numbered list."
- **The Fix:** Be relentlessly specific about the structure. Use phrases like: "Format the output as a three-column table with the headers 'X,' 'Y,' and 'Z'." or "The final output should be a single paragraph of no more than 150 words."

3. The Problem: The output doesn't follow the rules.

- **Description:** The response is too long, the tone is wrong, or it includes information you specifically wanted to avoid.
- **Likely Cause:** Missing or weak **Constraints**.
- **Diagnosis:** You didn't set clear boundaries for the AI. You may have forgotten to specify a word count, or your tone instruction was too subtle.
- **The Fix:** Add a dedicated "Constraints" or "Rules" section to your prompt. Use negative prompting to be explicit about what the AI should not do. For example, "Constraint: The

tone must be formal. Do not use contractions or casual language."

4. The Problem: The AI did the wrong thing entirely.

- **Description:** You asked for a summary, but it wrote an analysis. You asked for a list of pros, but it gave you a list of cons.
- **Likely Cause:** An ambiguous or unclear **Task**.
- **Diagnosis:** Your action verb was not precise enough. A word like "handle" or "address" is open to interpretation. The AI made its best guess, and it guessed wrong.
- **The Fix:** Use a single, strong, unambiguous action verb. "Summarize," "Analyze," "Translate," "Rewrite," "Brainstorm," "Compare," "Create." Leave no room for misinterpretation.

Professional Scenario: Debugging a Flawed Prompt

Let's walk through a real-world example. A junior marketing manager, Alex, is tasked with creating a short brief for a freelance graphic designer to create a new promotional image for a software product.

Alex's First Prompt (The Flawed Prompt):
"I need some ideas for a promotional graphic for our new software, 'TaskFlow.' It's a project management tool. Just give me some concepts for the designer."
The AI's Output (The Flawed Output):
"Here are some concepts for a promotional graphic for TaskFlow:

1. **A stylized checklist:** This represents task completion and organization. The checkmarks could be in the company's brand colors.
2. **An abstract network diagram:** This visualizes the idea of connecting different parts of a project together.

3. **A simple, bold typographic poster:** Just the name 'TaskFlow' with a powerful tagline like 'Project Management, Perfected.'"

Alex's Analysis (The Debugging Process):
Alex looks at the output. It's not terrible, but it's far too generic to be useful. A designer would still have many questions. Alex runs through the diagnostic checklist:

- **Generic Output?** Yes. Very. **Diagnosis: Missing Context.** The AI has no idea who the target audience is, what the key benefit of the software is, or where this graphic will be used.
- **Wrong Structure?** Not really, a list is fine. **Diagnosis: Format is okay.**
- **Doesn't Follow Rules?** There were no rules to follow. **Diagnosis: Missing Constraints.** The AI doesn't know the dimensions, the required text, or the desired feeling of the graphic.
- **Did the Wrong Thing?** It did provide "concepts," so the task was understood at a high level. **Diagnosis: Task is okay, but could be clearer.**

Alex's Second Prompt (The Refined Prompt):
"

Act as a senior marketing manager writing a creative brief for a freelance graphic designer. We are creating a promotional graphic for our new project management software, 'TaskFlow.' Our target audience is freelance project managers and small agency owners who are overwhelmed by their workload. The key benefit of TaskFlow is that it simplifies complex projects into a clear, visual timeline. The graphic will be used primarily in social media ads on LinkedIn.

Create a design brief for a promotional graphic.

The brief should have three distinct sections with the following headers: 'Objective,' 'Key Message,' and 'Visual Requirements.'

Under 'Visual Requirements,' specify that the graphic should feel clean, modern, and professional, and must include our company logo (placeholder for now) and the tagline 'From Chaos to Clarity.' The dimensions should be 1200x628 pixels. Do not suggest using stock photos of office workers."

This refined prompt is a night-and-day improvement. It will produce a detailed, actionable brief that a designer can actually use, saving hours of back-and-forth communication. The 60 seconds Alex spent diagnosing and fixing the prompt will save a huge amount of time and confusion down the line.

The Iterative Refinement Process

In Chapter 3, we introduced the concept of iterative prompting as a core part of the creative process. Here, we will look at it through the lens of debugging. Iterative refinement is your primary tool for fixing a prompt that is almost, but not quite, right.

The key principle is to **make one change at a time.**

When you get a flawed output, it's tempting to write a follow-up prompt that tries to fix everything at once. "Okay, that's wrong. Make the tone more formal, add a section about the budget, shorten the introduction, and format it as a table." This approach often leads to more confusion. The AI might fix two of your points but ignore the other two, or the combination of new instructions might produce an even stranger result.

A more effective method is to treat it like a scientific experiment. Change only one variable at a time, observe the result, and then proceed to the next variable. This gives you a much clearer understanding of how your instructions are affecting the output.

The Step-by-Step Iterative Refinement Workflow:

1. **Run Your Initial Prompt (V1):** Start with your best possible prompt.
2. **Analyze the Output:** Read the AI's response carefully. Identify the *single biggest flaw*. Don't try to fix everything at once. Is the tone the biggest problem? Is it a missing piece of information?
3. **Craft a Targeted Follow-Up Prompt:** Write a simple, direct follow-up prompt that addresses only that one flaw.
    - "That's a good start, but the tone is too casual. Please rewrite it in a more formal and professional voice."
    - "Excellent. Now, please add a new section titled 'Budget Considerations' and write a brief paragraph about the estimated costs."
    - "Great. The content is good, but now please reformat the entire response into a table with two columns: 'Problem' and 'Solution'."
4. **Analyze the New Output (V1.1):** Did the follow-up prompt successfully fix the problem? If yes, great. Now identify the *next* biggest flaw and repeat the process.
5. **Continue Until Satisfied:** Continue this cycle of small, targeted refinements until the output meets your standards of quality.

This methodical process might seem slower, but in practice, it is almost always faster and more reliable than trying to fix everything in one go. You are carefully guiding the AI toward your desired destination, one clear turn at a time.

A/B Testing Different Prompt Approaches

For your most important or most frequent tasks, it's worth investing a little extra time to find the absolute best way to prompt the AI. A/B testing, a concept borrowed from marketing and product design, is a simple way to do this. The idea is to create two different versions of a prompt (Prompt A and Prompt B) for the same task, run them both, and then compare the outputs side-by-side to see which approach works better.

This is not something you need to do for every email you write. This is a technique for optimizing your high-stakes "power prompts," the ones that form the basis of your most valuable templates.

How to Conduct a Prompt A/B Test:

1. **Identify a High-Value Task:** Choose a recurring task where a high-quality output is critical. Examples: writing a project proposal summary, generating a weekly sales report analysis, or creating a new marketing campaign concept.
2. **Formulate a Hypothesis:** Think about two different ways you could instruct the AI. Your hypothesis might be, "I think a prompt that uses a very specific persona will produce a better result than one that uses a more generic chain-of-thought approach."
3. **Write Prompt A and Prompt B:** Craft your two distinct prompts. They should both aim for the same final goal but use different techniques.
    - **Prompt A** might heavily rely on a detailed persona and tone instructions.

    - **Prompt B** might use a multi-step, chain-of-thought process with explicit instructions on the reasoning steps.
    - **Prompt A** could use a zero-shot approach (no examples).
    - **Prompt B** could use a few-shot approach (with examples of the desired output).
4. **Run Both Prompts in Separate Chat Sessions:** It's important to use new, clean chat windows for each prompt to ensure that context from one test doesn't leak into the other.
5. **Compare the Outputs:** Evaluate the two responses based on clear criteria:
    - **Quality:** Which one is better written, more accurate, and more insightful?
    - **Completeness:** Which one came closer to a finished product with less need for editing?
    - **Speed/Efficiency:** Which prompt was easier to write and got you to the desired result faster?
6. **Declare a Winner and Save It:** The winning prompt becomes your new gold-standard template for that task.

Professional Scenario: A/B Testing a Prompt for Competitive Analysis

A product manager wants to create a reusable prompt for quickly analyzing competitor product announcements.

Hypothesis: A prompt that forces the AI to think like different specialists will produce a more well-rounded analysis than a single, generic analysis prompt.

Prompt A (The Single Persona Prompt):
"Act as a senior product marketing manager. I am going to paste the text of a press release from our main competitor announcing a new product feature. Your task is to write a concise analysis of

this announcement. The analysis should cover the key new capabilities, the likely target audience, and the potential impact on our market position."
[Paste competitor press release]
Prompt B (The Multi-Persona A/B Test):
"I am going to paste the text of a press release from our main competitor. I want you to analyze it from three different expert perspectives.

1. **As a Product Manager:** Summarize the core new features and how they address user needs.
2. **As a Sales Director:** Identify the key talking points their sales team will likely use against us and suggest one potential counter-argument.
3. As a Marketing Strategist: Analyze the language and positioning in the press release. What is the key message they are trying to send to the market?
   Please format your response with three clear sections, one for each persona's analysis."
   [Paste competitor press release]

By running this test, the product manager will likely discover that Prompt B, while slightly more complex to write, produces a far richer and more actionable analysis. It breaks the problem down and provides strategic insights from multiple angles. Once validated, this multi-persona approach becomes their go-to template for this critical task.

When to Start Over Versus When to Refine

You are working on a prompt, and the results are just not getting there. You've tried a few follow-up refinements, but the output is still fundamentally flawed. Now you face a critical decision: do you continue to try to fix the current conversation, or do you cut your losses and start over with a completely new prompt in a new chat window?

Knowing when to quit is a crucial skill. Continuing to refine a fundamentally broken prompt is a waste of time. It's like trying to patch up a building with a cracked foundation.

Here is a simple decision-making framework:

You should REFINE the prompt when:

- The AI has correctly understood the core **Task** and **Context**.
- The overall structure and content are about 60% or more of the way to your goal.
- The flaws are related to specific details: the **tone** is slightly off, a specific piece of data is missing, the **format** needs tweaking, or you want to add or remove a specific section.
- **Analogy:** The house is built and standing, but you want to repaint a room, move some furniture, and add a window. These are renovations.

You should START OVER when:

- The AI has fundamentally misunderstood the **Task**. You asked for a summary, and it wrote a poem. You asked for a marketing plan, and it wrote a technical manual.
- The output is completely off-topic or irrelevant to the **Context** you provided.
- The output is less than 20% useful. You find yourself wanting to delete almost everything it wrote.
- You realize after seeing the first output that your initial approach was completely wrong and you need to rethink the entire structure of your request.
- **Analogy:** You asked for a two-story house, and the builder

gave you a one-story bungalow. You can't fix this by repainting. You need to tear it down and start again with a new blueprint.

Time-Saving Technique: The "Fresh Eyes" Restart
When you decide to start over, don't just copy and paste your old, flawed prompt. The AI's bad first attempt often reveals a weakness in your instructions. Take 30 seconds to think about why the AI got it so wrong. Was your Task verb ambiguous? Was your Context confusing? Use that insight to write a brand new, fundamentally better prompt from scratch. This "fresh eyes" approach is often the fastest way to get to a great result.

Building a Personal Prompt Library

As you debug, refine, and A/B test, you will start to produce some truly exceptional prompts. These are your "master prompts" – the perfectly crafted, battle-tested instructions that reliably produce high-quality outputs for your most common tasks.

Do not let these gems disappear into your chat history. You must save them.

A personal prompt library is a curated collection of your best prompts, organized in a way that makes them easy to find, reuse, and share. This is arguably the single most important system you can build for long-term AI productivity. It turns your past efforts into a compounding asset. Why reinvent the wheel every time you need to create a meeting agenda when you have a perfect, optimized prompt ready to go?

How to Organize Your Prompt Library:
There are many ways to do this, and the best system is the one you will actually use. Here are a few popular methods:

- **By Task Type:** Create folders or documents for categories like "Emails," "Reports," "Meeting Management," "Brainstorming," etc. This is the most common and intuitive method.
- **By Project:** If you work on distinct projects, you can keep a dedicated prompt library for each one. This is useful for keeping all project-related templates in one place.
- **By Persona:** You might create a collection of prompts for when you are "Acting as a Project Manager" or "Acting as a Marketing Analyst."

Tools for Building Your Library:

- **Simple Text Files:** The simplest solution. Create a folder on your computer and save each master prompt as a separate `.txt` file with a clear, descriptive name (e.g., `Weekly_Team_Update_Email_Prompt.txt`).
- **Note-Taking Apps (The Best Option for Most People):** Tools like Notion, Evernote, Obsidian, or Microsoft OneNote are perfect for this. You can create a dedicated "Prompt Library" notebook and use pages, tags, and folders to organize your prompts in a searchable and structured way.
- **Dedicated Prompt Manager Tools:** As AI becomes more integrated into our work, specialized tools are emerging that are designed specifically for saving, sharing, and managing prompts.

What to Save in Your Library:
For each entry, save more than just the prompt itself. Create a mini-template:

- **Title:** A clear, descriptive name for the task (e.g., "Monthly Project Status Report Prompt").
- **The Prompt:** The full, optimized text of your master prompt,

often with bracketed placeholders for the parts that will change each time (e.g., [Project Name], [Key Metric]).

- **Notes:** A brief sentence or two explaining the context for the prompt, or any tips for using it effectively (e.g., "This prompt works best when you provide at least three specific data points.").

Version Control for Your Best Prompts

This is a slightly more advanced practice, but it's incredibly valuable for professionals who rely on AI for critical, repeatable workflows. Version control is the idea of keeping a historical record of your most important prompts as you modify and improve them over time.

Why is this important?
AI models are not static. They are constantly being updated and changed by the companies that build them. A prompt that works perfectly today with Model X might produce a slightly different or lower-quality result when Model X.1 is released next month. If you have a record of how your prompt has evolved, it's much easier to adapt it to changes in the underlying AI.
A Simple, Non-Technical Approach to Version Control:
You don't need complex developer tools for this. A simple file-naming convention is all you need.
When you create your first master prompt, save it as:
Competitive_Analysis_Prompt_v1.0.txt
A few weeks later, you have an idea to improve it by adding a negative prompt. You test it and it works better. You save the new version as:
Competitive_Analysis_Prompt_v1.1.txt
In the new file, you can add a small "Changelog" note at the top:

- **v1.1 (2025-10-02):** Added a negative prompt to exclude analysis of our own company.

This simple practice creates a historical record that allows you to track what works and why. If a future AI model update "breaks" your v1.1 prompt, you can easily go back to v1.0 as a starting point for your new debugging process. It's a professional habit that future-proofs your most valuable productivity systems.

Key Takeaways from This Chapter

- When a prompt fails, don't get frustrated. Get analytical. Use the **CTFC diagnostic checklist** to systematically identify the likely flaw in your instructions.
- Refine your prompts **iteratively**. Make one small, targeted change at a time to carefully guide the AI's output.
- For your most critical and recurring tasks, use **A/B testing** to experiment with different prompting techniques and discover the most effective approach.
- Know when to **refine versus when to start over**. If the AI has fundamentally misunderstood the task, a fresh start is usually more efficient.
- The goal of debugging is to create a master prompt. **Save these optimized prompts** in a personal library to create a compounding productivity asset.
- For your most important prompts, use a simple **version control** system to track changes and future-proof your workflows.

You have now completed Part II of this book. You have not only mastered the core skills of prompting but also learned how to troubleshoot, refine, and systematize your interactions with AI. You are no longer just a user; you are becoming an architect of AI-powered workflows. In Part III, we will take all of these foundational skills and apply them to a wide range of specific professional roles and career-defining tasks.

Part III: Professional Applications – Career-Specific Use Cases

Chapter 7: AI Prompts for Business Professionals

Welcome to Part III. In the first two parts of this book, we built your workshop. You've learned about your tools (the AI models), mastered the techniques for using them (the prompting frameworks), and developed the skills to troubleshoot and refine your work. You have established a solid foundation.

Now, it is time to build something with it.

Part III is where we move from the workshop to the worksite. This section is dedicated to practical, career-specific applications. We will take all the foundational skills you've learned—the CTFC framework, iterative prompting, multi-step workflows, and advanced strategies—and apply them directly to the real-world tasks that define modern professional life. Each chapter in this part will act as a dedicated playbook for a specific role or industry, filled with targeted examples, scenarios, and ready-to-use prompt templates.

We begin with the role that forms the backbone of countless organizations: the business professional. This chapter is for the project managers, the consultants, the analysts, the team leads, the department heads, and every professional who navigates the daily landscape of corporate communication, strategic planning, and project execution. The work of a business professional is diverse, demanding a constant shift between communication, analysis, and planning. It is also a role filled with repetitive tasks that are perfectly suited for AI automation.

In this chapter, we will cover the core competencies of the modern professional workplace. We will start with the most fundamental and time-consuming task: writing compelling emails and professional correspondence. From there, we will move to creating the content for persuasive presentations and slide decks. We will revolutionize your meeting workflow, covering everything from preparation and agenda creation to post-meeting summaries and action items. You will learn to draft high-impact reports and executive summaries in a fraction of the time. We will then elevate your strategic contribution by using AI for business analysis and competitive research. Finally, we will provide a framework for using AI as a partner in project planning and milestone tracking.

This chapter is your new operational manual. By the end of it, you will have a suite of powerful, practical, and immediately applicable prompts that will not only save you hours each week but also improve the quality and impact of your most important work.

Writing Compelling Emails and Professional Correspondence

Email is the circulatory system of the modern workplace. It is also one of the biggest drains on our time and mental energy. Crafting the right message with the right tone for the right audience can be a painstaking process. This is where AI can have the most immediate and profound impact on your daily productivity. By mastering prompts for email, you can transform yourself from an email writer into an email editor and strategist, focusing your energy on the message, not the mechanics.

The key to effective email prompting is to provide a detailed brief that covers the purpose, the audience, and the desired outcome of the communication.

Professional Scenario: Delivering Difficult News

Let's tackle one of the most challenging email types: delivering bad news. You need to inform a key stakeholder that a project milestone will be delayed. A vague prompt would be disastrous here, but a well-structured prompt can produce a draft that is professional, proactive, and strategically sound.

- **The Goal:** You are a project manager. You need to email a client, Ms. Chen, to inform her that the delivery of the project's beta version will be delayed by one week due to an unforeseen technical issue. You need to maintain her confidence and present a clear path forward.
- The Prompt:
  "Act as a senior project manager with excellent client communication skills. I need to write a difficult email to a key client, Ms. Chen.
  Context: The project is the 'Orion Platform Development.' We were scheduled to deliver the beta version this Friday, October 10th. Due to an unexpected issue with a third-party data integration, we need to delay the delivery by one week to Friday, October 17th. The issue is identified, and our engineering team has a clear solution that is already being implemented.
  Task: Draft a professional email to Ms. Chen.
  Format: The email should have a clear subject line, a brief opening, a paragraph explaining the situation, a paragraph outlining our solution and new timeline, and a concluding paragraph that reaffirms our commitment to the project's success.

Constraints: The tone must be professional, transparent, and proactive. Do not sound overly apologetic or defensive. The focus should be on the solution, not the problem. Do not blame the third-party vendor. Reassure the client that this delay will not impact the final project launch date of November 30th. End the email by offering to set up a brief call to discuss this further."

- **Analysis of the Prompt:** This prompt uses the CTFC framework perfectly for a sensitive communication.
    - **Context:** It provides the persona, the project name, the client's name, the specific dates, and the root cause of the problem.
    - **Task:** The instruction to "Draft a professional email" is clear and direct.
    - **Format:** It dictates the precise paragraph-by-paragraph structure of the email.
    - **Constraints:** This is the most critical part. The instructions on tone ("transparent and proactive," "not overly apologetic") and content ("focus on the solution," "reassure about the final launch date") are what will ensure the AI produces a strategically sound message.

Productivity Technique: The "Three Bullet Points" Email

For your routine internal communications, you don't always need such a detailed prompt. A powerful shortcut is the "three bullet points" method. For any standard email, just provide the AI with the three most important pieces of information you need to convey.

- The Prompt:
  "Act as a team lead. Write a brief and friendly email to my team about our upcoming Q4 planning session.

Please include these three key points:

- The meeting is scheduled for this Thursday at 10 AM in Conference Room 3.
- The goal is to finalize our top three priorities for the next quarter.
- Ask everyone to come prepared with at least one strategic suggestion.

The tone should be conversational and action-oriented."

This simple technique can handle 80% of your daily email needs, turning a five-minute writing task into a 30-second prompting task.

Creating Presentations and Slide Deck Content

Creating a compelling presentation is one of the most high-stakes activities in a professional's career. It's a chance to influence decision-makers, align teams, and drive action. It can also be a time-consuming and stressful process. While AI cannot design your slides (yet), it is an exceptionally powerful tool for generating the most important part of any presentation: the narrative and the content.

The most effective way to build a presentation with AI is to use a multi-step prompting approach, breaking the process down into logical phases.

Step 1: Brainstorming the Core Narrative

Before you even think about slides, you need a story. What is the key message you want your audience to walk away with?

- **The Goal:** You need to create a presentation for the leadership team to get approval for a new internal software procurement.

- The Prompt (Step 1):
  "Act as a strategic communications consultant. I need to create a persuasive presentation for our executive team.
  Context: The goal of the presentation is to convince them to approve a $50,000 annual budget for a new customer relationship management (CRM) software called 'ConnectSphere.' Our current system is outdated and inefficient, leading to lost sales opportunities and frustrated account managers.
  Task: Using the Problem-Agitate-Solve framework, create a core narrative for this presentation. Outline the key points for each of the three sections.
  Format: Present the output as three distinct sections with the headers: 'The Problem,' 'The Consequences (Agitate),' and 'Our Proposed Solution.'"

Step 2: Creating a Slide-by-Slide Outline

Once you have your core narrative, you can translate it into a presentation structure.

- The Prompt (Step 2):
  "That's a perfect narrative. Now, take that Problem-Agitate-Solve structure and expand it into a detailed, slide-by-slide outline for a 10-slide presentation deck.
  Task: Create a slide-by-slide outline.
  Format: For each slide, provide a clear slide title and 3-4 bullet points summarizing the key content or data that should be on that slide.
  Constraints: The outline should logically flow from the problem to the solution. Include a slide for the budget request and a final slide with a clear call to action (approving the procurement)."

Step 3: Generating Speaker Notes

With a solid outline, you can now generate the detailed content. A great technique is to ask the AI to write your speaker notes, which you can then summarize onto the slides themselves.

- The Prompt (Step 3):
  "This outline is excellent. Now, let's focus on Slide 4, which is titled 'The Hidden Costs of Our Current System.'
  Context: The bullet points for this slide are: 'Wasted employee time on manual data entry,' 'Missed follow-up opportunities with key clients,' and 'Lack of accurate sales forecasting.'
  Task: Write a compelling and detailed paragraph of speaker notes for this specific slide.
  Constraints: The notes should be written in a conversational, confident speaking style. Use data where possible (you can use plausible placeholders like 'an estimated 10 hours per week' or 'a potential 15% revenue loss'). The goal is to make the leadership team feel the tangible cost of inaction."

By following this three-step process, you methodically build a high-quality presentation from the ground up. You use your strategic input to guide the narrative and structure, while delegating the heavy lifting of content generation to the AI.

Meeting Preparation and Agenda Creation

Meetings are another area where a small amount of AI-assisted preparation can yield massive productivity gains. An effective meeting is almost always the result of a clear agenda and a shared understanding of the goals. AI can help you create both in minutes.

Crafting a Purpose-Driven Agenda

A good agenda doesn't just list topics; it frames them as questions to be answered or decisions to be made. This is a perfect task for AI.

- **The Goal:** You need to create an agenda for a one-hour weekly project check-in meeting.
- The Prompt:
  "Act as an expert project manager and meeting facilitator. I need to create an agenda for our weekly 'Project Phoenix' check-in meeting.
  Context: The team is currently working on the user testing phase. The meeting is one hour long and will include the project manager, two developers, and one designer. The primary goal of this week's meeting is to resolve a key roadblock and plan the next sprint.
  Task: Create a detailed meeting agenda.
  Format: The agenda should include the meeting title, date, attendees, and overall objectives. Then, create a timed list of agenda items. For each item, list the topic, the person leading that discussion point, and the intended outcome (e.g., 'A decision on X,' 'A list of action items for Y').
  Constraints: Allocate specific time slots for each topic, including 5 minutes at the beginning for a quick recap and 5 minutes at the end for summarizing action items. The main discussion topic, 'Resolving the User Feedback Roadblock,' should be allocated the most time."
- **Benefit:** This prompt will produce a professional, outcome-oriented agenda that ensures your meeting stays on track and achieves its goals. By specifying the format, you get a document that is ready to be sent out to the team

immediately.

Post-Meeting Workflow: From Transcript to Action Items

As we touched on in Chapter 4, one of the most powerful AI automations is summarizing meeting transcripts.

- The Prompt:
  "Act as a highly efficient executive assistant. I have pasted the raw transcript from a project meeting below.
  Task: Please review the entire transcript and perform the following two actions:
  1. Write a concise, one-paragraph summary of the key discussion points and the final decisions that were made.
  2. Create a separate, bulleted list of all the specific action items that were assigned. For each action item, clearly state the task and the name of the person it was assigned to.
     Format: The final output should have two sections with the headers 'Meeting Summary' and 'Action Items.'
     Constraints: Ignore any small talk or off-topic conversations in the transcript. Focus only on the substantive parts of the discussion.

###TRANSCRIPT###[Paste the full, raw meeting transcript here]"

This single prompt can save you 30-60 minutes of post-meeting administrative work, allowing you to focus on executing the action items rather than just documenting them.

Report Writing and Executive Summaries

Writing detailed reports and summarizing long documents are core tasks for many business professionals. They are also incredibly time-consuming. AI is exceptionally good at both, particularly at the task of distillation, which is the heart of any good executive summary.

Creating a High-Impact Executive Summary

The key to a good summary is to ground the AI in the source text and give it a clear audience and purpose.

- **The Goal:** You have a dense, 20-page market analysis report, and you need to create a one-page executive summary for your department head.
- The Prompt:
  "Act as a professional business analyst. I am providing you with a 20-page market analysis report.
  Task: Write a one-page executive summary of this report. The summary must be concise, strategic, and easy for a busy executive to understand.
  Format: The summary should begin with a single sentence stating the most important conclusion of the report. It should then be followed by 3-4 key bullet points, with each bullet point summarizing a major finding or recommendation from the report. Conclude with a single paragraph outlining the strategic implications for our business.
  Constraints: The summary must be based only on the information contained in the provided report. Do not introduce any external information. The tone should be objective and data-driven. The total length should not exceed 400 words.
  ###REPORT TEXT###
  [Paste the full text of the 20-page report here]"
- **Why This Works:** The "grounding" constraint is critical here. By forbidding the AI from using outside knowledge, you ensure the summary is a faithful representation of the source

document. The specific format instructions (opening sentence, bullet points, concluding paragraph) force the AI to create a well-structured and scannable summary, which is exactly what a busy executive needs.

Business Analysis and Competitive Research

This is where you can begin to use AI for higher-level strategic work. By feeding the AI specific business documents or public information, you can ask it to perform foundational business analysis tasks, acting as a tireless junior analyst.

Conducting a SWOT Analysis

A SWOT (Strengths, Weaknesses, Opportunities, Threats) analysis is a classic strategic framework. You can use AI to perform a preliminary analysis by providing it with the right raw materials.

- **The Goal:** You want to conduct a quick SWOT analysis of your own department based on the past quarter's performance reports and team feedback.
- The Prompt:
  "Act as a senior business strategist. I am going to provide you with several internal documents, including our Q3 performance report and anonymous feedback from a recent team survey.
  Task: Based only on the information in these documents, conduct a SWOT analysis for our department. Identify 2-3 key points for each of the four categories.
  Format: Present the analysis in four distinct sections with the headers: 'Strengths,' 'Weaknesses,' 'Opportunities,' and 'Threats.' Use bullet points for the items under each header.
  Constraints: For each point you list, briefly explain your

reasoning based on the provided text. For example, if you list 'High Team Morale' as a strength, you should follow it with a note like '(Reasoning: The team survey showed a 95% satisfaction score).'"
###INTERNAL DOCUMENTS###
[Paste the text from your reports and survey feedback here]"

- **Strategic Value:** The AI is not going to have a groundbreaking strategic insight. However, what it can do with incredible efficiency is read, synthesize, and categorize large amounts of information. This prompt gives you a well-organized first draft of your analysis in minutes, allowing you to spend your valuable time interpreting the findings and developing the actual strategy.

Project Planning and Milestone Tracking

AI can be an invaluable partner in the initial, and often most difficult, phase of project planning: breaking down a large, ambiguous goal into a structured set of manageable tasks.

Deconstructing a Project Goal

- **The Goal:** You have been tasked with planning a small office move to a new floor in your building, to be completed in 60 days. You need to create an initial project plan.
- The Prompt:
  "Act as a highly experienced facilities project manager. I need to create a high-level project plan for a small office move.
  Context: Our team of 20 people is moving from the 3rd floor to the 5th floor of our current building. The entire project must be completed within the next 60 days. The goal is to execute the move with minimal disruption to daily work.

Task: Break this project down into logical phases and key tasks.
Format: Create a project plan with a clear, hierarchical structure. Use main headings for the major phases (e.g., 'Phase 1: Planning and Preparation'). Under each phase, use a bulleted list for the key tasks.
Constraints: The phases should be in chronological order. Include tasks related to logistics, IT setup, employee communication, and vendor coordination. For at least five of the key tasks, suggest a potential deadline (e.g., 'Day 15,' 'Day 30')."

- **Benefit:** The blank page is often the hardest part of project planning. This prompt gives you a comprehensive, well-structured first draft of your entire plan. It will include tasks you might have forgotten and provide a logical sequence to build upon. You can then take this outline, refine it with your team, and input it into your official project management software.

20+ Ready-to-Use Prompt Templates for Business Professionals

Here is a collection of copy-and-paste templates based on the concepts we've discussed in this chapter. Remember to replace the bracketed [text] with your own specific details.

Emails and Correspondence

1. **Meeting Follow-Up:** "Act as a [Your Role]. Draft a follow-up email to [Recipient Name] after our meeting today about [Topic]. The goal is to summarize the key decisions and reiterate the action items. The key decision was [Key Decision]. The action items are: [Action Item 1 for Person A],

[Action Item 2 for Person B]. The tone should be professional and efficient."

2. **Request for Information:** "Act as a [Your Role]. Draft a polite and concise email to [Recipient Name/Team] requesting the following information: [Specific Information Needed]. I need this information by [Date] in order to complete [Your Task]. The tone should be friendly and professional."
3. **Difficult "No" Email:** "Act as a [Your Role]. I need to write a polite but firm email declining a request from [Requester Name]. The request was to [The Request]. I need to decline because [Reason for Declining]. Offer an alternative solution if possible: [Alternative Solution]. The tone should be empathetic but clear and direct."
4. **Delegating a Task:** "Act as a manager. Draft an email to [Team Member Name] delegating the task of [Task to Delegate]. Provide the necessary context: [Brief Background]. Clearly state the desired outcome and the deadline of [Date]. Offer your support and ask them to confirm they have received the task. The tone should be clear, supportive, and encouraging."

Presentations and Slide Decks
5. Presentation Outline: "Act as a strategic consultant. Create a 7-slide outline for a presentation titled '[Presentation Title].' The audience is [Audience Description] and the goal is to [Goal of Presentation]. The outline should include a compelling title for each slide and 3-4 bullet points of key content for each."
6. Opening Story: "Act as a presentation coach. Write a compelling, one-paragraph opening story for a presentation about [Topic]. Use the Problem-Agitate-Solve framework. The problem is [Problem]. The consequence is [Agitation]. Our solution is

[Solution]."

7. Speaker Notes for a Data-Heavy Slide: "Write the speaker notes for a slide titled '[Slide Title].' The slide contains a chart showing [Describe the Chart/Data]. The key takeaway from this data is [The Main Point]. Explain what the data shows and what it means for the business in simple, clear language for a non-technical audience."

Meeting Management

8. Brainstorming Meeting Agenda: "Act as a meeting facilitator. Create an agenda for a 60-minute brainstorming session on [Topic]. The goal is to generate at least 15 new ideas. Structure the agenda with time slots for introductions, a 10-minute 'blue sky thinking' phase, a 30-minute structured idea-generation phase, and a 10-minute phase for grouping and prioritizing the top ideas."

9. Decision-Making Meeting Agenda: "Act as a team lead. Create an agenda for a 45-minute meeting to make a final decision on [The Decision to be Made]. The agenda should list the 2-3 options we are considering, allocate time for discussing the pros and cons of each, and have a final 10-minute slot dedicated to making the final decision."

10. Meeting Invitation Email: "Draft a clear and concise calendar invitation email for a meeting about [Topic]. The goal of the meeting is [Meeting Goal]. Include the agenda as a bulleted list. The meeting is on [Date] at [Time] via [Link/Location]."

Reports and Summaries

11. Weekly Status Report from Notes: "Act as a project manager. I have a list of raw notes from the past week. Organize these notes into a structured weekly status report. The report should have three sections: 'Accomplishments This Week,' 'Challenges Encountered,' and 'Priorities for Next Week.'

###NOTES###

[Paste your unstructured weekly notes]"
12. Summarize Article for Team: "Summarize the key takeaways from the following article for my team of [Team Description]. The summary should be a short, easy-to-read paragraph followed by 3 key bullet points that are most relevant to our work on [Project/Field].
###ARTICLE###
[Paste article text]"
13. Executive Summary of Internal Document: "Act as a business analyst. Write a one-paragraph executive summary of the attached internal proposal. The summary should state the core proposal, the main benefit, and the total cost. It is for a senior executive who has only 60 seconds to read it.
###PROPOSAL###
[Paste proposal text]"
Business Analysis
14. Competitor Website Analysis: "Act as a market intelligence analyst. Review the text from the homepage of our main competitor, [Competitor Name]. Based only on this text, what are their top 3 value propositions? What seems to be their primary target audience? And what is the main call to action?
###WEBSITE TEXT###
[Paste competitor homepage text]"
15. Risk Brainstorming: "Act as a senior risk manager. We are about to launch a new project: [Project Description]. Brainstorm a list of 10 potential risks for this project. Categorize the risks into three groups: 'Technical Risks,' 'Operational Risks,' and 'Market Risks.'"
Project Planning
16. Project Kick-Off Email: "Draft a project kick-off email to the new project team for '[Project Name].' The email should welcome them to the team, briefly state the project's primary goal, mention

that the full project plan is attached, and announce the date and time of the kick-off meeting."

17. Milestone Definition: "Our project goal is to [Project Goal]. Break this goal down into 4-5 high-level, sequential milestones. For each milestone, give it a clear name and a one-sentence description of what will be completed to achieve it."

18. Task Breakdown: "Let's focus on the first milestone: '[Milestone 1 Name].' Break this milestone down into 5-7 specific, actionable tasks that need to be completed. For each task, suggest a potential owner role (e.g., 'Developer,' 'Designer,' 'Marketing')."

19. Follow-Up on Action Item: "Draft a short and friendly email to [Person's Name] to follow up on an action item from our last meeting. The action item was [The Action Item]. Ask for a quick status update and if they are facing any roadblocks."

20. Project Closure Report Summary: "Act as a project manager. I am providing you with notes on the outcomes of '[Project Name].' Draft a summary for the project closure report. The summary should include a brief overview of the project's initial goals, a summary of the final outcomes (including key metrics), and a list of 2-3 key 'lessons learned' that we can apply to future projects.

###PROJECT NOTES###

[Paste your notes]"

Chapter 8: AI Prompts for Marketing and Sales

In the previous chapter, we established a comprehensive toolkit for the modern business professional, covering the essential tasks of communication, planning, and analysis that are fundamental to any corporate role. Now, we sharpen our focus and step into one of the most dynamic, fast-paced, and critical functions of any organization: the engine of growth itself, marketing and sales.

If business professionals use AI to improve operational efficiency, marketers and salespeople use it to scale creativity and persuasion. The core of their work revolves around understanding human psychology, crafting compelling messages, and building relationships at scale. These are tasks that require a delicate balance of art and science, and they are areas where a well-guided AI can become an indispensable partner. The sheer volume of content creation, customer research, and communication required in these roles makes them perfectly suited for AI augmentation.

This chapter is a dedicated playbook for the marketing and sales professional. We are moving from internal communications to external persuasion, from project plans to campaign strategies. We will explore how to use AI to craft marketing copy and ad campaigns that capture attention and drive action. You will learn to build a robust social media content pipeline, saving hours on creation and scheduling. We will dive deep into one of the most fundamental marketing tasks: developing detailed customer personas from raw data.

For sales professionals, we will cover how to refine sales scripts and pitches, and how to prepare for and overcome common customer objections. We will explore the creation of high-impact email campaigns and newsletters, from brainstorming subject lines to structuring entire automated sequences. We will also touch on the technical side of marketing, showing you how to use AI for foundational SEO optimization and keyword research, as well as for conducting market research and trend analysis to keep you ahead of the competition.

By the end of this chapter, you will have a powerful set of prompts and workflows designed specifically to meet the high demands of a marketing or sales career. You will be able to generate higher quality creative content faster, understand your customers more deeply, and communicate your value proposition more effectively.

Crafting Marketing Copy and Ad Campaigns

At the heart of all marketing is the copy. It is the set of words on your website, in your ads, and on your social media that must do the heavy lifting of grabbing attention, building interest, and persuading someone to take action. Writing effective copy is a difficult skill that combines psychology, strategy, and creativity. While AI cannot replace the strategic insight of a great copywriter, it can act as an incredibly powerful assistant, helping you brainstorm angles, draft variations, and overcome the dreaded blank page.

To get high-quality copy from an AI, you must provide it with a proven copywriting framework. Simply asking it to "write an ad" will produce generic results. Asking it to write an ad using a structure like AIDA (Attention, Interest, Desire, Action) will produce a strategic and persuasive draft.

Professional Scenario: Writing Ad Copy for a New B2B Service

- **The Goal:** You are a marketing manager for a B2B tech company. You need to write short-form ad copy for a LinkedIn campaign to promote a new cybersecurity service for small businesses.
- The Prompt (Using the AIDA Framework):
  "Act as an expert direct-response copywriter specializing in B2B technology. I need you to write three variations of short-form ad copy for a LinkedIn campaign.
  Context: The product is a new service called 'SecureShield SMB.' It is an all-in-one cybersecurity subscription designed specifically for small businesses (10-50 employees) that do not have a dedicated IT department. It protects them from common threats like phishing and ransomware.
  Task: Write three distinct ad variations using the AIDA (Attention, Interest, Desire, Action) framework.
  Format: For each variation, clearly label the four sections: Attention (the headline), Interest (the opening line), Desire (the benefits), and Action (the call to action).
  Constraints: The tone should be professional, slightly urgent, and reassuring. Focus on the peace of mind that the service provides. The call to action for each ad should be 'Get a Free Security Audit.'"
- **Analysis of the Prompt:** This prompt is effective because it doesn't just ask for an ad. It provides a professional persona, deep context about the product and audience, and most importantly, a clear creative framework (AIDA). This forces the AI to structure its response in a way that is

psychologically persuasive. It also asks for three variations, which pushes the AI to come up with different angles and gives you options to test.

Productivity Technique: The "Variation Generator"
Once you have an ad or piece of copy that is performing well, you can use AI to scale that success. This technique helps you avoid creative fatigue by generating fresh variations on a proven theme.

- The Prompt:
  "Act as a senior copywriter. The following ad has been very successful for us.
  ###SUCCESSFUL AD###
  Headline: Is your small business one click away from a disaster?
  Body: 90% of cyberattacks target small businesses. SecureShield SMB provides enterprise-grade protection that's affordable and easy to manage.
  CTA: Get a Free Security Audit.
  ###END AD###
  Your task is to write 5 new headlines for this ad. The headlines should maintain the same sense of urgency and target the same audience, but use different emotional angles (e.g., fear, curiosity, benefit-driven)."

This is a high-leverage way to quickly create new ad creatives for A/B testing, helping you optimize your campaigns without having to start from scratch each time.

Social Media Content Creation and Scheduling

The demand for a constant stream of high-quality social media content can be overwhelming for any marketing team. AI can serve as your tireless content engine, helping you brainstorm ideas, draft posts, and even structure an entire content calendar. The key is to think in terms of content pillars and repurposing.

A Step-by-Step Workflow for a Week of Social Media Content

Let's use a multi-step prompting workflow to plan and create content for a professional services firm.

Step 1: Establishing Content Pillars
Content pillars are the 3-5 core themes you will consistently talk about. They ensure your content stays focused and relevant to your audience.

- The Prompt (Step 1):
  "Act as a senior social media strategist. My company is a management consulting firm that advises mid-sized businesses on improving their operational efficiency. Our target audience is CEOs and COOs of these companies.
  Task: Brainstorm and define four distinct 'content pillars' for our LinkedIn presence.
  Format: For each pillar, provide a name and a one-sentence description of the type of content it will include."

Step 2: Generating Post Ideas
Once you have your pillars, you can use them to generate an endless stream of specific post ideas.

- The Prompt (Step 2):
  "This is an excellent list of content pillars. Now, let's focus on the pillar you named 'Process Optimization Frameworks.'
  Task: Generate five specific and engaging post ideas for LinkedIn that would fall under this pillar. For each idea, write a one-sentence summary of the post's core message."

Step 3: Drafting a Specific Post

Now that you have a list of approved ideas, you can delegate the drafting of individual posts.

- The Prompt (Step 3):
  "Great ideas. Let's write the post for the idea: 'Explaining the 'Five Whys' technique for root cause analysis.'
  Task: Draft a short, engaging LinkedIn post (around 150 words) explaining this technique.
  Format: The post should start with a relatable question to hook the reader, explain the 'Five Whys' concept in simple terms, give a brief business example (e.g., a manufacturing defect), and end with a question to encourage comments.
  Constraints: The tone should be authoritative but accessible. Avoid overly academic language. Include 3-4 relevant hashtags at the end."

By following this three-step process, you have created a sustainable system for content creation. You use your strategic input to define the pillars and select the ideas, and then you use AI for the heavy lifting of drafting.

Customer Persona Development

All effective marketing and sales starts with a deep understanding of the customer. A customer persona is a semi-fictional representation of your ideal customer based on market research and real data. Creating these personas can be a time-consuming process of synthesizing research. AI is the perfect tool for taking unstructured data and transforming it into a structured, usable persona document.

Professional Scenario: Creating a Persona from Interview Notes

- **The Goal:** You are a product marketer. You have just

completed a series of interviews with potential customers and have a document full of raw, unstructured notes. You need to synthesize these notes into a clear customer persona.

- The Prompt:
  "Act as an expert market researcher. I am going to provide you with a collection of raw notes and direct quotes from interviews with potential customers for a new budget-planning software for freelancers.
  Task: Your task is to read all of the provided information and create a detailed customer persona document.
  Format: The persona should be named 'Alex, the Freelance Designer.' The document must be organized with the following exact headers:
  - **Background:** A short paragraph summarizing their professional background and business.
  - **Goals:** A bulleted list of their top 3-4 professional goals.
  - **Challenges:** A bulleted list of the top 3-4 challenges they face, particularly regarding finances.
  - **How We Help:** A short paragraph explaining how our budget-planning software would directly address their main challenges.
  - A Representative Quote: Select a single, powerful quote from the notes that best summarizes their core frustration.
    Constraints: The persona must be based only on the information provided in the notes below. Do not invent any new information.

  ###INTERVIEW NOTES###[Paste all of your unstructured interview notes, quotes, and observations here]"
- **Benefit:** This prompt gives the AI a clear template to pour the unstructured information into. It does the tedious work of

reading, categorizing, and summarizing, presenting you with a well-organized persona that your entire team can use. This saves hours of manual synthesis and ensures your marketing efforts are grounded in real customer insights.

Sales Scripts and Pitch Refinement

For a sales team, consistent and effective messaging is key to success. While a great sales conversation is always a natural dialogue, having a strong foundational script for common scenarios is invaluable. AI can help you draft these baseline scripts, refine your value proposition, and even prepare you for handling difficult questions and objections.

Professional Scenario: Developing an Objection Handling Script

- **The Goal:** You are a sales manager. Your team sells a premium project management software, and a common objection they hear from potential customers is, "It's too expensive compared to competitors like Asana or Trello." You need to create a script to handle this objection effectively.
- The Prompt:
  "Act as an expert sales coach and trainer. I need help creating a script for my sales team to handle a common price objection.
  Context: Our product is 'ProjectFlow,' a premium project management software that costs $50 per user per month. It's more expensive than some competitors because it offers advanced features like automated reporting and budget tracking. Our target customers are mid-sized creative agencies.

The Objection: 'Your product looks great, but it's much more expensive than what we pay for our current tool.'
Task: Draft a three-part response to this objection using the 'Acknowledge, Reframe, Resolve' framework.
Format: Structure the response with three clear paragraphs, labeled 'Acknowledge,' 'Reframe,' and 'Resolve.'

- **Acknowledge:** Start by validating the customer's concern.
- **Reframe:** Shift the conversation from price to value and return on investment.
- Resolve: Ask a question that moves the conversation forward to discuss the value in their specific context. Constraints: The tone should be confident and consultative, not defensive."

- **Strategic Value:** This prompt doesn't just ask for a response; it asks for a response based on a proven sales methodology. This guides the AI to produce a script that is not only well-written but also strategically sound, equipping your team with a powerful and repeatable way to handle a critical part of the sales process.

Email Campaigns and Newsletter Content

Email remains one of the most effective channels for nurturing leads and retaining customers. AI can be your partner in every step of the process, from brainstorming compelling subject lines to drafting the content for a multi-part email sequence.

Professional Scenario: Outlining a Lead Nurturing Campaign

- **The Goal:** You are a digital marketer. A potential customer has just downloaded a free e-book from your website. You want to create a 3-part automated email series to nurture this new lead with the ultimate goal of getting them to sign up for a product demo.

- The Prompt:
  "Act as an expert in email marketing automation. I need to design a 3-part lead nurturing email campaign.
  Context: The lead is a marketing manager who just downloaded our e-book, 'The Ultimate Guide to SEO.' Our company sells an advanced SEO analytics software called 'RankRight.' The goal of the campaign is to build trust and persuade them to book a free demo of our software.
  Task: Outline the entire 3-email sequence.
  Format: For each email in the sequence, provide the following:
  - **Email #:** (e.g., Email 1)
  - **Timing:** (e.g., 1 day after download)
  - **Core Goal:** (e.g., Provide value and build trust)
  - **Subject Line Idea:** (e.g., A catchy subject line)
  - **Brief Content Summary:** (A 1-2 sentence summary of the email's content)
  - **Call to Action:** (The specific action you want them to take)"
- **Benefit:** This prompt allows you to strategically map out your entire campaign before you write a single word of copy. The AI acts as a strategist, helping you design a coherent journey for your new lead. From here, you can use follow-up prompts to draft the full text for each email in the sequence.

Productivity Technique: "The Subject Line Synthesizer"
"Act as a world-class email copywriter. I am about to send a newsletter with the following content: [Briefly summarize the newsletter content]. The goal is to maximize the open rate. Generate a list of 10 compelling subject lines for this email.

Please categorize them into three types: 'Benefit-Oriented,' 'Curiosity-Driven,' and 'Direct & Clear.'" This technique gives you a range of high-quality options to test, which can dramatically improve the performance of your email campaigns.

SEO Optimization and Keyword Research

Search Engine Optimization (SEO) is the art and science of getting your content to rank highly in search engine results. While dedicated SEO tools are essential for deep technical analysis and rank tracking, AI is a fantastic partner for the content strategy side of SEO. It can help you explore keywords, understand user intent, and structure content in a way that is friendly to both users and search engines.

Professional Scenario: Creating an SEO-Friendly Content Brief

- **The Goal:** You are a content marketer. You want to write a blog post that will rank for the keyword "remote team productivity software." You need to create a detailed brief for a writer (or for yourself) to ensure the article is comprehensive and well-optimized.
- The Prompt:
  "Act as an expert SEO content strategist. I am planning to write a comprehensive blog post targeting the primary keyword 'remote team productivity software.'
  Context: The target audience for this post is managers and team leads who are newly managing remote teams and are looking for software solutions. They are likely in the 'information gathering' stage of their search.
  Task: Create a detailed content brief for this blog post.
  Format: The brief should be structured with the following sections:

- Suggested Title: A catchy, SEO-friendly title that includes the primary keyword.
  - **Meta Description:** A compelling, 155-character description for search engine results.
  - **Primary Keyword:** 'remote team productivity software'
  - **Secondary Keywords:** A bulleted list of 5-7 related keywords and long-tail phrases to include naturally in the article (e.g., 'best tools for remote teams,' 'how to manage remote team tasks').
  - **Content Outline:** A detailed outline for the article using H2 and H3 headings. The outline should cover key topics like 'What to Look For in Productivity Software,' 'Top 5 Software Categories,' and 'Implementation Best Practices.'"
- **Benefit:** This prompt transforms a simple keyword into a complete strategic roadmap for a piece of content. The AI generates a structure that is designed to comprehensively answer the questions a user searching for that keyword is likely to have. This dramatically increases the chances of the content ranking well and provides immense clarity for the writer.

Market Research and Trend Analysis

Staying ahead of the curve is critical in both marketing and sales. AI can act as your personal research assistant, helping you synthesize information from articles, reports, and industry news to identify key trends and understand the competitive landscape.

Professional Scenario: Summarizing Competitor News

- **The Goal:** You need to prepare a quick briefing for your team on the latest activities of your top three competitors.

You have found a few recent news articles for each.

- The Prompt:
  "Act as a professional competitive intelligence analyst. I am going to provide you with the text from several recent news articles about our main competitors.
  Task: Your task is to read all of the provided articles and write a consolidated 'Competitor Briefing' summary.
  Format: The summary should be a single, concise document organized by competitor. For each competitor, create a section with their name as the header. Under each header, provide a bulleted list summarizing their key recent activities, focusing on new product launches, pricing changes, strategic partnerships, or quotes from their leadership.
  Constraints: The summary must be factual and based only on the information in the articles provided.
  ###COMPETITOR A: ARTICLE 1###
  [Paste text of first article]
  ###COMPETITOR A: ARTICLE 2###
  [Paste text of second article]
  ###COMPETITOR B: ARTICLE 1###
  [Paste text of third article]
  ...and so on."
- **Benefit:** This is a massive time-saver. Instead of you needing to read, digest, and manually summarize hours' worth of articles, the AI does the heavy lifting of extraction and consolidation. The use of delimiters (###) keeps the information organized and makes the prompt easy for the AI to understand. This allows you to spend your time on the high-value work of analyzing the implications of this news for your own strategy.

25+ Ready-to-Use Prompt Templates for Marketing

and Sales

Here is a collection of copy-and-paste templates to get you started. Remember to customize the bracketed [text] with your specific details.

Marketing and Ad Copy

1. **AIDA Ad Copy:** "Act as a copywriter. Write ad copy for [Product/Service] using the AIDA framework. The target audience is [Audience Description]. The key benefit is [Benefit]. The call to action is [CTA]."
2. **PAS Ad Copy:** "Act as a copywriter. Write ad copy for [Product/Service] using the Problem-Agitate-Solve framework. The problem is [Problem]. The agitation is [Negative Consequence]. The solution is our product."
3. **Website Headline Ideas:** "Brainstorm 10 compelling headlines for a website homepage that sells [Product/Service]. The headlines should be short, benefit-focused, and target [Audience]."
4. **Value Proposition Refinement:** "Our current value proposition is: '[Your Value Proposition].' Act as a brand strategist and rewrite this to be more clear, concise, and compelling for an audience of [Audience]."
5. **Product Description:** "Write a 150-word product description for [Product Name]. It is a [Product Category] that helps [Audience] solve [Problem]. Mention these three key features: [Feature 1], [Feature 2], [Feature 3]."

Social Media
6. LinkedIn Post from Article: "Act as a social media manager. Read the following article and write an engaging LinkedIn post summarizing the key takeaway for an audience of [Audience].

Start with a hook and end with a question. ###ARTICLE### [Paste Article]"

7. Content Calendar Ideas: "Act as a content strategist. Generate a list of 10 content ideas for the Instagram account of a [Type of Business]. The content should be a mix of educational, behind-the-scenes, and promotional posts."

8. Twitter Thread Outline: "Outline a 5-tweet thread based on the core idea that '[Core Idea].' Each tweet should build on the last and the final tweet should have a call to action to [CTA]."

Customer and Market Research

9. Persona from Data: "Act as a market researcher. Create a customer persona based on the following survey data. The persona document should include sections for Goals, Challenges, and Motivations. ###DATA### [Paste Survey Data]"

10. Survey Question Brainstorm: "Brainstorm 10 unbiased survey questions to help us understand why customers choose our [Product Type] over competitors. The questions should be a mix of multiple-choice and open-ended."

11. Trend Analysis: "Summarize the top 3 emerging trends discussed in the following industry report. For each trend, explain its potential impact on a business like ours ([Your Business Type]). ###REPORT### [Paste Report Text]"

Sales Enablement

12. Cold Email Template: "Act as a sales development representative. Write a cold email template to a [Job Title] at a [Industry] company. The email should be short, personalized, and focused on solving [Problem] with our [Product/Service]. The goal is to book a 15-minute introductory call."

13. Discovery Call Questions: "Generate a list of 10 powerful, open-ended discovery call questions for a salesperson selling [Product/Service] to ask a potential customer."

14. Follow-Up Email after Demo: "Draft a follow-up email to be

sent after a product demo of [Our Product]. The email should thank the prospect, summarize the key value points discussed, and outline the clear next steps."

15. Voicemail Script: "Write a concise and compelling 30-second voicemail script for a salesperson following up on a lead. The script should state their name, company, the reason for calling, and a clear call to action."

Email Marketing

16. Newsletter Ideas: "Brainstorm 5 engaging article ideas for the next monthly newsletter for our [Type of Business]. The audience is [Audience Description]."

17. Welcome Email: "Write the first email in a welcome series for new subscribers to our newsletter. The email should confirm their subscription, thank them, and provide one piece of high-value content, like a link to our most popular guide."

18. Re-engagement Email: "Write a 'we miss you' re-engagement email for subscribers who have not opened our emails in 90 days. The tone should be friendly. Offer them an exclusive resource or discount to entice them back."

19. Subject Line Test: "Generate 5 different subject lines for an email announcing a [Type of Announcement, e.g., '20% off sale']. The subject lines should test different angles like urgency, benefit, and curiosity."

SEO and Content Marketing

20. Keyword Brainstorm: "Act as an SEO specialist. My business sells [Product/Service]. Brainstorm a list of 15 keywords and long-tail phrases that a potential customer might search for."

21. Blog Post Outline: "Create a detailed outline for a blog post titled '[Blog Post Title].' The outline should include H2 and H3 headings and cover the key points needed to make it a comprehensive guide for [Audience]."

22. Meta Description: "Write a compelling meta description (under

160 characters) for a blog post about [Topic]. The description should include the keyword '[Keyword]' and entice users to click."

23. Content Repurposing: "I have a blog post about [Topic]. Suggest 3 ways to repurpose this content into other formats (e.g., a short video script, an infographic, a LinkedIn post)."

24. Internal Linking Suggestions: "Read the following blog post. Suggest 3-4 natural places within the text where I could add internal links to other articles on my site about [Related Topic 1] and [Related Topic 2]. ###POST### [Paste Post Text]"

25. Call to Action Ideas: "Brainstorm 5 different calls to action (CTAs) to place at the end of a blog post about [Topic]. The CTAs should be varied, including soft CTAs (e.g., 'download a guide') and hard CTAs (e.g., 'book a demo')."

Chapter 9: AI Prompts for Content Creators and Writers

In the preceding chapters, we've explored how AI can amplify the effectiveness of business professionals and the persuasive power of marketing and sales teams. We've seen how structured prompts can streamline communication, planning, and strategy. Now, we turn our attention to a group of professionals for whom the written word is not just a tool, but the very essence of their craft: content creators and writers.

This chapter is a dedicated playbook for the journalists, copywriters, technical writers, bloggers, scriptwriters, and authors who spend their days wrestling with the blank page. For writers, the rise of AI can feel particularly disruptive, sometimes even threatening. It's natural to wonder what role is left for a human when a machine can generate thousands of words in seconds.

The answer, as we will explore in detail, is that AI is not a replacement for a writer. It is a collaborator. It is a research assistant that never sleeps, an editor that is never fatigued, and a brainstorming partner with access to a near-infinite library of patterns and ideas. The true value of AI for a writer is not in replacing the act of creation, but in automating the tedious, time-consuming, and often frustrating tasks that surround it. This allows the human writer to dedicate their precious energy to what truly matters: creativity, critical thinking, storytelling, and developing a unique, authentic voice.

In this chapter, we will break down the entire writing process and show you where AI can be your most powerful ally. We will start at the very beginning, using AI to create robust blog post outlines and article structures to conquer the blank page. We will discuss how to use AI as a research assistant, while emphasizing the critical importance of human fact-checking. You will learn to build sophisticated editing and proofreading workflows that go far beyond a simple grammar check. We will dive into generating dozens of compelling headlines and titles for any piece of content. We'll build on our previous discussion of SEO, focusing specifically on how writers can optimize their content for search. We'll cover the high-leverage strategy of repurposing a single piece of content across multiple platforms. Finally, we will provide a set of practical techniques for using AI to break through the most persistent enemy of any writer: writer's block.

By the end of this chapter, you will not see AI as a competitor, but as an essential part of your professional toolkit, one that empowers you to produce higher-quality work, more consistently, and with less friction.

Blog Post Outlines and Article Structures

For any writer, the most intimidating part of a new project is often the blank page. The blinking cursor on an empty screen represents a sea of infinite possibilities, which can lead to paralysis. A well-structured outline is the map that turns that intimidating void into a manageable journey. This is one of the most immediate and powerful applications of AI for any writer. By providing the core idea and the target audience, you can generate a comprehensive, logical structure in minutes, freeing you to focus on filling in that structure with your own insights and voice.

To get a truly useful outline, you must guide the AI with a clear goal and a defined structure. Don't just ask for an outline; ask for an outline that will achieve a specific objective for a specific reader.

Professional Scenario: Structuring a Comprehensive Guide

- **The Goal:** You are a content marketer for a SaaS company that sells business intelligence software. You need to write a definitive guide titled "How to Choose the Right Business Intelligence Tool for Your Company." It needs to be a cornerstone piece of content that attracts organic traffic and establishes your company as an expert.
- **A Multi-Step Workflow for Creating a "Skyscraper" Outline**

This workflow is designed to create a long-form, highly detailed article outline, often called a "skyscraper" post in the content marketing world, because it aims to be the best and most comprehensive piece on the topic.

Step 1: Define the Audience and the Core Questions
Before you can create an outline, you need to understand who you're writing for and what they need to know.

- The Prompt (Step 1):
  "Act as a senior content strategist. I am planning a comprehensive guide for our company blog about choosing the right business intelligence (BI) software.
  Context: Our target audience is non-technical business leaders (e.g., department heads, COOs) at mid-sized companies. They are likely feeling overwhelmed by data and are looking for a solution, but they are not data scientists. They are beginners in this space.
  Task: Based on this audience, brainstorm a list of the top 10

most important questions they would have when researching BI software. Frame these as direct questions."

Step 2: Transform Questions into a Logical Outline
Once you have the core questions, you can use them as the building blocks for your article's structure.

- The Prompt (Step 2):
  "This is a fantastic list of questions. Now, take these 10 questions and organize them into a logical, hierarchical article outline.
  Task: Create a detailed outline for a long-form blog post.
  Format: The outline should use a clear structure with H2 and H3 headings. Group related questions under logical H2 sections like 'Understanding Your Needs,' 'Key Features to Compare,' and 'Implementation and Adoption.' The final H2 section should be a subtle call to action for our product.
  Constraints: The flow should take the reader on a journey from understanding their problem to making a confident decision."

Step 3: Fleshing Out a Section with Talking Points
With the high-level structure in place, you can drill down and get the AI to help you build out the substance of each section.

- The Prompt (Step 3):
  "This outline is perfect. Let's expand on the H2 section, 'Key Features to Compare.' The H3s you suggested were 'Data Visualization and Dashboards,' 'Data Source Connectors,' and 'Reporting and Analytics.'
  Task: For each of these three H3 sections, generate 3-4 key talking points or sub-topics that I should cover. These should be specific aspects a non-technical leader should consider for each feature."
- **Benefit of the Workflow:** In three strategic steps, you have

moved from a broad topic to a highly detailed, reader-focused article structure. You have a comprehensive blueprint that ensures your final article will be thorough, logical, and incredibly helpful to your target audience. The "blank page" problem is completely solved.

Research and Fact-Checking Assistance

This is an area where AI can be a writer's best friend, but it comes with a critical, non-negotiable warning.

A Crucial Note on Accuracy: AI language models are not databases of facts. They are pattern-matching engines. This means they can, and frequently do, "hallucinate" or invent information, statistics, and sources that sound plausible but are entirely false. **You must treat an AI as a research assistant, not as a source of truth.** Your credibility as a writer is on the line. Every single verifiable claim generated by an AI must be independently fact-checked by you using reliable primary sources.

With that critical caveat in mind, AI can still be an incredible tool for accelerating the research process.

Prompting for High-Level Summaries

You can use AI to quickly get the gist of a long article, academic paper, or report to decide if it's relevant to your work.

- The Prompt:
  "Act as a professional researcher. I am providing you with the text of a 10-page market research report. Please read it and write a concise, one-paragraph summary of the report's methodology, key findings, and main conclusion. This is to help me quickly determine if I should read the full document.
  ###REPORT TEXT###

[Paste the full report text here]"

A Workflow for Verifiable Claims
Instead of asking the AI for facts, use it to create a checklist of facts you need to find yourself. This is a much safer and more professional way to use AI for research.

- **The Goal:** You have written a draft of an article and want to ensure all your claims are well-supported.
- The Prompt:
  "Act as a professional fact-checker. I have written the draft of an article below. Your task is to read the entire text and extract a bulleted list of every specific, verifiable claim made in the article. For example, if the text says 'sales increased by 25%,' you should list that. If it says 'the system is more efficient,' that is a subjective claim and should not be listed.
  Task: Create a checklist of all factual claims I need to verify and cite. Do not attempt to verify them yourself.
  ###DRAFT TEXT###
  [Paste your full article draft here]"
- **Benefit:** This prompt cleverly uses the AI's ability to parse text to create a to-do list for your manual fact-checking process. It saves you the time of having to re-read your own work to identify the claims, making your research process more rigorous and efficient.

Editing and Proofreading Workflows

Modern grammar checkers are good, but AI offers a level of editing that is far more sophisticated. You can instruct it to act as different types of editors, each with a specific focus. This allows you to run your draft through multiple "lenses" to catch different kinds of issues and dramatically improve the quality of your writing.

The Three Essential AI Editors

1. The "Conciseness" Editor
This editor's only job is to make your writing tighter and more powerful by cutting out the fluff.

- The Prompt:
  "Act as a ruthless copy editor whose only goal is to improve clarity and conciseness. I am going to provide you with a paragraph of text. Please rewrite it to be more direct and impactful.
  Your task is to:
  - Eliminate all filler words and redundant phrases.
  - Replace passive voice with active voice.
  - Break up long, complex sentences into shorter, clearer ones.
  - Aim to reduce the word count by at least 20% without losing the core message.
    ###TEXT###
    [Paste your paragraph or section here]"

2. The "Clarity" Editor
This editor is focused on making sure your message is easy for your target audience to understand.

- The Prompt:
  "Act as an editor who specializes in simplifying complex topics. My target audience for this text is [Audience Description], who are not experts in this field.
  Task: Please review the following text and identify any technical jargon, acronyms, or overly complex concepts. For each one you find, suggest a simpler explanation or a more accessible analogy.
  ###TEXT###

[Paste your text here]"

3. The "Tone" Editor
This editor helps ensure your writing strikes the right emotional chord with your reader.

- The Prompt:
  "Act as an expert brand voice editor. Our company's brand voice is '[e.g., helpful, authoritative, and slightly playful].' I have written a draft of a blog post, but I'm worried it sounds too dry and academic.
  Task: Please read the draft and suggest 3-5 specific changes to make the tone more aligned with our brand voice. You can suggest rephrasing sentences, adding more engaging questions, or changing specific word choices.
  ###DRAFT###
  [Paste your draft here]"

By running your text through these three distinct prompts, you can perform a multi-pass edit in a fraction of the time it would take to do it manually.

Headline and Title Generation

The headline or title is the single most important part of most written content. It's the gatekeeper to your work. A great headline can lead to thousands of readers, while a weak one can ensure your brilliant article goes unread. Because it's so high-stakes, it's worth generating a large number of options to choose from. This is a perfect task for AI.

The "Headline Matrix" Technique
This technique pushes the AI to generate a wide variety of headlines by forcing it to brainstorm across different proven copywriting angles.

- **The Goal:** You have written an article about the productivity benefits of a four-day work week.
- The Prompt:
  "Act as a world-class copywriter and headline specialist. I have written an article about the benefits of a four-day work week for corporate teams. The main argument is that it increases focus and reduces burnout, leading to higher quality output.
  Task: Generate 20 headline ideas for this article.
  Format: Organize the headlines into four categories, with five headlines in each category. The categories are:
    - **Benefit-Driven:** (Focuses on the positive outcome for the reader)
    - **Curiosity Gap:** (Piques interest without giving away the answer)
    - **Direct & Clear:** (Says exactly what the article is about)
    - **Provocative/Question:** (Challenges a common belief or asks a compelling question)"
- **Benefit:** Instead of getting 20 variations on the same theme, you get a rich palette of creative options. This allows you to see your article from different angles and choose the headline that best fits the platform and audience you are targeting.

SEO Content Optimization

We touched on creating SEO content briefs in the previous chapter. Now, let's focus on how a writer can use AI during the actual writing and editing process to improve on-page SEO.

The "Keyword Integration" Assistant
Once you have your list of primary and secondary keywords, you need to weave them into your text naturally. This can sometimes

feel forced. AI can act as an assistant to help you find the most logical places for them.

- The Prompt:
  "Act as an SEO editor. I have written a draft of a blog post. My primary keyword is '[primary keyword].' My list of secondary keywords is: [list of 3-5 keywords].
  Task: Please read the draft and suggest 3-4 natural-sounding ways to integrate the secondary keywords into the text. Do not force them in. Suggest rephrasing sentences where necessary to make the inclusion smooth. Also, tell me if I have used the primary keyword too many times.
  ###DRAFT###
  [Paste your draft here]"

Optimizing for "People Also Ask"

The "People Also Ask" (PAA) section in Google search results is a goldmine for content ideas. You can use AI to structure parts of your article to directly answer these questions, increasing your chances of being featured.

- The Prompt:
  "Act as an SEO content strategist. My article is about [Topic]. I have identified three common questions from Google's 'People Also Ask' section:
  1. [Question 1]
  2. [Question 2]
  3. [Question 3]
     Task: Create a new 'Frequently Asked Questions (FAQ)' section for the end of my article. Use these three questions as H3 headings and, for each one, write a clear, concise, and direct answer (around 50-75 words) based on the information in my article draft below.
     ###DRAFT###

[Paste your draft here]"

Repurposing Content Across Platforms

The "create once, distribute many" model is the secret to a successful content strategy. A single, well-researched piece of content like a whitepaper or a long blog post is a valuable asset that can be "transmuted" into dozens of other formats for different platforms. AI is the ultimate engine for this process.

A Step-by-Step Workflow for Content Repurposing

- **The Goal:** You have just published a 2,000-word blog post, "The 2025 Guide to Sustainable Business Practices." You want to create a full content campaign from it.
- **Step 1: The LinkedIn Article**
  - **Prompt:** "Act as a B2B content editor. Take my blog post, 'The 2025 Guide to Sustainable Business Practices,' and repurpose it into a 600-word article for LinkedIn. The audience is business executives. Focus on the high-level strategic takeaways and the financial benefits of sustainability. Keep the tone professional and authoritative. [Paste Blog Post]"
- **Step 2: The Twitter (X) Thread**
  - **Prompt:** "Act as a social media expert. Convert the key ideas from my blog post into a compelling 6-part Twitter thread. The first tweet should be a strong hook. Each subsequent tweet should reveal one key statistic or tip. The final tweet should link back to the full blog post. [Paste Blog Post]"
- **Step 3: The Explainer Video Script Outline**
  - **Prompt:** "Act as a video scriptwriter. Create an outline for a 3-minute animated explainer video based on my

blog post. The outline should have three sections:

1. **Introduction:** A hook that presents the problem.
2. **Main Body:** Three key points from the article, simplified for a visual medium.
3. Conclusion: A summary and a clear call to action. [Paste Blog Post]"

- **Step 4: The Email Newsletter Blurb**
    - **Prompt:** "Act as an email marketer. Write a short, 150-word blurb for our weekly newsletter to promote our new blog post. The goal is to get subscribers to click through and read the full article. Focus on the most surprising or valuable insight from the post. [Paste Blog Post]"
- **Benefit:** With a series of targeted prompts, you have turned one piece of content into at least five, dramatically increasing its reach and return on investment with minimal additional effort.

Overcoming Writer's Block

Every writer experiences it. The ideas won't come, the words won't flow, and the cursor just blinks. AI can be an incredibly effective tool for breaking this frustrating state by acting as a creative sparring partner that can help you see your topic from a new perspective.

The "Angle Finder" Prompt
When you feel like you have nothing new to say about a topic, ask the AI to find new angles.

- The Prompt:
  "I have to write an article about [Topic], but I feel stuck. I've already written about [Angle 1] and [Angle 2] in the past.
  Task: Brainstorm 5 fresh, unexpected, or counter-intuitive angles for an article about [Topic]. For each angle, write a

one-sentence description of the main argument."

The "Opening Line" Generator
Sometimes, just getting the first sentence down is the hardest part.

- The Prompt:
  "I'm trying to start an article about [Topic]. I am struggling with the opening paragraph.
  Task: Please give me three different opening paragraph options to get me started.
  - **Option 1:** Start with a surprising or shocking statistic.
  - **Option 2:** Start with a short, relatable story or hypothetical scenario.
  - **Option 3:** Start with a thought-provoking question that challenges a common assumption."

The "Interview Me" Technique
This advanced technique turns the AI into an interviewer to help you generate your own raw content.

- The Prompt:
  "Act as a professional journalist. You are interviewing me for an article about [Your Topic of Expertise]. I am an expert in this field. Your task is to ask me a series of 5 insightful, open-ended questions that will help me explain the most important aspects of this topic. After I answer each question, you will ask a relevant follow-up question. Start with your first question now."

You then answer the questions in the chat. The conversation that follows can serve as a transcript of your own thoughts, which you can then edit and structure into a finished article.

20+ Ready-to-Use Prompt Templates for Content

Creators and Writers

Here is a collection of copy-and-paste templates based on the concepts we've discussed.

Outlines and Structures

1. **Blog Post Outline:** "Create a detailed outline for a blog post titled '[Title].' The target audience is [Audience]. The outline should include a logical flow of H2 and H3 headings."
2. **Listicle Outline:** "Generate an outline for a listicle titled '10 Ways to [Achieve Goal].' For each of the 10 points, provide a brief one-sentence description."
3. **Book Chapter Structure:** "Structure a chapter for a non-fiction book on the topic of [Topic]. The chapter's goal is to [Goal]. Break it down into 3-4 key sections with descriptive headings."

Research and Explanation
4. Concept Simplifier: "Explain the concept of [Complex Concept] in simple terms, as if you were explaining it to a high school student. Use an analogy to make it easier to understand."
5. Fact-Check Checklist: "Read the following text. Extract a bulleted list of all specific, verifiable factual claims that I need to check and cite. [Paste Text]"
Editing and Proofreading
6. Conciseness Edit: "Rewrite the following paragraph to be at least 20% shorter without losing the core message. Remove filler words and convert passive voice to active voice. [Paste Paragraph]"
7. Clarity Edit: "Review the following text for jargon and complex sentences. Suggest simpler alternatives for an audience of [Audience]. [Paste Text]"

8. Tone Adjustment: "The following text is too [Current Tone, e.g., 'formal']. Rewrite it to have a more [Desired Tone, e.g., 'conversational and friendly'] tone."

Headlines and Titles

9. Headline Brainstorm: "Generate 15 headline ideas for an article about [Topic]. The key takeaway is [Key Takeaway]. Categorize the headlines by different angles (e.g., benefit-driven, curiosity, direct)."

10. Email Subject Lines: "Write 10 subject lines for an email newsletter about [Topic]. The goal is to maximize the open rate."

SEO and Optimization

11. Keyword Integration: "My primary keyword is '[Keyword].' Read my draft and suggest 3 natural places to include this keyword or a variation of it. [Paste Draft]"

12. Meta Description: "Write a compelling meta description (under 160 characters) for a blog post titled '[Title].' It should be engaging and include the keyword '[Keyword].'"

13. FAQ Section: "Create an FAQ section for my article on [Topic]. Write clear, concise answers to the following three questions: [Question 1], [Question 2], [Question 3]."

Repurposing Content

14. Article to LinkedIn Post: "Convert the key points from the following article into a 200-word LinkedIn post. Start with a strong hook and end with a question to drive engagement. [Paste Article]"

15. Article to Video Outline: "Create a script outline for a 3-minute YouTube video based on the following article. The outline should have sections for an intro, three main points, and a conclusion with a call to action. [Paste Article]"

16. Blog Post to Twitter Thread: "Outline a 5-tweet thread summarizing the main arguments of this blog post. [Paste Blog Post]"

Overcoming Writer's Block

17. Idea Generation: "I need to write about [Topic]. I'm feeling uninspired. Give me 5 interesting or contrarian angles on this topic that most people don't consider."
18. Opening Paragraphs: "Give me three different opening paragraph ideas for an article about [Topic]. One should use a statistic, one an anecdote, and one a question."
19. Metaphor and Analogy Finder: "I'm trying to explain the concept of [Concept]. Can you brainstorm 5 simple metaphors or analogies to help make it more relatable?"
20. Next Sentence Suggester: "I'm stuck in the middle of a paragraph. Here is what I have written so far: '[Paste your incomplete paragraph].' Can you give me three different options for the next sentence to keep the momentum going?"

Chapter 10: AI Prompts for Developers and Technical Professionals

As we journey through the various professional landscapes transformed by AI, we now arrive at a domain that is both the architect and a primary beneficiary of this technological shift: the world of developers and technical professionals. In the previous chapters, we've seen AI act as a communications assistant, a marketing strategist, and a creative partner. Here, we will explore its role as a pair programmer, a tireless quality assurance engineer, and a hyper-efficient technical writer.

For software developers, data scientists, systems architects, and other technical professionals, the core work involves logic, structure, and precision. The daily tasks are a cycle of creation, debugging, documentation, and optimization. This cycle, while intellectually stimulating, is filled with repetitive, time-consuming, and often frustrating tasks that are perfectly suited for AI assistance. Code is, after all, just another language, and modern AI models are exceptionally fluent.

The apprehension in the technical community is understandable. If an AI can write code, what does that mean for the future of a developer's career? The reality, as we will demonstrate, is that AI is not a replacement for a skilled developer. It is a force multiplier. It automates the boilerplate, accelerates the debugging process, and handles the tedious documentation, freeing up the human professional to focus on the truly complex and valuable work: system architecture, creative problem-solving, strategic thinking, and elegant algorithm design. A developer who embraces AI will not be replaced by it; they will be the one who replaces the developer who does not.

In this chapter, we will provide a comprehensive playbook for integrating AI into every stage of the development lifecycle. We will begin with the most direct application: code generation and debugging, treating the AI as an intelligent coding partner. We will then tackle one of the most significant productivity drains: the creation of thorough documentation and API references. You will learn how to use AI as a first-pass code reviewer, offering optimization suggestions and catching common errors. We will explore how AI can be a personal tutor for learning new programming languages and frameworks faster than ever before. We will cover the practical applications of generating database queries from natural language and brainstorming testing scenarios to build more robust systems. Finally, we will touch upon the critical but often overlooked skill of technical writing and architecture documentation.

By the end of this chapter, you will have a suite of powerful prompts and workflows that can be immediately integrated into your daily coding and system management routines. You will be equipped to write better code faster, build more reliable systems, and spend more of your valuable time solving the hard problems that drive innovation.

Code Generation and Debugging

This is the most direct and, for many, the most exciting application of AI for technical professionals. The ability to describe a function in plain English and receive a working code snippet in seconds feels like a genuine leap forward. However, it is also the area that requires the most diligence and professional oversight.

A Critical Warning: AI Code is a First Draft

Before we write a single prompt, we must establish a foundational rule: Never, under any circumstances, should you copy and paste AI-generated code directly into a production environment without a thorough review, understanding, and testing process. AI models are trained on vast amounts of public code, which can be outdated, insecure, or inefficient.

Think of the AI as a brilliant but sometimes naive junior developer. It can generate code that is syntactically correct and often works for the happy path, but it does not understand the broader context of your application, your security requirements, or your performance standards. You, the senior developer, are always responsible for the quality, security, and reliability of the code you commit.

With that vital disclaimer in place, let's explore how to use this powerful tool responsibly.

Generating Boilerplate and Utility Functions

One of the best use cases for AI code generation is automating the creation of "boilerplate" or common utility functions. These are the small, repeatable pieces of code that are necessary but don't require deep, creative problem-solving.

Key Prompt Elements for Code Generation:

- **Programming Language:** Be explicit. "Write a script in Python 3."
- **The Goal/Task:** Clearly describe what the code should

accomplish. "Write a function that takes a string as input..."

- **Inputs and Outputs:** Define the function's signature. "...and returns True if the string is a valid email address, and False otherwise."
- **Logic and Constraints:** Explain the core logic or any specific rules the code must follow. "It should check for the presence of an '@' symbol and a '.' in the domain part."
- **Libraries/Dependencies:** Specify any libraries, frameworks, or modules that should be used. "Use the re module for regular expressions."

Professional Scenario: Creating a Data Validation Function

- **The Goal:** You are building a web application and need a simple function in JavaScript to validate that a user-provided phone number is in a standard format.
- The Prompt:
  "Act as a senior JavaScript developer. I need a utility function for form validation.
  Task: Write a JavaScript function named isValidPhoneNumber that takes a string as input.
  Logic: The function should return true if the string matches the format (XXX) XXX-XXXX and false otherwise. It should only validate the format, not whether the number is real.
  Constraints: Write the function using modern ES6 syntax. Do not use any external libraries."
- **Analysis of the Prompt:** This is a perfect example of a well-defined, low-risk task. The logic is explicit, the language is specified, and the constraints are clear. The AI will generate a small, self-contained function that you can quickly read, understand, and test before integrating it into your larger application.

AI as Your Debugging Partner

Debugging can be one of the most frustrating parts of a developer's day. Staring at an error message for an hour only to find a simple typo can be maddening. AI can act as a "rubber duck" with a photographic memory of nearly every error message ever posted online. By providing the code and the error, you can often get an explanation and a solution in seconds.

The "Code + Error" Debugging Prompt

This is a simple but incredibly effective two-part prompt structure.

- **The Goal:** You have a piece of Python code that is throwing a `TypeError`, and you don't immediately see why.
- The Prompt:
  "Act as an expert Python debugger. I am getting an error in my code and I need help understanding why and how to fix it. First, here is the Python code that is causing the problem:

```
def calculate_total_price(items):
  total = 0
  for item in items:
    total = total + item['price']
  return "Total price is: " + total

order_items = [{'price': 10}, {'price': 20}]
print(calculate_total_price(order_items))
```

  Second, here is the exact error message I am receiving:
  TypeError: can only concatenate str (not "int") to str
  Task:
  1. Explain in simple terms what this `TypeError` means in the context of my code.

2. Identify the exact line of code that is causing the error.
3. Provide a corrected version of the code that fixes the error."

- **Benefit:** This prompt is highly effective because it provides all the necessary context. The AI can see the code, see the error, and immediately connect the two. It will correctly identify that you are trying to add an integer (total) to a string ("Total price is: ") and will suggest converting the integer to a string before concatenation, saving you potentially significant debugging time.

Documentation Writing and API References

This is arguably the most powerful and productivity-boosting application of AI for developers. Writing good documentation is critically important for team collaboration and long-term project maintainability, but it is also a tedious task that many developers dislike. AI is exceptionally good at this, and by automating documentation, you can free up enormous amounts of time while dramatically improving the quality of your project's resources.

Generating Line-by-Line Code Comments

Clear comments make code easier to understand and maintain. AI can add these comments to existing code with incredible speed.

- The Prompt:
  "Act as a senior developer who writes excellent, clear code comments.
  Task: Add clear and concise line-by-line comments to the following Python function. The comments should explain the purpose of each logical step in the code.
  def get_user_data(user_id):

```
  db_conn = connect_to_database()
  query = "SELECT * FROM users WHERE id = %s"
  user_record = db_conn.execute(query, (user_id,))
  if user_record:
    return {'id': user_record[0], 'name': user_record[1]}
  else:
    return None
```"
```

### Creating Professional Function Docstrings

A docstring is a more formal piece of documentation that explains what a function does, its parameters, and what it returns. Most IDEs can read these docstrings to provide helpful information to developers using the function.

- The Prompt:
  "Act as a software engineer who follows best practices for documentation.
  Task: Write a comprehensive docstring for the following JavaScript function.
  Format: The docstring should follow the JSDoc format. It must include:
  - A brief, one-sentence summary of what the function does.
  - A description for each parameter, including its type and purpose.
  - A description of the return value, including its type.

```
function calculateTax(amount, taxRate) {
  if (typeof amount !== 'number' || typeof taxRate !== 'number')
{
    return 0;
```
```

```
  }
  return amount * taxRate;
}
```"

- **Benefit:** The AI will generate a perfectly formatted JSDoc block that you can paste directly above your function. This creates professional, machine-readable documentation in seconds, a task that might have taken 5-10 minutes to write manually.

Writing High-Level README Files

A good README file is the front door to your project. AI can help you create a great first draft.

- The Prompt:
  "Act as a technical writer. I need to create a README.md file for a new open-source project.
  Context: The project is a command-line tool written in Go called 'LogParser.' It reads server log files and generates a summary report in JSON format.
  Task: Write a draft for the README.md file.
  Format: The document should be in Markdown and must include the following sections with these exact H2 headings:
  - ## About The Project (A brief, one-paragraph description)
  - ## Getting Started (Instructions for installation)
  - ## Usage (A simple example of how to run the tool from the command line)"

Code Review and Optimization Suggestions

AI can be used as a preliminary step in the code review process. By asking an AI to review your code before you submit it to your team, you can catch common mistakes, improve readability, and get suggestions for performance enhancements. This saves your human colleagues time and allows them to focus on more significant architectural and logical issues.

The "AI Code Reviewer" Prompt

- **The Goal:** You have just finished writing a new function and you want a quick, automated review before creating a pull request.
- The Prompt:
  "Act as a senior software architect and expert code reviewer.
  I am going to provide you with a C# code snippet.
  Task: Please perform a code review on this snippet. Your review should focus on three specific areas:
  1. **Readability and Style:** Are the variable names clear? Does the code follow standard C# conventions?
  2. **Potential Bugs:** Do you see any potential for null reference exceptions, off-by-one errors, or other common bugs?
  3. Performance Optimization: Can you suggest any ways to make this code more efficient or performant?
     Format: Please structure your feedback with three clear headings for each of the areas listed above.

```
// C# code snippet to be reviewed
public List<string> GetActiveUserNames(List<User> users)
{
    var result = new List<string>();
    for (int i = 0; i <= users.Count; i++)
    {
        if (users[i].IsActive == true)
        {
            result.Add(users[i].Name);
```

```
            }
        }
        return result;
    }
```"

- **Analysis of Output:** The AI will provide structured feedback. It will praise the clear function name but suggest using a foreach loop for better readability instead of a for loop. It will immediately identify the critical "off-by-one" error in the loop condition (i <= users.Count should be i < users.Count), which would cause an IndexOutOfRangeException. For performance, it might suggest using LINQ (users.Where(u => u.IsActive).Select(u => u.Name).ToList()) as a more concise and potentially more performant alternative. This automated first pass is incredibly valuable.

Learning New Programming Languages and Frameworks

AI is a revolutionary tool for learning and development. You can use it as a personalized tutor that is available 24/7. One of the most effective techniques is to use analogies from a language you already know well.

The "Teach Me Like I Know X" Prompt

- **The Goal:** You are an experienced Python developer, and you need to learn Rust. You are confused by Rust's core concept of "ownership."
- The Prompt:
  "Act as a computer science professor who is an expert in both Python and Rust.

Task: Explain the concept of 'ownership' in Rust to me.
Context: I am an experienced Python developer. I am used to Python's automatic garbage collection and how it manages memory.
Constraints: Please explain Rust's ownership model by contrasting it directly with how memory is managed in Python. Use simple analogies and provide a short, comparative code snippet in both Python and Rust to illustrate the key difference."

- **Benefit:** This prompt leverages your existing knowledge, making the new concept much easier to grasp. The AI can bridge the gap between what you know and what you need to learn, creating a personalized and highly efficient learning experience.

Database Queries and Data Manipulation

Writing complex database queries can be challenging and error-prone. AI is exceptionally good at translating natural language questions into structured query languages like SQL. This can be a huge time-saver for both developers and data analysts.

The "Natural Language to SQL" Prompt

- **The Goal:** You need to get a specific set of data from your database, but you're not a SQL expert.
- The Prompt:
  "Act as an expert SQL database administrator. I need you to write a SQL query for me.
  Context: I have a database with two tables:
  1. customers (with columns: customer_id, name, signup_date)
  2. orders (with columns: order_id, customer_id,

order_amount, order_date)
Task: Write a single SQL query that returns a list of the names of all customers who signed up in the year 2024 and have placed at least one order with an order_amount greater than $100.
Format: Provide only the complete, runnable SQL query."

- **Benefit:** The AI will translate your plain English request into a correctly formatted SQL query with the necessary JOIN and WHERE clauses. This is not only faster but also helps you learn the correct syntax by example.

Testing Scenarios and Edge Case Identification

Good software is robust software, and robustness comes from thorough testing. A common blind spot for developers is thinking only about the "happy path" where everything works as expected. AI can be a great partner in brainstorming the "unhappy paths" and edge cases that can cause bugs.

The "Find the Edge Cases" Prompt

- **The Goal:** You have written a function, and you want to make sure your unit tests are comprehensive.
- The Prompt:
"Act as a senior Quality Assurance (QA) engineer. I have written the following Python function that calculates the average of a list of numbers.

```
def calculate_average(numbers):
  return sum(numbers) / len(numbers)
```

Task: Brainstorm a comprehensive list of test cases and edge cases that I should write unit tests for.
Format: Organize the list into categories like 'Standard Input,'

'Edge Cases,' and 'Invalid Input.' For each test case, describe the input and the expected output."

- **Probable Output:** The AI would generate a list like:
  - **Standard Input:**
    - Input: [1, 2, 3] -> Expected Output: 2.0
    - Input: [10, 20, 30, 40] -> Expected Output: 25.0
  - **Edge Cases:**
    - Input: [] (an empty list) -> Expected Output: ZeroDivisionError (This is a great catch!)
    - Input: [5] (a list with a single number) -> Expected Output: 5.0
    - Input: [-1, 0, 1] (a list with negative and zero values) -> Expected Output: 0.0
  - **Invalid Input:**
    - Input: ['a', 'b', 'c'] (a list of strings) -> Expected Output: TypeError
    - Input: None -> Expected Output: TypeError
- **Benefit:** The AI has quickly identified a critical bug (dividing by zero with an empty list) and several other important test cases that you might have overlooked, leading to more robust and reliable code.

Technical Writing and Architecture Documentation

Beyond documenting specific code, technical professionals often need to write higher-level documents that explain system architecture, proposals for new technology, or technical specifications. AI can help translate complex technical concepts into clear, structured documents for various audiences.

The "Architectural Summary" Prompt

- **The Goal:** You need to write a high-level summary of your application's architecture for a new team member. You have a set of rough technical notes.

- The Prompt:
  "Act as a technical writer who specializes in creating clear software architecture documentation.
  Context: I have a set of rough notes describing the architecture of our web application. The audience for this summary is a new developer joining our team who is unfamiliar with our system.
  Task: Transform my notes into a clear, well-structured architectural overview.
  Format: The document should have the following sections:
    - **Frontend:** Describe the technology stack and its primary role.
    - **Backend API:** Describe the language, framework, and its main responsibilities.
    - **Database:** Describe the type of database and what kind of data it stores.
    - Deployment: Briefly explain how the application is deployed.
      Constraints: The tone should be clear and concise. Avoid overly deep technical details and focus on the high-level components and how they interact.
      ###TECHNICAL NOTES###
      [Paste your raw, unstructured notes about the architecture here]"

25+ Ready-to-Use Prompt Templates for Developers

Code Generation

1. **Utility Function:** "Write a [Language] function named [FunctionName] that takes [Input] and returns [Output]. It

should [Logic]. Use the [Library] library."

2. **API Endpoint Stub:** "Act as a [Framework, e.g., 'FastAPI'] expert. Write the boilerplate code for a new API endpoint at /users/{user_id} that handles a GET request and returns a JSON object with the user's details."
3. **Data Structure:** "Define a class or struct in [Language] named [ClassName] to represent [Concept]. It should have the following properties: [Property1: Type], [Property2: Type]."
4. **Regular Expression:** "Write a regular expression that validates a [Type of String, e.g., 'hex color code']. It should match [Example 1] but not [Example 2]."
5. **Configuration File:** "Generate a boilerplate [e.g., Dockerfile] for a standard [e.g., Node.js with Express] application."

Debugging

6. Error Explanation: "I have this [Language] code: [Code Snippet]. I am getting this error: [Error Message]. Explain what the error means and how to fix it."

7. Logic Debugging: "I have written this function in [Language] to [Goal], but it's producing the wrong output. For the input [Input], it's returning [Actual Output] when I expect [Expected Output]. Can you help me find the logical error in the code? [Code Snippet]"

Documentation

8. Function Docstring: "Write a docstring for the following [Language] function in [Format, e.g., 'Google-style Python docstring']. It should describe the function, its arguments, and what it returns. [Code Snippet]" 9. **README Generation:** "Create a README.mdfor a project named[Project Name]that[Description]. Include sections for 'Features,' 'Installation,' and a 'Quick Start' example." 10. **API Reference:**

"Write the API documentation for the following endpoint. Describe the resource, the supported HTTP method, any URL parameters, and provide an example of the expected JSON response. [Code Snippet]`"

Code Review and Refactoring

11. Code Review: "Act as a senior developer. Review the following [Language] code for readability, potential bugs, and performance. Provide feedback in a bulleted list. [Code Snippet]"
12. Refactoring: "Take the following [Language] code and refactor it to be more modern and idiomatic. For example, use [Modern Feature] instead of [Old Feature]. [Code Snippet]"
13. DRY Principle: "Analyze this code and identify any repeated logic. Suggest a way to refactor it to follow the Don't Repeat Yourself (DRY) principle by creating a reusable function. [Code Snippet]"

Learning

14. Concept Explanation: "Explain [Complex Concept] in [Language A] to an experienced developer who knows [Language B]. Use analogies from [Language B] to help me understand."
15. Code Translation: "Translate the following code snippet from [Language A] to [Language B]. Add comments to the [Language B] code to explain any significant syntactical or idiomatic differences."

Database and Data

16. Natural Language to SQL: "I have a table named [Table] with columns [Columns]. Write a SQL query to [Your Goal in Plain English]."
17. Schema Design: "Design a simple database schema for a [Type of App, e.g., 'blog']. It needs to store users, posts, and comments. Describe the tables and the relationships between them."
18. Data Transformation Script: "Write a [Language] script that

reads a CSV file named input.csv, removes the column named [Column to Remove], and saves the result to a new file named output.csv."

Testing

19. Unit Test Generation: "Act as a QA engineer. Write a basic unit test for the following [Language] function using the [Testing Framework] framework. The test should check that for the input [Input], the output is [Expected Output]. [Code Snippet]"

20. Edge Case Brainstorm: "Brainstorm a list of edge cases to test for a function that [Function's Purpose]."

21. Mock Data Generation: "Generate a small JSON array of 5 mock [e.g., user] objects for testing. Each object should have the keys [key1], [key2], and [key3] with realistic-looking fake data."

Technical Writing

22. Architectural Overview: "Transform my technical notes into a high-level architectural summary for a non-technical manager. Focus on the 'what' and 'why,' not the deep 'how.' [Paste Notes]"

23. Technical Proposal: "Write the outline for a technical proposal to [Goal, e.g., 'migrate our database from MySQL to PostgreSQL']. The outline should include sections for 'Problem Statement,' 'Proposed Solution,' 'Benefits,' and 'High-Level Timeline.'"

24. Commit Message: "Write a clear and concise git commit message for a change that [Description of Change]. Follow the conventional commit message format."

25. Simplifying Technical Explanations: "I need to explain [Technical Concept] to our marketing team. Take the following technical description and rewrite it in a simple, easy-to-understand way using an analogy. [Paste Technical Description]"

Chapter 11: AI Prompts for Students and Researchers

Throughout this guide, we have explored a diverse range of professional roles, from business and marketing to writing and software development. Now, we turn our focus to a group for whom the management of information, the synthesis of complex ideas, and the pressure of deadlines are a constant reality: students and academic researchers.

The world of academia is an environment of intellectual rigor and high stakes. It is a place where your ability to absorb, analyze, and articulate complex information is the very measure of your success. It is also a world of immense pressure: looming exam dates, demanding research projects, and the ever-present challenge of producing high-quality written work. For students and researchers, the primary challenge is not a lack of information, but an overabundance of it. The task is to find the signal in the noise.

This chapter is a dedicated playbook for navigating the academic landscape with AI as your personal research assistant, study partner, and writing tutor. It is crucial, however, that we begin with a clear and unwavering ethical framework. In an academic context, the line between using a tool for assistance and using it for plagiarism is absolute. This chapter is not about how to get an AI to write your essays or do your homework for you. Submitting AI-generated work as your own is unethical, academically dishonest, and ultimately, it robs you of the very learning process that education is designed to provide.

Instead, this chapter will show you how to use AI ethically and effectively to manage the *process* of learning and research. We will treat the AI as a tool to augment your own intellect, not replace it. You will learn how to use AI to explore and refine research topics, to manage vast amounts of reading through intelligent summarization, and to conquer the blank page by developing structured, logical outlines for your essays and papers. We will explore how AI can become a personalized tutor, explaining complex concepts in simple terms and generating study guides tailored to your specific needs. We will also cover practical, time-saving applications like formatting citations and preparing for exams.

The goal is to use AI to handle the logistical and organizational burdens of academic life, freeing up your mental energy to focus on what truly matters: critical thinking, original analysis, and the deep understanding of your subject matter. By the end of this chapter, you will have a powerful and ethical toolkit for using AI to learn more effectively, conduct research more efficiently, and produce better work with less stress.

Research Topic Exploration and Literature Reviews

Every great academic project begins with a single, compelling question. Yet, finding that question can be one of the most challenging steps. Staring at a broad subject area and trying to narrow it down to a focused, researchable topic can be daunting. AI can act as an excellent brainstorming partner, helping you explore different facets of a subject and formulate interesting questions.

A Critical Note on AI for Research: Remember the warning from Chapter 9: AI models can and do invent facts and sources.

This is a critical danger in an academic setting where citations and accuracy are paramount. **Never use an AI to find primary sources.** Use your university's library databases, Google Scholar, and other vetted academic search engines to find your papers. Use the AI to help you *make sense* of the material you have already found.

Professional Scenario: Narrowing Down a Research Topic

- **The Goal:** You are a university student in an introductory course on sustainable urban development. You need to propose a topic for your final research paper, but the subject feels too broad.
- The Prompt:
  "Act as a university professor specializing in urban development. I am a student in an introductory course and need to brainstorm a research paper topic. My general area of interest is 'sustainable urban development.'
  Task: Generate 5 distinct and focused research questions related to this topic that would be appropriate for a 15-page undergraduate paper.
  Format: For each research question, provide a brief, one-sentence description of the potential focus or angle of a paper based on that question.
  Constraints: The topics should be contemporary and focus on practical policy or design challenges, not purely historical analysis."
- **Analysis of the Prompt:** This prompt assigns a clear expert persona ("university professor") and provides crucial context ("introductory course," "15-page paper"). This guides the AI to produce topics of appropriate scope and complexity. It moves you from a vague interest to a list of concrete,

researchable questions that can serve as the foundation for your project.

Using AI for Literature Reviews (The Right Way)

A literature review requires you to synthesize the findings and arguments of multiple academic sources. This is a high-level analytical task. Instead of asking an AI to "write a literature review," which is both academically dishonest and likely to be filled with fabricated sources, use it to find the connections between the sources *you* have already gathered.

A Step-by--Step Workflow for Synthesizing Research:

Step 1: You Find the Sources
Use your library's academic databases to find 5-7 relevant peer-reviewed articles on your chosen topic.
Step 2: You Provide the Abstracts to the AI
The abstract of an academic paper is a dense summary of its core argument, methodology, and findings.

- The Prompt (Step 2):
  "Act as a graduate-level research assistant. I am going to provide you with the abstracts from six academic papers on the topic of 'The use of carbon capture technology in industrial manufacturing.'
  Task: Your task is to perform a thematic analysis of these abstracts.
  1. First, for each abstract, write a single, concise sentence that summarizes the paper's main argument or finding.
  2. Second, after analyzing all six summaries, identify and describe 3-4 major themes, debates, or recurring points of discussion that appear across the papers.
     ###ABSTRACT 1###

[Paste the first abstract here]
###ABSTRACT 2###
[Paste the second abstract here]
...and so on."

- **Benefit:** This workflow keeps you in complete control of your sources. You are using the AI not as a search engine, but as a pattern-recognition tool. It does the heavy lifting of reading and comparing the dense academic language, helping you quickly identify the key conversations happening in the scholarly literature on your topic. This provides an excellent starting point for structuring your literature review.

Note-Taking and Summarization Techniques

The sheer volume of reading required in any academic program can be overwhelming. AI's ability to summarize long texts is one of its most powerful applications for students. This isn't about skipping the reading; it's about creating tools that help you review and retain the information more effectively.

Professional Scenario: Summarizing a Dense Academic Chapter

- **The Goal:** You have been assigned a 30-page chapter from a textbook. You have read it, but you want to create a concise set of study notes to help you remember the key points.
- The Prompt:
  "Act as an academic tutor. I am providing you with the full text of a textbook chapter on 'The Principles of Aerodynamics.'
  Task: Read the entire chapter and create a one-page summary in the format of a study guide.

Format: The study guide must have two distinct sections:

1. **Key Concepts:** A bulleted list that summarizes the 5-7 most important principles or concepts explained in the chapter. Each bullet point should be no more than two sentences.
2. Key Terminology: A list of the top 10 most important technical terms or vocabulary introduced in the chapter, along with a simple, one-sentence definition for each.
   Constraints: The language used in the summary should be clear and easy for a second-year engineering student to understand.
   ###CHAPTER TEXT###
   [Paste the full text of the chapter here]"

- **Benefit:** This prompt transforms a dense block of text into a structured, high-value study asset. It saves you hours of manual note-taking and provides a perfect document for quick review before an exam.

Organizing Messy Lecture Notes

Whether you take notes by hand or on a laptop, they are often a chaotic mix of ideas, abbreviations, and half-finished thoughts. AI can instantly bring order to this chaos.

- The Prompt:
  "Act as a diligent student. I have just finished a lecture and my notes are very messy. Please organize them for me.
  Task: Take my raw lecture notes and structure them into a clean, hierarchical outline.
  Format: Use headings for the main topics discussed in the lecture. Under each heading, use indented bullet points for the key details, examples, and supporting points. At the very end, create a separate section called 'Professor's Questions'

and list any questions the professor posed to the class.
###RAW NOTES###
[Paste your messy, unstructured lecture notes here]"

Essay Outlining and Structure Development

As with professional writing, the blank page is often the most significant hurdle in academic writing. Using AI to build a strong, logical outline is an ethical and highly effective way to get started. A good outline is a roadmap that ensures your final essay is well-structured, coherent, and effectively argues your thesis.

Professional Scenario: Creating an Argumentative Essay Outline

- **The Goal:** You need to write a 2,000-word history paper on the economic factors leading to the fall of the Roman Empire. You have a thesis statement but need to structure the body of the essay.
- The Prompt:
  "Act as a professor of history who is an expert in academic writing. I need to develop an outline for an argumentative essay.
  Thesis Statement: 'While military defeats and political instability played a role, the fall of the Western Roman Empire was primarily driven by unsustainable economic factors, including over-reliance on conquest, currency debasement, and the collapse of trade networks.'
  Task: Create a detailed outline for a five-paragraph essay structure that argues in favor of this thesis statement.
  Format: The outline should include:
  1. **Introduction:** Briefly describe the historical context and end with my thesis statement.

2. **Body Paragraph 1 (Topic Sentence):** A topic sentence focusing on the economic problems caused by the cessation of territorial expansion. Suggest 2-3 points of evidence to discuss.
3. **Body Paragraph 2 (Topic Sentence):** A topic sentence focusing on the issue of currency debasement and inflation. Suggest 2-3 points of evidence to discuss.
4. **Body Paragraph 3 (Topic Sentence):** A topic sentence focusing on the breakdown of internal and external trade. Suggest 2-3 points of evidence to discuss.
5. **Conclusion:** A plan to briefly summarize the arguments and restate the thesis in a compelling way."

- **Benefit:** This prompt doesn't ask the AI to write the essay, but to create the logical skeleton for it. It forces you to think through the structure of your argument and the evidence you will need for each section. This makes the actual writing process much faster and more focused.

Study Guides and Concept Explanations

One of the most powerful uses of AI for learning is to transform it into a personalized, on-demand tutor. It can explain complex topics from different angles until you understand them and can help you create custom study materials based on your own course content.

Using AI as a Concept Explainer

- The Prompt:
  "Act as a physics tutor. I am a first-year university student and I am having trouble understanding the concept of 'entropy.'
  Task: Explain the concept of entropy to me in three different

ways:
1. A simple, technical definition.
2. A real-world analogy that helps illustrate the concept.
3. A brief explanation of why it is an important concept in physics."

- **Benefit:** By asking for multiple explanations, you increase the chances that one of them will click with your personal learning style. The use of an analogy is particularly effective for translating abstract concepts into concrete understanding.

Creating a Personalized Study Guide

- The Prompt:
  "Act as an academic coach. I have a final exam next week for my 'Introduction to Macroeconomics' course. I am providing you with the syllabus and my collected notes from the semester.
  Task: Based on all the provided material, create a comprehensive study guide for the final exam.
  Format: The study guide should be organized by the major units listed in the syllabus. For each unit, it must include:
  - A one-paragraph summary of the core concepts.
  - A bulleted list of the key terms and their definitions.
  - Three practice short-answer questions that I can use to test my knowledge.
    ###SYLLABUS###
    [Paste the course syllabus]
    ###COURSE NOTES###
    [Paste your combined notes from the semester]"

Problem-Solving for Math and Science

For quantitative subjects, the goal is not just to find the right answer, but to understand the process of getting there. When using AI for help with problem sets, you must constrain it to act as a tutor, not just a calculator.

The "Show Your Work" Prompt

- **The Goal:** You are stuck on a calculus problem and need help, but you want to learn the method, not just get the solution.
- The Prompt:
  "Act as a calculus tutor. I need help solving the following integration problem.
  Problem: [Paste the mathematical problem here]
  Task: Please provide the final answer, but more importantly, give me a detailed, step-by-step explanation of how you arrived at the solution. For each step, explain the rule or theorem you are applying. My goal is to understand the process so I can solve similar problems on my own."
- **Benefit:** The constraint "show your work" is the key. This prompt turns the AI from a simple answer key into a powerful teaching tool, guiding you through the logical steps required to solve the problem.

Citation Formatting and Bibliography Management

This is a perfect example of a low-risk, high-value task to delegate to AI. Manually formatting citations and bibliographies is tedious, time-consuming, and prone to error. AI can do it in seconds.

A Crucial Note on Accuracy: Just as with facts, AI can make small mistakes in citation formatting. It might miss a comma, get the capitalization wrong, or use an outdated version of a style guide. **You must always double-check the AI's output** against an official source like the Purdue Online Writing Lab (OWL) or your university's style guide. However, the AI's draft will be 99% correct and save you a huge amount of time.

The "Citation Formatter" Prompt

- **The Goal:** You have the details for a source and need to format it in two different academic styles.
- The Prompt:
  "Act as a university librarian who is an expert in academic citation styles.
  Task: I will provide you with the information for a scholarly article. Please format it as a citation in two different styles:
  1. APA 7th Edition
  2. Chicago Manual of Style (17th Edition)
     Source Information:
  - Authors: Jane Doe, John Smith
  - Year of Publication: 2023
  - Article Title: The Impact of Geothermal Energy on Urban Power Grids
  - Journal Name: Journal of Sustainable Energy
  - Volume: 45
  - Issue: 2
  - Page Numbers: 112-128
  - DOI: 10.1234/jse.2023.5678"
- **Benefit:** This is a simple, direct prompt that automates one of the most tedious parts of academic writing, allowing you to focus on your research and arguments.

Exam Preparation Strategies

Beyond creating study guides, AI can also help you with the meta-skill of planning and strategizing for your exams, ensuring you use your study time as effectively as possible.

The "Exam Study Plan" Prompt

- **The Goal:** It's the week before final exams, and you feel overwhelmed. You need a structured plan to tackle your studying.
- The Prompt:
  "Act as an academic success coach. I have three final exams next week and I need to create a study plan.
  Context:
  - **Exam 1:** European History (Monday)
  - **Exam 2:** Chemistry (Wednesday)
  - Exam 3: Statistics (Friday)
    I estimate that Chemistry is my most difficult subject, followed by Statistics, and then History. I have about 20 hours of dedicated study time available between now and the first exam on Monday.
    Task: Create a detailed study schedule for me from today (Thursday) until next Friday.
    Format: The schedule should be a day-by-day list. For each day, break down the study time into focused blocks (e.g., '2-hour block') and assign a specific subject and a study method to each block (e.g., 'Review notes,' 'Do practice problems,' 'Create flashcards').
    Constraints: The plan should prioritize my most difficult subjects and incorporate principles of effective studying, like spaced repetition and active recall."
- **Benefit:** This prompt takes the stress and guesswork out of planning. The AI acts as a neutral third party, creating a logical, balanced schedule that helps you allocate your time efficiently and reduces the feeling of being overwhelmed.

20+ Ready-to-Use Prompt Templates for Students

and Researchers

Research and Ideation

1. **Topic Brainstorm:** "Act as a professor in [Subject]. I am in an [undergraduate/graduate] course. My general interest is [Topic]. Brainstorm 5 focused research questions suitable for a [Number]-page paper."
2. **Thesis Statement Refinement:** "My current working thesis is: '[Your Thesis].' Act as a writing tutor and help me refine it to be more specific, arguable, and concise."
3. **Synthesize Abstracts:** "Act as a research assistant. I have provided 5 abstracts below on [Topic]. Summarize each one in a single sentence, then identify 3 common themes that connect them. [Paste Abstracts]"

Note-Taking and Summarization
4. Textbook Chapter Summary: "Summarize the key concepts from the provided textbook chapter on [Topic] into a one-page study guide with bullet points and a list of key terms. [Paste Text]"
5. Lecture Note Organizer: "Organize my messy lecture notes into a structured outline with headings and sub-bullets. Create a separate list of key definitions. [Paste Notes]"
6. Article Summary for Audience: "Summarize the following academic article for someone who is not an expert in the field. Focus on the main findings and their real-world implications. [Paste Article]"
Writing and Outlining
7. Essay Outline: "Create a detailed outline for a [Number]-word argumentative essay on the topic '[Topic].' The outline should include a thesis statement, topic sentences for three body paragraphs, and ideas for supporting evidence."
8. Paragraph Expansion: "I have a topic sentence: '[Your Topic

Sentence].' Please expand this into a full paragraph of about 150 words, providing a hypothetical example to illustrate the point."

9. Counterargument Brainstorm: "My main argument in my essay is '[Your Argument].' Act as a critical reader and brainstorm 3 potential counterarguments or objections that I should address in my paper."

Studying and Learning

10. Concept Explainer: "Explain the concept of '[Complex Concept]' to me as if I were a high school student. Use a simple analogy."

11. Study Guide Creator: "Based on my course notes, create a study guide for my upcoming exam on [Subject]. Include summaries, key terms, and 5 practice questions. [Paste Notes]"

12. Flashcard Generation: "Generate a list of 10 flashcards (term on one side, definition on the other) based on the key terminology in the provided text. Format it as a two-column table. [Paste Text]"

13. Self-Correction Prompt: "I am trying to solve this problem: [Problem]. Here is my attempted solution: [Your Solution]. Please review my work, identify any mistakes I made, and explain the correct way to solve it."

Problem Solving

14. Math/Science Tutor: "Act as a [Subject] tutor. Walk me through the solution to this problem step-by-step, explaining the reasoning behind each step. [Paste Problem]"

15. Proofreading Code for Logic: "I've written a simple script in [Language] to [Goal]. Please review it for logical errors or inefficiencies and suggest improvements. [Paste Code]"

Formatting and Preparation

16. Citation Formatter: "Format the following source information in [e.g., MLA 9th edition] style. [Paste Source Info]"

17. Bibliography Organizer: "I have a list of sources. Please

alphabetize them and format them as a complete bibliography in [e.g., APA 7th edition] style. [Paste List]"

18. Exam Study Plan: "Create a 7-day study plan for my exams in [Subject 1], [Subject 2], and [Subject 3]. I have [Number] hours to study. Prioritize based on difficulty."

19. Presentation Outline: "Create an outline for a 10-minute academic presentation on my research paper, '[Paper Title].' The outline should structure the talk into an introduction, main points, and a conclusion with time for questions."

20. Abstract Writing Assistant: "I have written a full research paper. Read the paper and write a concise, 150-word abstract that summarizes the research question, methodology, key findings, and conclusion. [Paste Paper]"

Chapter 12: AI Prompts for Entrepreneurs and Freelancers

In our journey through the modern professional landscape, we have explored how AI can serve as a powerful assistant for business professionals, marketers, writers, developers, and students. Now, we turn our attention to the ultimate generalists, the professionals who must embody all of these roles at once: entrepreneurs and freelancers.

If you are an entrepreneur building a company from the ground up or a freelancer managing your own solo business, you know the reality of wearing multiple hats. On any given day, you are the chief executive officer, the head of marketing, the lead salesperson, the finance department, the customer service representative, and the project manager. The sheer breadth of responsibility is immense, and your most valuable resource is not money, but time. Every minute spent on administrative overhead is a minute not spent on growing your business, serving your clients, or developing your core product or service.

This is where AI becomes more than just a productivity tool. It becomes your strategic partner, your tireless administrative assistant, your on-demand consultant, and your creative collaborator. It is the force multiplier that allows a single individual or a small team to operate with the efficiency and reach of a much larger organization. For the entrepreneur and the freelancer, mastering AI prompting is not just about being more productive, it is about gaining a fundamental competitive advantage.

This chapter is your dedicated playbook for leveraging AI across the full spectrum of entrepreneurial and freelance activities. We will start at the very beginning, using AI to develop and refine the cornerstone of any new venture: the business plan. You will learn how to craft a compelling brand identity and translate it into consistent messaging. We will provide detailed workflows for writing persuasive client proposals, a critical skill for any freelancer. We'll dive into the often-intimidating world of pricing strategy and financial modeling, using AI to analyze options and build forecasts.

We will then shift to the daily operational challenges, using AI to master time management and prioritize your overwhelming to-do list. You will get practical templates for networking and outreach, helping you build connections and win new business. We will break down the process of creating a professional investor pitch deck and show you how to streamline your customer service with AI-assisted responses.

The goal of this chapter is to equip you with the prompts and strategies to automate the routine, accelerate the strategic, and amplify your ability to focus on what you do best. By integrating these tools into your workflow, you can reclaim your time, reduce administrative friction, and dedicate your energy to the high-value work that will truly grow your business.

Business Plan Development and Refinement

A business plan is the foundational document for any new venture. It is your roadmap, your strategic guide, and the document you will use to secure funding, attract partners, and align your own thinking. However, writing one from scratch can be an intimidating process. AI can act as an expert business consultant, helping you structure the document and think through each critical section.

This is a perfect task for a multi-step, iterative prompting workflow. You start with the high-level structure and then dive deeper into each component.

A Multi-Step Workflow for Building Your Business Plan

Step 1: Create the High-Level Outline
Before you write a single word, you need a solid structure.

- The Prompt (Step 1):
  "Act as a seasoned business consultant who has helped hundreds of startups write their business plans.
  Task: Generate a comprehensive, section-by-section outline for a traditional business plan.
  Context: The business is a direct-to-consumer e-commerce company that will sell high-quality, sustainable kitchenware.
  Format: The outline should be a numbered list of the main sections (e.g., Executive Summary, Company Description, Market Analysis, etc.). For each main section, include a bulleted list of the key topics and questions that should be addressed within that section."

Step 2: Draft the Executive Summary
The executive summary is the most important part of your business plan. It's the first thing investors or partners will read. You should draft it after you have thought through the other sections.

- The Prompt (Step 2):
  "Act as a business plan writer. I have outlined the key points of my business. Please synthesize them into a compelling, one-page Executive Summary.

Context: Our company, 'EcoKitchen,' will sell sustainable kitchenware online. Our target market is environmentally conscious millennials. Our key differentiator is our lifetime warranty and minimalist design. We project reaching $500,000 in revenue by year three. We are seeking $50,000 in seed funding for inventory and marketing.
Task: Write a professional and persuasive Executive Summary that covers our mission, product, target market, competitive advantage, financial highlights, and funding request."

Step 3: Flesh Out the Market Analysis Section
Now, you can use the AI to help you think through specific parts of your plan.

- The Prompt (Step 3):
  "Act as a market research analyst. I am writing the Market Analysis section of my business plan for 'EcoKitchen.'
  Context: Our target audience is eco-conscious millennials (ages 25-40) in urban areas. Our main competitors are 'GreenPans' and 'EarthlyWares.'
  Task: Help me structure my market analysis. Brainstorm three key points I should discuss for each of the following sub-sections:
  1. **Target Market:** (e.g., demographic details, psychographic profiles, purchasing habits)
  2. **Market Size and Growth:** (e.g., what kind of data should I look for to show the market is growing?)
  3. **Competitive Analysis:** (e.g., what factors should I compare between my company and my competitors?)"
- **Benefit of the Workflow:** This iterative process breaks down a massive project into manageable steps. You use the AI as a thinking partner at each stage, from structuring the

document to drafting its most critical components.

Brand Identity and Messaging

Your brand is more than just a logo. It's the personality of your business. It's how you communicate, what you value, and the feeling you want your customers to have when they interact with you. AI can help you codify this identity.

Professional Scenario: Defining Your Brand's Core

- **The Goal:** You are a freelance graphic designer starting your own business. You need to define your brand identity before you build your website and marketing materials.
- The Prompt:
  "Act as a brand strategist. I am a freelance graphic designer, and I need to define my brand identity.
  Task: Guide me through a brand discovery process by asking me five key questions. The questions should help me clarify my mission, my unique value proposition, my target client, and my brand's personality. After I answer your questions, synthesize my answers into a concise, one-paragraph brand statement."
- **How it Works:** The AI will ask you questions like, "What is the primary goal you help your clients achieve?" or "What three words would you want your clients to use to describe working with you?" You answer these in the chat, and the AI then combines your own words into a powerful summary statement that becomes the foundation of your brand messaging.

Developing a Messaging Style Guide

Consistency is key to a strong brand. A messaging style guide ensures you use the same tone and voice across all your communications.

- The Prompt:
  "Act as a brand voice expert. Based on the following brand statement, create a simple messaging style guide.
  Brand Statement: 'My freelance design business helps innovative tech startups create clean, minimalist, and user-friendly visual identities. My approach is collaborative, professional, and focused on delivering strategic value, not just pretty visuals.'
  Task: Create a style guide with three sections:
  1. **Brand Personality:** A list of 5 adjectives that describe the brand voice.
  2. **Voice Do's and Don'ts:** A bulleted list of 3 things to do (e.g., 'Use clear, concise language') and 3 things to avoid (e.g., 'Avoid overly casual slang').
  3. **Example Snippet:** Write a short (50-word) example of a LinkedIn post that perfectly captures this brand voice."

Client Proposal Writing

For many freelancers, writing proposals is a constant, time-consuming necessity. A well-structured proposal can be the difference between winning and losing a project. AI can help you create a professional, persuasive template that you can quickly customize for each new client.

The Ultimate Proposal Generation Prompt

This prompt is designed to be a comprehensive template that you can save and reuse. You simply fill in the bracketed information for each new project.

- The Prompt:
  "Act as an expert business proposal writer for freelancers.
  Task: Write a comprehensive and persuasive client proposal based on the following information.
  Context:
  - **My Services:** I am a freelance [Your Profession, e.g., 'Web Developer'].
  - **Client Name:** [Client's Name or Company]
  - **Project Name:** [Name of the Project]
  - **Client's Problem:** [Briefly describe the challenge the client is facing, as you understand it].
  - **Proposed Solution:** [Briefly describe how your services will solve their problem].
  - **Key Deliverables:** [List 3-5 specific things you will deliver, e.g., 'A 5-page responsive website,' 'A complete branding guide,' 'Monthly SEO reports'].
  - **Project Timeline:** [Estimated duration, e.g., '6 weeks'].
  - Project Price: [Your total project fee].
    Format: The proposal must be structured with the following clear sections and headings:
  1. **Prepared for: [Client Name]**
  2. **Introduction:** A brief, professional opening.
  3. **Understanding Your Needs:** A paragraph that shows you've listened and understand their problem.
  4. **Proposed Solution:** A detailed description of your solution and the value it will bring.
  5. **Project Deliverables:** A bulleted list of the key deliverables.
  6. **Timeline and Investment:** State the timeline and the project price clearly.
  7. Next Steps: A clear call to action (e.g., 'To proceed, please sign and return this proposal...').

Constraints: The tone should be professional, confident, and client-focused. Emphasize the benefits of your solution, not just the features."

- **Benefit:** By creating this master prompt, you turn the proposal writing process from a multi-hour chore into a 15-minute task. You simply update the context for each new client, and the AI generates a polished, professional draft.

Pricing Strategy and Financial Modeling

Setting your prices and forecasting your finances are two of the most challenging aspects of running your own business. AI can act as a neutral consultant, helping you analyze different models and create simple financial projections.

Brainstorming Pricing Models

- The Prompt:
  "Act as a business consultant for creative freelancers. I am a freelance [Your Profession, e.g., 'videographer'] and I am struggling with how to price my services.
  Task: Describe three common pricing models for my profession:
  1. Hourly Rate
  2. Per-Project Fixed Fee
  3. Value-Based Pricing
     Format: For each of the three models, create a bulleted list of its main pros and cons from the perspective of the freelancer."
- **Benefit:** This prompt gives you a structured way to think through your options. It lays out the strategic advantages and disadvantages of each model, helping you make a more informed decision that fits your business goals.

Creating a Simple Financial Forecast

- The Prompt:
  "Act as a small business financial advisor. I need to create a simple 12-month financial forecast for my first year of business.
  Context: I am a freelance consultant. I plan to charge an average of $3,000 per project. I realistically expect to complete 1 project in my first month, and then increase to 2 projects per month from month 2 onwards. My estimated monthly business expenses are $500.
  Task: Create a simple 12-month financial projection.
  Format: Present the information as a month-by-month list. For each month, calculate and show the 'Projected Revenue,' 'Estimated Expenses,' and 'Projected Profit.'"

Time Management and Task Prioritization

The entrepreneur's to-do list is infinite. The key to staying sane and making progress is ruthless prioritization. You can use AI to apply proven productivity frameworks to your daily tasks.

The "Eisenhower Matrix" Prompt

The Eisenhower Matrix is a simple tool for categorizing tasks into four quadrants to help you decide what to focus on.

- **The Goal:** You have a long, jumbled list of tasks and you feel paralyzed, not knowing where to start.
- The Prompt:
  "Act as an expert productivity coach. I am feeling overwhelmed with my to-do list. Please help me prioritize my tasks using the Eisenhower Matrix.
  Task: Take the following list of my tasks and categorize each

one into one of four quadrants:

1. **Urgent & Important (Do First):** Tasks to do immediately.
2. **Not Urgent & Important (Schedule):** Tasks to schedule time for.
3. **Urgent & Not Important (Delegate):** Tasks that could be delegated or automated.
4. Not Urgent & Not Important (Eliminate): Tasks to eliminate.
   Format: Present the output as four distinct lists with clear headings for each quadrant.
   ###TASK LIST###
   - Finish the proposal for the big new client (deadline tomorrow).
   - Research new accounting software for next quarter.
   - Respond to a non-urgent client email.
   - Update my portfolio with my latest project.
   - Fix a minor typo on my website's contact page.
   - Brainstorm ideas for my long-term business strategy.
   - Scroll through industry news feeds."

- **Benefit:** This prompt forces you to take a step back and look at your tasks strategically. The AI acts as an objective third party, applying the framework and giving you a clear, actionable plan for your day.

Networking and Outreach Templates

Building your network and finding new clients is essential for growth. AI can help you draft professional, non-generic outreach messages that get responses.

The "LinkedIn Connection" Prompt

- The Prompt:

"Act as a professional networking coach.
Task: Write a short, personalized LinkedIn connection request message (under 300 characters).
Context:

- **My Role:** I am a [Your Role, e.g., 'founder of a supply chain startup'].
- **Their Role:** I want to connect with a [Their Role, e.g., 'logistics manager at a major retail company'].
- Reason for Connecting: I admire their work on [Specific Project or Article they wrote] and I believe my startup's solution could be relevant to their challenges.
  Constraints: The tone should be respectful and professional, not a hard sales pitch. It should focus on shared interests and potential value."

Pitch Deck Creation

For entrepreneurs seeking investment, the pitch deck is a critical storytelling tool. AI can help you structure your narrative and draft the content for each slide.

The "10-Slide Pitch Deck" Outline Prompt

- The Prompt:
  "Act as a venture capital pitch coach. I am creating an investor pitch deck for my startup.
  Startup Idea: [A one-sentence description of your startup].
  Task: Create a slide-by-slide outline for a classic 10-slide investor pitch deck.
  Format: For each slide (from Slide 1 to Slide 10), provide the standard title for that slide (e.g., 'The Problem,' 'The Solution') and a bulleted list of 2-3 key points that should be covered on that slide."

Drilling Down on a Specific Slide

- The Prompt:
  "This outline is great. Now, let's draft the content for Slide 4: 'The Solution.'
  Context: Our startup, 'FlowMetrics,' is a SaaS platform that provides real-time inventory management for small e-commerce businesses.
  Task: Write three concise bullet points for the 'Solution' slide. Each bullet point should clearly and simply describe a core feature and the primary benefit it provides to the user."

Customer Service Responses

Providing excellent customer service is crucial for retention and reputation. AI can help you create a library of professional, empathetic, and consistent responses to common inquiries, saving you time and ensuring quality.

The "Customer Complaint" Response Prompt

- **The Goal:** A customer has emailed to complain about a delayed shipment. You need to respond professionally and helpfully.
- The Prompt:
  "Act as a highly skilled customer service manager.
  Task: Draft a professional and empathetic email response to a customer complaint.
  Context: A customer named Sarah Miller is upset because her order, #[Order Number], which was promised for delivery yesterday, has not yet arrived. The tracking information shows it is delayed by two days.
  Format: The email should have three parts:
  1. Acknowledge her frustration and sincerely apologize for

the delay.
2. Explain the situation clearly (the tracking shows a carrier delay) and provide the new expected delivery date.
3. Offer a gesture of goodwill (e.g., a 15% discount on her next purchase) to compensate for the inconvenience.
Constraints: The tone must be apologetic and helpful, not defensive."

25+ Ready-to-Use Prompt Templates for Entrepreneurs and Freelancers

Business Planning and Strategy

1. **Business Plan Outline:** "Act as a business consultant. Create a detailed outline for a business plan for a [Type of Business]."
2. **Executive Summary:** "Synthesize these key points into a one-page executive summary for my business plan: [Paste Key Points]."
3. **Mission Statement:** "Help me craft a powerful one-sentence mission statement for my company that provides [Product/Service] for [Target Audience] to achieve [Outcome]."
4. **SWOT Analysis:** "Act as a business strategist. Conduct a SWOT (Strengths, Weaknesses, Opportunities, Threats) analysis for my [Type of Business]."
5. **Elevator Pitch:** "Write a compelling 30-second elevator pitch for my business, '[Business Name],' which [What your business does]."

Branding and Marketing
6. Brand Voice Guide: "Based on these three adjectives ([Adjective 1, 2, 3]), create a simple brand voice guide with 'Do's and Don'ts'."

7. Client Persona: "Create a detailed customer persona for my ideal client. The business is [Business Type] and the client is likely a [Client Role]."
8. Content Ideas: "Brainstorm 10 blog post ideas for my [Industry] business that would attract my target audience of [Audience]."
9. LinkedIn Bio: "Write a professional and engaging LinkedIn 'About' section for me. I am a [Your Role] specializing in [Your Specialty]."

Proposals and Sales

10. Proposal Template: "Create a reusable client proposal template with sections for Introduction, Understanding Needs, Proposed Solution, Deliverables, Timeline, and Investment."
11. Cold Outreach Email: "Write a concise and personalized cold outreach email to a potential client. My service is [Service], and I want to offer help with their [Client's Potential Problem]."
12. Follow-Up Email: "Draft a polite follow-up email to a potential client I haven't heard from in a week after sending a proposal."

Finance and Pricing

13. Pricing Model Analysis: "Analyze the pros and cons of hourly vs. fixed-project pricing for a freelance [Your Profession]."
14. Simple Financial Forecast: "Create a simple 12-month profit and loss forecast based on projected monthly revenue of [$X] and monthly expenses of [$Y]."
15. Invoice Reminder: "Write a polite but firm reminder email to a client whose invoice is 7 days past due."

Productivity and Operations

16. Eisenhower Matrix: "Organize the following to-do list into an Eisenhower Matrix: [Paste List]."
17. Meeting Agenda: "Create an agenda for a 30-minute client kick-off meeting for a [Project Type] project."
18. Onboarding Checklist: "Generate a checklist of the key steps for onboarding a new freelance client."

19. Standard Operating Procedure (SOP): "Write an outline for a Standard Operating Procedure (SOP) for my process of [A recurring business process]."

Client Communication

20. Customer Service Response: "Draft an empathetic response to a client who is unhappy with a recent deliverable."

21. Testimonial Request: "Write a friendly email to a happy client asking them for a testimonial for my website."

22. Project Update: "Write a concise weekly project update email for a client. The update should cover what was completed this week, what is planned for next week, and any potential blockers."

Pitching and Networking

23. Pitch Deck Outline: "Create a slide-by-slide outline for a 10-slide investor pitch deck."

24. Networking Introduction: "Write a short, memorable self-introduction for me to use at a professional networking event. I am a [Your Role]."

25. Informational Interview Request: "Draft a respectful email asking an experienced professional in my field for a brief, 20-minute informational interview."

Chapter 13: AI Prompts for Human Resources and Management

As we continue our exploration of AI's role across various professions, we now arrive at the very heart of any organization: its people. The work of Human Resources professionals and managers is uniquely complex. It is a field built on communication, empathy, structure, and strategy. The goal is to build, support, and guide the teams that drive the business forward.

This noble objective, however, is often buried under a mountain of administrative work. Managers and HR professionals spend countless hours writing job descriptions, preparing for performance reviews, creating onboarding materials, developing training programs, and documenting policies. These tasks are essential for creating a fair, consistent, and well-run workplace, but they are also incredibly time-consuming. Every hour spent wordsmithing a policy document is an hour not spent mentoring a promising employee. Every evening spent preparing performance review scripts is an evening not spent thinking about long-term team strategy.

This is where AI offers a truly profound opportunity. For managers and HR leaders, AI is not a tool for replacing human judgment, but for liberating it. It is your on-demand administrative partner, your communications assistant, and your instructional designer. By delegating the first draft of these essential but repetitive tasks to an AI, you can reclaim your most valuable asset, your time, and reinvest it in the work that only you can do:

building culture, resolving complex interpersonal issues, providing mentorship, and leading with vision.

A critical note before we begin: The topics in this chapter, such as performance, conflict, and hiring, are among the most sensitive in any organization. AI should be used as a preparation and drafting tool, never as a decision-making one. The final judgment, the empathetic delivery, and the strategic oversight must always be human. The AI can provide the script, but you are the director.

In this chapter, we will provide a comprehensive playbook for integrating AI into the core functions of management and HR. We will start with the talent acquisition pipeline, from writing compelling job descriptions to creating structured candidate screening frameworks. We will then tackle the often-dreaded performance review cycle, showing you how to use AI to prepare more efficiently and deliver more constructive feedback. You will learn how to generate comprehensive onboarding materials and 30-60-90 day plans in minutes. We will explore how to use AI as an instructional design assistant to develop effective training programs. We will even touch upon how to use AI to prepare for difficult conversations and brainstorm conflict resolution strategies. Finally, we will cover team communication and the essential work of policy documentation.

By the end of this chapter, you will be equipped to transform your workflow, automating the administrative burdens of leadership and freeing yourself to be the strategic, people-focused leader your team needs.

Job Description Writing and Candidate Screening

Attracting and hiring the right talent is the single most important driver of an organization's success. It all starts with a clear, compelling, and inclusive job description.

Writing Compelling Job Descriptions

A great job description does more than just list requirements. It sells the role and the company to top candidates. It reflects your culture and sets clear expectations. However, writing them from scratch for every new role is a repetitive chore. AI can create an excellent first draft that is 90% of the way there.

Key Prompt Elements for Job Descriptions:

- **Persona:** "Act as a senior recruiter at a [Company Type, e.g., 'fast-growing fintech startup']."
- **Role Details:** The job title, department, and who the role reports to.
- **Core Responsibilities:** 3-5 key duties of the role.
- **Key Qualifications:** Must-have skills and experience.
- **Company Culture:** A few words describing your work environment (e.g., "collaborative," "data-driven," "remote-first").

Professional Scenario: Creating a Job Description for a Data Analyst

- **The Goal:** You need to hire a mid-level Data Analyst for your marketing team. You want a description that is professional but also reflects your dynamic company culture.
- The Strong Prompt:
  "Act as an experienced tech recruiter. I need to create a job description for a new 'Data Analyst' position on our Marketing team.
  Context: Our company is a SaaS business in the B2B

marketing analytics space. Our culture is highly data-driven, collaborative, and fast-paced. This role reports to the Director of Marketing Analytics.
Task: Write a complete job description.
Format: The description must include the following sections with these exact headings:
  - ## About the Role
  - ## What You'll Do (as a bulleted list based on the responsibilities below)
  - ## What You'll Bring (as a bulleted list based on the qualifications below)
  Key Responsibilities:
  - Analyze marketing campaign performance data to identify trends.
  - Build and maintain dashboards in our business intelligence tool.
  - Present findings and recommendations to the marketing leadership.
  - Collaborate with the sales team on lead quality analysis.
  Key Qualifications:
  - 3+ years of experience in a data analytics role.
  - Expert proficiency in SQL and a business intelligence tool (like Tableau or Power BI).
  - Excellent communication and presentation skills.
  Constraints: The tone should be professional yet energetic. It should appeal to a candidate who is passionate about using data to drive business growth."
- **Benefit:** This prompt gives the AI all the necessary context to create a detailed, well-structured, and culturally aligned job description in under a minute.

Using AI for Inclusive Language

After you have a draft, you can use a follow-up prompt to make it more inclusive.
"Review the job description I just created. Identify any language that might be considered non-inclusive or could unintentionally discourage certain groups from applying. For each identified phrase, suggest a more inclusive alternative."
Creating Frameworks for Candidate Screening

Ethical Warning: AI should never be used to make hiring decisions or to "score" candidates' resumes automatically. This is a high-risk area for bias. However, you can use AI to help you create a *consistent human-led screening framework* to ensure all candidates are being evaluated against the same objective criteria.

- The Prompt:
  "Act as an HR specialist focused on fair hiring practices. I have provided a job description for a 'Customer Support Representative' below.
  Task: Based only on the requirements in this job description, create a structured candidate screening scorecard for our interview team to use.
  Format: The scorecard should be a list of 5 key evaluation criteria (e.g., 'Communication Skills,' 'Problem-Solving Ability,' 'Experience with CRM Software'). For each criterion, create three sub-bullets describing what 'Exceeds Expectations,' 'Meets Expectations,' and 'Does Not Meet Expectations' would look like in an interview.
  ###JOB DESCRIPTION###
  [Paste the full job description here]"
- **Benefit:** This prompt helps you translate a job description into a consistent evaluation tool. It reduces unconscious bias

by forcing interviewers to assess every candidate against the same predefined, role-relevant criteria.

Performance Review Preparation

Performance reviews are one of the most high-stakes and time-consuming responsibilities for any manager. Gathering examples, structuring feedback, and finding the right words for a constructive conversation is challenging. AI can be an invaluable partner in the preparation process.

Organizing Your Feedback and Notes
Throughout a performance cycle, managers often accumulate a scattered collection of notes. AI can bring order to this chaos.

- The Prompt:
  "Act as an experienced management coach. I am preparing for a quarterly performance review with a team member. I have a list of my raw notes from the past three months.
  Task: Please organize these notes into a structured summary for my private preparation.
  Format: Create three distinct sections with the following headings:
  1. **Key Accomplishments & Strengths:** (List achievements and positive attributes)
  2. **Areas for Growth & Development:** (List opportunities for improvement)
  3. Specific Examples & Data Points: (Extract concrete examples from the notes to support the points above)
     ###RAW NOTES###
     [Paste your jumbled notes, e.g., 'Did a great job on the Q3 report, numbers were very clear. Needs to be more proactive in team meetings, sometimes waits to be asked for input. Client X sent a positive email about their quick

response on the support ticket last month. Was late on the initial draft of the project plan. Helped onboard the new intern and was very patient.']"

- **Benefit:** This prompt instantly transforms your raw observations into a structured document, making it much easier to see the key themes of the employee's performance.

Drafting Performance Review Talking Points

Once your thoughts are organized, you can use AI to help you script the conversation itself, ensuring it is balanced, constructive, and forward-looking.

- The Prompt:
  "Act as a leadership coach specializing in communication. Based on the structured feedback summary below, create a set of talking points for me to use in a performance review meeting.
  Task: Write a script outline for a 45-minute performance review conversation.
  Format: The outline should have sections for:
  - **Opening:** A positive and welcoming opening statement.
  - **Celebrating Successes:** Talking points to praise their key accomplishments, using specific examples from the summary.
  - **Discussing Growth Opportunities:** Constructive and forward-looking talking points for the development areas. Frame them as opportunities, not criticisms.
  - **Collaborative Goal Setting:** A series of open-ended questions to facilitate a discussion about goals for the next quarter.
  - Closing: A supportive and encouraging closing statement.
    Constraints: The tone must be constructive and motivating. Use a 'we' and 'us' framing where possible to

emphasize partnership.
###FEEDBACK SUMMARY###
[Paste the organized summary from the previous prompt]"

Employee Onboarding Materials

A great onboarding experience is critical for retaining new hires and getting them productive quickly. AI can help you standardize and accelerate the creation of these essential materials.

Generating Role-Specific Onboarding Plans

- The Prompt:
  "Act as an experienced HR onboarding specialist.
  Task: Create a comprehensive 30-60-90 day plan for a new hire in the role of 'Junior Financial Analyst.'
  Format: The plan should be structured with three main headings: 'First 30 Days,' 'First 60 Days,' and 'First 90 Days.'
  Under each heading, create bulleted lists for three sub-categories:
  1. **Learning Goals:** (What they should know)
  2. **Performance Goals:** (What they should be able to do)
  3. Key Relationships: (Who they should meet)
     Context: The role involves preparing financial reports, assisting with budget forecasting, and analyzing monthly financial data."
- **Benefit:** This creates a structured, professional roadmap for your new hire, setting them up for success from day one. It turns a multi-hour task into a five-minute one.

Training Program Development

Designing effective training is a specialized skill. AI can act as your instructional design assistant, helping you outline training sessions and even draft the content.

Outlining a Management Training Session

- The Prompt:
  "Act as a corporate trainer and instructional designer. I need to develop a 90-minute training workshop for newly promoted managers. The topic is 'Delegating Effectively.'
  Task: Create a detailed agenda and outline for this workshop.
  Format: The outline should include:
    - **Learning Objectives:** (3-4 clear goals for what participants will learn)
    - **Agenda with Timings:** (A minute-by-minute breakdown, e.g., '10:00-10:15: Introduction')
    - **Key Talking Points:** (For each agenda item, list the main concepts to cover)
    - **Interactive Exercise:** (Describe a simple role-playing exercise or group discussion to help participants practice the skill)"

Conflict Resolution Scenarios

Important Note: AI is not a mediator. However, it is an excellent private tool for managers to prepare for difficult conversations by brainstorming communication strategies and thinking through different angles.

Preparing to Mediate a Disagreement

- The Prompt:
  "Act as an executive coach specializing in conflict resolution. I am a manager who needs to facilitate a discussion between two senior team members, Alex and Ben.
  Context: Alex wants to adopt a new, experimental software

development methodology to increase speed. Ben is concerned this will compromise product quality and stability. The disagreement has created tension on the team.
Task: Help me prepare for a mediation meeting with them.

1. First, define the core interests of each person (what does Alex really want? what does Ben really want?).
2. Second, brainstorm three open-ended, non-judgmental questions I can ask to get the conversation started.
3. Third, suggest a potential 'win-win' compromise that I could guide them toward."

- **Benefit:** This prompt helps the manager move from a reactive to a strategic mindset. It uses the AI as a private sounding board to prepare for a high-stakes conversation, increasing the likelihood of a positive outcome.

Team Communication and Feedback

Clear and consistent communication is the hallmark of a great manager. AI can help draft routine communications, freeing up mental energy for more strategic tasks.

Drafting a Team Announcement

- The Prompt:
  "Act as a team lead. I need to write a clear and concise announcement to my team.
  Task: Draft an announcement for our team's communication channel.
  Context: We have just successfully completed 'Project Phoenix.'
  Key Points to Include:
  - Congratulate the team on their hard work and collaboration.

    - Mention one specific positive outcome (e.g., 'We delivered two days ahead of schedule').
    - Announce that as a reward, the company is giving everyone a bonus day off to be used next month.
    - State that the project retrospective meeting is scheduled for next Tuesday.
      Constraints: The tone should be celebratory, appreciative, and clear."

Policy Documentation

Writing company policies is a critical but dry task. It requires clarity, precision, and comprehensive coverage of key issues.

Ethical and Legal Disclaimer: AI is not a lawyer. Any policy document generated by an AI is a first draft and **must** be reviewed by qualified legal counsel before implementation.

Drafting a Company Policy

- The Prompt:
  "Act as a senior HR policy writer.
  Task: Write a first draft of a 'Use of Company Equipment' policy.
  Context: The company is a 100-person tech firm that provides laptops and mobile phones to employees.
  Format: The policy should be a formal document with numbered sections covering:
  1. **Purpose of the Policy**
  2. **Equipment Covered**
  3. **Employee Responsibilities** (including security and care)
  4. **Policy on Personal Use**
  5. Procedure for Lost or Damaged Equipment
     Constraints: The language must be clear, professional,

and unambiguous."

20+ Ready-to-Use Prompt Templates for HR and Management

Recruiting and Hiring

1. **Job Description:** "Act as a recruiter. Create a job description for a [Job Title] role, reporting to the [Manager Title]. Include sections for responsibilities and qualifications based on these points: [Paste 3-5 key points for each]."
2. **Interview Questions:** "Generate a list of 10 behavioral interview questions for a [Job Title] role, focusing on the core competencies of [Competency 1] and [Competency 2]."
3. **Screening Scorecard:** "Based on the attached job description, create a screening scorecard with 5 key criteria and descriptions for what 'Meets' vs. 'Exceeds' expectations looks like."
4. **Rejection Email:** "Write a polite and professional rejection email template to send to candidates who were interviewed but not selected for the [Job Title] position."

Performance Management
5. Feedback Organizer: "Organize my raw performance notes on an employee into three categories: 'Strengths,' 'Development Areas,' and 'Specific Examples.' [Paste Notes]"
6. Performance Review Script: "Create a talking points outline for a performance review, including a positive opening, a section for strengths, a section for growth opportunities, and a collaborative goal-setting section."
7. 360-Degree Feedback Questions: "Create a set of 5 anonymous 360-degree feedback questions for peers to rate a team member's collaboration and communication skills."
Onboarding and Training

8. 30-60-90 Day Plan: "Create a 30-60-90 day plan for a new [Job Title], outlining learning goals, performance objectives, and key relationships to build."
9. Onboarding Checklist: "Generate a comprehensive onboarding checklist for a new employee's first week, broken down by day."
10. Welcome Email: "Write a warm and welcoming email to a new hire, to be sent the week before their start date. Include information about their first-day schedule and what to expect."
11. Training Outline: "Create a detailed outline for a 60-minute training session on [Topic] for [Audience]. Include learning objectives, key topics, and an idea for a practical exercise."

Team Management and Communication

12. Meeting Agenda: "Create an agenda for our weekly 45-minute team sync meeting. Include sections for project updates, roadblocks, and action items."
13. Project Kick-off Email: "Draft a project kick-off email to the team for '[Project Name].' The email should outline the project's goals, key milestones, and team roles."
14. Team Announcement: "Write a clear and positive announcement to the team about [A new process or change]."
15. Survey Questions: "Generate 5 anonymous survey questions to gauge team morale and identify areas for improvement in our team's workflow."

Difficult Conversations and Development

16. Conflict Prep: "Act as a management coach. Help me prepare to mediate a disagreement between two employees about [Topic]. Brainstorm three open-ended questions I can ask to facilitate a constructive conversation."
17. Career Development Conversation Starter: "Create a list of 5 questions I can ask an employee to start a conversation about their long-term career goals and aspirations."

Policy and Documentation

18. Policy Draft: "Act as an HR policy writer. Draft a first draft of a [e.g., 'Social Media Use'] policy for our company. [LEGAL REVIEW REQUIRED]"
19. Process Documentation: "Write a simple, step-by-step Standard Operating Procedure (SOP) for our team's process of [A recurring task, e.g., 'submitting weekly status reports']."
20. Exit Interview Questions: "Create a list of 7 confidential exit interview questions to gather constructive feedback from a departing employee."

Part IV: Workflow Integration – Building AI into Your Daily Routine

Chapter 14: Designing Your Personal AI Workflow

Welcome to Part IV. In the preceding sections of this book, we have systematically built your AI prompting capabilities from the ground up. In Part I, we established the foundational understanding of what AI is and how it works. In Part II, we mastered the core skills and advanced strategies for crafting powerful prompts. In Part III, we put those skills to the test with an exhaustive tour of career-specific applications, providing you with a library of templates for almost any professional scenario.

You now have the tools. You have the techniques. You understand the "what" and the "how." Now, we begin the most transformative part of our journey: integrating these skills into the very fabric of your daily professional life. This is where we move from using AI as an occasional, ad-hoc tool to building a systematic, repeatable AI-powered workflow. The goal is no longer just to complete a single task more efficiently, but to fundamentally redesign how you approach your entire workday.

Think of it this way: so far, you have been learning how to use individual power tools. You know how to operate the drill (text generation), the sander (summarization), and the saw (data organization). In this chapter, you will learn how to design the layout of your entire workshop. We will build a system where the right tool is always within reach, where your processes are streamlined, and where the friction between having an idea and producing a result is reduced to a minimum.

This chapter is about moving from conscious effort to

unconscious habit. We will begin by conducting a personal audit of your daily work, identifying the repetitive, low-creativity tasks that are prime candidates for AI automation. You will learn how to create a "Task Automation Inventory," a personalized roadmap of your biggest time-saving opportunities. From there, we will design a set of simple but powerful AI-driven routines for your morning, midday, and evening, creating a rhythm that embeds productivity into your schedule.

We will also address the practicalities of integrating AI into the software you already use and discuss the crucial strategic balance between using AI for speed versus using it for quality. Finally, and perhaps most importantly, we will explore how to measure the impact of these new workflows, so you can see, in concrete terms, how much time you are saving and how much more you are accomplishing.

By the end of this chapter, you will have a clear, actionable plan for creating your own personal AI workflow. You will no longer be simply a user of AI, but an architect of your own productivity system.

Identifying Repetitive Tasks Suitable for Automation

The first step in designing your AI workflow is to identify the raw materials. You cannot automate a process until you are consciously aware of it. Many of our most time-consuming daily tasks are so ingrained in our routines that we barely notice them. Our goal in this section is to bring them into the light.

Not all tasks are good candidates for AI assistance. A creative brainstorming session with your team, a sensitive mentoring conversation with a direct report, or a high-stakes strategic decision are all activities that rely on uniquely human skills like empathy, intuition, and nuanced judgment. We are not looking to automate these. Instead, we are hunting for the tasks that are repetitive, structured, and consume your time without leveraging your core talents.

The Automation Suitability Checklist

As you look at your to-do list, ask yourself if a task meets the following criteria. The more "yes" answers you have, the better a candidate it is for AI-powered automation.

- **Is it frequent?** Do you perform this task daily or weekly? Automating a task you do once a year provides minimal return on investment. Automating a task you do every day, like drafting status update emails, can save you hours every month.
- **Is it rule-based?** Does the task follow a predictable pattern or a set of rules? Creating a weekly report that always has the same sections is rule-based. Coming up with a completely novel marketing campaign slogan is not.
- **Does it involve a standard format?** Does the output usually take the form of an email, a list, a table, a summary, or another structured format? AI excels at filling in these templates.
- **Is it a "first draft" task?** Does the task involve creating a starting point that you then review and refine? AI is the world's greatest first-draft generator. Writing the initial outline for a presentation, the first version of a project plan, or the initial draft of a policy document are all perfect examples.
- **Is it a summarization or organization task?** Does the task involve taking a large amount of information (like meeting notes or a long article) and distilling it into a more organized

or concise form? This is a core strength of AI.
- **Is it a low-creativity task?** Does it feel more like administrative work than creative problem-solving? Tasks like reformatting data, drafting routine correspondence, or creating meeting agendas fall squarely into this category.

A Quick Self-Audit Exercise

For the next two workdays, keep a simple log. On a piece of paper or in a digital note, jot down every distinct task you work on for more than five minutes. Do not overthink it. At the end of the two days, you will have a raw list of your actual, day-to-day activities.

Now, go through that list with the Automation Suitability Checklist in mind. Put a star next to every task that gets three or more "yes" answers. You might be surprised at what you find. That "quick" 15-minute report you write every afternoon, the 10 minutes you spend organizing notes after every client call, the 20 minutes you spend drafting a project update email every Friday, these all add up. These starred items are the building blocks of your new AI workflow.

Creating a Task Automation Inventory

Once you have identified your high-potential automation tasks, the next step is to organize them into a structured inventory. This document will become your personal AI playbook, a reference guide that turns abstract ideas about productivity into concrete, actionable prompts.

Creating this inventory is a one-time investment that will pay dividends for years to come. It serves three primary purposes:

1. **It provides clarity.** It forces you to articulate exactly what the task is and why it's a good candidate for AI.
2. **It serves as a prompt library.** It's where you will store the "master prompts" for your recurring tasks, saving you from having to rethink them every time.
3. **It helps you track progress.** It gives you a baseline, allowing you to measure the time you save as you implement your new workflows.

The Structure of Your Inventory

You can create this inventory in a simple spreadsheet or a document. For each task you identified in your self-audit, create an entry with the following five components:

- **Task Name:** A brief, clear description of the task (e.g., "Draft Weekly Project Status Email").
- **Frequency:** How often you do it (e.g., "Weekly," "Daily," "3-5 times per week").
- **Time Spent (Before AI):** Your best estimate of how long the task currently takes you each time (e.g., "25 minutes").
- **Automation Potential:** Your assessment of its suitability (High, Medium, or Low).
- **Master AI Prompt:** This is the heart of the inventory. Here, you will write a detailed, reusable prompt for the task, complete with placeholders for the information that changes each time.

A Professional Scenario: "Alex the Project Manager's" Inventory

Let's look at a sample inventory for a fictional project manager named Alex.

Task Name: Draft Weekly Project Status Email

- **Frequency:** Weekly (every Friday)
- **Time Spent (Before AI):** 30 minutes
- **Automation Potential:** High
- Master AI Prompt:
  "Act as a senior project manager. Draft a weekly status update email for 'Project Titan' to be sent to our key stakeholders. The tone should be professional, concise, and confident. The email must have three sections with these exact headings:
  1. **## Key Accomplishments This Week**: [I will provide a bulleted list of completed tasks here]
  2. **## Priorities for Next Week**: [I will provide a bulleted list of upcoming tasks here]
  3. ## Potential Risks or Blockers: [I will provide any risks or blockers here. If there are none, state that the project is on track.]
     Please synthesize the provided points into clear, professional prose under the appropriate headings."

Task Name: Organize Client Meeting Notes

- **Frequency:** 3-4 times per week
- **Time Spent (Before AI):** 15 minutes
- **Automation Potential:** High
- Master AI Prompt:
  "Act as a diligent executive assistant. I have just finished a client meeting and my notes are unstructured. Please organize them into a clean summary. The output must have two sections with these exact headings:
  1. **## Key Decisions Made**: (A bulleted list of any final decisions)

2. ## Action Items: (A table with three columns: 'Task,' 'Owner,' and 'Due Date')
   ###RAW NOTES###
   [I will paste my raw meeting notes here]"

Task Name: Brainstorm Agenda for Team Sync

- **Frequency:** Weekly
- **Time Spent (Before AI):** 10 minutes
- **Automation Potential:** Medium
- Master AI Prompt:
  "Act as a team facilitator. Create a draft agenda for our 45-minute weekly team sync meeting. The agenda should include time slots for the following standard topics: 'Quick Wins & Kudos,' 'Project Updates,' and 'Roadblocks Discussion.' Based on the following key priority for this week, suggest one additional 15-minute 'Deep Dive' topic.
  This Week's Priority: [I will insert the main priority here, e.g., 'Finalizing the Q4 budget proposal.']"

Your Turn: Build Your Inventory
Take the starred items from your self-audit exercise and create your own Task Automation Inventory. Don't worry about perfecting the prompts right away. Just get the structure in place. This document will be a living guide that you will refine and add to over time.

Building Morning, Midday, and Evening AI Routines

With your inventory in hand, you can now start to build habits. The most effective way to ensure you are consistently leveraging AI is to build it into your daily schedule. By creating simple routines for the beginning, middle, and end of your day, you create specific, recurring moments to deploy your new AI-powered workflows.

Think of these routines as the scaffolding that supports your productivity. They are not meant to be rigid or restrictive, but rather to provide a default structure that reduces cognitive load and makes efficiency your new normal.

The Morning Routine: Your Daily Launchpad (5-10 Minutes)

The goal of the morning routine is to move from a reactive state (drowning in overnight emails) to a proactive one. These prompts are designed to give you clarity and prepare you for the day ahead.

- Prompt 1: The Daily Briefing.
  "Act as my executive assistant. Review my calendar for today, [Paste calendar appointments]. For each meeting, provide a one-sentence summary of its purpose. Then, based on my master to-do list [Paste to-do list], identify and list the Top 3 Most Important Tasks I need to accomplish today to make the day a success."
- Prompt 2: The Inbox Triage.
  Identify the 2-3 types of emails you get most often (e.g., routine questions from colleagues, meeting requests, status inquiries). Use your master prompts to draft responses to these in a single batch, clearing out the clutter so you can focus on the truly important messages.
- Prompt 3: The Knowledge Digest.
  If your role requires you to stay on top of industry news, create a prompt to accelerate that process. "Scan the headlines from these five articles: [Paste links or article titles]. Write a three-bullet-point summary of the most important trends or news that I should be aware of today."

The Midday Routine: The Productivity Accelerator (Used as

Needed)

The midday routine is not a single block of time, but a series of go-to workflows you can deploy to tackle your core work. This is where you will pull heavily from your Task Automation Inventory.

- **The "Blank Page" Buster:** Before starting any writing task (a report, a presentation, a proposal), use your master prompt to generate the first-draft outline.
- **The "Data Wrangler":** Before trying to make sense of raw data or notes, use your master prompt to organize it into a structured table or list.
- **The "Meeting Maximizer":** Immediately after a meeting, use your master prompt to process the transcript or your notes into a clean summary with action items, while the context is still fresh in your mind.

The Evening Routine: Your Daily Wrap-Up (5-10 Minutes)

The goal of the evening routine is to achieve closure on the current day and set yourself up for a smooth start the next day. This helps you mentally disconnect from work, knowing that everything is organized and prepared.

- Prompt 1: The "End of Day" Report.
  "Act as my productivity partner. Based on my list of completed tasks for today, [Paste list of what you did], and my calendar for tomorrow, [Paste tomorrow's calendar], draft a brief 'End of Day' summary. It should include a bulleted list of today's key accomplishments and a prioritized list of the top 3 tasks for tomorrow morning."
- Prompt 2: The "Clean Slate" Communication.
  Are there any final status updates or confirmation emails you need to send before logging off? Use your master prompts to

draft them quickly, ensuring your stakeholders are informed and you can start the next day with a clean communication slate.

Integrating AI into Existing Tools and Platforms

To make your AI workflow truly seamless, you should strive to reduce the friction of using it. The goal is to make calling on your AI assistant as natural as opening a new browser tab. While later chapters will touch on more advanced technical integrations, you can achieve a great deal with simple workflow design.

The "Prompt Hub" Method

Your Task Automation Inventory is more than just a planning document; it's a practical tool. Keep it open in a pinned browser tab, a digital note-taking app (like Notion, Evernote, or OneNote), or a simple text file on your desktop. When you encounter a recurring task, instead of typing a prompt from scratch, you simply:

1. **Copy** the master prompt from your "Prompt Hub."
2. **Paste** it into the AI interface.
3. **Fill in** the placeholders with the specific details for that day's task.

This "copy-paste-fill" workflow saves mental energy and ensures you are using a well-crafted, effective prompt every single time.

Meeting the AI Where You Work

The AI ecosystem is evolving rapidly. Many of the software tools you already use are beginning to integrate AI capabilities directly into their platforms.

- **In Your Documents:** Tools like Google Docs and Microsoft Word now have integrated AI features. This means you can highlight a paragraph and prompt the AI to "make this more concise" or "rewrite this in a more formal tone" without ever leaving your document.
- **In Your Email:** Some email clients are integrating AI to help you draft responses, summarize long threads, and check your tone before you send.
- **In Your Browser:** AI-powered browser extensions can allow you to summarize web pages, draft social media posts, or get explanations of complex topics without switching contexts.

The key is to be an active observer. As you use your primary work tools, look for these emerging AI features. Adopting them can create an even more integrated workflow, further reducing the time it takes to move from task to completion.

Time-Saving Versus Quality: Finding the Right Balance

As you become more proficient with AI, you will realize that every prompt involves a strategic trade-off between speed and quality. Not every task requires a perfectly polished, ready-to-publish output. Learning to recognize this distinction is a critical productivity skill.

A Framework for Choosing Your Approach

Think of your tasks as falling into two broad categories:

1. High-Stakes Tasks (Optimize for Quality)
These are tasks where the output will be seen by important stakeholders (clients, executives, the public) and where the

quality of the work directly reflects on you and your organization.

- **Examples:** Client proposals, investor updates, final reports, articles for publication, performance reviews.
- **Your AI Workflow:**
    - **Use Detailed Prompts:** Invest the extra time to write a comprehensive prompt using all the CTFC elements and a strong persona.
    - **Use an Iterative Process:** Treat the first AI output as a strong first draft. Plan to spend time in a follow-up conversation with the AI, refining and improving the content.
    - **Perform a Thorough Human Review:** This is non-negotiable. You are the final quality check. Edit for nuance, voice, and strategic alignment.

2. Low-Stakes Tasks (Optimize for Speed)
These are tasks where the output is primarily for internal use, for organizing your own thoughts, or for routine communication where "good enough" is genuinely good enough.

- **Examples:** Organizing your personal notes, drafting a quick team reminder, creating a first-pass agenda for an internal meeting, summarizing an article for your own understanding.
- **Your AI Workflow:**
    - **Use Simple Prompts:** Focus on a clear Task and Format. Don't spend too much time on detailed context or constraints.
    - **Accept the 80% Solution:** If the AI output is clear, accurate, and serves its purpose, resist the urge to wordsmith it to perfection. Copy it, use it, and move on.
    - **Trust but Briefly Verify:** Give it a quick scan for obvious errors, but don't spend significant time editing. The goal is speed.

By consciously deciding which category a task falls into *before* you write the prompt, you can allocate your own time and energy much more effectively.

Measuring Productivity Gains

The ultimate test of your new workflow is whether it is actually making a difference. Tracking your progress provides powerful motivation and helps you identify which parts of your workflow are delivering the biggest returns.

Quantitative Measurement: The Time Audit
Go back to your Task Automation Inventory. Add a new column called "Time Spent (After AI)." For the next two weeks, as you complete your automated tasks, make a realistic estimate of the new time it takes.

Task	**Time (Before)**	**Time (After)**	**Time Saved (Weekly)**
Draft Status Email	30 mins	5 mins	25 mins
Organize Meeting Notes	15 mins (x4)	2 mins (x4)	52 mins
Draft Meeting Agenda	10 mins	2 mins	8 mins

Total			**1 hour 25 mins**

Seeing this data in black and white is incredibly powerful. The 30-45 minutes you invested in creating your inventory and master prompts are now paying you back with over an hour of saved time *every single week*.

Qualitative Measurement: The Focus Audit

Productivity is not just about time saved; it's about the quality of the time you have. At the end of each week, ask yourself two simple questions:

1. **What low-value, administrative work did I successfully delegate to my AI this week?**
2. **What high-value, strategic work did I have more time and mental energy for as a result?**

Perhaps you spent less time bogged down in your inbox and more time mentoring a team member. Maybe you spent less time formatting reports and more time analyzing their strategic implications. This qualitative assessment is often just as important as the quantitative one. It measures not just efficiency, but effectiveness.

Key Takeaways from This Chapter

- A personal AI workflow moves you from ad-hoc AI use to a systematic, habit-driven approach.
- Begin by identifying frequent, rule-based, and repetitive tasks, and organize them into a **Task Automation Inventory**.
- This inventory serves as your personal playbook and a library for your "master prompts."

- Build simple **AI routines** for your morning, midday, and evening to embed these workflows into your daily schedule.
- Find the right balance between **speed and quality**, optimizing for quality on high-stakes tasks and for speed on low-stakes ones.
- **Measure your progress**, both quantitatively (time saved) and qualitatively (focus on high-value work), to stay motivated and refine your system.

You now have a complete framework for designing a personal productivity system that works for you. This is not a rigid, one-size-fits-all solution, but a flexible set of principles that you can adapt to your unique role and work style. In the next chapter, we will build on this by exploring how to scale these benefits through batching, automation, and the creation of reusable systems.

Chapter 15: Batching and Automating with AI

In the last chapter, we designed the blueprint for your personal AI workflow. You learned how to identify tasks ripe for automation, create a structured inventory of your most common processes, and build simple routines to weave AI into the fabric of your workday. You have the layout for your new, highly efficient workshop. Now, it is time to build the assembly line.

This chapter is about scaling your productivity. We are moving beyond one-off efficiency gains and into the realm of systematic automation. The goal is to take the principles we have learned and apply them at a larger scale, creating systems that save you not just minutes, but hours. If the previous chapter was about building your first AI-powered car, this chapter is about building the factory that can produce a dozen cars a day with less effort and higher consistency.

The core concept we will explore is "batching," a classic productivity technique supercharged by AI. We will learn how to group similar tasks and execute them in a single, focused session, obliterating the mental friction of context switching. You will learn how to transform the "master prompts" from your inventory into true, reusable systems that combine a powerful prompt with a simple, repeatable process.

From there, we will apply these systems to your most common recurring tasks, looking at the weekly and monthly cadences that define our professional lives. We will also introduce a powerful advanced technique: building prompt sequences. This is where you will learn to break down large, complex projects into a series of interconnected prompts, with the output of one step becoming the input for the next. It is a method for tackling your most intimidating projects with clarity and confidence.

Finally, we will apply these automation and batching strategies to two of the biggest productivity drains in any professional's life: calendar management and the never-ending battle for a clear email inbox.

By the end of this chapter, you will have a new set of mental models for approaching your work. You will see opportunities not just to do tasks faster, but to build intelligent systems that handle entire categories of your work, freeing you to focus on the strategic, creative, and high-impact activities that truly drive your career forward.

Batch Processing Similar Tasks Efficiently

One of the biggest hidden costs to our productivity is a phenomenon known as "context switching." Every time you shift your focus from one type of task to another, say, from writing a report to answering an email to planning a meeting, your brain has to disengage from the previous context and load up a new one. This switching process is not instantaneous. It costs mental energy and time. Even a brief switch can take several minutes to fully recover from. When your day is a constant stream of different tasks, you are paying this mental tax over and over again.

Batch processing is the antidote. The concept is simple: group similar tasks together and do them all in one dedicated session. Instead of writing one email now, another in an hour, and three more in the afternoon, you handle all five in a single 20-minute block. This allows your brain to stay in one "zone," which is far more efficient.

AI amplifies the power of batching exponentially. The AI can execute the core work of each task so quickly that the time it takes to complete a batch of five items is often not much longer than the time it would have taken to do one manually.

A Professional Scenario: The Social Media Manager's Weekly Batch

Imagine you are a social media manager for a small company. You need to create five posts for LinkedIn for the upcoming week.

The Old Workflow (High Context Switching):

- **Monday:** Spend 20 minutes thinking about and writing Monday's post.
- **Tuesday:** Spend another 20 minutes on Tuesday's post.
- **Wednesday:** Get busy, forget to post.
- **Thursday:** Scramble to create a post in 15 minutes.
- **Total Time:** An hour or more, spread throughout the week, with inconsistent quality.

The New AI-Powered Batching Workflow (Low Context Switching):
On Monday morning, you dedicate one 30-minute block to creating all the content for the week.

- **Step 1: Gather Your Inputs (5 minutes).** You decide on the topics for the week: a post about a new product feature, a link to a recent company blog post, a post sharing a relevant industry statistic, a "behind-the-scenes" post about a company process, and a post asking a question to engage the audience.

- **Step 2: Use a "Batch Prompt" (2 minutes).** You use a single, comprehensive prompt to generate all five drafts at once.
- **Step 3: Review and Schedule (15 minutes).** You review the five AI-generated drafts, make minor edits to ensure they match your brand's voice, and load them into your scheduling tool.

The "Batch Prompt" for Social Media Posts:

"Act as a senior social media manager specializing in B2B content for LinkedIn. Our company sells project management software to mid-sized businesses. Our brand voice is helpful, professional, and slightly informal.

Task: Generate five distinct LinkedIn posts for this week based on the following topics. For each post, create a compelling hook, a short body text (under 150 words), and suggest 3-5 relevant hashtags.

- **Post 1 (Product Feature):** Announce our new 'Automated Reporting' feature, which saves project managers time.
- **Post 2 (Blog Post):** Promote our new blog post titled '5 Ways to Prevent Project Scope Creep.'
- **Post 3 (Industry Statistic):** Share the statistic that 'effective project management can reduce project costs by up to 30%.'
- **Post 4 (Process Insight):** A 'behind-the-scenes' look at how our product team uses agile sprints to develop new features.
- **Post 5 (Engagement Question):** Ask a question like, 'What's the single biggest challenge you face in your weekly project planning?'"

The Result: In one focused 30-minute session, you have

accomplished what used to take over an hour of scattered effort. The quality is more consistent, and your mental energy for the rest of the week is preserved for other tasks.

Creating Reusable Prompt Templates and Systems

In the last chapter, you created a Task Automation Inventory filled with "master prompts." Now, we will elevate those prompts into full-fledged systems.

A prompt is an instruction. A system is a prompt combined with a process. It is a simple, repeatable workflow that takes a recurring task from start to finish. Building these systems is the key to making your AI-powered productivity gains permanent and effortless.

How to Build a Prompt System: A 4-Step Guide

Let's use the common task of "summarizing a long article" as our example.

- **Step 1: Identify the Core Task.** The task is to take a long article and create a concise summary for sharing with your team.
- **Step 2: Create the "Master Prompt."** This is the heart of the system. You want a prompt that is detailed enough to be consistent but has clear placeholders for the information that changes each time.
    - Master Prompt: "Act as a research assistant. I am going to provide you with the text of an article. Your task is to write a summary for my internal team. The summary should be in the form of five key bullet points. Each bullet point should be a complete sentence. After the bullet points, add a concluding sentence that explains the

single most important takeaway for our company, which is in the [Our Industry] industry.
###ARTICLE TEXT###
[PASTE ARTICLE TEXT HERE]"

- **Step 3: Define the Process.** A system includes the simple steps you take before and after running the prompt.
  1. Copy the full text of the article I need to summarize.
  2. Open my "Prompt Hub" document.
  3. Copy the "Article Summary System" master prompt.
  4. Paste the prompt into the AI chat interface.
  5. Paste the article text into the [PASTE ARTICLE TEXT HERE] placeholder.
  6. Review the AI-generated summary for accuracy.
  7. Copy the summary and paste it into the team's communication channel.
- **Step 4: Store and Name the System.** Give your system a clear, action-oriented name and save it in your Prompt Hub (your central document or note for all your master prompts). A good name would be "System: Create Team Summary from Article."

By turning a prompt into a system, you eliminate the need to think. You simply follow your own pre-defined, high-efficiency process.

Using AI for Recurring Weekly and Monthly Tasks

Our professional lives run on a rhythm of recurring tasks. These are often the most tedious parts of our jobs, but because they are predictable, they are also the most perfect candidates for systematic AI automation.

Automating Weekly Recurring Tasks

Think about your work week. What are the tasks you have to do every single Monday or Friday?

- **Preparing for a weekly team meeting.**
- **Writing a weekly project status report.**
- **Summarizing your team's key metrics for leadership.**

Let's build a robust system for that last one.

Professional Scenario: The Weekly Metrics Summary System

- **The Goal:** Every Friday, you need to send a brief email to your director summarizing your team's performance against its three key performance indicators (KPIs) for the week.
- **The System:**
  1. **Process Step 1:** Gather the three key data points for the week: KPI 1 value, KPI 2 value, and KPI 3 value.
  2. **Process Step 2:** Copy the "Master Prompt" from your Prompt Hub.
  3. Master Prompt:
     "Act as a business analyst reporting to a senior director. My team's three weekly KPIs are 'New Leads,' 'Conversion Rate,' and 'Customer Satisfaction Score.' Our weekly targets are 100 new leads, a 5% conversion rate, and a 95% satisfaction score.
     Task: Write a short, professional summary email about this week's performance. The email should have a clear subject line. The body should first state the numbers for each of the three KPIs, noting whether we were above or below target for each. Then, add one paragraph of analysis, highlighting our biggest success and one area to focus on next week.
     This Week's Data:
     - New Leads: [Enter this week's number]

        - Conversion Rate: [Enter this week's percentage]
        - Customer Satisfaction Score: [Enter this week's percentage]
        This Week's Context:
        - Our biggest success was [Briefly describe one success, e.g., 'a strong performance from the new ad campaign'].
        - Our focus for next week will be [Briefly describe one focus area, e.g., 'improving the follow-up process for new leads']."
    4. **Process Step 3:** Paste the prompt into your AI tool, fill in the bracketed information, and run it.
    5. **Process Step 4:** Review the draft and send it.
- **Benefit:** What might have been a 25-minute task of data gathering, analysis, and careful writing is now a 5-minute task of data entry and review.

Automating Monthly Recurring Tasks

The same principle applies to less frequent, but often larger, monthly tasks.

- **Generating a monthly client report.**
- **Drafting an internal company newsletter.**
- **Outlining a monthly business review presentation.**

By creating a system for these, you ensure consistency and save significant time on tasks that can often take half a day or more.

Building Prompt Sequences for Complex Workflows

So far, we have focused on using a single prompt to complete a single, well-defined task. But what about your biggest, most complex projects? The kind of work that takes days or weeks, like developing a new marketing strategy, creating a comprehensive business proposal, or planning a major project.

For these, we use a technique called "prompt sequencing" or "prompt chaining." This is the process of breaking a large project down into a series of smaller, logical steps, and using a dedicated AI prompt for each step. Critically, the output from one prompt often becomes the context or input for the next prompt in the sequence.

This is arguably the most powerful technique in this entire book for tackling high-level strategic work.

A Professional Scenario: Developing a New Product Launch Plan

Let's say your complex project is to "create the marketing launch plan for a new product." A single prompt for this would be too vague. Instead, you build a sequence.

- **Product Context:** The new product is "FlowState," a premium, minimalist coffee maker designed for home office workers who value both quality and aesthetics.

The Prompt Sequence:

- Step 1: The Audience Analysis Prompt
  "Act as a market research analyst. Our new product is 'FlowState,' a premium coffee maker for design-conscious home office workers.
  Task: Identify the top 3 target audience segments for this product. For each segment, describe their likely psychographics (values, interests), their pain points related to their current coffee routine, and the social media platforms

they are most likely to use."

  - *Output of this prompt will be a detailed description of your target customers.*

- Step 2: The Core Messaging Prompt
  "Act as a brand strategist. I am developing the messaging for a new coffee maker called 'FlowState.' Based on the target audience analysis below, please craft a core messaging framework.
  Task: The framework should include:
  1. A primary tagline (under 7 words).
  2. Three key benefit statements (e.g., 'Perfect Coffee, Effortlessly').
  3. A short, one-paragraph brand story.
     ###AUDIENCE ANALYSIS###
     [Paste the full output from Step 1 here]"
  - *Output of this prompt will be your core marketing language.*

- Step 3: The Content Strategy Prompt
  "Act as a content marketing manager. We are launching 'FlowState,' a new coffee maker. We have our target audience and core messaging defined below.
  Task: Brainstorm 5 specific content ideas (e.g., blog posts, videos, social media campaigns) that we could create to promote the launch. For each idea, briefly explain how it connects with our audience and messaging.
  ###AUDIENCE & MESSAGING###
  [Paste the key outputs from Steps 1 and 2 here]"
  - *Output of this prompt will be a list of actionable marketing tactics.*

- Step 4: The Final Plan Assembly Prompt
  "Act as a marketing director. I have conducted research and brainstorming for the launch of our new product, 'FlowState.'

Task: Please assemble all the information below into a concise, one-page launch plan document. The document should have clear headings for 'Target Audience,' 'Core Messaging,' and 'Key Marketing Initiatives.'
###ALL NOTES###
[Paste the synthesized outputs from all the previous steps here]"

By chaining these prompts together, you have used the AI as a strategic partner at every stage of the process. You have turned an overwhelming project into a series of clear, manageable steps, and the final output is far more detailed and well-reasoned than what any single prompt could have produced.

Calendar and Schedule Optimization

While AI tools cannot directly access your live calendar for privacy reasons, you can provide them with the data to act as a powerful scheduling assistant. This is about using AI to help you plan your time more intentionally.

The "Ideal Week" Template Prompt

- The Prompt: "Act as a world-class productivity coach. I want to design my ideal weekly template. My role is a [Your Role]. My top three most important responsibilities are [Responsibility 1, 2, 3]. I want to block out time for 'deep work' on these priorities. I also have recurring weekly meetings on [List recurring meetings and times].
  Task: Create a sample weekly calendar template (Monday to Friday, 9 am to 5 pm) that allocates specific blocks of time for my key responsibilities, meetings, and includes protected 'deep work' sessions. Also include blocks for administrative tasks like email."

The "Cluttered Day" Triage Prompt

- The Prompt: "Act as an executive assistant. Tomorrow is going to be a very busy day. Here are my meetings and my to-do list.
  Meetings: [Paste list of meetings and times]
  To-Do List: [Paste list of tasks]
  Task: Suggest a realistic schedule for tomorrow that slots my to-do list items into the available time between meetings. Group the smaller, 15-minute tasks together into an 'Admin Block.' Identify any tasks that are unlikely to get done and suggest moving them to the next day."

Email Management and Inbox Zero Strategies

For many professionals, the email inbox is the single greatest source of stress and lost productivity. AI, combined with the batching principle, can help you finally achieve and maintain "inbox zero," or more accurately, a state of "inbox control."

The AI-Powered Email Processing Workflow

Instead of checking email constantly, schedule 2-3 dedicated "email batch" sessions per day (e.g., at 9 am, 1 pm, and 4 pm). During these sessions, your goal is to process every new email by applying one of these four actions, often with AI assistance:

1. **Delete/Archive (1 second):** If no action is needed, get it out of your inbox immediately.
2. **Reply (1-2 minutes with AI):** If an email requires a response and you can provide it quickly, use an AI master prompt.
   - **Scenario:** A colleague asks for a status update you have already prepared.

    - **Prompt:** "Draft a quick, friendly email to my colleague, Sarah, letting her know that the project is on track and that the full status report will be sent out on Friday as planned."
3. **Delegate (1-2 minutes with AI):** If the request is better handled by someone else on your team.
    - **Prompt:** "Draft a short email to my team member, David. Forward the email below to him and ask him to please handle this customer inquiry. Let him know he should follow up with me if he has any questions."
4. **Defer (30 seconds):** If an email is tied to a significant task that will take more than 2 minutes, don't leave it in your inbox. Convert it into a task on your to-do list or an event on your calendar, and then archive the email.

By systematically applying this workflow during your email batches, you prevent your inbox from becoming a secondary, disorganized to-do list.

The "Summarize This Thread" Prompt

You open your inbox to find a 25-email-long chain. Before you spend 20 minutes reading it, copy the entire thread and use this prompt: "Read the entire email thread below. Summarize the key issue being discussed, what the final resolution was (if any), and if there is a specific action item required from me."

Key Takeaways from This Chapter

- **Batching** similar tasks (like writing emails or social media posts) is a powerful way to reduce mental friction and increase efficiency.
- Elevate your master prompts into **reusable systems** by combining them with a simple, repeatable process.
- Apply these systems to your recurring **weekly and monthly**

tasks to automate the most predictable parts of your job.

- Use **prompt sequencing**—breaking large projects into a series of interconnected prompts—to tackle your most complex and strategic work.
- Leverage AI as a planning assistant to optimize your **calendar and schedule** for more intentional, high-impact work.
- Combine the batching principle with AI-powered drafting and summarization to achieve a state of **inbox control**.

You have now moved beyond single prompts and are thinking in terms of systems and workflows. You have the tools to automate not just tasks, but entire processes. In the next chapter, we will explore how to take these individual productivity gains and scale them to your entire team.

Chapter 16: Collaborative Prompting for Teams

Over the past two chapters, we have been intensely focused on building your personal AI-powered productivity system. You have learned how to identify high-value automation opportunities in your own work, create a personal library of master prompts, and build routines and systems that make efficiency a daily habit. You have designed your workshop and built your assembly line. The result is a significant increase in your individual output, quality, and focus.

But what happens when you multiply that power by five, ten, or a hundred?

Welcome to the next level of AI-driven productivity: collaborative prompting. This chapter is about taking the principles of personal efficiency and scaling them across your team and your entire organization. The goal is to move from being a solo practitioner of AI to becoming a leader and a catalyst, creating a shared ecosystem that elevates the performance of everyone you work with.

Think of it as the difference between a single craftsperson building a fine piece of furniture and an entire workshop of artisans all working from the same set of master blueprints. While the individual's work is valuable, the collective output of the workshop is far greater, more consistent, and more impactful. When a team adopts a shared approach to AI, the productivity gains are not additive, they are exponential.

In this chapter, we will lay out the complete playbook for transforming your team into an AI-powered productivity engine. We will start with the foundational step: creating and sharing a team-wide prompt library, your organization's single source of truth for high-quality AI instructions. From there, we will discuss the critical importance of establishing clear standards and best practices to ensure that everyone is speaking the same language.

We will then provide a practical guide for training your colleagues, turning you into an effective AI champion who can empower others with these new skills. We will explore powerful workflows for using AI in collaborative document creation, enabling your team to produce high-quality work faster than ever before. Finally, we will address the essential topics of quality control and the practical realities of managing AI-generated content in a shared professional environment.

This chapter is for the leaders, the team players, and the forward-thinkers who see that the future of work is not just about individual skill, but about collective capability. By learning how to prompt together, your team can build a formidable competitive advantage.

Sharing Prompt Libraries Across Organizations

The "master prompts" you developed in your personal Task Automation Inventory are valuable assets. When you are the only one who has them, they save you time. When your entire team has them, they create a shared standard of excellence and efficiency. The first step in scaling AI productivity is to move your prompts from a private document to a shared, accessible resource. We will call this the "Team Prompt Hub."

The Power of a Shared Prompt Hub

- **Consistency:** When everyone uses the same master prompt to write a client follow-up email, the company's voice remains consistent, regardless of who is sending the message.
- **Efficiency:** A new team member doesn't need to spend weeks learning how to write a perfect project report. They can use the team's master prompt on day one and produce a high-quality draft instantly.
- **Knowledge Sharing:** When a marketing specialist develops a brilliant prompt for analyzing competitor ad copy, sharing it in the hub immediately gives that capability to the entire marketing team.
- **Continuous Improvement:** A shared library becomes a living resource. Team members can suggest improvements to existing prompts, creating a virtuous cycle of refinement.

Choosing the Right Platform for Your Team Prompt Hub

The best tool for your hub is one your team already uses every day. The goal is to minimize friction. Here are a few excellent options:

- **Company Wiki (e.g., Confluence, SharePoint):** A great choice for creating a structured, searchable knowledge base. You can create a dedicated space for "AI Prompts" and build out a library with nested pages for each department or task type.
- **Shared Documents (e.g., Google Docs, Microsoft Word Online):** The simplest option to get started. A single, well-organized document with a clear table of contents can serve as an effective prompt library for a smaller team.
- **Knowledge Management Tools (e.g., Notion, Slite, Coda):** These platforms are ideal. They combine the structure of a

wiki with the flexibility of a document and often have database features, allowing you to create a sophisticated, sortable, and taggable prompt library.

- **Team Communication Channels (e.g., Slack, Microsoft Teams):** You can create a dedicated channel (e.g., #ai-prompts) where team members can share their best prompts. You can then pin the most important "master prompts" for easy access. This is great for informal sharing but can be harder to keep organized.

How to Structure Your Team Prompt Hub

Regardless of the platform you choose, a well-structured hub is an effective hub. For each prompt you add to the library, include the following fields:

- **Prompt Name:** A clear, searchable name using a consistent naming convention (e.g., EMAIL-Client_Project_Kickoff).
- **Goal/Purpose:** A one-sentence description of what this prompt is designed to achieve.
- **The Master Prompt:** The full text of the prompt itself, with clear, standardized placeholders for the information that needs to be filled in (e.g., [Insert Client Name Here]).
- **Example of Use:** A brief description of a scenario where this prompt would be used.
- **Author/Maintainer:** The name of the team member who created or is responsible for keeping the prompt up to date.

You can organize the library by department (Marketing, Sales, HR) or by task type (Emails, Reports, Analysis). Start with the structure that feels most intuitive for your team.

Creating Team Prompt Standards and Best Practices

A library full of prompts is a good start, but without a shared set of rules, it can quickly become a chaotic mess of inconsistent and low-quality instructions. To build a truly effective system, your team needs a simple, clear set of standards for how prompts are written and used. This ensures that every prompt in your hub is built for maximum quality and efficiency.

Think of this as your team's "AI Style Guide." It does not need to be a long, complicated document. A single page of best practices is often enough to create alignment.

Key Components of Your Team's AI Style Guide:

1. **The "Team CTFC" Mandate:** The first and most important rule. Every prompt added to the Team Prompt Hub must be structured with the four essential elements:
    - **Context:** Who are we, and what is the background?
    - **Task:** What is the specific action to be performed?
    - **Format:** How should the output be structured?
    - **Constraints:** What are the rules to follow?
2. **Standardized Placeholders:** Agree on a single, consistent format for placeholders in your prompts. This makes them instantly recognizable and easy to use. The most common convention is square brackets. For example: [Insert Project Name Here].
3. **Defined Personas:** Create a short list of the standard "personas" your team should use when prompting the AI. This ensures that the AI's output is aligned with your team's function.
    - **Example for a Marketing Team:**
        - "Act as a 'Brand A' social media manager."
        - "Act as a technical SEO analyst."
        - "Act as a direct-response copywriter."

4. **Official Tone and Voice Guidelines:** Instead of having each team member define the tone in their own words, create a set of standard tone descriptors that are aligned with your company's brand.
    - **Example:** "Our company's primary brand voice is 'Helpful, Professional, and Confident.' Please use these words when defining the tone in your prompts for external communications."
5. **A Clear Naming Convention:** A simple naming system makes the prompt hub searchable and easy to navigate. A good formula is [CATEGORY]-[Task_Description].
    - EMAIL-Weekly_Status_Report
    - REPORT-Monthly_Client_Summary
    - ANALYSIS-Customer_Feedback_Themes

Workplace Script: A Team Lead Introducing the Style Guide
"Hi Team, To help us all get the most out of our new AI tools, I've put together a simple one-page 'AI Prompting Style Guide' and saved it in our shared drive. It just covers a few best practices, like using the CTFC framework and our new prompt naming convention. Taking two minutes to follow these guidelines when you save a new prompt to our Team Hub will make the library much easier for everyone to use. Let me know if you have any questions!"

Training Colleagues on Effective AI Use

You cannot simply build a prompt library and a style guide and expect everyone to use them effectively. To truly scale the benefits of AI, you need to invest in training your colleagues. Your goal is not just to show them *what* to do, but to help them understand *why* it works. By turning your teammates into confident and skilled prompters, you create a team of force multipliers.

You do not need to be a formal "trainer" to do this. A simple, informal "Lunch and Learn" session or a demonstration in a team meeting can be incredibly effective.

A Step-by-Step Guide to an Informal Team Training Session (45 Minutes)

- **Step 1: Start with the "Why" (5 minutes).** Begin by showing a powerful "before and after" example that is directly relevant to your team's work.
    - **Show a vague prompt:** "Write a social media post about our new product."
    - **Show the generic, unhelpful output.**
    - **Show a prompt from the new Team Hub:** "Using our SOCIAL-LinkedIn_Product_Launch template..."
    - **Show the high-quality, on-brand output.** This immediately demonstrates the value of what you are about to teach them.
- **Step 2: Introduce the Core Concepts (10 minutes).** Briefly explain the CTFC framework. Do not treat it like a dry academic lesson. Use a real example from your team's work to illustrate what Context, Task, Format, and Constraints look like in practice.
- **Step 3: Tour the Team Prompt Hub (10 minutes).** Show them where the new shared library lives. Walk them through the structure and demonstrate how to find and use a prompt for a common task. Explain the naming convention and the style guide.
- **Step 4: Live, Interactive Demo (15 minutes).** Ask for a volunteer who has a real task they need to do that day. Work with them in front of the team to find a relevant prompt in the hub, fill in the placeholders, and generate a first draft. This

makes the process feel real and achievable.

- **Step 5: Q&A and Call to Action (5 minutes).** Answer any questions and end with a clear, simple call to action: "This week, I encourage each of you to try using just one prompt from the Team Hub for one of your daily tasks and let us know how it goes!"

Appoint "Prompt Champions"
Identify one or two people on your team who are naturally enthusiastic about these new tools. Officially designate them as "Prompt Champions." Their role is to be the friendly, go-to resource for their colleagues' questions, and to take the lead in maintaining and improving the Team Prompt Hub. This distributes the responsibility and fosters a culture of shared ownership.

Collaborative Document Creation with AI

One of the most powerful applications of a shared prompting methodology is in the collaborative creation of large, complex documents like business proposals, strategic plans, or in-depth reports. By using a shared set of prompts, a team can work together to produce a single, cohesive document with a consistent voice, even when different people are writing different sections.

The "AI-Assisted Divide and Conquer" Workflow

- **Step 1: The AI-Generated Master Outline.** The team lead or project manager starts the process by using a detailed prompt to create a comprehensive outline for the entire document.
    - **Prompt:** "Act as a management consultant. We need to create a comprehensive business proposal for a new client in the manufacturing sector. The goal of the

proposal is to win a six-month project focused on process optimization. Create a detailed document outline, including all the standard sections like 'Executive Summary,' 'Understanding the Challenge,' 'Proposed Solution,' 'Project Timeline,' 'Budget,' and 'About Us.'"

- **Step 2: Assign Sections and Standard Prompts.** The lead assigns different sections of the AI-generated outline to individual team members. Crucially, they also assign a specific "master prompt" from the Team Hub that should be used to draft each section.
    - **Example:** "Sarah, you're assigned the 'Proposed Solution' section. Please use the PROPOSAL-Solution_Section prompt from the hub to generate your first draft."
- **Step 3: Individual AI-Assisted Drafting.** Each team member uses the assigned master prompt to create a high-quality first draft of their section. Because they are all starting from a similar set of instructions, the tone, voice, and format of their individual sections will already be highly consistent.
- **Step 4: Human Assembly and Final Polish.** The team lead gathers all the AI-assisted drafts and assembles them into a single document. The final stage is a human-led review. At this point, the editor is not bogged down in basic writing and formatting. Instead, they can focus their energy on the highest-value work: refining the strategic narrative, ensuring a seamless flow between sections, and adding the final layer of human nuance and polish.

This workflow dramatically accelerates the creation of complex documents and leads to a more coherent and professional final product.

Quality Control and Review Processes

When your team starts using AI to generate content, a formal quality control process is not just a good idea, it is an absolute necessity. Remember, AI is a powerful tool, but it is not infallible. It can make mistakes, misunderstand nuance, and generate text that is factually incorrect. A clear review process protects your team's reputation and ensures the quality of your work.

A Simple Three-Layer Review System for AI-Generated Content

1. **Layer 1: The Self-Review (The Prompt Operator).** The person who runs the prompt is the first and most important line of defense. They have the most context on the task. Their responsibility is to perform an initial review, checking for:
    - **Accuracy:** Are all the facts, figures, and names correct?
    - **Relevance:** Does the output directly address the goal of the prompt?
    - **Clarity:** Is the language clear and easy to understand?
2. **Layer 2: The Peer Review (A Fresh Pair of Eyes).** For any important document, especially those intended for an external audience, a peer review is critical. A colleague who was not involved in the prompt creation can often spot awkward phrasing or "AI-isms" that the original creator might miss. Their focus is on:
    - **Tone and Voice:** Does this sound like our brand?
    - **Readability:** Is the document easy to follow?
    - **Coherence:** Does it make a logical and persuasive argument?
3. **Layer 3: The Final Sign-Off (The Project Owner).** The manager or project lead has the final say. Their review is

less about the details of the text and more about the strategic big picture. They ask the ultimate question:

  - **Does this document achieve its business objective?**

The AI Content Review Checklist

Create a simple checklist and save it in your Team Hub. Encourage your team to use it as part of their review process.

- [ ] **Fact-Checked:** All specific data points (statistics, dates, names) have been verified against a reliable source.
- [ ] **On-Brand Voice:** The tone and style align with our company's official communication guidelines.
- [ ] **Edited for "AI-isms":** The text has been reviewed to remove any generic or robotic-sounding phrases.
- [ ] **Achieves its Goal:** The content successfully fulfills the purpose for which it was created (e.g., to persuade, to inform, to instruct).
- [ ] **Confidentiality Check:** The content does not contain any sensitive or confidential company information that should not be shared.

Managing AI-Generated Content in Team Environments

Finally, let's cover a few practical tips for managing the files and workflows when your team is collaborating with AI.

- **Establish a Clear Version Control System.** When drafts are being generated and edited quickly, things can get confusing. A simple file naming convention can save you from a lot of headaches.
  - ProjectProposal_v1_AI-Draft.docx
  - ProjectProposal_v2_Human-Edit-Sarah.docx
  - ProjectProposal_v3_Final.docx

- **Be Transparent Internally.** Within your team, it is a healthy practice to be open about which content was generated with AI assistance. This fosters a culture of learning and helps the team get better at identifying and editing AI-generated text.
- **Be Strategic About External Attribution.** For external-facing content, the final product represents your company as a whole. Once a document has been through your team's rigorous human review and editing process, it becomes a human work product. There is generally no need to disclose the use of AI as a drafting tool, just as you would not disclose the use of a calculator or a grammar checker.
- **Reiterate Your Company's Data Security Policy.** This is the most critical point of all. Remind your team that public AI tools are not secure environments for sensitive information. Unless your company has an enterprise-level AI platform with a strict data privacy agreement, no confidential company, client, or employee data should ever be pasted into a prompt.

Key Takeaways from This Chapter

- Moving from personal to collaborative prompting unlocks exponential productivity gains for a team.
- A centralized **Team Prompt Hub** is the foundation for consistency, efficiency, and shared knowledge.
- **Team standards and best practices**, including a shared style guide, ensure that all prompts are high-quality and effective.
- **Training your colleagues** is essential for adoption and empowers everyone on the team with new skills.
- The **"AI-Assisted Divide and Conquer"** workflow enables teams to create complex documents faster and with greater consistency.
- A formal **quality control and review process** is non-

negotiable for managing AI-generated content and protecting your team's reputation.

You now have a complete framework for leading your team into a new era of productivity. You are not just an AI user; you are an AI leader. In the next chapter, we will broaden our view even further, looking at the wider ecosystem of AI tools and integrations that can connect with your core productivity platforms.

Chapter 17: AI Tools Integration and Ecosystem

In the last three chapters, we have constructed a powerful, multi-layered productivity system. We started in Chapter 14 by designing your personal AI workflow, turning ad-hoc prompting into a daily habit. In Chapter 15, we built on that foundation by creating an assembly line, using batching and prompt sequencing to automate entire categories of your work. Then, in Chapter 16, we scaled that system to your entire team, creating a collaborative framework for shared efficiency and excellence.

You now have a robust methodology for using AI as a dedicated assistant within a chat interface. But the true future of AI-powered productivity lies beyond the chat window. The next leap in efficiency comes when we no longer have to consciously "go to the AI" to get work done. It comes when the AI is already there, deeply integrated into the tools and platforms where we already spend our entire workday.

This chapter is about building that seamless ecosystem. The goal is to weave AI so deeply into your digital environment that using it becomes as natural and unconscious as using spellcheck. We will move from thinking of AI as a single destination to seeing it as an ambient layer of intelligence that enhances every application you use.

Think of it this way: you have built an incredibly efficient power plant (your prompting skill). Now, it is time to build the electrical grid that delivers that power directly to every house, office, and appliance that needs it. The less friction there is between the source of the power and its point of use, the more useful it becomes.

We will begin by exploring the rapidly growing world of native AI integrations, looking at how your favorite productivity apps like Notion, Trello, and Slack are building AI directly into their core features. We will then cover the power of browser extensions, which act as a universal AI layer for the entire web. We will also look at how to leverage voice-to-text and mobile AI to stay productive when you are away from your desk.

Finally, we will look toward the exciting future of this field, touching on the power of API integrations and the rise of "no-code" automation platforms that allow anyone, regardless of technical skill, to build custom, multi-step AI workflows that can handle complex processes for you in the background.

By the end of this chapter, your perspective will have shifted. AI will no longer be just a tool you use, but a fundamental part of the environment in which you work.

Connecting AI with Productivity Apps (Notion, Trello, Slack, etc.)

The most significant development in workplace AI is its integration directly into the software we rely on daily. Instead of copying text from your project management tool, pasting it into a separate AI chat window, and then pasting the result back, these "native integrations" allow you to perform the entire workflow in one place. This is the definition of a frictionless experience.

Knowledge Management Tools: Your "Second Brain," Now with a Brain

Platforms like Notion, Coda, and Slite are designed to be a central hub for notes, documents, and project plans. The addition of AI turns them from static storage into dynamic workspaces.

- **On-the-Fly Summarization:** You can highlight a long page of meeting notes and, with a single click, ask the integrated AI to "Summarize this page." The summary appears right there in the document.
- **Content Generation:** You can create an outline for a report on a page, then ask the AI to "Write a first draft based on this outline."
- **Data Structuring:** You can paste a block of unstructured text and prompt the AI to "Turn this into a database with columns for 'Task,' 'Status,' and 'Owner'." The tool will create a fully functional, sortable database for you.

Professional Scenario: Planning a Project in Notion
A product manager is starting a new project plan in Notion.

1. She creates a new page and types out a simple outline for the project's phases.
2. She highlights the outline and uses the integrated Notion AI with the prompt: "Expand these points into a detailed project plan. For each phase, include a list of key deliverables and potential risks."
3. The AI generates a comprehensive plan within the Notion page.
4. She then highlights a paragraph describing the key deliverables and prompts the AI: "Create a to-do list from this paragraph." The AI converts the text into a checklist.
5. Finally, she highlights the entire plan and prompts: "Create a one-paragraph executive summary of this project plan." She places this summary at the very top of the document.

The entire process of outlining, drafting, and summarizing happens in one place, creating a seamless and incredibly fast workflow.

Project Management Tools: Your AI-Powered Taskmaster

In tools like Trello, Asana, and ClickUp, AI is being integrated to help manage the flow of work itself.

- **Automated Task Creation:** You can paste an email or a paragraph of notes into a task description and ask the AI to "Create a checklist of sub-tasks based on this description."
- **Smart Suggestions:** Some tools use AI to suggest the next logical step in a project or to identify potential bottlenecks based on the current status of tasks.

Professional Scenario: Managing Tasks in Trello
A team lead receives a detailed email from a stakeholder with a list of requested changes for a website.

1. She creates a new Trello card titled "Implement Stakeholder Feedback."
2. She pastes the entire body of the email into the card's description field.
3. She uses an AI-powered plugin (a "Power-Up" in Trello's terminology) and highlights the pasted email text.
4. She gives it a simple prompt: "Extract every distinct requested change from this text and create a checklist of action items."
5. The AI instantly generates a clean, actionable checklist within the Trello card, which she can then assign to her team.

Communication Hubs: Cutting Through the Noise

Platforms like Slack and Microsoft Teams are the central nervous system of many organizations, but they can also be a source of constant distraction and information overload. AI integrations are designed to solve this problem.

- **Channel Summarization:** You can ask an AI bot to "Summarize the last 50 messages in the #marketing-campaign channel" to quickly get caught up on a conversation.
- **Thread Summarization:** If a single message has a long thread of replies, you can get a summary of the discussion and its conclusion.
- **Drafting Assistance:** You can draft messages and ask the AI to "Make this sound more professional" or "Rewrite this to be more concise" before you send it.

This allows you to stay informed without having to read every single message, a massive time-saver in a busy organization.

Browser Extensions and AI-Powered Plugins

While native integrations are powerful, they only work within a specific application. What about the rest of your digital life? The articles you read, the research you do, the emails you write in your browser. This is where AI-powered browser extensions come in.

An AI browser extension is a small piece of software you add to your web browser (like Chrome, Firefox, or Safari) that makes an AI assistant available on any webpage you visit. It usually appears as a small icon in your browser's toolbar or as a feature that activates when you highlight text. This creates a universal AI layer that follows you across the web.

Common Use Cases for AI Browser Extensions:

- **Web Page and Article Summarization:** This is the most common and powerful use case. You can be on a long news article, a technical blog post, or a dense Wikipedia page, and simply click the extension's icon to get a bulleted summary of the key points.
- **Email Drafting (in any web-based email):** Whether you use Gmail, Outlook.com, or another service, an AI extension can read the context of an email thread and help you draft a reply directly in the compose window.
- **Content Improvement and Rewriting:** You can highlight a sentence or paragraph you have written in any text box on the web (a social media post, a blog comment, a forum reply) and ask the extension to improve it.
  - "Make this more persuasive."
  - "Fix the grammar and spelling."
  - "Translate this to Spanish."
- **Quick Research and Explanation:** You can highlight a term or concept you don't understand on a webpage and ask the AI to "Explain this concept to me in simple terms."

Professional Scenario: A Consultant Conducting Market Research

A strategy consultant is researching a new industry. Her workflow is supercharged by a browser extension.

1. She finds a 30-page industry report published as a PDF on a website. Instead of downloading and reading the whole thing, she uses her AI extension to generate a one-page summary, immediately identifying the most relevant sections.
2. While reading a competitor's blog, she comes across an industry-specific acronym she doesn't recognize. She highlights it and asks the extension to "Define this acronym."
3. She finds a key statistic she wants to share with her team.

She highlights it and uses the extension to "Draft an email to my team summarizing this statistic and explaining why it's important for our project."
4. She opens LinkedIn to post about the trend. She writes a quick draft, highlights it, and prompts the extension, "Rewrite this LinkedIn post to have a more professional and authoritative tone, and suggest 5 relevant hashtags."

In this scenario, the consultant never had to leave her browser or switch contexts. The AI was a constant, ambient partner in her research and communication process.

Voice-to-Text and Mobile AI Applications

Some of our best ideas and most important thoughts come to us when we are not sitting at our desks. They come to us while we are walking, commuting, or exercising. Mobile and voice-powered AI tools are designed to capture this value, ensuring that your productivity is not tethered to your keyboard.

The "Capture and Refine" Voice Workflow

The single most powerful use of mobile AI is a two-step process we call "Capture and Refine."

- **Step 1: Capture (Using Your Phone's Native Voice-to-Text).** Every modern smartphone has a built-in voice dictation feature. It is a fantastic tool for raw, unstructured "brain dumps." The next time you have a complex idea or need to think through the outline of a document, don't try to type it on your phone.
  1. Open any simple notes app.
  2. Tap the microphone icon on the keyboard.
  3. Speak. Don't worry about punctuation, grammar, or

perfect sentences. Just talk through your ideas in a stream of consciousness. Capture the raw thoughts.

- **Step 2: Refine (Using AI).** Later, when you are back at your desk, take that messy, unstructured block of dictated text and paste it into an AI tool. This is where the organization happens.
    - **Prompt:** "Act as an editor. The following text was dictated via voice-to-text and is very messy. Please clean it up by fixing all grammar and punctuation, removing filler words, and structuring it into a coherent document. Format the output as a well-organized outline with a main heading and a series of bullet points."

This workflow allows you to be highly creative and productive in moments that would otherwise be lost, turning a walk around the block into a productive outlining session.

Mobile AI Apps for On-the-Go Tasks

Dedicated AI applications on your smartphone offer the power of a desktop AI in your pocket.

- **Brainstorming on the Fly:** "I'm a marketing manager. Give me 10 ideas for a social media campaign for a new brand of eco-friendly coffee."
- **Quick Email Drafts:** "Draft a quick, informal email to my team letting them to know I'm running 15 minutes late for the morning meeting due to traffic."
- **Image Analysis:** Some mobile apps allow you to take a photo of a whiteboard after a meeting and ask the AI to "Transcribe the text from this whiteboard and organize it into a list of action items."

The key is to think of your mobile AI as a tool for starting tasks, capturing ideas, and handling quick communications, which you can then develop further when you return to your primary workstation.

API Integrations for Custom Workflows

This section is a brief look into a more advanced topic, but it is essential for understanding the full potential of an AI ecosystem. Do not worry if you are not a technical person; the goal here is to understand the concept, not to learn how to code.

An API, or Application Programming Interface, is simply a secure and standardized way for two different software applications to talk to each other and exchange information.

When a company like OpenAI provides an API for its language model, it means that other software developers can build that AI's capabilities directly into their own applications. Every "native integration" we discussed earlier is built using an API.

But for companies with technical resources, an API allows them to build completely custom workflows that are tailored to their unique business processes.

Examples of Custom API Workflows:

- **Automated Customer Support Triage:** A company could connect their customer support email inbox to an AI via an API. The custom workflow could be:
  1. When a new support email arrives, send its text to the AI.
  2. The AI analyzes the email's content and categorizes it (e.g., "Billing Question," "Technical Issue," "Sales Inquiry").
  3. The system then automatically routes the email to the

correct department's queue.

- **Automated Sales Proposal Generation:** A sales team could build a tool where they fill out a simple form with a client's name, industry, and needs. This data is sent to an AI via an API with a master prompt, which then generates a complete, customized first draft of a sales proposal and saves it in a shared folder.

While you may not build these systems yourself, understanding that they are possible is important. It helps you see the strategic potential of AI not just as a personal assistant, but as a core component of your company's business processes.

The Future of No-Code AI Automation

For the vast majority of professionals who are not developers, the most exciting frontier of AI integration lies in "no-code" automation platforms. These are tools like Zapier or Make that have a simple, visual interface, allowing you to connect the apps you use every day and create automated workflows without writing a single line of code.

These platforms are now deeply integrating AI into their systems, allowing you to build incredibly powerful, custom automations.

The "Trigger -> Action" Model
The logic of these platforms is very simple. You define a "Trigger" (an event that happens in one app) and a resulting "Action" (an event that should happen in another app).

A Simple Example (Without AI):

- **Trigger:** When I save a new file to a specific folder in my Dropbox...
- **Action:** ...automatically send a message to a Slack channel

to notify my team.

A Powerful Example (With AI):
Now, let's inject an AI step into the middle of that workflow.
Professional Scenario: Automating First-Response to Web Leads
A small business owner wants to ensure that every potential client who fills out the "Contact Us" form on her website gets a fast, personalized response.
She uses a no-code tool to build this three-step workflow:

- **Trigger:** A new submission is received from the website contact form.
- Step 2 (The AI Action): The data from the form (name, company, and the message from the potential client) is automatically sent to an AI model with the following prompt: "Act as a helpful business development assistant. A potential new client has submitted the inquiry below. Please draft a warm, professional, and personalized first-response email. Acknowledge their specific question and let them know that I will be following up with them personally within 24 business hours.
  Client Name: [Data from the 'Name' field of the form]
  Client's Message: [Data from the 'Message' field of the form]"
- **Step 3 (The Final Action):** The email generated by the AI is automatically saved as a draft in her Gmail account.

Now, her process is transformed. When a new lead comes in, a perfectly drafted, personalized response is sitting in her drafts folder, waiting for her to give it a quick one-over and hit "send." This is a truly automated, intelligent system that saves time, improves customer experience, and allows the business owner to focus on more important work.

This is the pinnacle of the AI ecosystem: a network of connected apps with an AI acting as the intelligent "glue" between them, handling entire processes for you in the background.

Key Takeaways from This Chapter

- The goal of AI integration is to move from a separate "AI destination" to an **ambient layer of intelligence** across all your tools.
- Prioritize using **native AI integrations** within the productivity apps you already use every day (Notion, Slack, Trello, etc.).
- Use **AI-powered browser extensions** to create a universal AI assistant that works on any webpage.
- Leverage **voice-to-text and mobile AI apps** to capture ideas and be productive when you are away from your desk, using the "Capture and Refine" workflow.
- Understand that **APIs** are the technology that enables these integrations, allowing for powerful custom workflows.
- The future for most professionals lies in **no-code automation platforms**, which allow you to build your own custom, multi-step AI-powered workflows without needing to code.

You are no longer just a prompter. You are an architect, designing a connected digital ecosystem that is custom-built to support you and your work. You have the power to not only use applications, but to connect them in intelligent ways. In the next part of the book, Part V, we will explore the new strategic capabilities that this powerful ecosystem unlocks. We will move beyond productivity and into the realm of using AI for high-level decision-making, learning, and career growth.

Part V: Advanced Applications – Specialized and Strategic Use

Chapter 18: AI for Decision-Making and Strategy

Welcome to Part V. Over the course of this journey, we have systematically transformed your relationship with your work. In Part IV, you became an architect, designing a personal AI-powered workflow, building systems for automation, scaling your success to your team, and integrating AI into your digital ecosystem. You have mastered the art of using AI to get your work done faster, more consistently, and with greater efficiency. You are now an expert in "doing the work right."

In this next section of the book, we will elevate our ambition. We are moving from the tactical to the strategic. The new goal is to use AI to ensure you are "doing the right work." This is a crucial distinction. Efficiency is about optimizing your processes. Strategy is about ensuring those processes are aimed at the correct destination.

This chapter marks the beginning of that shift. We will explore how to use AI not just as an assistant that follows instructions, but as a strategic partner that can help you think, plan, and decide. You will learn to use AI as your on-demand consultant, a tireless analyst that can help you see around corners, challenge your assumptions, and make better, more informed decisions.

Think of it like this: up until now, you have been using AI to help you drive your car more effectively, navigating the streets with perfect precision and speed. Now, you will learn how to use AI to look at the entire map, to analyze the traffic patterns across the whole city, and to decide on the best possible destination before you even start the engine.

We will begin by exploring how to use AI for scenario analysis, a powerful technique for stress-testing your plans against multiple potential futures. We will then dive into the world of classic strategic frameworks like SWOT analysis, showing you how AI can apply these time-tested models to your unique business challenges in seconds. We will cover how to build a more robust risk assessment and mitigation plan, and how AI can provide data-driven support for your most critical decisions. Finally, we will look at how to leverage AI for competitive intelligence and long-term strategic planning.

By the end of this chapter, you will have a new set of tools for your professional arsenal. You will be able to approach complex, ambiguous challenges with a new level of clarity and confidence, using AI to augment your own strategic thinking and amplify your impact as a leader and decision-maker in your field.

Scenario Analysis and Planning

In a world of constant change and uncertainty, one of the most valuable strategic skills is the ability to think through multiple potential futures. This is the essence of scenario analysis. Instead of betting everything on a single, linear forecast, you create a handful of different, plausible stories about what the future might hold. This allows you to build more resilient strategies that can adapt and succeed in a variety of conditions.

However, humans are often not very good at this. We are susceptible to a range of cognitive biases. We suffer from "optimism bias," where we tend to assume the best-case scenario will happen. We are influenced by "recency bias," where we overweight the importance of recent events when thinking about the future.

This is where AI can be an incredibly powerful partner. By instructing it to take on different perspectives, you can force a more disciplined and objective exploration of the future. AI has no emotional attachment to the "best-case" outcome. It can dispassionately generate a range of scenarios, helping you see possibilities you might have otherwise overlooked.

A Step-by-Step Guide to AI-Powered Scenario Planning

1. **Define Your Core Strategic Question.** Start with the central decision you are facing. This should be a significant, high-stakes question. Examples include: "Should we expand our business into the European market?" or "Should we invest in developing a new flagship software product?"
2. **Identify the Key Uncertainties.** What are the 2-3 most critical and unpredictable variables that will determine the success or failure of your decision? These are the "drivers" of your scenarios. For expanding into Europe, the drivers might be "regulatory changes" and "competitor response." For developing a new product, they might be "customer adoption rate" and "disruptive technology shifts."
3. **Craft a Role-Based Scenario Prompt.** This is where you bring it all together. Assign the AI a clear role and task it with creating a set of distinct scenarios based on your key uncertainties.

Professional Scenario: A Logistics Company Considers Automation

A mid-sized logistics company is facing a major strategic decision: whether to make a significant capital investment in automating its primary warehouse.

- **Core Strategic Question:** Should we invest $5 million in a new robotic automation system for our main warehouse?
- **Key Uncertainties:**
  1. The future cost and stability of the human labor market.
  2. The speed of improvement in automation technology.
- The Scenario Generation Prompt:
  "Act as a senior business strategist and futurist. I am the CEO of a mid-sized logistics company. We are considering a $5 million investment in a new robotic automation system for our main warehouse.
  The success of this decision depends on two key uncertainties: the future cost of human labor and the pace of technological change in robotics.
  Task: Create three distinct, plausible scenarios for the next five years. For each scenario, give it a memorable name, a one-paragraph description of the future world it represents, and a concluding sentence explaining the implication for our investment decision.
  The three scenarios should be:
  1. **'Steady Evolution' (The Most Likely Case):** Labor costs rise moderately, and automation technology improves incrementally.
  2. **'Labor Shock' (A Challenging Case):** A sudden shortage of labor drives wages up dramatically, while technology development remains steady.
  3. **'Tech Leap' (An Opportunity Case):** Labor costs remain stable, but a breakthrough in robotics makes the next generation of automation twice as effective and 30% cheaper than today's systems."

The Power of the AI's Output

The AI will generate three clear, concise narratives. The "Steady Evolution" scenario might suggest the investment is sound. The "Labor Shock" scenario would frame the investment as a critical, defensive necessity. The "Tech Leap" scenario, however, might reveal a hidden risk: by investing in today's technology, the company might be unable to afford the far superior technology that becomes available in three years.
This output does not make the decision for the CEO. Instead, it provides a richer, more nuanced landscape for that decision. It allows the leadership team to ask better questions, like "How can we structure our investment to avoid being locked out of future technological leaps?" The AI has successfully broadened their strategic perspective.

SWOT Analysis and Strategic Frameworks

The business world has developed a rich toolkit of strategic frameworks to help leaders analyze their situation and make decisions. These are structured methods for thinking through complex problems. While it takes a human years to master the application of these frameworks, an AI has been trained on the vast library of business literature where they are discussed. As a result, it can apply them with remarkable speed and accuracy.

The Classic SWOT Analysis
A SWOT analysis is a foundational strategic exercise. It involves identifying an organization's internal Strengths and Weaknesses, and its external Opportunities and Threats.
The key to getting a high-quality SWOT analysis from an AI is to provide it with rich, detailed context. The more relevant background you provide, the more insightful the analysis will be.

Professional Scenario: A Direct-to-Consumer Startup Prepares for Growth

An innovative startup that sells high-quality, modular office furniture directly to consumers is preparing its strategy for the next year.

- The Prompt:
  "Act as a seasoned business consultant specializing in e-commerce startups. Conduct a comprehensive SWOT analysis for my company.
  Context:
  - **Company:** 'Urban Desks,' a direct-to-consumer brand.
  - **Product:** High-quality, minimalist, modular office furniture made from sustainable materials.
  - **Target Market:** Design-conscious professionals working from home.
  - **Known Strengths:** We have a strong brand identity on social media, excellent customer reviews, and a unique, patented modular design.
  - **Known Weaknesses:** Our supply chain is dependent on a single overseas supplier, our marketing budget is small, and we have a limited product range.
  - Market Conditions: The work-from-home trend is a major tailwind. However, several large, established furniture companies are now entering the market.
    Task: Generate a SWOT analysis.
    Format: Present the analysis with four clear headings: Strengths, Weaknesses, Opportunities, and Threats. Under each heading, provide at least three distinct bullet points with a brief explanation for each."

The Value of the Output

The AI will not only reflect back the strengths and weaknesses you provided, but it will also use its vast training data to identify opportunities and threats you may not have considered.

- **Opportunities:** It might suggest things like "Partnerships with interior design influencers" or "Expanding into the corporate home-office outfitting market."
- **Threats:** It might identify "Rising costs of sustainable materials" or "The risk of knockoff designs from low-cost competitors."

The AI-generated analysis becomes a rich, well-organized document that can serve as the foundation for a productive team strategy session.

Applying Other Key Frameworks
The same principle applies to dozens of other strategic frameworks.

- **PESTLE Analysis:** To understand the macro-environment.
    - **Prompt:** "Act as a market analyst. Conduct a PESTLE (Political, Economic, Social, Technological, Legal, Environmental) analysis for the luxury electric vehicle market in North America."
- **Porter's Five Forces:** To analyze industry competition.
    - **Prompt:** "Act as a professor of business strategy. Analyze the global streaming service industry using Porter's Five Forces framework."

Risk Assessment and Mitigation

Every new project or business initiative comes with a set of risks. The most successful leaders are not those who avoid risk, but those who identify, understand, and plan for it. AI can be an invaluable partner in this process, helping you brainstorm a much broader and more comprehensive set of potential risks than you might come up with on your own.

A Two-Step Workflow for Risk Management

This process involves a prompt sequence, where the output of the first step becomes the input for the second.

- Step 1: The Risk Identification Prompt
  The first goal is to generate a comprehensive list of potential risks. A good technique is to ask the AI to categorize them, which ensures a more thorough analysis.
- Professional Scenario: Launching a New Software Application
  A tech company is preparing to launch a new mobile productivity app.
- The Prompt:
  "Act as a veteran risk management officer. We are a software company planning the launch of a new mobile productivity app called 'TaskFlow.'
  Project Context: The app is designed for freelancers and small business owners. It will be a subscription-based service. The launch is scheduled for three months from now and will be supported by a digital marketing campaign.
  Task: Identify a comprehensive list of potential risks associated with this product launch. Please categorize the risks under the following headings:
    - Technical Risks (e.g., bugs, server issues)
    - Market Risks (e.g., competitor actions, poor adoption)
    - Financial Risks (e.g., cost overruns, low sales)
    - Reputational Risks (e.g., negative reviews, security concerns)"
- Step 2: The Mitigation Brainstorming Prompt
  Once you have the list of risks, the next step is to plan how you will deal with them. You can use a follow-up prompt in

the same conversation.

- The Follow-Up Prompt:
"That is an excellent list of risks. Now, for the top two most critical risks you identified under each of the four categories, brainstorm three potential mitigation strategies for each one. A mitigation strategy is a specific action we can take before the launch to reduce the likelihood or impact of the risk. Format your response as a bulleted list."

The Strategic Advantage
This two-step process provides a structured and actionable risk management plan. It moves you from a state of vague anxiety about "what could go wrong" to a state of prepared confidence. You not only have a clear view of the potential pitfalls, but you also have a playbook of proactive steps you can take to navigate them.

Data-Driven Decision Support

The best business decisions are not based on gut feelings alone; they are supported by data. While AI should never be used with sensitive or proprietary company data in a public tool, it is exceptionally good at analyzing qualitative data like customer feedback, which can provide a strong foundation for your decisions.

Important Security Reminder: The techniques described here are for use with anonymized, non-confidential qualitative data. Never paste customer lists, financial records, or any other sensitive information into a public AI tool unless your company has a specific enterprise-grade version with a data privacy guarantee.

Professional Scenario: Making a Product Roadmap Decision

A product manager is trying to decide which major feature to prioritize for the next development cycle. She has a document containing 200 pieces of anonymized feedback from a user survey.

- **The Goal:** To analyze the qualitative feedback to see which requested feature is mentioned most often and with the most urgency.
- The Prompt:
  "Act as a senior product analyst. I am going to provide you with a collection of 200 anonymized user feedback comments about our software.
  Task: Read through all of the comments and perform the following analysis:
  1. First, identify all mentions of requests for new features.
  2. Group these requests into thematic categories (e.g., 'Requests for better reporting tools,' 'Requests for third-party integrations,' 'Requests for improved mobile access').
  3. Count how many unique user comments fall into each category.
  4. Finally, write a brief summary report. The report should list the top three most-requested feature categories, ranked by the number of user comments. For each category, include a representative quote that captures the essence of the user need."

The Decision-Making Power

The AI's output is not just a summary; it is a quantitative analysis of qualitative data. The product manager can now go to her team with a clear, data-supported recommendation: "Users are requesting better reporting tools more than twice as often as any other feature. This should be our top priority." The AI has transformed a mountain of unstructured text into a clear, actionable insight that directly supports a critical business decision.

Competitive Intelligence Gathering

Staying aware of your competitors' strategies, products, and market positioning is a fundamental part of any healthy business strategy. AI can act as your personal competitive intelligence analyst, helping you gather and synthesize publicly available information with incredible speed.

Important Disclaimer: Always remember that a standard AI model's knowledge is not real-time. It is based on the data it was trained on, which has a specific cut-off date. For the most up-to-the-minute information, you need an AI tool that is integrated with a live web search capability.

A Suite of Competitive Intelligence Prompts

- The Competitor Profile:
  "Create a detailed business profile of our competitor, 'Global Tech Inc.' Based on publicly available information up to your last update, cover their primary product lines, their stated target market, their key marketing messages, and their geographic focus."
- The Feature-by-Feature Comparison:
  "Create a detailed feature comparison table. Compare our 'Product Alpha' with 'Global Tech's Product Beta.' The columns in the table should be 'Feature,' 'Product Alpha,' and 'Product Beta.' In the cells for each product, briefly describe how it implements the feature or state if the feature is absent."
- The Marketing Analysis:

"Analyze the marketing and branding strategy of 'Global Tech Inc.' Based on the tone of their website copy, their social media presence, and their press releases, what appears to be their core value proposition and their target customer persona?"

By running these types of prompts on a regular basis (e.g., quarterly), you can build a living, breathing repository of competitive intelligence, allowing you to spot shifts in the market and anticipate your competitors' moves.

Long-Term Planning and Forecasting

This is the area where it is most important to be clear about the AI's limitations. AI cannot predict the future. It does not have genuine insight or foresight. Any "forecast" it generates is simply an extrapolation based on the patterns in its training data.

With that crucial caveat in mind, AI can still be a valuable partner in the *process* of long-term planning. You can use it to structure your thinking, brainstorm possibilities, and pressure-test your strategic vision.

Using AI for Trend Extrapolation and Implication Brainstorming

- The Prompt:
  "Act as a strategic foresight consultant. I am the leader of a company in the corporate training and professional development industry.
  Context: Here are three major trends currently impacting our industry:
  1. A shift from in-person workshops to virtual and hybrid learning models.

2. The rise of 'micro-learning' and on-demand skill development.
3. Increasing demand for skills in data science, AI, and automation.
   Task: Based on the logical extension of these three trends, brainstorm a list of 5 potential new product or service ideas that our company could develop to be successful five years from now."

Using AI to Refine Vision and Mission

- The Prompt:
  "Act as a branding and strategy expert. Our company's current mission statement feels outdated.
  Current Mission: [Insert current mission statement]
  Company Context: We are a financial technology company that provides simple, powerful budgeting tools for small businesses. Our core values are empowerment, clarity, and integrity.
  Task: Rewrite our mission statement to be more modern, inspirational, and concise (under 25 words). Generate five different options."

In both of these examples, you are not asking the AI for "the answer." You are using it as a creative and strategic sounding board. The AI's output is not the end of the process, but the beginning of a high-level strategic conversation with your human team.

Key Takeaways from This Chapter

- Move beyond using AI for tactical execution and begin leveraging it as a **strategic thinking partner**.
- Use **scenario analysis** to pressure-test your plans against a

range of plausible futures and build more resilient strategies.

- Apply classic **business frameworks like SWOT** analysis by providing the AI with rich context to get insightful, structured analysis in return.
- Employ a two-step process of **risk identification and mitigation brainstorming** to proactively manage uncertainty in your projects.
- Leverage AI for **data-driven decision support** by asking it to analyze and summarize qualitative data like customer feedback.
- Use AI as a **competitive intelligence analyst** to gather and synthesize publicly available information about your competitors.
- Remember that AI cannot predict the future, but it can be a powerful partner for **long-term planning** by helping you extrapolate trends and brainstorm ideas.

You have now entered the highest tier of AI-powered professional work. You are using these tools not just to enhance your productivity, but to enhance your judgment. This is a critical skill for any current or aspiring leader. In the next chapter, we will continue this theme by exploring how you can use AI to design personalized learning paths and accelerate your own skill development.

Chapter 19: AI for Learning and Skill Development

In the last chapter, we elevated our use of AI, moving from a focus on tactical productivity to the realm of high-level strategy and decision-making. You learned how to use AI as your on-demand consultant, a partner to help you analyze complex situations, pressure-test your plans, and make better, more data-informed choices. You are now using AI to ensure you are not just "doing the work right," but that you are "doing the right work."

Now, we take that strategic mindset and turn it inward. The most valuable asset you have in your career is not your current knowledge set, but your capacity to learn and adapt. In a world of rapid technological change and shifting business landscapes, the commitment to continuous learning is the ultimate career insurance policy. Your ability to acquire new skills quickly and effectively is what will keep you relevant, valuable, and in demand for years to come.

This chapter is about using AI to become a master learner. We will explore how to transform your AI assistant from a work tool into a personalized, world-class tutor that is available to you 24/7. This is a fundamental shift in how we approach professional development. No longer are you limited by the fixed curriculum of a corporate training program or the slow pace of a generic online course. You can now create a bespoke learning journey that is perfectly tailored to your goals, your schedule, and your unique learning style.

Think of it this way: if Chapter 18 was about using AI to draw the map for your business, this chapter is about using AI to draw the map for your own growth. You will become the architect of your own expertise.

We will begin by showing you how to create a comprehensive, personalized learning path for any skill you want to acquire. From there, we will dive into the practical techniques for using AI as an interactive tutor, helping you master new subjects faster than ever before. We will cover specific applications for language learning and professional certification preparation, two high-value areas where AI can provide a significant advantage.

We will also explore how to use AI for technical skill development and, for those who want to achieve true mastery, we will introduce a powerful method for using Socratic questioning to develop a deeper, more critical understanding of any topic.

By the end of this chapter, you will see that AI is not just a tool for producing work, but a powerful engine for personal and professional transformation. You will have a complete toolkit for accelerating your own skill development, making you a more capable, confident, and future-proof professional.

Creating Personalized Learning Paths

The traditional "one-size-fits-all" approach to learning is inefficient. A senior manager does not need the same introductory material as a new intern, and a visual learner will struggle with a purely text-based curriculum. The first and most powerful application of AI in skill development is its ability to act as a personalized curriculum designer, creating a learning plan that is built just for you.

An AI can take your current role, your future career goals, your preferred learning style, and your available time commitment, and synthesize that information into a structured, step-by-step learning path.

A Step-by-Step Guide to Generating Your Learning Path

1. **Define Your Learning Goal.** Be specific. "Learn about marketing" is too vague. "Acquire the foundational skills to become a data-driven digital marketing manager" is a clear, actionable goal.
2. **Provide Your Professional Context.** Who are you, and what is your starting point? Include your current role, your years of experience, and any existing knowledge you have on the topic. This helps the AI calibrate the starting difficulty of the curriculum.
3. **Specify Your Learning Style.** Do you learn best by reading, watching videos, or doing hands-on projects? Tell the AI your preference so it can recommend the right types of resources.
4. **Set Your Time Constraints.** How much time can you realistically dedicate to this each week? This allows the AI to create a practical and achievable schedule.
5. **Craft the Master Prompt.** Combine all of this information into a single, comprehensive prompt that assigns the AI the role of a career development coach.

Professional Scenario: A Project Manager Wants to Learn About AI

A project manager with five years of experience in the construction industry sees the increasing importance of AI and wants to understand how it can be applied to her field.

- **Learning Goal:** To gain a practical understanding of AI and machine learning concepts in order to identify opportunities for their application in construction project management.

- **Context:** "I am a project manager with 5 years of experience in commercial construction. I am not a technical person and have no background in coding."
- **Learning Style:** "I learn best from a mix of reading clear, non-technical articles and watching short, explanatory videos. I would also like some practical exercises or thought experiments."
- **Time Commitment:** "I can dedicate 3-4 hours per week to learning."
- The Learning Path Generation Prompt:
  "Act as an expert career development coach and curriculum designer. I want to create a personalized 4-week learning path for myself.
  My Goal: To gain a practical understanding of AI and machine learning concepts so I can identify opportunities to apply them in my field of construction project management.
  My Background: I am a project manager with 5 years of experience in commercial construction. I have a strong understanding of project lifecycles but I am not a technical person and have no background in coding or data science.
  My Learning Style: I learn best from a mix of reading clear, non-technical articles, watching short explanatory videos, and working through simple, practical thought experiments.
  My Time Commitment: I can dedicate 3-4 hours per week.
  Task: Create a detailed, week-by-week learning plan for the next four weeks. For each week, provide a clear learning objective, a list of 3-4 specific topics to cover, and a suggestion for a simple practical exercise.
  Format: Structure the output with clear headings for 'Week 1,' 'Week 2,' 'Week 3,' and 'Week 4.' Under each week, use subheadings for 'Objective,' 'Topics to Cover,' and 'Practical

Exercise.'"

The Power of the AI's Output
The AI will not just generate a list of topics. It will create a structured, progressive curriculum.

- **Week 1** might focus on "Demystifying AI Terminology," with topics like "What is the difference between AI, Machine Learning, and Deep Learning?" and an exercise to identify three manual processes in construction that could be automated.
- **Week 2** could move on to "Common AI Applications," with topics like "Predictive Maintenance for Equipment" and "AI for Site Safety Monitoring."
- **Week 3** might cover "The Data Foundation," explaining the importance of data collection on a construction site.
- **Week 4** could conclude with "Building a Business Case," with an exercise to create a one-page proposal for a pilot AI project.

This output is a clear, actionable, and, most importantly, personalized roadmap. It meets the project manager exactly where she is and provides a realistic path to where she wants to be.

Mastering New Subjects Faster with AI Tutoring

Once you have your learning path, you can use AI as your personal, on-demand tutor to help you master the topics within it. The key to effective AI tutoring is to treat it as an interactive conversation, not a one-way lecture. Ask questions, request examples, and test your own understanding.

Core Techniques for AI Tutoring

- **The "Explain It Like I'm..." Technique:** This is the single most powerful tool for understanding complex subjects. If you encounter a concept that feels too abstract or technical, you can use this simple prompt formula to get an explanation that is tailored to your level of understanding.
  - **Prompt:** "Explain the concept of 'blockchain' to me like I'm a project manager who understands supply chains."
  - **Prompt:** "Explain 'machine learning regression models' to me like I'm a high school student who is good at math."
- **The "Give Me an Analogy" Technique:** Analogies are a powerful learning tool because they connect a new, abstract idea to a familiar, concrete one.
  - **Prompt:** "I'm having trouble understanding the difference between an API and an SDK. Can you give me a simple analogy to help me understand the relationship between them?"
- **The "Test My Understanding" Technique:** After you have read an article or watched a video on a new topic, you can ask the AI to quiz you. This is a form of active recall, which is scientifically proven to be a highly effective way to solidify new knowledge.
  - **Prompt:** "I have just learned about the core principles of the Agile project management methodology. Please ask me five questions to test my understanding of the key concepts."

Professional Scenario: Learning a New Financial Concept
An account manager needs to understand a new financial regulation that will impact her clients. The official documentation is dense and full of legal jargon.
Her AI Tutoring Workflow:

1. **Paste and Simplify:** She pastes a section of the legal

document into the AI.
    - **Prompt:** "Act as a financial compliance expert. Please explain the following section of this new regulation in simple, plain English. Focus on the key takeaway for a small business owner."
2. **Ask for an Example:** After getting the simplified explanation, she wants to see it in action.
    - **Prompt:** "That's helpful. Now, can you give me a practical, step-by-step example of how a small retail business would comply with this specific requirement?"
3. **Test Her Knowledge:** She wants to make sure she can explain it to a client.
    - **Prompt:** "Okay, I think I understand. Now, pretend you are my client. Ask me three common questions a business owner might have about this new regulation so I can practice my answers."

This interactive process transforms a passive reading task into an active learning session, leading to a much deeper and more durable understanding of the material.

Language Learning and Translation Assistance

Whether you are preparing for an international business trip or working with a global team, AI can be an incredibly powerful language learning and translation partner.

Using AI as a Translation Tool
Modern AI models are excellent at translation, but you can go beyond simple word-for-word translation by providing context.

- Contextual Translation Prompt:
  "Translate the following English phrase into professional, formal German. This phrase will be used in a business email

to a potential new client.
Phrase: 'We're excited to explore a potential partnership with you.'"

Using AI as a Language Tutor

- Vocabulary Building:
  "I am an English speaker learning Japanese for a business trip. My industry is software development. Give me a list of 20 essential Japanese business vocabulary words related to technology and project management. Please format it as a table with three columns: 'Japanese Word (Romaji),' 'Japanese Word (Kanji),' and 'English Meaning'."
- Grammar Correction and Explanation:
  "I am writing an email in Spanish. Please correct any grammatical errors in the sentence below. After the corrected sentence, please explain why the changes were necessary. Sentence: [Paste your Spanish sentence]"
- Conversational Practice:
  "I am preparing for a business dinner in Paris. I need to practice some basic conversational French. Let's role-play. You be the French host, and I will be the visiting American colleague. Start the conversation by asking me about my trip."

Professional Certification Preparation

Preparing for a professional certification, such as a PMP (Project Management Professional) or a cloud computing certification, is a significant undertaking that requires memorizing a large body of knowledge. AI can act as your personal study partner, helping you to organize the material, identify your weak spots, and prepare for the exam format.

An AI-Powered Certification Study Workflow

1. **Create the Study Plan:** Find the official exam syllabus or topic outline online. Paste it into the AI.
    - **Prompt:** "Act as an expert instructor for the [Certification Name] exam. Based on the official topic outline provided below, create a comprehensive 8-week study plan. Assume I can study for 5 hours per week. Break down the plan week by week, assigning specific topics from the syllabus to each week."
2. **Explain Complex Concepts:** As you work through the study plan, use the "Explain It Like I'm..." and "Give Me an Analogy" techniques to clarify any topics you find difficult.
3. **Generate Practice Questions:** This is one of the most valuable uses of AI in exam prep.
    - **Prompt:** "You are an exam question writer for the [Certification Name] certification. Based on the topic of 'Risk Management Processes,' please generate 10 multiple-choice practice questions in the style of the official exam. For each question, provide four answer choices (A, B, C, D) and then, after all the questions, provide a separate answer key with a brief explanation for why the correct answer is right."
4. **Create Custom Study Aids:**
    - **Prompt:** "Based on my study notes about the 'Five Phases of the Project Lifecycle,' create a set of digital flashcards. For each card, provide a key term on one side and a concise definition on the other. Format this as a two-column table."

Technical Skill Development

The principles we have discussed apply equally to the

development of technical skills, such as learning a new software platform, a business intelligence tool, or a new coding framework.

Key Prompts for Technical Learning

- The "Step-by-Step Guide":
  "Act as a software instructor. I am a beginner trying to learn how to use [Software Name]. I want to perform a specific task: [Describe the task, e.g., 'creating a pivot table in Microsoft Excel that shows sales by region']. Please provide a clear, step-by-step, numbered list of instructions on how to do this. Start from the very beginning, assuming I have the software open but have not done anything yet."
- The "Troubleshooting Partner":
  "Act as a senior developer. I am trying to run this Python script, but I am getting an error message. Here is the script and the error. Can you please explain what the error means in simple terms and suggest a possible solution?
  Script: [Paste your code]
  Error Message: [Paste the error message]"
- The "Best Practices" Consultant:
  "I have written a basic database query that works, but I want to make sure it is efficient. Act as a database administrator. Please review my SQL query and suggest any improvements based on industry best practices for performance and readability.
  Query: [Paste your SQL query]"

Socratic Questioning for Deeper Understanding

This is the most advanced technique in this chapter, and it is designed for those who want to move beyond mere knowledge acquisition to true critical thinking. The Socratic method is a form of disciplined dialogue. Instead of providing answers, the "tutor" asks a series of probing questions that are designed to help the learner examine their own underlying assumptions and arrive at a more profound understanding.

You can instruct the AI to act as your Socratic partner, a powerful way to pressure-test your own ideas and deepen your strategic thinking.

The Socratic Dialogue Prompt

- Prompt:
  "Act as a Socratic dialogue partner. Do not give me direct answers. Instead, your goal is to help me think more deeply about a topic by asking probing, open-ended questions. I will make a statement, and you will respond only with a question that challenges my assumptions, asks for evidence, or explores the logical implications of my statement. Let's begin.
  My Statement: I believe that the most important strategic priority for our company next year should be to expand into the Asian market."

The Power of the AI's Response
The AI will not agree or disagree. It will respond with a question designed to make you think.

- AI's Question: "What specific evidence have you seen that suggests the Asian market represents a better opportunity than further penetration of your existing markets?"
  You would then answer that question, and the AI would respond with another question, and so on. This disciplined process forces you to build a much more robust and well-reasoned argument, significantly strengthening your strategic thinking.

Key Takeaways from This Chapter

- Shift your view of AI from a work assistant to a **personalized, on-demand tutor** for skill development.
- Use AI to create **personalized learning paths** that are tailored to your specific goals, background, and learning style.
- Master new subjects faster by using AI as an interactive tutor, employing techniques like **"Explain It Like I'm..."** and asking it to **test your understanding**.
- Leverage AI for practical **language learning** tasks, from contextual translation to conversational role-playing.
- Accelerate your **professional certification preparation** by using AI to create study plans, generate practice questions, and explain complex topics.
- For those seeking true mastery, use AI as a **Socratic partner** to challenge your assumptions and develop deeper critical thinking skills.

Your professional value is a direct reflection of the skills you possess. By integrating AI into your learning process, you have given yourself a powerful tool to accelerate your growth and, by extension, your career. In the next chapter, we will build on this by exploring how to use AI to manage your professional brand, from optimizing your resume to preparing for high-stakes interviews.

Chapter 20: AI for Personal Brand and Career Growth

In the last two chapters, we have explored how to use AI for high-level strategic work. In Chapter 18, you learned to use AI as a business consultant, a partner to help you analyze markets, assess risks, and make better decisions. In Chapter 19, you turned that strategic lens inward, using AI as a personal tutor to design learning paths and accelerate your own skill development. You now have a robust system for doing the right work and for continuously improving your ability to do it.

Now, we will address the final, critical piece of the puzzle: ensuring that the professional world *knows* about your skills and value. Having exceptional talent is one thing; effectively communicating that talent is another. This is the work of personal branding and active career management. It is the process of crafting a clear, compelling, and consistent narrative about who you are, what you do, and the value you bring to the table.

This chapter is about using AI as your personal career coach and public relations agent. We will move from the internal work of skill acquisition to the external work of career advancement. In today's competitive job market, it is not enough to simply be good at your job. You must also be good at telling the story of your work. This means having a resume that gets noticed, a professional profile that engages, and the confidence to navigate high-stakes career conversations.

Think of it this way: the previous chapters helped you build a remarkable, high-performance professional engine. This chapter is about designing the sleek, aerodynamic body that goes around it and crafting the powerful marketing campaign that makes everyone want to see what is under the hood.

We will start with the foundational documents of any career: your resume and cover letter. You will learn a powerful workflow for tailoring these documents to any job application in minutes, not hours. We will then turn our attention to your digital storefront, your LinkedIn profile, and show you how to transform it from a static career history into a dynamic professional brand.

From there, we will cover the entire job search and career advancement lifecycle. We will explore how to build a personal website, how to use AI as an unflappable interview practice partner, and how to prepare for the often-daunting task of salary negotiation. We will even look at how to use AI for long-term career planning, helping you map out a potential career pivot and identify the skills you need to get there.

By the end of this chapter, you will have a complete set of AI-powered tools to manage every aspect of your professional brand. You will be able to approach your career growth with the same strategic, systematic, and efficient mindset that you now apply to your daily work.

Resume and Cover Letter Optimization

For many professionals, the resume is a source of constant, low-grade anxiety. We know we are supposed to tailor it for every single job application, but the process is so tedious and time-consuming that we often resort to sending out a generic version and hoping for the best. This is one of the single biggest mistakes a job seeker can make, and it is a problem that AI is perfectly suited to solve.

The modern hiring process is often a two-stage challenge. First, you must get past the Applicant Tracking System (ATS), the software that scans your resume for keywords and qualifications before a human ever sees it. Second, you must capture the attention of a human recruiter who might spend only a few seconds glancing at your document. AI can help you win on both fronts.

The AI-Powered Resume Tailoring Workflow

This workflow will transform the way you apply for jobs. It turns a multi-hour process into a focused, 15-minute exercise. The core idea is to create a single, comprehensive "Master Resume" and then use AI to create targeted variations of it for each application.

Step 1: Create Your "Master Resume."
Before you even touch an AI tool, create a single, detailed resume document that contains everything you have ever done: every job, every project, every skill, every certification. For each role, write down as many accomplishment-oriented bullet points as you can think of. Do not worry about length. This document is for your eyes only. It is your personal career database.
Step 2: Let the AI Analyze the Job Description.
For any new job you want to apply for, your first step is to understand exactly what the employer is looking for. Copy the entire job description from their website.

- The Prompt:
  "Act as a professional recruiter and an expert in Applicant Tracking Systems (ATS). I am going to provide you with a job description for a role I want to apply for. Please analyze it

and perform two tasks:

1. Extract a list of the top 10 most important keywords and key phrases from this description. These should include both technical skills (like 'data analysis,' 'SQL') and soft skills (like 'stakeholder management,' 'cross-functional collaboration').
2. Write a one-paragraph summary of the ideal candidate profile based on this description.
   Job Description: [Paste the entire job description here]"

Step 3: Provide Your Master Resume and Generate Tailored Bullet Points.

Now, you will provide the AI with the relevant sections of your Master Resume and ask it to rewrite them in the language of the job description.

- The Prompt:
  "That analysis is very helpful. Now, act as a professional resume writer. I am going to provide you with the bullet points from my 'Master Resume' for a specific role. Your task is to rewrite these bullet points to be more impactful and to strategically incorporate the keywords you identified in the previous step.
  For each rewritten bullet point, use the STAR method (Situation, Task, Action, Result) to frame it as a clear accomplishment. Focus on quantifiable results wherever possible.
  Keywords to Incorporate: [Paste the list of keywords the AI generated]
  My Original Bullet Points: [Paste the relevant bullet points from your Master Resume]"

Professional Scenario: A Financial Analyst Applying for a Senior Role

Let's say a financial analyst's Master Resume has a bullet point like this: "Was responsible for the quarterly budget report." After the AI has analyzed a job description that emphasizes "variance analysis" and "stakeholder presentation," the rewritten bullet point might look like this:

- **AI's Rewritten Bullet Point:** "Led the quarterly budgeting process, performing detailed variance analysis to identify a 15% cost-saving opportunity, and presented the findings to senior stakeholders, leading to a successful reallocation of resources."

This is a world apart. It is active, data-driven, and speaks directly to the needs expressed in the job description. By repeating this process for your most relevant past roles, you can assemble a highly tailored, keyword-optimized resume in a matter of minutes.

From Resume to Compelling Cover Letter

Once your resume is tailored, you can use the exact same source materials to generate a powerful cover letter. The cover letter is your opportunity to connect the dots for the hiring manager, telling the story that the resume bullet points can only hint at.

- The Master Cover Letter Prompt:
  "Act as a career coach and expert storyteller. Using the job description and my newly tailored resume provided below, write a compelling and professional cover letter.
  The cover letter should be structured in three paragraphs:
  1. **Paragraph 1 (The Hook):** State the specific role I am applying for and express genuine enthusiasm for the company, mentioning something specific about their work or mission that resonates with me.
  2. **Paragraph 2 (The Bridge):** Highlight my 2-3 most relevant accomplishments from my resume and explicitly

connect them to the top requirements listed in the job description. This paragraph should answer the question: 'Why am I the perfect fit for this specific role?'
3. Paragraph 3 (The Close): Reiterate my interest and include a clear call to action, such as expressing my eagerness to discuss my qualifications in an interview.
Job Description: [Paste the job description]
My Tailored Resume: [Paste your newly tailored resume]"

This systematic approach removes the guesswork and the writer's block from the application process, allowing you to create high-quality, customized applications at scale.

LinkedIn Profile Enhancement

Your LinkedIn profile is your professional home on the web. It is often the first place a recruiter, a potential client, or a new business contact will look for you online. While your resume is a formal document tailored for specific applications, your LinkedIn profile is your broader professional narrative. It should be engaging, comprehensive, and optimized to attract opportunities.

AI can help you transform your profile from a simple work history into a powerful branding tool.

Crafting a Magnetic Headline
Your headline is the most important piece of real estate on your LinkedIn profile. It appears next to your name in search results and is your single best opportunity to communicate your value proposition in a few seconds.

- The Prompt:
  "Act as a personal branding expert and LinkedIn specialist. I

am a [Your Current or Desired Role] with expertise in [Your Top 3 Skills or Specialties]. My career goal is to [Your Goal, e.g., 'help SaaS companies scale their marketing efforts']. Based on this, write 5 compelling and keyword-rich LinkedIn headlines for me. The headlines should be no more than 220 characters."

Writing a Narrative "About" Section

The "About" section is your chance to tell your professional story in your own voice. It should be more personal and narrative-driven than a resume.

- The Prompt:
  "Act as a professional storyteller and career coach. Write a compelling 'About' section for my LinkedIn profile, written in the first person.
  Context: [Provide 2-3 sentences about your current role and what you enjoy about it].
  My Career Journey: [Provide a brief, chronological summary of your career path].
  My Core Skills: [List your top 5-7 skills].
  What I'm Passionate About: [Mention what drives you professionally, e.g., 'I'm passionate about using data to simplify complex business problems'].
  Task: Weave this information into a cohesive and engaging narrative of about 200-250 words. The tone should be confident, approachable, and professional. The final paragraph should include a call to action, such as inviting people to connect or discussing potential collaborations."

Enhancing Your Experience Descriptions

You can use the tailored bullet points from your resume as a starting point, but on LinkedIn, you have more space to elaborate.

- The Prompt:

"Take the following accomplishment-oriented bullet points from my resume and rewrite them as a short, two-paragraph description for the 'Experience' section of my LinkedIn profile. The description should be more narrative in style, summarizing my key responsibilities and my single most significant achievement in the role.
My Resume Bullet Points: [Paste 3-5 tailored bullet points]"

Personal Website and Portfolio Content

For many professionals, especially freelancers, consultants, creatives, and entrepreneurs, a personal website is an essential tool for building credibility and attracting clients. AI can be an invaluable assistant in overcoming the "blank page" problem and generating the core content for your site.

Drafting Key Website Pages

- The Homepage "Value Proposition":
  "Act as a branding and copywriting expert. I am a [Your Profession] who helps [Your Target Audience] to [The Result You Provide]. Draft three different options for a concise, powerful 'hero' section for my personal website's homepage. Each option should include a main headline (under 10 words) and a sub-headline (under 25 words) that clearly communicates my value proposition."
- The "Services" Page:
  "Act as a marketing consultant. I offer three primary services: [Service 1, Service 2, Service 3]. For each service, write a brief, client-focused description. The description should have a clear title, a one-sentence summary of what the service is, and a bulleted list of 3 key benefits for the client. The tone should be helpful and persuasive."

- The Portfolio Case Study:
  This is one of the most powerful uses of AI for a personal site. You provide the raw facts of a project, and the AI weaves them into a compelling story.
  "Act as a business writer. I need to create a portfolio case study for a successful project. Please use the following information to write a 400-word case study.
  Structure: Please organize the case study with these four headings: The Challenge, The Process, The Solution, and The Results.
  The Raw Information:
    - **Client:** [Client Name and Industry]
    - **Challenge:** [Describe the problem the client was facing in 1-2 sentences]
    - **Process:** [List the key steps you took to address the problem]
    - **Solution:** [Describe the final deliverable or outcome]
    - **Results:** [List the key quantifiable results, e.g., 'Increased website traffic by 40%,' 'Reduced operational costs by 15%']"

Interview Preparation and Practice

An interview is not just a test of your qualifications; it is a performance. And like any performance, it is a skill that improves dramatically with practice. AI can serve as your tireless, on-demand interview coach, helping you anticipate questions, craft strong answers, and rehearse your delivery.

The AI-Powered Interview Prep Workflow

Step 1: Generate a List of Likely Questions.
Do not walk into an interview blind. Use the job description to

generate a highly specific list of questions you are likely to face.

- The Prompt:
  "Act as a senior hiring manager for a [Company Type, e.g., 'fast-growing tech startup']. I am preparing for an interview for the [Job Title] role. Based on the job description provided below, generate a list of 15 likely interview questions. Please include a mix of:
  - 5 Behavioral Questions (e.g., 'Tell me about a time...')
  - 5 Situational Questions (e.g., 'What would you do if...')
  - 5 Technical or Role-Specific Questions
    Job Description: [Paste the job description]"

Step 2: Craft Your Answers Using a Framework.
For every behavioral question, you should have a story prepared. The STAR method (Situation, Task, Action, Result) is the gold standard for structuring these stories.

- The Prompt:
  "Act as an interview coach. I need to prepare an answer for the common behavioral question: 'Tell me about a time you had to deal with a difficult stakeholder.' Help me structure my answer using the STAR method.
  Here are the details of the story I want to tell:
  - **Situation:** [Briefly describe the context of the project and the stakeholder's role]
  - **Task:** [Describe what you were trying to achieve]
  - **Action:** [List the specific steps you took to handle the situation]
  - Result: [Describe the positive outcome of your actions]
    Task: Please weave these points into a clear, concise, and compelling two-paragraph story that I can use as my interview answer."

Step 3: Conduct a Mock Interview.

This is where the AI becomes a true practice partner.

- The Prompt:
  "Let's conduct a mock interview for the [Job Title] role. You will act as the interviewer. Please ask me one question at a time from the list you generated earlier. I will type out my full answer. After I submit my answer, you will provide me with constructive feedback on it. The feedback should assess my answer based on the STAR method, its clarity, its impact, and its relevance to the job description. After giving the feedback, ask me the next question. Let's begin with the first question."

This process of generating questions, structuring your answers, and actively rehearsing them will give you a level of preparation and confidence that is impossible to achieve by simply thinking about the questions in your head.

Salary Negotiation Scripts

Salary negotiation is one of the highest-stakes conversations in any professional's career, and many people avoid it because they feel unprepared or uncomfortable. AI can help you replace that anxiety with a clear, data-driven, and well-rehearsed plan.

An AI-Powered Negotiation Workflow

Step 1: Conduct Your Research.
A successful negotiation is built on data. If your AI tool has live web access, you can use it for this step. If not, use traditional salary websites and bring the data to the AI.

- The Prompt (for a web-enabled AI):
  "Act as a professional compensation analyst. Based on the most current data available, what is the typical salary range

(including the 25th, 50th, and 75th percentiles) for a [Job Title] with [X] years of experience located in [City, State]? Please provide links to your sources."

Step 2: Build Your Negotiation Script.
Once you have your data, you can build your case.

- The Prompt:
  "Act as an expert career coach and negotiation specialist. I have received a job offer for [Job Title] with a salary of [$X]. My research shows that the market average for this role is closer to [$Y].
  My Key Qualifications:
  - [List your years of experience]
  - [Mention a key skill or certification that is highly relevant to the role]
  - [Mention one major accomplishment from your past role that demonstrates your value]
    Task: Write a professional, polite, and firm script that I can use to negotiate a higher salary. The script should be for a phone conversation. It must:
  1. Express sincere enthusiasm for the role and the company.
  2. State my appreciation for the offer.
  3. Confidently make my case for a higher salary based on the market data and my specific qualifications.
  4. Clearly state my desired salary ([$Y]) or a desired range.
  5. End on a collaborative and positive note."

You can also ask for variations: "Now, give me a response I can use if they say their budget is fixed." This preparation allows you to enter the conversation with a calm, professional, and persuasive script.

Career Pivot Planning and Skill Gap Analysis

As your career progresses, you may decide you want to move into a new field or a different type of role. This can feel like a daunting leap into the unknown. AI can act as your personal career strategist, helping you to explore your options, identify the gaps in your skills, and build a plan to bridge them.

An AI-Powered Career Pivot Workflow

Step 1: Explore Your Options.

- The Prompt:
  "Act as a career development coach. I am currently working as a [Your Current Role] and have a strong background in [Skill 1, Skill 2, Skill 3]. I am interested in pivoting to a new career that leverages my analytical skills but involves more creative problem-solving. Based on my background, suggest 5 potential new career paths that I should research. For each path, provide a brief description and explain why my current skills would be a good foundation for it."

Step 2: Conduct a Skill Gap Analysis.
Once you have identified a promising new career path, you need to understand what it will take to get there.

- The Prompt:
  "That's a helpful list. Let's focus on the career path of a 'User Experience (UX) Designer.' Act as a technical recruiter for UX roles. Compare my current skill set ([Skill 1, Skill 2, Skill 3]) with the skills you would typically look for in a mid-level UX Designer candidate.
  Task: Create a detailed skill gap analysis. Format it as a table with three columns: 'Essential UX Skill,' 'My Current Status,' and 'Learning Priority (High, Medium, Low).'"

Step 3: Create a Reskilling Plan.
This step connects directly back to the techniques we learned in the previous chapter.

- The Prompt:
"Based on the skill gap analysis you just created, design a 6-month personalized learning plan to help me acquire the skills with a 'High' learning priority. For each skill, suggest a learning module with key topics, recommended resource types (e.g., online courses, books, project-based learning), and a practical exercise to build a portfolio piece."

Networking Message Templates

Effective networking is a cornerstone of career growth, but reaching out to strangers can be intimidating. AI can help you draft concise, professional, and effective outreach messages that increase your chances of getting a positive response.

Master Prompts for Networking

- The "Cold" LinkedIn Connection Request:
"Act as a networking expert. Draft a concise (under 300 characters) LinkedIn connection request to [Name], who is a [Their Role] at [Their Company]. I am a [Your Role] and I admire their work in [Specific Area]. The goal is simply to connect and follow their work. The tone should be respectful and professional, not demanding."
- The Follow-Up After an Event:
"Draft a brief follow-up email to [Name], whom I met yesterday at the [Event Name]. I enjoyed our conversation about [Specific Topic]. The goal is to reinforce the connection and suggest a brief virtual call next week to continue the conversation. The tone should be warm and professional."

- The Informational Interview Request:
  "Draft a polite and concise email to [Name], a professional in my target field of [Field]. The goal is to request a 15-minute virtual informational interview to learn more about their career path and their experience at [Their Company]. I should make it clear that I am seeking advice, not asking for a job. The tone must be highly respectful of their time."

Key Takeaways from This Chapter

- Your career is your most important project. Proactive **personal branding and career management** are essential for long-term success.
- Use the **AI-Powered Resume Tailoring Workflow** to customize your resume and cover letter for every application in minutes.
- Transform your **LinkedIn profile** from a static resume into a dynamic branding tool by using AI to craft a compelling headline, "About" section, and experience descriptions.
- Use AI as your tireless **interview coach** to generate likely questions, craft strong answers using the STAR method, and conduct mock interviews.
- Replace negotiation anxiety with data-driven confidence by using AI to research salaries and prepare **professional negotiation scripts**.
- Plan a **career pivot** systematically by using AI to explore options, conduct a skill gap analysis, and create a targeted reskilling plan.

You are now equipped with a powerful suite of AI-driven strategies to manage your professional narrative and actively guide your career path. You have learned to apply the same principles of efficiency and automation to your personal growth that you apply to your daily work. In our final chapter of this section, we will explore the exciting frontier of using AI for creative problem-solving, unlocking new ways to innovate and generate breakthrough ideas.

Chapter 21: Creative Problem-Solving with AI

We have reached the final and most advanced application in our strategic journey. Over the last three chapters, you have learned to use AI as a business strategist, a personal tutor, and a career coach. You have built systems to make better decisions, accelerate your learning, and actively manage your professional brand. These are the skills that separate high-impact professionals from the rest.

This chapter is the capstone. It is about leveraging AI for what is arguably the most valuable and uniquely human skill of all: creative problem-solving. In a world where routine tasks are increasingly automated, the ability to generate novel, innovative, and effective solutions to complex problems is the ultimate career differentiator. It is the engine of progress, the source of competitive advantage, and the hallmark of a true leader.

But what does it mean to use a logical, pattern-matching machine to enhance something as intuitive and unpredictable as creativity? This is a crucial point. We are not going to ask the AI to "be creative" for us. True creativity, the kind that involves genuine insight, emotional intelligence, and a deep understanding of the human condition, remains firmly in our domain. Instead, we are going to use the AI as a powerful catalyst for our *own* creativity.

Think of it like this: your mind is a garden where ideas can grow. Over time, you tend to create well-worn paths in that garden, and you naturally walk down them again and again. This is "vertical thinking," and it is very efficient for solving familiar problems. But when you face a new or stubborn challenge, those old paths lead to the same old, tired solutions. This chapter is about using AI to blast new paths through your garden. It is a tool for systematically breaking out of your conventional thinking patterns and forcing you to look at your problems from entirely new and unexpected angles.

We will explore a suite of powerful techniques designed to do exactly that. We will begin with lateral thinking exercises, using AI to introduce randomness and challenge your core assumptions. We will then learn how to reverse engineer solutions from a desired future state, a powerful method for clarifying complex plans. You will discover how to use analogical reasoning, leveraging the AI's vast cross-disciplinary knowledge to borrow breakthrough ideas from completely unrelated fields. We will even see how applying artificial constraints can, counterintuitively, unlock greater creativity.

Most importantly, we will introduce a framework for the ultimate partnership, combining the AI's strength in machine-scale idea generation with your unique human ability to provide insight, judgment, and synthesis. By the end of this chapter, you will have a toolkit for innovation, a reliable process for getting "unstuck," and a new appreciation for the exciting frontier of human-AI collaboration.

Lateral Thinking and Innovation Exercises

For most of our professional lives, we are trained to think vertically. This is a logical, step-by-step, analytical approach. We define a problem, analyze the data, and move sequentially towards a solution. This is an incredibly effective method for optimizing existing systems and solving well-defined problems. However, it is often a barrier to true innovation.

Lateral thinking, a term coined by Edward de Bono, is the opposite. It is about solving problems through an indirect and creative approach, using reasoning that is not immediately obvious. It involves disrupting your normal thought patterns to come at the problem from a new direction. This is where we can use the AI as a deliberate agent of chaos, a tool to jolt us out of our comfortable cognitive ruts.

The "Random Input" Technique

One of the most effective ways to break a creative logjam is to introduce a random, unrelated concept and force your brain to make a connection. The AI, with its vast and diverse training data, is the perfect random concept generator.

Professional Scenario: A Marketing Team Tackles a "Boring" Product
A marketing team is tasked with creating a new advertising campaign for their company's accounting software. All their ideas so far have been predictable and bland, focusing on "efficiency," "accuracy," and "cost savings." They are stuck in a vertical thinking pattern.

- **The Goal:** To generate a completely fresh, unexpected marketing angle.
- The Prompt:
  "Act as a creative facilitator using the 'random input' technique for lateral thinking. Our team is trying to find a new marketing angle for our accounting software, which helps small businesses manage their finances. Our current ideas

are all stuck on the themes of efficiency and cost savings.
Task:

1. First, provide me with a list of 5 completely random, unrelated, concrete nouns.
2. Then, for each of those 5 nouns, I want you to brainstorm three potential marketing campaign slogans or concepts that use the noun as a metaphor to describe a key benefit of our accounting software.
   The goal is not to find a perfect answer, but to spark unconventional ideas."

The Power of the AI's Output
The AI might generate random words like: "A Bridge," "A Compass," "A Lighthouse," "An Anchor," and "A Key." Then, it would begin to force connections:

- **For "A Bridge":**
  - "Our software is the bridge between your daily transactions and your long-term business strategy."
  - "Campaign Concept: An image of a beautifully designed bridge connecting an island of messy receipts to an island of a clean, organized city skyline."
  - "Slogan: 'Bridge the gap to financial clarity.'"
- **For "A Lighthouse":**
  - "In the fog of financial uncertainty, our software is your lighthouse, guiding you to safe harbor."
  - "Campaign Concept: A video ad showing a small business owner navigating a stormy sea of paperwork, then looking up to see our software's logo shining like a lighthouse beam."

Suddenly, the conversation has shifted. The team is no longer talking about spreadsheets and data entry. They are talking about clarity, safety, and vision. The random input did not provide the final answer, but it broke the creative logjam and opened up a whole new field of more emotional and compelling marketing concepts.

The "Assumption Reversal" Technique

Another powerful lateral thinking technique is to identify the core, unstated assumptions you have about a problem and deliberately reverse them. This forces you to question your foundational beliefs and explore the opposite perspective.

- The Prompt:
  "Act as a provocative business strategist whose job is to challenge a team's core assumptions. Our team is designing a new project management application.
  Our Core Assumptions:
  1. Project management tools must be focused on tasks, deadlines, and timelines.
  2. The target user is a professional project manager.
  3. The goal of the tool is to increase team productivity.
     Task: For each of these three assumptions, I want you to write a 'reversed' assumption. Then, for each reversed assumption, brainstorm two radical new product features that would make sense if that reversal were true."

The AI's Disruptive Output:

- **Assumption 1 Reversed:** "Project management tools should be focused on team energy, communication flow, and morale, not tasks and deadlines."
  - **Feature 1:** An "Energy Dashboard" that visualizes team communication patterns and flags potential burnout risks.
  - **Feature 2:** An integrated "Kudos" system that automatically prompts for and highlights positive feedback between team members.

This exercise forces the team to think about the human element of project management, potentially leading to a product that is not just another task tracker, but a true team collaboration hub.

Reverse Engineering Solutions

This technique flips the conventional planning process on its head. Instead of starting with your current problem and trying to build a path forward, you start by defining your ideal future state in vivid detail and then work backward to the present, identifying the necessary steps. This is incredibly effective for complex, long-term goals where the path forward is unclear. AI can help you both to paint the picture of the future and to map the path back to the present.

An AI-Powered Reverse Engineering Workflow

Professional Scenario: Becoming a Top Employer
A mid-sized company has set a bold strategic goal: to be recognized as the "best place to work" in their industry within the next three years. The leadership team knows the goal, but they are unsure of the specific steps to get there.
Step 1: Define the Destination in High Resolution.

- The Prompt:
  "Act as an expert in organizational development and corporate culture. Our company's goal is to be ranked as a '#1 Best Place to Work' in the tech industry.
  Task: Describe, in vivid detail, what the day-to-day internal reality of a company that has achieved this status looks like. Use headings to structure your description. Cover the following areas:
  - Communication and Transparency

  - Leadership and Management Style
  - Employee Growth and Development Opportunities
  - Compensation and Benefits Philosophy
  - Work-Life Balance and Flexibility"

This prompt forces the AI to create a rich, detailed vision of the target. It moves the goal from an abstract slogan to a concrete, tangible description of a future reality.

Step 2: Identify the Major Milestones.
With the destination clearly in view, you can now ask the AI to map out the major landmarks on the journey back to today.

- The Follow-Up Prompt:
  "That is an excellent and inspiring description. Now, based on that vision, identify the 5 most critical, high-level strategic milestones a company would need to achieve to transform itself from an 'average' workplace into the one you just described. For each milestone, give it a clear name and a one-sentence description of the outcome."

Step 3: Define the Immediate Next Actions.
Once you have the major milestones, you can zoom in on the very first one and use the AI to break it down into an actionable, short-term plan.

- The Final Prompt in the Sequence:
  "Let's focus on the first milestone you identified: 'Establish a Culture of Radical Transparency.' Act as a change management consultant. What are the first 5 specific, actionable steps our leadership team needs to take in the next 90 days to begin making progress on this milestone?"

This reverse engineering process, guided by AI, transforms a daunting, multi-year vision into a clear, manageable, 90-day action plan. It makes the impossible feel achievable.

Analogical Reasoning for Breakthrough Ideas

Some of the greatest innovations in history have come from analogical reasoning: borrowing a concept from one domain to solve a problem in a completely different one. Johannes Gutenberg combined the mechanics of a wine press with the concept of a coin punch to invent the printing press. This is a uniquely human spark of insight, but AI can be a powerful tool to fuel it. Because an AI has been trained on a massive dataset spanning virtually every field of human knowledge, it can be prompted to find and explain analogies that you would never encounter on your own.

Professional Scenario: Improving a Warehouse Process
A logistics company is looking for a breakthrough idea to improve the speed and accuracy of the package sorting process in their warehouses. Their team is stuck thinking about conveyor belts, scanners, and human workers—the traditional components of their industry.

- The Prompt:
  "Act as an innovation consultant who specializes in cross-domain analogies. Our goal is to find a breakthrough idea to improve the efficiency of a package sorting warehouse. To break our team out of our conventional thinking, please provide detailed descriptions of how three completely different complex systems solve a similar 'sorting and routing' problem.
  The three systems are:
  1. **A Biological Cell:** How does a human cell sort, package, and transport thousands of different proteins to their correct destinations?
  2. **A Large-Scale Library System:** How does a national

library system categorize, store, and retrieve millions of unique books efficiently?
3. A Computer Network: How does the internet's TCP/IP protocol break down information into packets, route them through a chaotic network, and reassemble them at their destination?
For each of these three analogies, first provide a simplified, one-paragraph explanation of the core mechanism. Then, brainstorm 3 specific, practical ideas that a logistics warehouse could 'borrow' from that system's logic."

The Power of the AI's Cross-Domain Output:

- **From the Biological Cell:** The AI might explain the role of "molecular tags" on proteins. This could spark an idea for using advanced, multi-purpose QR codes on packages that contain not just the destination, but also information about priority, fragility, and optimal routing paths.
- **From the Library System:** The AI might describe the Dewey Decimal System's hierarchical structure. This could lead to a redesign of the warehouse layout, moving from a simple grid to a hierarchical system where broad categories of goods are stored in one zone, with sub-zones for more specific destinations, reducing search and travel time.
- **From the Computer Network:** The AI might explain the concept of "packet switching," where data is broken up and sent via multiple routes to be reassembled later. This could inspire a new system where large, multi-item orders are not picked all at once by a single worker, but are broken into individual items that are picked and routed independently and then consolidated at the final packing station.

The AI did not invent these solutions. It acted as a bridge, connecting the logistics team's problem to a vast world of other complex systems, providing the raw material for a human-led innovative breakthrough.

Constraint-Based Creativity

It is a common misconception that creativity requires absolute freedom. In reality, some of the most innovative solutions arise when we are faced with tight constraints. When the usual options are taken off the table, our brains are forced to find new and more inventive paths. You can use AI to deliberately impose and explore the creative possibilities of such constraints.

Professional Scenario: Overcoming "Analysis Paralysis"
A product design team at a furniture company is tasked with designing a new, innovative ergonomic office chair. They have been given an almost unlimited budget and a flexible timeline. Instead of feeling liberated, they are paralyzed by the sheer number of possibilities. They are suffering from "analysis paralysis."

- The Prompt:
  "Act as a world-class industrial design coach. My product design team is stuck in the early stages of designing a new ergonomic office chair. To help us break out of our creative paralysis, I want you to use the 'constraint-based creativity' method.
  Task: Propose three different, highly restrictive, and artificial design constraints. For each constraint, I want you to generate three initial, high-level design concepts that would emerge if we were forced to work within that constraint.
  The goal is to generate unexpected ideas, not finished

designs."

The AI's Creativity-Inducing Constraints:

- **Constraint 1: Extreme Material Limitation.** "The chair must be constructed from only two materials: bent plywood and a single piece of woven fabric."
  - **Concept A:** A 'suspension' design where the fabric is stretched across a minimalist plywood frame like a hammock.
  - **Concept B:** A 'living hinge' design where the plywood itself is cut in a way that allows it to flex and provide support.
- **Constraint 2: No-Tool Assembly.** "The chair must be shippable in a flat box and fully assemblable by the end-user in under 60 seconds without using any tools."
  - **Concept A:** An interlocking design where the pieces of the frame slot and lock into each other like a 3D puzzle.
  - **Concept B:** A design that uses integrated, high-tension elastic cords to snap the frame into place.

By forcing the team to solve these smaller, more focused problems, the AI helps them discover innovative structural and material solutions they would have never considered in their "anything is possible" state.

Combining AI Suggestions with Human Insight

This is the most important section of this chapter. It is the master framework that governs all the techniques we have discussed. AI is an incredible tool for generating a vast quantity of ideas, options, and possibilities. It can do this at a scale and speed that no human team can match. However, it lacks genuine understanding, strategic context, and taste. Your role as the human professional is to be the curator, the editor, the strategist, and the final decision-maker.

The most effective creative process is a dance between the AI and the human mind, a cycle of divergence and convergence.

A Framework for the Human-AI Creative Partnership

Step 1: Diverge (The AI's Primary Role)
The goal of this first phase is to make the "solution space" as large as possible. You want to generate the maximum number of ideas, from the practical to the absurd. This is where you deploy the techniques we have discussed.

- Use **Lateral Thinking** prompts to generate unexpected angles.
- Use **Analogical Reasoning** prompts to bring in ideas from other domains.
- Use **Constraint-Based Creativity** prompts to explore unconventional paths.

At the end of this phase, you might have a document with 50, 100, or even 200 raw, unfiltered ideas.

Step 2: Cluster (The AI's Organizational Role)
A list of 200 ideas is overwhelming. The next step is to use the AI to find the patterns and create some structure.

- **The Prompt:** "Act as a research analyst. I have provided you with a list of 150 raw ideas we generated for our marketing campaign. Please analyze this entire list and group all the ideas into 5 to 7 distinct thematic clusters. For each cluster, provide a descriptive name and a list of the specific ideas that fall within it."

This step turns a chaotic list into a manageable, structured mind map of your creative territory.

Step 3: Converge (The Human's Primary Role)
This is where your professional expertise becomes irreplaceable. Read through the clusters and the ideas within them. Your brain, armed with your unique experience, intuition, and strategic understanding of your company's goals, will start to see connections and possibilities that the AI cannot.

- **Your Task:** Select the 2-3 clusters that feel the most promising. Within those clusters, highlight the 5-10 individual ideas that spark your interest the most. You are the curator, applying the filter of human judgment and strategic relevance to the AI's raw output.

Step 4: Synthesize and Refine (The Human-AI Partnership)
Now, you return to the AI, but with a much more focused goal. You take the handful of promising ideas you have selected and use the AI to develop them further, or even combine them.

- **The Prompt:** "We have decided to focus on the cluster you named 'Metaphors of Security and Guidance.' Take the two ideas I liked most—the 'Lighthouse' concept and the 'Anchor' concept—and combine them into a single, cohesive campaign idea. Draft a one-page creative brief for this new, hybrid concept. The brief should include a campaign title, a target audience, a core message, and two examples of potential ad copy."

This four-step process creates a powerful loop. The AI provides scale and novelty, you provide strategic direction and taste, and together, you build innovative solutions that are far better than what either of you could have created alone.

Case Studies of Innovative AI-Assisted Solutions

Let's look at two fictional but realistic scenarios of this process in action.

Case Study 1: The Stagnant Software Company

- **The Problem:** A B2B software company's growth has flatlined. Their product is solid, but their business model feels dated.
- **The AI Process:** The CEO uses an **analogical reasoning** prompt. "Act as a business model innovation expert. Analyze the business models of three highly successful subscription services from outside the B2B software world: Netflix (media), Peloton (fitness), and a subscription box service for gourmet food. For each one, explain its core retention strategy. Then, brainstorm how a B2B software company could adapt those strategies."
- **The AI's Output:** The AI explains Netflix's content release strategy, Peloton's community-building features, and the food box's element of curated discovery.
- **The Human Insight:** The CEO realizes they have been thinking only about their software's features, not the user's experience. Inspired by the analogies, the human leadership team develops a new strategy that includes:
    - A "Netflix-style" regular release of small, valuable new feature modules to keep the product feeling fresh.
    - A "Peloton-style" online community and certification program to build user engagement and loyalty.
- **The Result:** The new model increases user retention by 30% and re-ignites company growth.

Case Study 2: The Inefficient Factory

- **The Problem:** A manufacturing plant is plagued by bottlenecks on its assembly line that no one can seem to pinpoint.

- **The AI Process:** The plant manager uses the **reverse engineering** workflow.
    1. **Define the Future:** She prompts the AI to describe a "perfectly optimized, zero-bottleneck assembly line" in detail, covering everything from inventory intake to final packaging.
    2. **Work Backward:** She then prompts the AI: "Based on that ideal state, what is the single most important data point we would need to be tracking at every stage of our line to identify where we are falling short of this ideal?"
- **The AI's Output:** The AI suggests that tracking the "wait time" of a component at each station is more critical than tracking the "work time."
- **The Human Insight:** The manager realizes they have been obsessed with how fast people work, not how long the product is sitting idle waiting for the next step. By shifting their focus and measurement to "wait time," they discover a non-obvious bottleneck at a quality control station that was holding up the entire line.
- **The Result:** A simple change in the quality control workflow increases overall line output by 18%.

Key Takeaways from This Chapter

- Creative problem-solving is a systematic skill that can be enhanced with AI, not a mysterious talent.
- Use **lateral thinking** techniques like "random input" and "assumption reversal" to break out of conventional thought patterns.
- Employ **reverse engineering** to bring clarity to complex, long-term goals by starting with the ideal future state and working backward.

- Leverage **analogical reasoning** to borrow innovative ideas from completely unrelated fields, using the AI's vast cross-domain knowledge.
- Embrace **constraint-based creativity** to turn limitations into a source of innovation.
- The most powerful model is a partnership: use the AI to **diverge** (generate many ideas), use it to **cluster** (organize the ideas), and then use your human insight to **converge** (select the best ideas) and **synthesize** them into a final solution.

You have now reached the summit of what is currently possible with AI as a professional productivity tool. You have moved from simple task execution to strategic planning, personal development, and now, creative innovation. You have a complete toolkit for augmenting not just your efficiency, but your intelligence and creativity. In the final part of this book, we will shift our focus to mastery and future-proofing, exploring how to develop your own prompt intuition, maintain quality control, and stay current in the rapidly evolving world of AI.

Part VI: Mastery and Future-Proofing

Chapter 22: Developing Your Prompt Intuition

Welcome to Part VI, the final stage of our journey together. Over the past five parts, we have built a comprehensive and powerful skill set. We started with the fundamentals, demystifying AI and learning the anatomy of a great prompt. We mastered core and advanced techniques, learning to craft instructions for any type of output. We applied these skills to dozens of real-world professional roles and scenarios. We designed systematic workflows to integrate AI into our daily routines. And finally, we elevated our use of AI to the highest strategic levels, using it for decision-making, skill development, career growth, and even creative problem-solving.

You have followed the roadmap from understanding, to crafting, to applying. You have the frameworks, the templates, and the techniques. You are now in the top tier of professionals who know how to effectively leverage AI as a productivity partner. The final part of this book is about securing that position and ensuring your skills remain valuable for the long term. This is the part about mastery and future-proofing.

This chapter is different from the ones that came before. It is less about learning a new list of techniques and more about developing a new way of thinking. It is about moving beyond the conscious, deliberate application of rules and frameworks to the fluid, effortless state of intuition.

Think of it like learning to cook. In the beginning, you follow a recipe meticulously. You measure every ingredient precisely. You check the instructions at every step. This is where you have been so far, learning the "recipes" for great prompts. It is an essential and effective way to get reliable results. But a master chef does not just follow recipes. A master chef has an *intuition*. They can feel when a dish needs a bit more acidity, they know instinctively how to substitute one ingredient for another, and they can create entirely new dishes by combining a deep understanding of foundational principles with their own creative flair.

That is our goal in this chapter: to turn you from a recipe-follower into a master chef of prompting. We will explore how to recognize the underlying patterns in successful prompts until they become second nature. We will focus on building "mental models," or cognitive shortcuts, that allow you to instantly know how to approach different categories of tasks. We will cover practical strategies for getting faster and more efficient with your prompting, moving it from a deliberate action to a rapid reflex.

Crucially, we will also discuss the strategic wisdom of knowing when to use AI and when to rely on your own human effort, a critical component of true mastery. We will encourage you to discover your own personal prompting style, because just like writing, there is no single "best" way for everyone. Finally, we will put it all together, charting the path from the structured use of templates to a state of true, intuitive command.

By the end of this chapter, the frameworks we have learned will begin to fade into the background, not because they are forgotten, but because they have been fully absorbed into your professional toolkit, ready to be used with speed, confidence, and a touch of your own personal style.

Pattern Recognition in Successful Prompts

The foundation of intuition is pattern recognition. A grandmaster in chess does not analyze every possible move on the board. Instead, they recognize thousands of patterns from past games, allowing them to intuitively grasp the strategic landscape and identify the most promising moves. Your journey to prompt intuition begins the same way: by learning to see the underlying patterns in effective prompts until they become second nature.

At this point, you have seen dozens, if not hundreds, of prompt examples throughout this book. They may have seemed different on the surface, tailored to different tasks and roles, but they all share a common DNA. They are all built upon the core principles we established in Part I. The first step toward developing intuition is to consciously practice deconstructing successful prompts to see this DNA for yourself.

Let's revisit our foundational CTFC framework (Context, Task, Format, Constraints) from Chapter 2, but with a new lens. Instead of seeing it as a rigid set of rules to follow, start seeing it as a diagnostic tool for understanding *why* a prompt works.

The Prompt Autopsy: A Practical Exercise

Take any of the "Strong Prompt" examples from a previous chapter. For instance, the prompt for creating a job description from Chapter 2:

"Act as a hiring manager for a mid-sized tech company that creates productivity software. We have a fast-paced, collaborative culture. Write a compelling job description for a 'Junior Project Coordinator' position. The description should include three sections: 'About the Role,' 'Key Responsibilities' (as a bulleted list), and 'Qualifications' (as a bulleted list). The tone should be energetic and encouraging, designed to attract ambitious, early-career candidates. Avoid overly formal corporate language. Mention that the role reports to the Senior Project Manager."

Now, perform an "autopsy" on it. Go through sentence by sentence and label the function of each piece.

- **"Act as a hiring manager for a mid-sized tech company that creates productivity software." -> Context (Persona & Environment)**
- **"We have a fast-paced, collaborative culture." -> Context (Culture)**
- **"Write a compelling job description for a 'Junior Project Coordinator' position." -> Task**
- **"The description should include three sections: 'About the Role,' 'Key Responsibilities' (as a bulleted list), and 'Qualifications' (as a bulleted list)." -> Format**
- **"The tone should be energetic and encouraging, designed to attract ambitious, early-career candidates." -> Constraint (Tone & Audience)**
- **"Avoid overly formal corporate language." -> Constraint (Negative Constraint)**
- **"Mention that the role reports to the Senior Project Manager." -> Constraint (Inclusion)**

By doing this exercise a few times, you will start to internalize the structure. Your brain will stop seeing a block of text and start seeing the functional components. You will begin to automatically recognize that a successful prompt almost always starts by setting the scene (Context), then gives a clear command (Task), then specifies the structure (Format), and finally, lays out the rules of the road (Constraints). This recognition is the first step in being able to construct such prompts automatically.

Building Mental Models for Different Tasks

Once you can recognize the patterns in a prompt, the next step is to build mental models. A mental model is a simple, internal representation of how something works. It is a cognitive shortcut that helps you make sense of the world and make decisions quickly. For example, "supply and demand" is a mental model for understanding economics. You do not need to be a Ph.D. economist to use it to make a reasonable prediction about what will happen to prices if a product becomes scarce.

In the context of AI prompting, a mental model is a pre-packaged "recipe" in your head for a specific category of task. When you encounter a task, instead of building a prompt from scratch using the CTFC framework, your brain will simply call upon the appropriate mental model. Let's define four essential mental models for the modern professional.

1. The "Analyst" Mental Model

- **When to Use:** Any task that involves making sense of existing information. This includes summarizing, analyzing, extracting, categorizing, or finding insights in a body of text or data.
- **Core Function:** To transform raw information into structured knowledge.
- **Key Prompt Ingredients (Your Internal Checklist):**
    - **Persona:** Start by assigning an expert analytical role (Act as a market researcher, Act as a financial analyst).

    - **The Data:** Clearly provide the raw information to be analyzed.
    - **The Specific Lens:** State exactly what you are looking for (Identify the top 3 themes, Extract all action items, What are the key risks?).
    - **The Structured Output:** Demand a specific, organized format (a bulleted list, a table, a one-paragraph summary).

Scenario: You have just read a long industry report.
Your Brain's "Analyst" Model Activates:

- *Okay, this is an analysis task. I need the Analyst model.*
-
    1. **Persona:** Act as a senior strategist.
-
    2. **Data:** Here is the report...
-
    3. **Lens:** Summarize the top 3 strategic threats for our company mentioned in this report.
-
    4. **Output:** Present them in a numbered list with a brief explanation for each.

2. The "Creator" Mental Model

- **When to Use:** Any task that involves generating new content from a concept or an idea. This includes brainstorming, drafting emails, writing reports, creating presentation content, or generating marketing copy.
- **Core Function:** To transform a blank page into a first draft.
- **Key Prompt Ingredients (Your Internal Checklist):**
    - **Persona:** Assign a creative or communicative role (Act as a marketing copywriter, Act as a project manager).

- **The Goal & Audience:** Clearly state the purpose of the content and who it is for.
- **The Core Message:** Provide the key points, ideas, or data that must be included.
- **The Voice & Tone:** Specify the desired style and emotional feel of the content.

Scenario: You need to draft an email announcing a project delay.
Your Brain's "Creator" Model Activates:

- *This is a creation task. I need the Creator model.*
-
  1. **Persona:** Act as a project manager.
-
  2. **Goal & Audience:** The goal is to inform the client about a one-week delay. The audience is the main project stakeholder, who values transparency.
-
  3. **Core Message:** The delay is due to an unexpected technical issue. We have a plan to resolve it. The new launch date is next Friday.
-
  4. **Voice & Tone:** The tone should be professional, apologetic but confident, and reassuring.

3. The "Organizer" Mental Model

- **When to Use:** Any task that involves taking unstructured information and imposing a clear structure on it. This is closely related to the Analyst model, but the primary focus is on formatting, not insight.
- **Core Function:** To transform chaos into order.
- **Key Prompt Ingredients (Your Internal Checklist):**
  - **The Command:** Start with a clear formatting instruction

(Organize this into a table, Create a checklist).
  - **The Raw Input:** Provide the messy notes or text.
  - **The Exact Structure:** This is critical. Define the precise column headers, the format of the list, or the sections of the document.

Scenario: You have a jumble of notes from a brainstorming meeting.
Your Brain's "Organizer" Model Activates:

- *This is an organization task. I need the Organizer model.*
-
  1. **Command:** Organize these notes into a table.
-
  2. **Input:** Here are my notes...
-
  3. **Structure:** The table must have three columns: 'Idea,' 'Potential Impact (High/Medium/Low),' and 'Estimated Effort (High/Medium/Low).'

4. The "Coach" Mental Model

- **When to Use:** Any task related to your own learning, skill development, or preparation. This includes interview practice, learning new concepts, or getting feedback.
- **Core Function:** To facilitate your own growth.
- **Key Prompt Ingredients (Your Internal Checklist):**
  - **Persona:** Assign an expert teaching or coaching role (Act as a career coach, Act as a Socratic tutor).
  - **Your Goal:** State your learning objective (Help me prepare for an interview, Explain this concept to me).
  - **The Process:** Define the rules of the interaction (Ask me one question at a time and then give feedback, Explain it using an analogy).

By consciously using these mental models for a few weeks, you will find that they become automatic. You will see a task and your brain will instantly categorize it and access the relevant "prompt recipe," allowing you to construct a high-quality prompt in seconds.

Speed Prompting: Getting Faster with Practice

As your intuition develops, your speed will naturally increase. You will spend less time consciously thinking about the structure of your prompts and more time focusing on the core task. However, there are a few practical techniques you can use to accelerate this process.

Use a Text Expander for Your Master Prompts
A text expander is a simple application that allows you to type a short abbreviation (a "snippet") and have it automatically expand into a longer block of text. This is one of the single greatest productivity hacks for any professional, and it is a game-changer for AI prompting.

1. **Go to Your Task Automation Inventory** (from Chapter 14). This is your library of pre-built, high-quality master prompts.
2. **Choose a High-Frequency Prompt,** like the one for organizing meeting notes.
3. **Create a Snippet.** In your text expander tool (many are available for free online), create a new snippet.
    - **Abbreviation:** !notes
    - **Expanded Text:** Act as a diligent executive assistant. I have just finished a client meeting and my notes are unstructured. Please organize them into a clean summary. The output must have two sections with these exact headings... [etc.]

4. **Deploy Instantly.** Now, the next time you finish a meeting, you can simply open your AI tool, type !notes, paste your raw notes, and hit Enter. You have just executed a perfect, multi-line prompt in about five seconds.

Develop "Prompt Skeletons"
For tasks that are less frequent and do not have a master prompt, you can still speed up the process by using a "prompt skeleton." This is a bare-bones template that you can quickly flesh out.
Keep this skeleton in a digital note for easy access.
Your Master Skeleton:
"Act as [EXPERT PERSONA].
The goal is to [DESIRED OUTCOME]. The audience is [TARGET AUDIENCE].
The task is to [ACTION VERB] the following input: [INPUT DATA/TEXT].
The output should be a [SPECIFIC FORMAT].
Constraints: The tone must be [TONE]. Do not [NEGATIVE CONSTRAINT]."
When you have a new task, you can copy this skeleton and simply fill in the bracketed information. This ensures you never forget a key component, even when you are moving quickly.

Knowing When to Use AI Versus Human Effort

True mastery is not just about knowing how to use a tool, but knowing *when* to use it. As you become more adept with AI, it can be tempting to use it for everything. However, the most productive professionals are discerning. They understand that their own time and cognitive effort are valuable resources, and they allocate them strategically.

Think of your professional tasks as existing on an "Augmentation

Spectrum."

1. Full Delegation (AI-Heavy)

- **Description:** These are the low-stakes, repetitive, rule-based tasks we identified in Chapter 14. The goal is maximum speed and efficiency.
- **AI's Role:** To produce a "good enough" output that can be used with minimal, if any, human review.
- **Examples:** Organizing your personal notes, getting a first-pass summary of an article for your own understanding, drafting a routine internal reminder email.
- **Your Intuitive Signal:** When a task feels like "administrative overhead."

2. Collaboration (Human-AI Partnership)

- **Description:** These are the high-stakes tasks that require a quality first draft. They are important enough to warrant your expertise, but the initial creation process is time-consuming.
- **AI's Role:** To do the heavy lifting of generating the initial structure and content.
- **Your Role:** To act as the strategist and editor, providing the initial detailed prompt, and then spending significant time refining, fact-checking, and infusing the AI's draft with your own voice and insight.
- **Examples:** Drafting a client proposal, creating a presentation for leadership, writing a performance review, generating a detailed project plan.
- **Your Intuitive Signal:** When a task requires both significant effort *and* a high degree of quality.

3. Inspiration (AI-Light)

- **Description:** These are highly creative or strategic tasks where you are not looking for a draft, but for a spark. You need to break out of your conventional thinking.

- **AI's Role:** To act as a catalyst for your own creativity. You use techniques like the "Random Input" or "Analogical Reasoning" from Chapter 21.
- **Your Role:** You are doing 99% of the cognitive work. You take the AI's strange and unexpected output and use your human intuition to find a novel connection or a breakthrough idea.
- **Examples:** Brainstorming a completely new product concept, developing a new business model, solving a stubborn, complex problem.
- **Your Intuitive Signal:** When you feel "stuck" or are facing a blank page on a major strategic challenge.

4. Human-Only

- **Description:** These are tasks where the core component is empathy, trust, nuanced human judgment, or a personal relationship.
- **AI's Role:** None. Using AI for these tasks is not only ineffective but can be damaging to your professional relationships.
- **Your Role:** To be fully present and human.
- **Examples:** Giving sensitive personal feedback to a direct report, a mentoring conversation, building rapport with a new client, making a final, high-stakes ethical judgment.
- **Your Intuitive Signal:** When the task is fundamentally about a human-to-human connection.

Your intuition will manifest as a quick, subconscious categorization of every task that comes across your desk. You will instantly "feel" whether a task is a "Delegation,"

"Collaboration," "Inspiration," or "Human-Only" task, allowing you to apply the right tool and the right amount of your own energy.

Developing a Personal Prompting Style

There is no one "correct" way to interact with an AI. As you gain experience, you will naturally gravitate toward a style that suits your personality and the nature of your work. Being aware of these styles can help you consciously lean into the one that feels most effective for you.

- **The Architect:** This is the style we have largely focused on in this book. The Architect likes to build a single, comprehensive, highly detailed prompt upfront. They invest the time to craft a perfect blueprint (Context, Task, Format, Constraints) because they want the AI to generate a near-final product on the first try. This style is excellent for high-stakes, repeatable tasks.
- **The Conversationalist:** This user treats the AI more like a true collaborative partner. They start with a simpler, more open-ended prompt and then build toward the final product through a series of iterative follow-up messages. Their process is a dialogue: "Give me some ideas for X," "Okay, I like idea #3, can you expand on it?", "Now rewrite that in a more formal tone." This style is excellent for creative and exploratory tasks where the final goal may not be perfectly clear at the start.
- **The Minimalist:** The Minimalist values speed above all else. They use short, direct prompts, often omitting detailed context when it's not absolutely necessary. They are masters of the "Quick Draft" and are comfortable with an 80% solution that they can quickly edit themselves. This style is effective for professionals who are very confident in their own editing

skills and are primarily using the AI to overcome the "blank page" problem.

Which one are you? There is no right answer. You might even find that you are an Architect for your weekly reports (a structured task) and a Conversationalist when brainstorming a new marketing campaign (a creative task). The key is to recognize which style feels most natural and efficient for you in different contexts.

Moving from Templates to True Mastery

We have now come full circle. The journey to mastery is a progression from conscious incompetence (not knowing what you don't know) to conscious competence (deliberately applying the rules and templates) and, finally, to unconscious competence (intuitive mastery).

This final stage is where all the pieces we have discussed in this chapter come together.

- You no longer think about CTFC; you just **naturally provide** the right information.
- You no longer consciously choose a mental model; you just **instantly know** how to approach the task.
- You no longer think about the Augmentation Spectrum; you just **instinctively feel** how much of your own effort a task deserves.
- You no longer worry about your style; you just **communicate** with the AI in the way that works best for you.

This is the point where the AI ceases to feel like an external tool you are operating and starts to feel like a true extension of your own mind. It is the seamless dance between human intent and machine execution. Reaching this stage is not the result of learning one final secret technique. It is the natural outcome of consistent, deliberate practice. Every prompt you write is a small step on the path to mastery.

Key Takeaways from This Chapter

- Prompt intuition is not a mysterious gift, but a skill built through **pattern recognition** and practice.
- Develop **mental models** ("Analyst," "Creator," "Organizer," "Coach") as cognitive shortcuts to instantly structure your prompts for different task categories.
- Use practical tools like **text expanders** to dramatically increase your prompting speed for recurring tasks.
- True mastery involves knowing when to use AI and when to use human effort. Learn to instinctively categorize tasks as **Full Delegation, Collaboration, Inspiration, or Human-Only**.
- Discover and embrace your **personal prompting style**, whether you are an Architect, a Conversationalist, or a Minimalist.
- The ultimate goal is to move from consciously using templates to **unconsciously competent** prompting, where the process becomes a fluid and natural part of your professional workflow.

You are now at the threshold of mastery. You have all the knowledge and frameworks required to develop a deep, intuitive command of AI as a professional tool. However, with great power comes great responsibility. The final chapters of this book will address the critical skills of quality control, ethical considerations, and how to stay current in this ever-changing field, ensuring that your AI-augmented career is not only productive but also responsible and future-proof.

Chapter 23: Quality Control and AI Output Verification

In the previous chapter, we explored the path to mastery, focusing on how to develop an intuitive, fluid relationship with AI. You learned how to internalize prompting frameworks, build mental models, and adapt your style to become a faster, more effective AI-augmented professional. Reaching that state of unconscious competence is the ultimate goal for productivity. However, with great speed and power comes an equally great responsibility: the duty of care.

This chapter is the essential counterbalance to the speed and ease of AI-powered creation. It is about building the critical habits of quality control, verification, and ethical diligence. If the previous chapter was about becoming a master chef who can create dishes intuitively, this chapter is about being the executive chef who is ultimately responsible for every single plate that leaves the kitchen. No matter how skilled your assistants are, the final sign-off is always yours. Your professional reputation depends on it.

We have established throughout this book that the most effective way to use AI is as a high-speed, highly capable assistant. But like any assistant, it is not infallible. It can misremember facts, misunderstand nuance, and generate content that is plausible-sounding but factually incorrect. To delegate a task to AI without implementing a robust quality control process is not just a productivity risk; it is a career risk.

In this chapter, we will construct a comprehensive framework for verifying and refining AI-generated content. We will begin with the most fundamental skill: fact-checking. You will learn a simple, repeatable process for identifying and verifying claims made by the AI. We will then dive into the phenomenon of "hallucinations," understanding why they happen and how to spot the red flags that signal an AI is inventing information.

From there, we will move from factual accuracy to stylistic integrity. You will learn how to edit AI content to infuse it with your own authentic voice and ensure it aligns with your professional brand. We will also tackle the important and often misunderstood topics of plagiarism and originality, providing clear guidelines on how to use AI-generated content responsibly.

Finally, we will zoom out to address the broader legal and ethical landscape. We will discuss the critical importance of data privacy, intellectual property, and adhering to company policies. We will conclude by establishing a clear framework for attribution and transparency, helping you understand when and how to disclose your use of AI in a professional context.

This chapter is your professional safety net. The habits you build here will give you the confidence to leverage AI to its fullest potential, knowing that you have a system in place to catch errors, maintain quality, and protect your hard-earned credibility.

Fact-Checking AI-Generated Content

The single most important rule of using AI for any task that involves factual information is this: **You are the fact-checker.** An AI language model is a text generator, not a truth generator. Its primary function is to create statistically probable sequences of words, which often results in text that is coherent, well-written, and completely wrong.

This is because the AI has no concept of "truth." It only has patterns. If it has been trained on millions of articles where a certain statistic is commonly cited, it will reproduce that statistic, regardless of whether the original sources were accurate or are still up-to-date. Therefore, you must approach every factual claim, every number, and every date generated by an AI with a healthy dose of professional skepticism.

The Three-Step Verification Workflow

For any AI-generated content that you plan to share with others, especially in a professional context like a report, presentation, or client email, you must perform a verification check.

Step 1: Isolate Verifiable Claims.
Read through the AI's output and highlight every statement that presents itself as an objective fact. This includes:

- **Quantitative Data:** Statistics, percentages, financial figures, dates.
- **Proper Nouns:** Names of companies, products, individuals, specific events.
- **Technical Specifications:** Features of a product, scientific claims, definitions.
- **Market Trends or Statements:** Claims about the state of an industry or consumer behavior.

Step 2: Go to the Source.
For each isolated claim, you must find a reliable, independent source to confirm it. Do not simply ask the same AI to "verify this fact," as it may just confidently repeat the same error.

- **For general knowledge and definitions:** Use a reputable encyclopedia or a major, well-regarded news source.
- **For industry statistics and market trends:** Look for reports

from established market research firms, government agencies, or major industry publications.

- **For company-specific information:** Go directly to the company's official website or their public financial filings.

If your AI tool has live web access and can provide source links, click on them. Do not just trust the summary; go to the linked page and verify that the information is actually there and is presented in the correct context.

Step 3: Attribute or Correct.
Once you have verified a claim, you can use it with confidence. If you are writing a formal report or article, it is good practice to keep a note of your source, even if you do not cite it directly in the text. If you find that the AI's claim is incorrect or outdated, replace it with the accurate information you found.

Professional Scenario: Verifying a Market Research Summary

- **The Task:** You asked an AI to generate a summary of current trends in the sustainable packaging industry for a client presentation.
- **The AI's Output (Excerpt):** "...The market for biodegradable plastics is growing at an astonishing rate of 25% annually, driven by new regulations in the European Union. Major players like EcoPack Global have seen their stock prices triple in the last year..."
- **Your Verification Process:**
  1. **Isolate Claims:**
     - Claim A: Market growth is 25% annually.
     - Claim B: The growth is driven by new EU regulations.
     - Claim C: "EcoPack Global" exists and its stock has tripled.

2. **Go to the Source:**
   - You perform a web search for "biodegradable plastics market growth rate report." You find a recent report from a major market research firm that states the compound annual growth rate (CAGR) is closer to 15%. The AI was likely referencing an older, more optimistic, or less reliable source.
   - You search for "new EU regulations on biodegradable plastics." You find information about the EU's Single-Use Plastics Directive, which does indeed impact the industry. This claim seems directionally correct.
   - You search for "EcoPack Global stock price." You find that there is no publicly traded company with that exact name. The AI has likely "hallucinated" a plausible-sounding company name.
3. **Attribute or Correct:** You rewrite the paragraph for your presentation based on your verified findings: "...The market for biodegradable plastics is projected to grow significantly, with some analysts forecasting a compound annual growth rate of around 15%, partly driven by regulations like the EU's Single-Use Plastics Directive. This trend has created significant opportunities for innovation in the sector..."

This process took a few extra minutes, but it saved you from presenting inaccurate data and a non-existent company to your client, a mistake that could have seriously damaged your professional credibility.

Detecting AI Hallucinations and Errors

An AI "hallucination" is a specific type of error where the model generates information that is not just incorrect, but is completely fabricated. It might invent a historical event, create a fake book title, or, as in the example above, invent a company name. These can be particularly dangerous because they are often presented with the same confident, authoritative tone as factual information.

Hallucinations happen because of how the AI works. When it doesn't have a direct, high-probability pattern to follow from its training data, it will sometimes "bridge the gap" by creating a new pattern that is statistically plausible but factually baseless. Learning to spot the signs of a potential hallucination is a critical skill.

Red Flags for AI Hallucinations

- **Overly Specific but Unsourced Details:** If the AI provides a very specific quote, statistic, or name of a person or study without any prompting to do so, be extra skeptical. For example, if it says, "According to a 2022 study by Dr. Alistair Finch at the University of Somerton..." and you have never heard of Dr. Finch or the University of Somerton, there is a high probability they do not exist.
- **Nonsensical or Circular Logic:** If you ask an AI to explain its reasoning and the explanation feels circular or doesn't make logical sense, it may be trying to justify a hallucinated fact.
- **Vague or Non-Existent Sources:** If you ask for sources and the AI provides a list of generic-sounding articles ("The Economics of Supply Chains") or broken links, it is a major red flag.

Prompting Strategies to Reduce Hallucinations

While you can never eliminate hallucinations entirely, you can use specific prompting techniques to reduce their likelihood.

- **Ask for Sources Upfront:** Include a constraint in your original prompt like, "For any factual claims, please provide a URL to a verifiable source." This forces the AI to ground its answers in specific data.
- **Use Chain-of-Thought Prompting:** For analytical tasks, ask the AI to "think step-by-step" and explain its reasoning before giving the final answer. This makes it harder for the AI to "jump" to a fabricated conclusion.
- **Provide the Source Material:** The single best way to prevent hallucinations is to not ask the AI to find facts, but to reason based on facts you provide. Instead of asking, "What are the key features of Product X?", it is far safer to go to the product's website, copy the features list, and then prompt the AI, "Based on this list of features that I am providing, summarize the top three benefits for a small business owner."

Editing AI Content for Authenticity and Voice

Beyond factual accuracy, the next layer of quality control is authenticity. The default writing style of most AIs is clean, competent, and often a bit generic. It lacks a distinct personality. Using this content "as is" for any communication that represents you or your brand can make your work feel impersonal and robotic.

Your professional voice is a valuable asset. It is the unique combination of your word choice, sentence structure, and tone that makes your communication recognizable as *yours*. Infusing an AI-generated draft with your own voice is a critical step in taking ownership of the work.

The Authenticity Editing Checklist

After you have fact-checked a draft from your AI, read it aloud. This is the fastest way to spot phrases and rhythms that do not sound like you. As you read, ask yourself these questions:

- **Is This How I Would Say It?** Are there any "corporate-speak" phrases or overly formal words that you would never use in a real conversation? (e.g., "henceforth," "utilize," "leverage the synergy"). Replace them with your own, more natural vocabulary.
- **Does It Match the Brand Voice?** If you are writing for your company, does the tone align with your brand's personality? Is it supposed to be playful and witty, or serious and authoritative? Adjust the language to match.
- **Is the Nuance Correct?** AI can sometimes miss the subtle social or political context of a situation. A draft of an email about a project delay might be technically correct but lack the right level of empathy or reassurance. Your job is to add that human layer of emotional intelligence.
- **Are There Any Personal Touches Missing?** Could you add a brief, personal anecdote or a reference to a shared experience to make the communication more relatable?

Professional Scenario: Personalizing a Team Announcement

- **The Task:** You are a manager who used an AI to draft an email announcing that your team has successfully hit its quarterly target.
- **The AI's First Draft:** "Team, This email is to inform you that we have successfully achieved our Q3 target of 150,000 units sold. This is a significant accomplishment that reflects

the hard work of all team members. Let's maintain this momentum as we enter Q4. Regards, The Management."

- **Your Editing Process (Adding Authenticity):**
  - **Voice:** "Inform you" is too formal. "Let's maintain this momentum" sounds generic.
  - **Nuance:** The message is correct but lacks genuine celebration or recognition.
  - **Personal Touches:** You remember a specific challenge the team overcame.
- **Your Final, Edited Version:** "Team, I'm absolutely thrilled to share that we didn't just meet our Q3 target—we smashed it, hitting over 150,000 units! This is a huge win, and it's all down to your incredible effort. I know how hard everyone worked to get the 'Phoenix' integration over the line in August, and that was the key to this success. Take a moment to be proud of what we've accomplished. We'll celebrate properly at our team lunch next week. Amazing work, everyone."

The second version has the same core message, but it is infused with a human voice, specific praise, and genuine emotion. It transforms a sterile corporate memo into an act of leadership.

Plagiarism and Originality Concerns

This is a topic that causes a great deal of anxiety for new AI users. The fear is understandable: if an AI is trained on the internet, is it just "copying and pasting" from other sources? The answer is more complex than a simple "yes" or "no."

An AI does not store a database of documents that it copies from. Rather, it has learned the statistical patterns of how words and sentences are put together from its training data. However, because some phrases, sentences, and ideas are extremely common in that data, it is possible for the AI to generate text that is identical or very similar to existing sources.

Differentiating Plagiarism from Unoriginal Content

- **Plagiarism** is an act of academic or professional dishonesty that involves the *intent* to pass off someone else's work as your own.
- **Unoriginal Content** generated by an AI is a statistical artifact. The AI has no "intent." It is simply generating a probable sequence of words.

The responsibility for avoiding plagiarism always rests with you, the human user. If you use AI to generate text for an academic paper or a professional article and submit it as your own without proper editing, citation, and added insight, you are responsible for the consequences.

A Practical Workflow for Ensuring Originality

1. **Always Treat AI Content as a Starting Point.** The most important rule is to never copy, paste, and publish. The process of editing for your own voice and adding your own insights is your first and best defense against unoriginal content.
2. **Use AI for Structure and Ideas, Not Final Prose.** One of the safest ways to use AI for writing is to have it generate outlines, bullet points, or rough drafts that you then completely rewrite in your own words.
3. **Use Plagiarism Checkers for High-Stakes Content.** If you are writing an article for publication, a major report, or any other document where originality is paramount, you should run your final, human-edited draft through a professional plagiarism detection tool. This is a standard part of the

writing and publishing process for many professionals, and it should be for you as well.

Legal and Ethical Considerations

Using AI in a professional context requires you to be aware of your ethical and, in some cases, legal obligations. While this book cannot provide legal advice, we can outline a clear set of ethical principles that will help you use these tools responsibly.

The Workplace Ethics Checklist for AI Use

- **Follow Company Policy.** This is the number one rule. Your employer may have specific guidelines about which AI tools are approved for use and what kind of information can be entered into them. If your company has a policy, you must follow it.
- **Protect Confidential Information.** Never paste sensitive, proprietary, or confidential information into a public AI tool. This includes internal financial data, unreleased product specifications, strategic plans, and, most importantly, any personal information about your customers or colleagues. Assume that any data you enter could be used to train the model and could, in theory, be seen by others.
- **Respect Client and Customer Privacy.** Never use AI to process personally identifiable information (PII) of your clients without their explicit consent and without using a secure, enterprise-grade AI platform that guarantees data privacy.
- **Understand Intellectual Property.** The legal landscape around who owns AI-generated content is still evolving. As a general rule for most public AI tools, you, the user, are the owner of the output. However, it is your responsibility to

understand the terms of service of the specific tool you are using. Furthermore, just because you own the output does not mean you can't be held liable for its content (e.g., if it is defamatory or infringes on a copyright).

Attribution and Transparency Best Practices

One of the most common ethical questions professionals have is, "Do I need to tell people I used AI?" The answer depends entirely on the context. There is no single rule, but we can establish a clear framework based on the principle of professional integrity.

A Framework for AI Disclosure

1. No Disclosure Needed (Your Personal Productivity)

- **Context:** You are using AI for your own internal work, to organize your thoughts, or to produce drafts for your own use.
- **Examples:** Summarizing an article for your own notes, organizing your to-do list, generating a first-pass draft of an email that you then heavily edit.
- **Reasoning:** In this context, AI is a tool, no different from a word processor's spell-checker or a calculator. You are not required to disclose every tool you use to do your job.

2. Informal Transparency Recommended (Internal Team Collaboration)

- **Context:** You are using AI to create content that will be used internally by your immediate team.
- **Examples:** Creating a draft project plan for team review, generating a first-pass agenda for a team meeting.
- **Reasoning:** While not strictly required, being open with your colleagues that you used AI to "get the first draft done" can foster a culture of efficiency and shared learning. It frames

the AI output as a starting point for discussion, not a final product.

3. Take Full Ownership (Final Deliverables)

- **Context:** You are submitting a final piece of work to a client, to leadership, or for public consumption. You have followed your quality control process, fact-checked, and edited the work into your own voice.
- **Examples:** A final client report, a published blog post, a presentation to the executive board.
- **Reasoning:** At this stage, the work is no longer "AI-generated." It is your work, augmented by AI. You are putting your professional reputation on it. You are responsible for its accuracy, its quality, and its impact. Just as a photographer does not attribute their work to their camera, you do not need to attribute your final, polished work to the AI tool you used in the process. The exception is if your company policy or the specific submission guidelines require such a disclosure.

Key Takeaways from This Chapter

- You are always the final checkpoint for quality. Your professional reputation depends on the accuracy and integrity of your work, regardless of the tools you use.
- Build a systematic **fact-checking workflow** for any AI-generated content that contains verifiable claims.
- Learn to spot the red flags of **AI hallucinations** (like overly specific but unsourced details) and use prompting techniques to minimize them.
- Go beyond factual accuracy by editing for **authenticity and voice**, infusing AI drafts with your unique professional persona.
- Understand that the responsibility for avoiding **plagiarism**

rests with you. Always treat AI content as a starting point to be significantly rewritten and refined.

- Adhere to a strict ethical code: follow company policy, protect confidential information, and respect customer privacy.
- Use a clear framework for **attribution**: take full ownership of your final, polished deliverables, while being transparent with colleagues about using AI as a collaborative tool.

You are now equipped with the essential safety and quality control systems to be a responsible, ethical, and effective AI-augmented professional. You have the skills to move fast, and the wisdom to know when to slow down and verify. In the next chapter, we will look to the horizon, discussing how to keep your skills sharp and relevant in the rapidly evolving landscape of artificial intelligence.

Chapter 24: Staying Current in the AI Landscape

We have come a long way. Over the past twenty-three chapters, you have built a powerful and comprehensive skill set for leveraging AI in your professional life. You have moved from understanding the fundamentals to mastering advanced prompting techniques, applying them to your specific career, building them into your daily workflows, and developing the critical habits of quality control. You are equipped with the knowledge, the frameworks, and the systems to be a highly effective, AI-augmented professional right now.

However, the landscape of artificial intelligence is not a static picture; it is a rapidly flowing river. The tools, techniques, and capabilities that are cutting-edge today will be standard tomorrow and potentially outdated the year after. This is not a cause for alarm. It is a call for adaptation. The final, and perhaps most crucial, element of future-proofing your career is building a sustainable habit of continuous learning.

This chapter is your guide to navigating that river. It is not about chasing every new headline or feeling overwhelmed by the pace of change. It is about developing a simple, manageable system for staying informed, adapting your skills, and maintaining your edge over the long term. If the rest of this book was about building your high-performance vehicle, this chapter is about learning how to be your own expert mechanic, capable of upgrading and maintaining it for the road ahead.

We will start by demystifying how AI models actually evolve, so you can understand the fundamental drivers of change. We will then translate that understanding into practical action, exploring how to adapt your prompting strategies to take advantage of new capabilities like larger context windows and multimodality.

Next, we will build your personal "AI intelligence system," a curated, low-effort toolkit of resources like newsletters, podcasts, and communities that bring the most important developments directly to you, saving you from having to hunt for them. We will establish a simple framework for experimenting with new tools and features in a structured, time-efficient way. Finally, we will tie it all together, discussing how to move beyond being just a skilled AI user to becoming an AI strategist, building a durable, AI-enhanced career that lasts.

The goal of this chapter is to replace anxiety about the future with a quiet confidence. You will finish it with a clear plan for keeping your skills sharp, your knowledge current, and your career trajectory pointed firmly upward.

How AI Models Evolve and Improve

To adapt to change, you first need to understand it. The evolution of AI models can seem like a series of random, dramatic leaps, but it is actually driven by a few predictable and understandable trends. Grasping these core trends will help you anticipate what is coming next and how it will impact your work.

Trend 1: They Get Bigger (More Parameters)
You will often hear about new models having billions or even trillions of "parameters." You do not need to understand the complex mathematics behind this. The simplest way to think about parameters is as the "knobs" that the AI can tune during its

training process. The more knobs it has, the more nuanced and complex are the patterns in language and logic it can learn.

- **What it means for you:** As models get bigger, they generally become more capable at complex reasoning, understanding subtlety, and generating higher-quality, more coherent text. Your prompts for analytical or creative tasks may require less hand-holding and refinement as the models' baseline capabilities improve.

Trend 2: They Are Trained on More Recent Data

Early AI models had a "knowledge cut-off" date. They could not tell you about anything that happened after their training data was collected. This is changing rapidly. Many AI tools now have the ability to access the live internet to supplement their internal knowledge.

- **What it means for you:** You can increasingly rely on AI for tasks that require up-to-date information, like market research on recent trends or summaries of the latest industry news. However, the principle of "trust but verify" from Chapter 23 remains absolutely critical. Always check the sources the AI provides.

Trend 3: Their "Short-Term Memory" Gets Longer (Larger Context Windows)

The "context window" is one of the most important concepts for a professional AI user. Think of it as the AI's short-term memory for your current conversation. If you provide a 10-page document but the AI's context window is only 5 pages, it will have effectively "forgotten" the first 5 pages by the time it reads the end. For years, this was a major limitation.

This is one of the fastest-improving areas of AI development. Context windows are expanding from a few thousand words to hundreds of thousands or even millions.

- **What it means for you:** This is a game-changer for professional productivity. Instead of feeding the AI small chunks of a report, you can now upload the entire 100-page document and ask for a comprehensive analysis. You can provide multiple documents at once for comparison. The nature of your prompts will shift from processing small pieces of information to analyzing entire projects or datasets in a single conversation.

Trend 4: They Are Becoming Multimodal (Beyond Text)
"Multimodality" simply means that the AI can understand and process more than just text. The latest generation of models can "see" and "hear." They can analyze images, understand charts, process audio, and even interpret videos.

- **What it means for you:** This opens up a vast new frontier of productivity use cases that were previously impossible. You can now take a screenshot of a data dashboard and ask, "What are the three most important trends in this chart?" You can upload a photo of a whiteboard from a brainstorming session and say, "Transcribe these notes and organize them into a project plan." This capability will fundamentally change how we interact with information.

Adapting Your Prompts to New AI Capabilities

Understanding these trends is the first step. The next is adapting your prompting techniques to leverage them. The core principles of CTFC (Context, Task, Format, Constraints) still apply, but the scale and type of information you provide will change.

Prompting for Long-Context Windows

When your AI tool has a large context window, you can move from single-document analysis to multi-document synthesis.

Old Way (Limited Context):
"Here is the sales report from Q1. Please summarize the key findings."
(New Prompt)
"Here is the sales report from Q2. Please summarize the key findings."
(New Prompt)
"Based on the summaries I provided, what are the differences between Q1 and Q2?"
New Way (Long Context):
"Act as a business analyst. I have uploaded two documents: the sales report for Q1 and the sales report for Q2. Your task is to perform a comparative analysis.
First, provide a three-bullet-point summary of the key findings for each quarter.
Second, identify the top three most significant trends or changes between Q1 and Q2.
Finally, based on the trends you identified, what is one potential risk we should be aware of for Q3?
Please format your response with clear headings for each section."
Notice how the task shifts from simple summarization to a much higher-value act of comparative analysis and strategic insight.

Prompting for Multimodality

Multimodal prompts combine text instructions with other forms of media, like images or audio.

Professional Scenario: Analyzing a Presentation Slide

- **The Task:** You are in a virtual presentation, and a speaker shows a complex slide with a chart and several bullet points.

You want to quickly understand it and formulate a smart question.

- **The Action:** You take a screenshot of the slide.
- The Multimodal Prompt:
  "I have uploaded an image of a presentation slide.
  Task 1: Summarize the main point of the bar chart in a single sentence.
  Task 2: Extract the key takeaways from the bullet points on the right.
  Task 3: Based on the information on this slide, suggest one insightful follow-up question I could ask the presenter."

This workflow, which takes about 30 seconds, allows you to instantly digest complex visual information and engage with it on a deeper level. It is a perfect example of how new AI capabilities can directly augment your professional performance.

Following AI Developments and Updates

You do not need to become a full-time AI researcher to stay current. The goal is to build a simple, efficient system that brings the most important news to you. This is about curation, not consumption of everything. You can build a powerful "intelligence system" with just three components that take no more than 15-20 minutes a day to scan.

1. Curated Newsletters

This is the most efficient way to stay informed. Let other experts do the hard work of sifting through the noise. Subscribe to one or two high-quality newsletters that specialize in summarizing AI news for a professional audience.

- **What to look for:** Look for newsletters that offer daily or weekly briefings. They should cover new feature launches from major platforms, interesting use cases, and links to the most important articles of the day.

- **How to use them:** Do not feel obligated to read every article they link to. Your goal is to scan the headlines and the one-sentence summaries. You are looking for pattern recognition. Is there a new feature that could help with a task from your Automation Inventory? Is there a new tool that seems particularly relevant to your industry? Only click through on the 1-2 items that are most directly applicable to your work.

2. Industry-Specific Podcasts

While newsletters are great for broad trends, podcasts are excellent for deep dives into how AI is specifically impacting your field.

- **What to look for:** Search on your favorite podcast app for terms like "AI in Marketing," "AI for Finance Professionals," or whatever your specialty is. Look for shows that feature interviews with practitioners who are actively using AI in their roles.
- **How to use them:** You can listen to these during your commute, while exercising, or during a break. You are listening for case studies and real-world examples. How are other people in your role solving problems with AI? This can spark ideas for new prompts and workflows you can adopt.

3. Official Company Blogs and Release Notes

This is the most direct way to find out about new features for the specific tools you use every day.

- **What to do:** Once a month, take 10 minutes to visit the official blogs or "What's New" pages for the 2-3 AI platforms you use most often.
- **Why this is important:** This is where you will find out about concrete updates like expanded context windows, new

analysis features, or multimodality. When you see a new feature, your first thought should be, "How does this impact the master prompts in my Task Automation Inventory?"

Community Resources and Learning Platforms

Beyond passively consuming news, actively engaging with communities is a powerful way to accelerate your learning.

- **Online Forums and Communities:** Websites like Reddit have dedicated communities (subreddits) for nearly every major AI tool. In these forums, users share their most effective prompts, troubleshoot problems, and showcase creative new workflows. Spending 15 minutes a week browsing one of these communities can be an incredibly high-yield learning activity.
- **Professional Networking Platforms:** On platforms like LinkedIn, follow AI researchers, productivity experts, and the official pages of AI companies. This will integrate AI news and best practices directly into a feed you are likely already scrolling through.
- **Online Courses:** If you want to do a "deep dive" into a specific new area (like using AI for data analysis or for coding), consider a short online course. This can be a more structured way to level up your skills in a targeted manner.

Experimenting with New AI Tools and Features

Staying current is an active process. Reading about a new feature is not enough; you have to try it for yourself. The key is to make this experimentation a low-effort, repeatable habit.

The 30-Minute Friday Sandbox

Set aside just 30 minutes every week, perhaps on a Friday

afternoon, for "AI Sandbox Time." This is not structured work; it is structured play. The goal is to experiment without the pressure of a specific deadline.

A Simple Experimentation Framework

During your sandbox time, follow this simple, four-step process:

1. **Identify One New Thing:** Based on your review of newsletters or blogs that week, pick one new tool or one new feature to test.
2. **Choose a Standard Task:** Go to your Task Automation Inventory and pick a common task with a master prompt you already use. This is your control case.
3. **Run a Head-to-Head Comparison:**
    - First, run your standard task through your usual tool and prompt.
    - Second, try to accomplish the exact same task using the new tool or feature. You may need to adapt your prompt slightly.
4. **Evaluate and Decide:** Compare the two outputs. Ask yourself:
    - **Was it faster?**
    - **Was the quality of the output significantly better?**
    - **Was the user experience more intuitive?**

If the answer to any of these is a clear "yes," then it is worth investing a little more time to update your master prompt and integrate the new tool into your workflow. If not, make a note of your findings and move on. You have lost nothing and gained valuable knowledge.

Professional Scenario: Testing a New Image-to-Text Feature

- **1. Identify New Thing:** Your favorite AI tool just launched a new feature that can analyze images.
- **2. Choose Standard Task:** You have a recurring task to summarize the key points from your manager's whiteboard sessions after team meetings.
- **3. Run Comparison:**
  - **Old Workflow:** Look at a photo of the whiteboard, manually type out the notes, and then feed the text into an AI with your "Organize Meeting Notes" master prompt. Total time: 10 minutes.
  - **New Workflow:** Upload the photo of the whiteboard directly into the AI and use a new prompt: "This is an image of our team's whiteboard notes. Please transcribe all the handwritten text and then organize it using my standard format: a bulleted list of 'Key Ideas' and a table of 'Action Items' with columns for 'Task' and 'Owner'." Total time: 2 minutes.
- **4. Evaluate and Decide:** The new workflow is dramatically faster and produces the same or better quality output. You decide to update your "Organize Meeting Notes" entry in your Task Automation Inventory to make this the new standard process.

Building an AI-Enhanced Career That Lasts

Everything we have discussed in this chapter, and indeed in this entire book, is about more than just saving time on daily tasks. It is about a fundamental shift in your professional identity. The skills of prompting, workflow design, quality control, and continuous learning are not just about efficiency; they are about long-term career resilience.

The Shift from "AI User" to "AI Strategist"

A skilled AI user knows how to get an AI to draft a good email.
An AI strategist knows how to design a system that reduces the entire team's email burden by 30%.
A skilled AI user can get an AI to summarize a report.
An AI strategist can use an AI to synthesize five different reports and identify a market opportunity that no one else has seen.
The goal of your continuous learning is not just to keep up, but to level up. As you become more comfortable with these tools, start thinking beyond your own to-do list. How could these capabilities solve a larger problem for your team? For your department? For your entire company? The professional who can answer those questions is not just future-proofing their job; they are defining their next promotion.

The Mindset of a Lifelong Learner

The technology will change. The platforms will evolve. But the foundational skills you have built will endure.

- **Clear Communication:** Your ability to break down a complex task into clear, logical instructions is a timeless skill.
- **Strategic Thinking:** Your ability to identify a problem and design a process to solve it is a timeless skill.
- **Quality Control:** Your commitment to accuracy, authenticity, and ethical diligence is a timeless skill.

AI is not a replacement for these skills. It is an amplifier for them. By committing to being a lifelong learner in this space, you are not just learning about AI. You are investing in a more durable and valuable version of your professional self.

Key Takeaways from This Chapter

- The AI landscape evolves along predictable trends: models

get bigger, their knowledge becomes more current, their context windows get longer, and they are becoming **multimodal**.

- Adapt your prompts to leverage these new capabilities, especially for **long-context analysis** and **multimodal tasks**.
- Build a simple, efficient **"intelligence system"** using curated newsletters, podcasts, and company blogs to stay informed without feeling overwhelmed.
- Make experimentation a habit. Use a **"30-Minute Sandbox"** each week to test new tools and features in a structured way.
- The ultimate goal is to transition from being a skilled **AI user** to an **AI strategist** who applies these tools to solve larger business problems.
- Committing to continuous learning is the single best way to build a resilient, future-proof career in the age of AI.

You now have a map and a compass for the road ahead. You have the skills to excel today and a plan to stay relevant tomorrow. In our final chapter, we will bring everything together, reflecting on the future of work and your new role as an AI-augmented professional.

Chapter 25: The Future of Work and AI Collaboration

We have reached the final chapter in our journey through the core principles of AI-powered productivity. In the last chapter, we built a system for staying current in this ever-evolving landscape. You now have a strategy for continuous learning, a framework for experimentation, and a mindset geared toward long-term career resilience. You are prepared not just for the AI of today, but for the AI of tomorrow.

As we conclude, it is time to zoom out from the specific skills of prompting and workflow design to the broader context of your career and the future of work itself. This is not a chapter about prompt templates or productivity hacks. This is a chapter about vision. It is about understanding the profound shifts that are happening in our industries and, more importantly, understanding your new role within them.

For decades, professional value was often defined by the knowledge you held and the tasks you could perform efficiently. The landscape is changing. AI is rapidly commoditizing the execution of routine tasks and the retrieval of standardized knowledge. This is not a cause for fear, but a catalyst for a fundamental redefinition of professional worth. The future of work is not a battle of human versus machine, but a partnership. Your success will not be determined by your ability to outperform AI, but by your ability to collaborate with it.

In this final chapter, we will explore this new reality. We will begin by examining how AI is reshaping entire industries and job roles, shifting the focus from task execution to strategic oversight. We will then identify the core set of skills that will remain uniquely and enduringly human, skills that AI cannot replicate but can amplify.

From there, we will define the concept of the "augmented professional," the new ideal of a human-AI partnership, and what that collaboration looks like in practice. We will provide a clear, actionable guide for preparing for these AI-driven workplace changes, so you can lead the transition rather than react to it. We will also address the critical topic of ethical leadership, outlining the responsibilities that come with wielding these powerful new tools.

Finally, we will provide you with a personal roadmap for your own continuous learning journey, ensuring that the skills and momentum you have built throughout this book are just the beginning. This chapter is the bridge from mastering a new tool to embracing a new professional identity. It is your guide to not just surviving, but thriving in the future of work.

How AI Is Reshaping Industries and Roles

The integration of AI into the workplace is not just another incremental technology update like the adoption of email or cloud computing. It represents a more fundamental shift in the division of labor between humans and technology. To navigate this shift, you must first understand its nature. The primary change is the move from a focus on *tasks* to a focus on *outcomes*.

For much of modern professional history, many jobs have been defined by a collection of tasks. A market analyst's job involved the tasks of gathering data, cleaning spreadsheets, creating charts, and writing summaries. A project manager's job involved the tasks of creating timelines, updating status reports, and sending reminder emails. AI is becoming exceptionally good at performing these discrete, rule-based tasks.

The result is that job roles themselves are being redefined away from the "how" (the tasks) and toward the "why" (the outcomes).

- The market analyst's role is shifting from *creating the report* to *using the AI-generated report to derive a strategic insight that drives business growth*.
- The project manager's role is shifting from *manually updating the project plan* to *directing an AI to maintain the plan and using the saved time to resolve complex interpersonal conflicts that are blocking progress*.

This is the great "unbundling" of professional work. The repetitive, process-oriented tasks are being unbundled from the job description and delegated to AI assistants. What remains is the core of human professional value.

The Three Major Workplace Shifts

1. The Shift from Information Retrieval to Insight Generation
Previously, a significant part of a knowledge worker's value was in their ability to find, recall, and synthesize information. Lawyers spent countless hours in discovery, consultants billed for weeks of market research, and developers scoured documentation. AI can now do this kind of work in seconds.

- **The Old Way:** A junior consultant spends a week gathering industry reports, manually extracting key statistics, and building a presentation on market trends.
- The New Way: A senior consultant uploads ten industry reports into a long-context AI and prompts it: "Act as a

leading industry strategist. Synthesize these reports and identify the top three counterintuitive or emerging trends that a new market entrant should be aware of. For each trend, provide supporting data points from the documents and outline a potential strategic opportunity."

The value is no longer in finding the information, but in asking the right, insightful question of the AI and then using the output to build a unique strategy.

2. The Shift from First-Draft Creation to Strategic Refinement

The "blank page" is one of the biggest drains on professional productivity. AI has effectively solved this problem. The initial, time-consuming work of creating the first draft of almost any document—be it a report, a legal contract, a piece of code, or a marketing plan—can now be done in moments.

- **The Old Way:** A marketing manager spends half a day writing the first draft of a comprehensive marketing plan for a new product launch.
- The New Way: The marketing manager uses a detailed master prompt, built from the principles in this book, to generate a comprehensive first draft in five minutes. She then spends the rest of the day using her deep industry knowledge to refine the strategy, challenge the AI's assumptions, and add a layer of creative nuance that the AI could never produce on its own.

  Her role shifts from "writer" to "editor and strategist." She is working on the plan, not just in the plan.

3. The Shift from Process Management to Exception Handling

Many professional roles involve managing predictable workflows and processes. AI and automation are increasingly capable of handling the standard, "happy path" scenarios. The human professional's role is becoming that of an expert "exception handler," stepping in only when a situation is too complex, too novel, or too emotionally charged for the automated system.

- **The Old Way:** A customer service manager spends most of their day answering routine inquiries about order status and return policies.
- The New Way: An AI-powered chatbot handles 90% of routine inquiries instantly. The customer service manager now focuses exclusively on the 10% of cases that are highly complex or involve a deeply dissatisfied customer, using their empathy and problem-solving skills to turn a negative experience into a positive one.
  The job becomes more challenging, more engaging, and ultimately, more valuable to the organization.

Understanding these shifts is the first step to positioning yourself on the right side of change. Your goal is to proactively move your own work from the "old way" to the "new way," delegating the tasks that are being commoditized and doubling down on the skills that are becoming more valuable.

Skills That Will Remain Uniquely Human

As AI automates the automatable, what is left? The answer is a suite of skills that are exceptionally difficult to replicate in a machine because they are not based on processing data, but on understanding context, emotion, and unstated meaning. These are the skills that you should be relentlessly cultivating in yourself and your teams. They are the new currency of professional value.

The Five Core Human Skills in the Age of AI

1. Strategic Judgment
An AI can analyze a dataset and tell you that a certain marketing

channel has the highest ROI. It can even recommend that you double your investment in that channel. What it cannot do is ask the critical follow-up questions. Is that ROI sustainable? Does that channel align with our long-term brand identity? What are our competitors doing in that space, and how might they react? Strategic judgment is the ability to take the data-driven output from an AI and overlay it with a deep understanding of the business context, competitive landscape, and long-term goals. It is the wisdom to know when the "obvious" answer is the wrong one.

2. Complex Communication and Negotiation
AI can draft a logically sound email, but it cannot navigate a tense negotiation with a key supplier. It cannot have a difficult but necessary conversation with an underperforming team member. It cannot build the personal rapport and trust with a client that is the foundation of a long-term business relationship.
These high-stakes conversations rely on reading body language, understanding emotional subtext, and building consensus through empathy and persuasion. These are deeply human abilities.

3. Creative Problem-Solving
While AI is an excellent partner for brainstorming and ideation, it is fundamentally a tool of derivation. It remixes and re-combines the patterns it has learned from its training data. It cannot have a truly original, "out of the blue" idea that is disconnected from its existing knowledge.
True creative problem-solving, the kind that leads to breakthrough innovations, often involves connecting disparate concepts from different fields, challenging the core assumptions of a problem, or having an intuitive leap of insight. Your ability to

think laterally and ask, "What if we approached this in a completely different way?" is a powerful creative advantage.

4. Emotional Intelligence and Empathy
This is perhaps the most enduringly human skill of all. Emotional intelligence is the ability to understand and manage your own emotions and to recognize and influence the emotions of others. It is the foundation of leadership, teamwork, and client service. An AI can be prompted to write in an "empathetic tone," but it cannot feel genuine empathy. It cannot sense the mood in a room. It cannot provide the authentic human connection that is essential for mentoring an employee, resolving a team conflict, or reassuring a nervous stakeholder.

5. Ethical Discernment
An AI operates based on its programming and the data it was trained on. It has no innate moral compass. It can be instructed to follow certain ethical rules, but it cannot make a nuanced ethical judgment in a novel situation with competing priorities.
For example, an AI might determine the most "efficient" way to implement a cost-cutting measure, but it cannot weigh that efficiency against the human impact on the employees who will be affected. That requires ethical discernment, a uniquely human capacity for moral reasoning.

Your career development plan for the next decade should be built around these five skills. Every time you successfully delegate a routine task to AI, you should immediately ask yourself, "How can I reinvest this saved time into developing my strategic judgment, my communication skills, my creativity, my emotional intelligence, or my ethical leadership?"

The Augmented Professional: Human + AI Partnership

The future does not belong to AI alone, nor does it belong to humans who resist AI. It belongs to the "augmented professional," the individual who seamlessly blends their own deep expertise and human skills with the speed and scale of artificial intelligence.

This is not a new concept. A grandmaster chess player who uses a chess engine to analyze positions and test strategies is an augmented professional. They are often referred to as a "centaur," combining the human torso of strategic thought with the powerful legs of computational analysis. This is the model for the modern knowledge worker.

What the Human-AI Partnership Looks Like in Practice

In a successful augmented workflow, the human and the AI each play to their strengths in a collaborative loop.

1. The Human Defines the Goal and Asks the Question.
The process always begins with human intent. You bring your strategic understanding of the problem and formulate the critical question. This is the art of prompting we have spent this entire book mastering. The quality of your question determines the quality of the collaboration.
2. The AI Generates the First Draft and Explores Possibilities.
The AI takes your prompt and does what it does best: it processes the information and generates a comprehensive first draft at a speed no human ever could. Whether it is an analysis, a report, a project plan, or a piece of code, the AI creates the raw material.

3. The Human Reviews, Refines, and Adds Nuance.
You now take over as the editor, the strategist, and the quality controller. You review the AI's output, using your expertise to spot errors, challenge assumptions, and add the layer of nuance and strategic insight that only you can provide. This is where you might use follow-up prompts to guide the AI, creating an iterative dialogue.
4. The AI Implements the Revisions.
Based on your feedback, the AI revises the draft, incorporating your strategic direction and making the requested changes instantly.
5. The Human Makes the Final Decision and Takes Ownership.
The loop concludes with a final human review and sign-off. You, the professional, are ultimately accountable for the work. You make the final judgment call and take ownership of the deliverable.

Professional Scenario: Creating a Business Proposal (Augmented Workflow)

- **1. Human Goal-Setting:** A business development manager needs to create a detailed proposal for a potential client. Her goal is to create a customized proposal that directly addresses the client's known pain points.
- **2. AI First-Draft Generation:** She uses a master prompt: "Act as a senior business consultant. Generate a draft proposal for 'Client Corp' for a project to overhaul their supply chain logistics. I have uploaded our standard proposal template, the notes from our last client call, and a case study from a similar project. Use this information to create a comprehensive first draft, ensuring you specifically address the client's stated concerns about 'inventory waste' and 'delivery delays'."

- **3. Human Review and Refinement:** She reads the draft. The AI has done an excellent job of structuring the proposal and incorporating the information. However, she knows this particular client is very data-driven. She gives the AI a follow-up prompt: "This is a strong start. Now, let's make the 'Expected Outcomes' section more quantitative. For each outcome, add a specific, projected KPI. For example, instead of 'Reduced Waste,' write 'Projected 15-20% Reduction in Inventory Waste'."
- **4. AI Revision:** The AI instantly revises the section to include the quantitative projections.
- **5. Human Ownership:** She does a final read-through, adjusts the tone in the executive summary to better match her personal communication style, and sends the proposal to the client with confidence.

In this scenario, a task that would have taken 4-5 hours of manual work is completed in under an hour, and the final result is arguably better because the manager was able to spend her energy on high-level strategy instead of low-level writing and formatting.

Preparing for AI-Driven Workplace Changes

Knowing that these changes are coming is one thing. Actively preparing for them is another. You cannot afford to be a passive observer. The professionals who will thrive in the coming years are those who take proactive steps to align their skills and their roles with the new realities of an AI-powered workplace.

A Personal Action Plan for Future-Proofing Your Career

1. Become the "Go-To" AI Expert on Your Team.

You have read this book. You are now far ahead of most of your colleagues in your understanding of these tools. Do not keep that knowledge to yourself. Volunteer to run a lunch-and-learn session. Share your best prompt templates. When a colleague is struggling with a tedious task, offer to show them how you would tackle it with an AI assistant. By becoming the resident expert, you make yourself invaluable to the team's overall productivity.

2. Proactively Redesign Your Own Job.

Do not wait for your manager to redefine your role. Start the process yourself. Go back to your Task Automation Inventory. For your three most time-consuming automatable tasks, create a one-page "process improvement plan." Document the old way, document your new AI-powered workflow, and quantify the time saved. Present this to your manager not as a way to do less work, but as a way to free up your time to focus on higher-value activities that you have also identified.

Workplace Script: Proposing a Workflow Change to Your Manager

"Hi, I've been experimenting with some ways to make my weekly reporting process more efficient. Right now, it takes me about three hours every Friday to manually pull the data and write the summary. I've developed a new workflow using our company's approved AI tool that can get the first draft done in about 20 minutes, with another 40 minutes for me to review, fact-check, and add my strategic analysis. By saving these two hours each week, I'd have more capacity to work on the that we discussed."

3. Shift Your Focus from "Doing" to "Directing and Reviewing."

Consciously change your mindset about what "work" looks like. For tasks that are suitable for AI, your job is no longer to perform the task, but to direct the AI and to rigorously review its output. This requires a different set of skills: clear communication, critical thinking, and a sharp eye for detail. This is the essence of becoming an editor and a strategist.

4. Build Your Portfolio of "Uniquely Human" Skills.

Make a concrete plan to develop your skills in the five core areas we identified earlier.

- **Strategic Judgment:** Volunteer to be part of a strategic planning committee.
- **Complex Communication:** Take a course on negotiation or public speaking.
- **Creative Problem-Solving:** Actively seek out the most challenging, unstructured problems in your department.
- **Emotional Intelligence:** Find a mentor who is a strong leader and ask them to coach you on giving feedback and managing team dynamics.
- **Ethical Discernment:** Read and participate in discussions about the ethical implications of technology in your industry.

Ethical Leadership in an AI-Powered World

With this great new power comes a new set of responsibilities, especially for those in leadership positions. As a manager or team lead, your role is not just to use AI, but to guide its use in a way that is effective, equitable, and ethical.

A Manager's Ethical AI Checklist

- **Promote Transparency, Not Mandates.** Encourage your team to experiment with AI, but be transparent about its limitations. Create a safe environment where team members can talk openly about what works and what does not.
- **Focus on Augmentation, Not Just Replacement.** Frame the adoption of AI as a way to augment the team's capabilities, freeing them from drudgery so they can focus on more engaging and valuable work.

- **Invest in Reskilling.** Use the productivity gains from AI to fund training and development for your team, helping them build the "uniquely human" skills that will be most valuable in the future.
- **Ensure Human Oversight on Critical Decisions.** Establish clear policies that any AI-assisted decisions related to hiring, performance reviews, or promotions must be rigorously reviewed and approved by a human.
- **Advocate for Data Privacy and Security.** Be the champion for ethical data handling. Ensure your team understands what company information is and is not appropriate to use in public AI tools.

Your Roadmap for Continuous AI Learning

The journey you have started with this book is the first, most important step on a longer path. Your goal now should be to build a sustainable, career-long habit of learning and adaptation.

A Three-Stage Personal Learning Roadmap

Stage 1: Foundation (Where You Are Now)

- **Goal:** Master the core principles of effective prompting and workflow integration.
- **Actions:** Complete the exercises in this book. Build and refine your Task Automation Inventory. Establish your daily AI routines.
- **Outcome:** You are a highly proficient AI user, capable of automating a significant portion of your daily tasks.

Stage 2: Specialization (The Next 6-12 Months)

- **Goal:** Become the go-to expert for applying AI within your specific job function or industry.

- **Actions:** Follow the industry-specific resources you identified in Chapter 24. Experiment with advanced, domain-specific prompts. Start sharing your expertise with your immediate colleagues.
- **Outcome:** You are an AI specialist, recognized for your ability to solve problems unique to your role using advanced AI techniques.

Stage 3: Strategy (1-3 Years and Beyond)

- **Goal:** Transition from a specialist to a strategist, using your AI expertise to drive broader business outcomes.
- **Actions:** Proactively identify opportunities to use AI to improve team-wide or department-wide processes. Lead pilot projects for new AI integrations. Mentor others and help shape your organization's AI strategy.
- **Outcome:** You are an AI strategist, a leader who is not just using AI to do their job, but is using it to redefine how the work gets done.

Key Takeaways from This Chapter

- AI is reshaping job roles by automating routine tasks, shifting the professional focus from **task execution** to **outcome-driven strategy**.
- The most valuable and durable professional skills are the ones that are uniquely human: **strategic judgment, complex communication, creative problem-solving, emotional intelligence, and ethical discernment.**
- The ideal professional model is the **"augmented professional,"** who combines their human expertise with the speed and scale of AI in a collaborative partnership.
- Proactively prepare for workplace changes by becoming a team expert, redesigning your own role, and focusing on

directing and reviewing AI-generated work.

- Ethical leadership is crucial. Focus on augmenting your team, reskilling employees, and ensuring human oversight on all critical decisions.
- Commit to a long-term **roadmap for continuous learning**, moving from foundation to specialization, and ultimately, to strategy.

You are standing at the beginning of a new era of professional work. The skills you have acquired are your ticket to not just participating in this transformation, but leading it. The future is a partnership between human talent and artificial intelligence, and you are now fully equipped to be a master of that collaboration. Your AI-powered future starts now.

Appendices

Appendix A: The Complete Prompt Template Library

Welcome to your central resource for AI-powered productivity. This appendix contains over 150 copy-and-paste prompt templates designed to handle a wide range of professional tasks. Think of this library not as a set of rigid rules, but as a collection of powerful starting points. The most effective way to use these templates is to adapt, customize, and refine them to fit your unique needs, industry, and communication style.

How to Use This Library

Each template is designed for immediate use. Simply find the task you need to accomplish, copy the template, and replace the bracketed information like [Your Topic] or [Specific Goal] with your own details. The real power of prompting comes from iteration. If the first result isn't perfect, don't start over. Instead, adjust the prompt with more context, clearer instructions, or specific examples until the AI delivers exactly what you need.

The templates are organized into logical categories that mirror common professional functions. Whether you're drafting an email, planning a project, creating marketing copy, or preparing for an interview, you'll find a structured prompt here to get you started. Use this library to save time, reduce mental friction, and produce higher-quality work, faster.

Section 1: Business Professionals – Core Operations and Communication

This section covers the fundamental tasks that drive daily

business operations, from communication and meetings to project management and analysis.

Email and Professional Correspondence

1. The Formal Email to a New Contact

- **Purpose:** To introduce yourself or your company to a new professional contact in a clear and respectful manner.
- Prompt Template:
  Act as a professional business communicator. Draft a formal email to [Recipient Name], [Recipient Title] at [Company Name]. The purpose of this email is to introduce myself, [Your Name], [Your Title] at [Your Company], and to [State the reason for contact, e.g., inquire about a partnership, request information, etc.].
  Key points to include:
    - A clear and concise subject line.
    - A brief introduction of myself and my company.
    - The specific reason for my outreach, referencing [How you found their contact information or a mutual connection, if applicable].
    - A clear call to action, such as [e.g., "schedule a brief 15-minute call next week," "request a copy of your latest report," "explore potential synergies"].

  The tone should be formal, respectful, and professional. Ensure the email is concise and easy to read.
- **Customization Guidelines:** Fill in all bracketed information. For the call to action, be as specific as possible to make it easy for the recipient to respond.
- **Real-World Usage Example:** You want to connect with a potential supplier you found through an industry directory. The prompt helps you draft an email that is professional and

gets straight to the point.

2. The Follow-Up Email After a Meeting

- **Purpose:** To summarize key discussion points and outline next steps after a meeting.
- Prompt Template:
  Draft a professional follow-up email to [Recipient Name(s)] regarding our meeting on [Date] about [Meeting Topic].
  The email should:
  1. Thank the attendees for their time and contribution.
  2. Briefly summarize the key decisions made: [Decision 1], [Decision 2].
  3. List the agreed-upon action items, clearly assigning responsibility and deadlines:
     - [Action Item 1] - [Owner] - [Due Date]
     - [Action Item 2] - [Owner] - [Due Date]
  4. Mention the next meeting date or the next milestone.

  The subject line should be "Follow-up: [Meeting Topic]". The tone should be proactive and collaborative.
- **Customization Guidelines:** Be precise with the action items, owners, and due dates. This creates accountability and clarity.
- **Real-World Usage Example:** After a project kickoff meeting, you use this prompt to send a summary that ensures everyone on the team is aligned on their responsibilities and deadlines.

3. The "Nudge" Email for a Non-Responsive Colleague

- **Purpose:** To gently remind a colleague about a pending task or request without sounding demanding.
- Prompt Template:
  Write a brief and friendly reminder email to [Colleague's

Name] about [The Task or Information Needed]. I am waiting on this to [Reason you need it, e.g., "complete the quarterly report," "move forward with the project plan"].
The email should be polite and assume they may have forgotten or are busy. Propose a soft deadline or ask if they need any help. The subject line could be "Quick question about [Topic]".

- **Customization Guidelines:** Adjust the tone based on your relationship with the colleague. A more casual tone might be appropriate for a teammate you work with daily.
- **Real-World Usage Example:** You need a data set from a colleague in another department to finish your presentation. This prompt helps you write a reminder that is professional and maintains a good working relationship.

4. The Email Declining an Invitation or Request

- **Purpose:** To politely decline a request, invitation, or proposal while maintaining a positive relationship.
- Prompt Template:
  Draft a professional and gracious email declining [The Invitation or Request] from [Sender's Name].
  The email should:
  1. Thank the sender for the opportunity or invitation.
  2. State clearly but politely that you are unable to accept or participate at this time. Provide a brief, professional reason if appropriate, such as "[e.g., a prior commitment, a current project deadline, not the right fit for our current strategic goals]".
  3. If possible, offer an alternative, such as "[e.g., suggesting a colleague who might be interested, proposing a different time, offering to connect in the future]".
  4. End on a positive and forward-looking note.

- **Customization Guidelines:** The key is to be polite and decisive. Avoid being vague, which can create false hope or confusion.
- **Real-World Usage Example:** You are invited to speak at an event but do not have the bandwidth. This prompt helps you craft a response that respectfully declines while keeping the door open for future collaboration.

5. The Request for Information Email

- **Purpose:** To clearly and concisely request specific information from a colleague, client, or partner.
- Prompt Template:
  Compose a professional email to [Recipient Name] at [Company Name] to request the following information:
    - [Information Item 1]
    - [Information Item 2]
    - [Information Item 3]

  Provide context for why this information is needed: [e.g., "to complete the financial audit," "for the upcoming project proposal," "to update our client records"]. Specify the desired format for the information, if any, such as [e.g., "a spreadsheet file," "a PDF document," "access to a shared folder"].Please state the deadline by which you need the information: [Date]. The subject line should be "Information Request: [Topic]".
- **Customization Guidelines:** Using a bulleted list for the requested items makes the email scannable and easy to act upon.
- **Real-World Usage Example:** A project manager needs updated budget figures from the finance department. This prompt ensures the request is specific, includes a deadline, and provides context.

6. The "Bad News" Delivery Email

- **Purpose:** To communicate negative news, such as a project delay or a change in plans, in a professional and empathetic way.
- Prompt Template:
  Act as a senior manager. Draft an email to [The Team or Stakeholder] to inform them about [The Bad News, e.g., a delay in the project timeline, a budget cut, a change in scope]. The email must:
  1. State the news clearly and directly, without excessive sugarcoating.
  2. Briefly explain the reason for the change: [Reason].
  3. Outline the impact this will have on [The Project, The Team, The Client].
  4. Propose a clear plan of action or next steps to mitigate the issue.
  5. Express confidence in the team's ability to navigate the challenge and offer your support.

  The tone should be transparent, responsible, and forward-looking, not defensive or alarmist.
- **Customization Guidelines:** Focus on the solution, not just the problem. This demonstrates leadership and helps maintain morale.
- **Real-World Usage Example:** A project lead has to inform stakeholders that a critical software launch will be delayed by two weeks. This prompt helps craft a message that is transparent and focuses on the revised plan.

7. The Introduction Email for Two Contacts

- **Purpose:** To introduce two professional contacts who could benefit from knowing each other.

- Prompt Template:
  Write an email to introduce [Person 1 Name], [Person 1 Title/Company] to [Person 2 Name], [Person 2 Title/Company].
  The email should:
    - Briefly introduce each person, highlighting their relevant expertise or role.
    - Explain why you are connecting them, stating the potential mutual benefit, such as "[e.g., they both work in the logistics industry and could share insights, Person 1 is looking for expertise that Person 2 has]".
    - Suggest a next step, but leave it to them to follow up (e.g., "I'll let you two take it from here.").
    - Make sure to get permission from both parties before making the introduction. This prompt assumes you already have it.
- **Customization Guidelines:** Keep it brief. Your job is to make the connection and then step out of the way.
- **Real-World Usage Example:** You know a freelance graphic designer and a startup founder who needs a new brand identity. This prompt helps you write a warm, professional introduction.

8. The Mass Communication Update Email

- **Purpose:** To provide a status update to a large group, such as a department or an entire company.
- Prompt Template:
  Draft a company-wide update email from [Your Name/Department Head] about [Topic of the Update, e.g., the successful launch of a new product, Q3 performance results, a new company policy].
  The email structure should be:

  - **Opening:** A clear statement of the announcement.
  - **Key Highlights:** Use bullet points to list the most important information or achievements.
  - **Impact/What This Means for Us:** Explain the significance of the update for employees.
  - **Call to Action/Next Steps:** Direct people to where they can find more information or what is expected of them.
  - **Closing:** A positive and forward-looking closing statement.

  The tone should be informative, engaging, and professional.
- **Customization Guidelines:** For mass emails, clarity and scannability are key. Use headings and bullet points to break up the text.
- **Real-World Usage Example:** The Head of IT needs to announce a planned system maintenance weekend. This prompt creates a clear, informative email that explains the what, why, when, and what to expect.

Meetings and Presentations

9. The Meeting Agenda Creator

- **Purpose:** To generate a structured and effective agenda for a meeting.
- Prompt Template:
  Create a detailed meeting agenda for a [Duration, e.g., 60-minute] meeting about [Meeting Topic]. The meeting objective is [Primary Goal of the Meeting].
  Attendees are: [List of Attendees and their Roles].
  The agenda should include:
  - Meeting Title, Date, Time, and Location/Link.
  - A list of required and optional attendees.
  - A brief statement of the meeting's objective.

    - Agenda items with a designated time allocation and a lead person for each topic. Example topics:
        - Welcome and Introductions (5 mins)
        - Review of Previous Action Items (10 mins)
        - [Main Topic 1 Discussion] (20 mins)
        - [Main Topic 2 Discussion] (15 mins)
        - Summary of New Action Items and Next Steps (10 mins)
    - A section for any pre-reading or preparation required.
- **Customization Guidelines:** Be realistic about time allocations. It's better to cover fewer topics well than many topics poorly.
- **Real-World Usage Example:** A manager is planning a weekly team check-in. This prompt helps create a structured agenda that keeps the meeting on track and productive.

10. The Presentation Outline Generator

- **Purpose:** To structure the content for a professional presentation.
- Prompt Template:
  Generate a presentation outline for a [Duration, e.g., 20-minute] presentation titled "[Presentation Title]". The target audience is [Audience Description, e.g., senior executives, a technical team, potential clients]. The main objective is to [Goal of the Presentation, e.g., get approval for a new project, explain the results of a recent analysis].
  The outline should include:
    - **Slide 1: Title Slide:** Title, presenter's name, date.
    - **Slide 2: Introduction/Hook:** A compelling opening and statement of purpose.
    - **Slide 3: Agenda:** What will be covered.
    - **Slides 4-7: Main Body:** Break down the core message

into 3-4 key points. For each point, list the main idea and supporting data or examples.
    - **Slide 8: Key Takeaways:** A summary of the most important messages.
    - **Slide 9: Call to Action/Next Steps:** What you want the audience to do.
    - **Slide 10: Q&A:** An invitation for questions.
- **Customization Guidelines:** Adjust the number of slides in the main body based on the complexity of your topic and the total time allotted.
- **Real-World Usage Example:** An analyst needs to present their quarterly findings to management. This prompt provides a logical flow for the presentation, ensuring all key points are covered.

11. Generating Talking Points for a Presentation

- **Purpose:** To create speaker notes or talking points for each slide of a presentation.
- Prompt Template:
  I am giving a presentation based on the following outline: [Paste your presentation outline here].
  For each section of the outline, generate concise and clear talking points. The tone should be [e.g., confident, informative, persuasive]. The audience is [Audience Description]. I want to emphasize [The Key Message you want to drive home].
  Focus on turning bullet points into conversational sentences. For each slide or section, provide 2-3 key sentences to deliver.
- **Customization Guidelines:** Pasting your actual outline provides the AI with the necessary context to generate relevant and coherent talking points.

- **Real-World Usage Example:** You have your presentation slides ready but need help articulating the key messages for each one. This prompt helps you develop a script that sounds natural and professional.

12. Brainstorming Questions for a Q&A Session

- **Purpose:** To prepare for potential questions from the audience after a presentation or meeting.
- Prompt Template:
  I am presenting on the topic of "[Presentation Topic]". My audience is [Audience Description], and my main argument is [Main Argument or Proposal].
  Generate a list of 15-20 potential questions that the audience might ask during the Q&A session. Categorize the questions into:
  - Clarifying questions (about the data or definitions).
  - Challenging questions (questioning my assumptions or conclusions).
  - Next-step questions (about implementation or future plans).
  - Financial questions (about budget or ROI).
- **Customization Guidelines:** The more context you provide about your topic and argument, the more relevant and insightful the generated questions will be.
- **Real-World Usage Example:** Before presenting a new project proposal to stakeholders, you use this prompt to anticipate tough questions about budget, timeline, and potential risks, allowing you to prepare thoughtful answers in advance.

13. The Meeting Minutes Template

- **Purpose:** To create a clear and professional summary of a meeting.

- Prompt Template:
  Act as a project manager. Based on the following raw notes from a meeting, generate formal meeting minutes.
  Raw Notes:
  - Meeting Topic: [Topic]
  - Date: [Date]
  - Attendees: [List of Names]
  - Discussed the new marketing campaign. John thinks we should focus on social media. Jane is concerned about the budget. Decision: we will move forward with a pilot program on two platforms. Action: John to create a project plan by Friday. Jane to provide a budget estimate by Wednesday. Next meeting is in two weeks.

  Format the output into a professional document with these sections:
  1. **Meeting Details:** (Topic, Date, Attendees)
  2. **Key Discussion Points:** (A brief, neutral summary of the conversation)
  3. **Decisions Made:** (A clear list of all decisions)
  4. **Action Items:** (A table with columns for Action, Owner, and Due Date)
- **Customization Guidelines:** Paste your own messy, raw notes into the template. The AI will organize and professionalize them for you.
- **Real-World Usage Example:** You were in charge of taking notes during a fast-paced brainstorming session. This prompt helps you quickly convert your jumbled notes into structured, shareable meeting minutes.

Reports, Analysis, and Documentation

14. The Executive Summary Generator

- **Purpose:** To summarize a long report or document for a senior leadership audience.
- Prompt Template:
  I have a long document about [Document Topic]. I need an executive summary of no more than [Word Count, e.g., 250 words]. The target audience is busy executives who need to understand the key findings and recommendations quickly. Here is the full text: [Paste the full text of your document here].
  The summary should cover:
  - The core problem or question addressed.
  - The main findings or analysis.
  - The key conclusions or recommendations.
  - The primary business impact or required decision.
- **Customization Guidelines:** For best results, paste the entire source text. If it's too long, provide a detailed summary of each section.
- **Real-World Usage Example:** You have written a 30-page market research report. You use this prompt to generate a concise one-page summary for the CEO and other executives.

15. The SWOT Analysis Framework

- **Purpose:** To analyze the Strengths, Weaknesses, Opportunities, and Threats for a project, product, or company.
- Prompt Template:
  Generate a SWOT analysis for [Subject of Analysis, e.g., a new software product, a proposed marketing strategy, our company's entry into a new market].
  Provide context:
  - **Product/Company:** [Brief description of the subject].
  - **Market:** [Description of the market environment and key

competitors].
    - **Goal:** [The strategic goal, e.g., to gain 10% market share in one year].

    Structure the output with four distinct sections:
    - **Strengths (Internal, Positive):** What are our inherent advantages?
    - **Weaknesses (Internal, Negative):** What are our internal limitations?
    - **Opportunities (External, Positive):** What external factors can we leverage?
    - **Threats (External, Negative):** What external factors could harm us?

  For each section, provide at least 4-5 bullet points.
- **Customization Guidelines:** The quality of the analysis depends heavily on the quality of the context you provide. Be detailed in your descriptions.
- **Real-World Usage Example:** A product manager is evaluating a new feature idea. This prompt helps them structure their thinking and present a balanced analysis to stakeholders.

16. The Project Plan Outline

- **Purpose:** To create a high-level project plan with phases, tasks, and milestones.
- Prompt Template:
  Create a project plan outline for [Project Name]. The project's main objective is [Project Goal]. The estimated duration is [e.g., 3 months].
  The plan should be broken down into the following phases:
  1. **Phase 1: Initiation & Planning:** (e.g., Define scope, assemble team, secure budget)

2. **Phase 2: Execution:** (e.g., Design, Development, Content Creation)
3. **Phase 3: Monitoring & Control:** (e.g., Weekly check-ins, budget tracking)
4. **Phase 4: Closure:** (e.g., Final delivery, retrospective)

For each phase, list the key tasks, major milestones, and estimated timelines. Also, identify potential risks and key stakeholders.

- **Customization Guidelines:** Adjust the phases to match your project's methodology (e.g., Agile sprints instead of waterfall phases).
- **Real-World Usage Example:** You have been assigned to lead a new website redesign project. This prompt helps you create the initial project charter and high-level plan to get stakeholder buy-in.

17. The Business Requirements Document (BRD) Outline

- **Purpose:** To outline the key sections of a document that details the business needs for a new project or system.
- Prompt Template:
  Generate an outline for a Business Requirements Document (BRD) for a new [System/Project Name, e.g., Customer Relationship Management (CRM) system]. The primary business problem this project solves is [Problem Statement]. The BRD outline should include standard sections like:
  - Introduction (Project Background, Business Objectives, Scope)
  - Business Process Analysis (Current State vs. Future State)
  - Functional Requirements (What the system must do, use categories like "User Management," "Reporting," "Data Entry")

- Non-Functional Requirements (e.g., Performance, Security, Usability)
    - Assumptions and Constraints
    - Glossary of Terms
- **Customization Guidelines:** This prompt provides a professional structure. You will need to fill in the detailed requirements for your specific project.
- **Real-World Usage Example:** A business analyst needs to document the requirements for a new internal software tool. This prompt creates a standard, comprehensive template to ensure nothing is missed.

18. The Data Analysis Request

- **Purpose:** To write a clear and specific request for a data analyst or team.
- Prompt Template:
  Draft a data analysis request for the analytics team.
    - **Business Question:** What is the primary question we are trying to answer? (e.g., "Which marketing channels drove the most valuable customers in Q3?")
    - **Hypothesis:** What do we believe the data will show? (e.g., "We hypothesize that email marketing has a higher ROI than social media ads.")
    - **Data Required:** What specific data sources, date ranges, and segments are needed? (e.g., "Sales data from July 1 to Sept 30, segmented by customer acquisition channel.")
    - **Desired Output:** What format should the analysis be in? (e.g., "A dashboard in our BI tool," "A spreadsheet with raw data and a summary tab," "A slide deck with key charts and insights.")
    - **Deadline:** [Date]
- **Customization Guidelines:** A clear hypothesis helps the

analyst understand your thinking and look for the right signals in the data.

- **Real-World Usage Example:** A marketing manager wants to understand campaign performance. This prompt helps them formulate a request that is specific enough for the data team to act on efficiently, avoiding back-and-forth communication.

19. Simplifying a Complex or Technical Topic

- **Purpose:** To explain a complex subject in simple, easy-to-understand terms for a non-technical audience.
- Prompt Template:
  Explain the concept of [Complex Topic, e.g., blockchain technology, machine learning, cloud computing] as you would to a [Target Audience, e.g., a marketing team, a new intern, the board of directors].
  Use an analogy to help clarify the main idea. Avoid jargon and technical terms. Focus on the "what" and "why it matters" rather than the "how it works" in minute detail. The explanation should be no more than [Word Count] words.
- **Customization Guidelines:** Specifying the audience is critical. An explanation for an intern will be different from one for a board of directors.
- **Real-World Usage Example:** An IT manager needs to explain the rationale for migrating to a new cloud-based server system to the entire company. This prompt helps them craft a clear, non-technical explanation for a company-wide email.

20. Creating a How-To Guide or Standard Operating Procedure (SOP)

- **Purpose:** To document a process in a step-by-step format.
- Prompt Template:

Write a Standard Operating Procedure (SOP) for the task of [Task Name, e.g., "Onboarding a New Client," "Processing a Customer Refund," "Publishing a Blog Post"].
The SOP should be written for a new employee and include the following sections:

- **Purpose:** A brief explanation of why this process is important.
- **Scope:** Who this process applies to.
- **Prerequisites:** What tools or information are needed before starting.
- **Step-by-Step Instructions:** A numbered list of clear, actionable steps. Start each step with a verb.
- **Verification:** How to confirm the task was completed successfully.
- **Escalation:** Who to contact if problems arise.

- **Customization Guidelines:** Be as granular as possible in the step-by-step instructions. What seems obvious to you may not be to a new team member.
- **Real-World Usage Example:** A team lead wants to standardize the way customer support tickets are handled. This prompt creates a clear SOP that can be used for training and ensuring consistent service quality.

21. The Professional Bio Writer

- **Purpose:** To write a professional biography for different lengths and platforms (e.g., LinkedIn, speaker bio, company website).
- Prompt Template:
  Write a professional bio for me, [Your Name], a [Your Job Title]. Key information:
  - **Experience:** [Number] years in [Your Industry].
  - **Expertise:** [Skill 1], [Skill 2], [Skill 3].

    - **Key Achievement:** [A notable accomplishment, e.g., "led a project that increased revenue by 15%"].
    - **Goal/Passion:** [What drives you professionally].

    Please generate three versions:
    1. A short, one-paragraph version for social media.
    2. A medium, two-paragraph version for a company website.
    3. A formal, third-person version for a conference speaker bio.
- **Customization Guidelines:** Providing a specific, quantifiable achievement makes your bio much more compelling.
- **Real-World Usage Example:** You've been asked to speak at an industry event and need to provide a bio for the event program. This prompt gives you multiple options to choose from.

22. The Stakeholder Communication Plan

- **Purpose:** To create a plan for keeping project stakeholders informed.
- Prompt Template:
  Create a stakeholder communication plan for [Project Name]. The key stakeholders are:
    - [Stakeholder 1, e.g., Project Sponsor]
    - [Stakeholder 2, e.g., Head of Engineering]
    - [Stakeholder 3, e.g., Marketing Team]

    For each stakeholder, create a plan that includes:
    - **Key Interest:** What do they care about most regarding this project?
    - **Communication Method:** (e.g., Email, Weekly Meeting, Dashboard).
    - **Frequency:** (e.g., Daily, Weekly, At Milestones).

    - **Content:** What information needs to be shared?
- **Customization Guidelines:** Be realistic about the frequency of communication. Over-communicating can be as problematic as under-communicating.
- **Real-World Usage Example:** A project manager is kicking off a complex project and uses this prompt to create a proactive communication plan, reducing surprises and ensuring alignment.

23. The Risk Assessment Matrix

- **Purpose:** To identify and categorize potential risks for a project.
- Prompt Template:
  Generate a risk assessment matrix for my project: [Project Name and Goal].
  Brainstorm potential risks in the following categories: Technical, Financial, and Operational.
  For each risk identified, assess its:
    - **Likelihood:** (High, Medium, Low).
    - **Impact:** (High, Medium, Low).
    - **Mitigation Strategy:** A brief plan to reduce the risk.

  Present the output in a structured list format.
- **Customization Guidelines:** Think about your specific project and add more context to help the AI brainstorm more relevant risks.
- **Real-World Usage Example:** Before finalizing a project budget and timeline, a team lead uses this prompt to identify potential roadblocks and plan for them in advance.

24. The Business Process Improvement Idea Generator

- **Purpose:** To brainstorm ways to make a current business process more efficient.

- Prompt Template:
  I want to improve our process for [Process Name, e.g., "handling customer support inquiries"].
  The current process is: [Briefly describe the current steps].
  The main problems are: [Problem 1, e.g., "it takes too long to respond"], [Problem 2, e.g., "different agents give different answers"].
  Brainstorm 5 ideas for improving this process. For each idea, explain how it addresses the problems and what the first step to implement it would be.
- **Customization Guidelines:** Clearly stating the current problems helps the AI focus on generating targeted and useful solutions.
- **Real-World Usage Example:** A manager wants to improve their team's efficiency and uses this prompt to generate actionable ideas for streamlining a key workflow.

25. The Elevator Pitch Refiner

- **Purpose:** To craft and refine a concise and compelling elevator pitch for a product, service, or idea.
- Prompt Template:
  Help me refine my elevator pitch for [Product/Idea Name].
  My current draft is: "[Paste your current pitch here]."
  The pitch should clearly and concisely answer these four questions:
  1. What is it?
  2. Who is it for?
  3. What problem does it solve?
  4. What makes it unique?

  Rewrite my draft into a smooth, 30-second pitch. Provide two different versions.
- **Customization Guidelines:** If you don't have a draft, just

describe your product or idea, and the AI will create a pitch from scratch.

- **Real-World Usage Example:** An entrepreneur is preparing for a networking event and uses this prompt to perfect a quick and memorable description of their startup.

Section 2: Marketing and Sales

This section focuses on prompts designed to create compelling marketing materials, develop sales strategies, and understand customer behavior.

Content and Copywriting

26. The AIDA Framework for Persuasive Copy

- **Purpose:** To write marketing or sales copy using the Attention, Interest, Desire, Action (AIDA) model.
- Prompt Template:
  Write a piece of marketing copy for [Product/Service Name], a [Brief description of the product/service]. The target audience is [Audience Description]. The goal is to get them to [Desired Action, e.g., sign up for a free trial, request a demo].
  Structure the copy using the AIDA framework:
  - **Attention:** A compelling headline or opening line to grab their attention.
  - **Interest:** Highlight interesting features or facts that appeal to their needs.
  - **Desire:** Explain the benefits and create an emotional connection. How will this make their life better?
  - **Action:** A clear and strong call to action.
- **Customization Guidelines:** The more you know about your audience's pain points, the more effective the "Interest" and

"Desire" sections will be.

- **Real-World Usage Example:** You are creating a landing page for a new project management software. This prompt helps you write persuasive copy that guides the visitor from initial interest to signing up.

27. The "Problem, Agitate, Solve" (PAS) Copywriting Formula

- **Purpose:** To create copy that resonates with a customer's pain points and presents a solution.
- Prompt Template:
  Write a [Type of Content, e.g., landing page section, email] for [Product/Service Name]. The audience is [Audience Description].
  Use the Problem, Agitate, Solve (PAS) formula:
  - **Problem:** Clearly state a problem the audience is experiencing.
  - **Agitate:** Elaborate on the problem. Why is it so frustrating? What are the consequences of not solving it?
  - **Solve:** Introduce your product/service as the clear solution to this problem.
- **Customization Guidelines:** This formula is powerful for audiences who are actively aware of their problem and seeking a solution.
- **Real-World Usage Example:** An e-commerce company selling ergonomic office furniture uses this prompt to write ad copy that highlights the problem of back pain from poor posture.

28. Generating Multiple Headlines for A/B Testing

- **Purpose:** To create several headline variations for a blog post, ad, or landing page to test which one performs best.

- Prompt Template:
  Generate 10 headline variations for an article about "[Article Topic]". The target audience is [Audience Description]. The article's main takeaway is [Main Takeaway].
  Create headlines that fit different styles:
  - Question-based (e.g., "Are You Making These Common Mistakes?")
  - Benefit-driven (e.g., "How to Achieve X in Half the Time")
  - Curiosity-driven (e.g., "The One Thing Top Performers Do Differently")
  - Direct and straightforward (e.g., "A Guide to X")
- **Customization Guidelines:** Specify the number of variations you want. You can also ask for headlines under a certain character count for social media or ads.
- **Real-World Usage Example:** A content marketer has written a blog post and uses this prompt to generate a list of potential titles to A/B test on their newsletter and social channels.

29. The Product Description Writer

- **Purpose:** To write clear, concise, and persuasive descriptions for e-commerce products or services.
- Prompt Template:
  Write a product description for "[Product Name]". It is a [Product Category] for [Target Customer].
  Key features:
  - [Feature 1]
  - [Feature 2]
  - [Feature 3]

    Translate each feature into a customer benefit. For example, "Feature: 10-hour battery life" becomes "Benefit: Work all day on a single charge without worrying about finding an outlet."The description should include:

- A short, engaging introductory paragraph.
- A bulleted list of 3-5 key benefits.
- Specifications (e.g., dimensions, materials, technical specs).

The tone should be [e.g., enthusiastic, professional, minimalist].

- **Customization Guidelines:** Providing a list of features is essential. The AI's strength is in translating those features into compelling benefits.
- **Real-World Usage Example:** An online store owner needs to write descriptions for a new line of office technology. This prompt helps create benefit-oriented descriptions that drive sales.

30. The Call to Action (CTA) Generator

- **Purpose:** To create clear and compelling calls to action for buttons, links, and ads.
- Prompt Template:
  Generate 10 different Call to Action (CTA) phrases for a [Button/Link] on a [Webpage/Email/Ad]. The goal is to get the user to [Desired Action, e.g., download an ebook, start a free trial, buy now].
  The context is a page about [Page Topic]. Create CTAs that are:
  - Benefit-oriented (e.g., "Get Your Free Guide")
  - Action-oriented (e.g., "Start Your Trial")
  - Urgency-driven (e.g., "Claim Your Spot Now")
- **Customization Guidelines:** Specify the context. A CTA on a pricing page will be different from one at the end of a blog post.
- **Real-World Usage Example:** A marketer is designing a new

landing page and needs effective text for the main conversion button. This prompt provides multiple options to test.

31. The "Features to Benefits" Translator

- **Purpose:** To turn a list of technical product features into customer-centric benefits.
- Prompt Template:
  I have a product with the following features. For each feature, write a clear benefit statement that explains its value to the customer.
  - **Feature:** [e.g., "Uses a proprietary encryption algorithm"]
  - **Feature:** [e.g., "Integrates with over 50 third-party apps"]
  - **Feature:** [e.g., "Built on a scalable cloud infrastructure"]

  The format for each should be: "**Feature:** [Feature Name] --> **Benefit:** [Benefit Statement]"
- **Customization Guidelines:** This is a fantastic exercise to shift from a product-centric to a customer-centric mindset in your marketing.
- **Real-World Usage Example:** A product marketing manager uses this prompt to create copy for a new landing page, ensuring the language focuses on "what's in it for the customer."

32. The Case Study Outline

- **Purpose:** To structure a compelling customer success story or case study.
- Prompt Template:
  Create an outline for a case study about our client, [Client Name], who used our product, [Product Name], to achieve [Result].
  The outline should follow a classic narrative structure:

1. **Title:** A compelling, benefit-oriented headline.
2. **Executive Summary:** A brief overview of the story.
3. **The Client:** A short introduction to the client's business.
4. **The Challenge:** What problem were they facing before they used our product?
5. **The Solution:** How did our product help them address the challenge?
6. **The Results:** What specific, quantifiable outcomes did they achieve? (e.g., "20% increase in productivity," "50% reduction in costs").
7. **Client Quote:** A powerful testimonial.

- **Customization Guidelines:** The most important part is the "Results" section. Use hard numbers and metrics whenever possible to make the case study credible.
- **Real-World Usage Example:** After a successful client project, a B2B company uses this prompt to create a case study for their website, providing social proof to potential new customers.

Social Media and Campaigns

33. The Social Media Content Calendar

- **Purpose:** To plan a week's worth of social media content around a specific theme or goal.
- Prompt Template:
  Create a one-week social media content calendar for [Company/Brand] on [Platform, e.g., LinkedIn, Twitter, Instagram]. Our target audience is [Audience Description]. The theme for the week is [Weekly Theme, e.g., "Productivity Tips," "Cybersecurity Awareness"].
  For each day (Monday to Friday), provide a post idea that includes:

    - **Post Topic:** A brief description of the content.
    - **Post Format:** (e.g., Text post, Image with caption, Poll, Link to blog post).
    - **Draft Caption:** A ready-to-use caption.
    - **Hashtags:** A list of 3-5 relevant hashtags.
- **Customization Guidelines:** Providing a clear theme helps the AI generate a coherent and focused content plan.
- **Real-World Usage Example:** A B2B technology company wants to plan its LinkedIn content for a week. This prompt helps them create a structured calendar with engaging post ideas.

34. The Ad Campaign Concept Brainstorm

- **Purpose:** To generate creative concepts for a new advertising campaign.
- Prompt Template:
  Brainstorm 5 creative concepts for an ad campaign for [Product/Service]. The target audience is [Audience Description]. The Unique Selling Proposition (USP) is [Product's Main Differentiator]. The campaign will run on [Channels, e.g., Facebook, Google Search, YouTube].
  For each concept, provide:
    - **Campaign Title/Slogan:** A catchy name.
    - **Core Message:** The main idea in one sentence.
    - **Visual Idea:** A brief description of the imagery or video concept.
    - **Key Channels:** Where this concept would work best.
- **Customization Guidelines:** The USP is the most important piece of context. It's what makes your product different and is the foundation of a good campaign.
- **Real-World Usage Example:** A marketing team is launching a new eco-friendly office supply product and needs fresh

ideas for their digital ad campaign. This prompt provides several distinct creative directions to explore.

35. Writing Ad Copy Variations

- **Purpose:** To generate different versions of ad copy for A/B testing.
- Prompt Template:
  Write 5 variations of ad copy for a [Platform, e.g., Google Search Ad, Facebook Ad].
  - **Product:** [Product Name]
  - **Target Audience:** [Audience Description]
  - **Key Benefit:** [The single most important benefit to highlight].
  - **Call to Action:** [Desired Action, e.g., "Learn More," "Shop Now"].

  For Google Search Ads, provide a Headline 1, Headline 2, and a Description. For Facebook Ads, provide a main text, a headline, and a link description.
- **Customization Guidelines:** Specify the platform to ensure the copy adheres to character limits and best practices for that channel.
- **Real-World Usage Example:** A digital marketer is setting up a new Google Ads campaign and uses this prompt to quickly generate multiple ad variations to test for the highest click-through rate.

36. The Email Newsletter Outline

- **Purpose:** To structure the content for a weekly or monthly newsletter.
- Prompt Template:
  Create an outline for our upcoming [Weekly/Monthly] newsletter. The target audience is [Audience Description].

The theme for this issue is [Newsletter Theme].
The newsletter should include these sections:

- **Subject Line:** Suggest 3 options.
- **Opening:** A brief, personal introduction.
- **Main Feature:** An article or update on [Main Topic].
- **Quick Tips/Links:** 2-3 bullet points with useful tips or links to external resources.
- **Company News:** A short update about [e.g., a new product, an upcoming event].
- **Call to Action:** What is the one thing we want readers to do?

- **Customization Guidelines:** A clear theme makes the newsletter feel cohesive rather than like a random collection of links.
- **Real-World Usage Example:** A consulting firm uses this prompt to plan their monthly client newsletter, ensuring it provides value and keeps their brand top-of-mind.

37. The A/B Test Hypothesis Generator

- **Purpose:** To generate clear, testable hypotheses for A/B testing.
- Prompt Template:
  I want to A/B test the [Element, e.g., "headline on our landing page," "color of our 'Buy Now' button"].
  The original version is [Description of Version A].
  My proposed change is [Description of Version B].
  The key metric I want to improve is [Metric, e.g., "click-through rate," "conversion rate"].
  Generate a formal hypothesis for this test using the format:
  "By changing [Element] from [Version A] to [Version B], we will [increase/decrease] [Metric] because [Your Rationale]."
- **Customization Guidelines:** The "because" part is the most

important. It forces you to articulate why you think the change will work, which leads to better testing ideas.

- **Real-World Usage Example:** A marketer wants to test a new headline. This prompt helps them frame the experiment with a clear hypothesis, making it easier to analyze the results.

38. The Social Media Poll and Question Idea Generator

- **Purpose:** To create engaging questions and polls for social media to boost interaction.
- Prompt Template:
  Generate 10 engaging poll questions for our [Platform, e.g., LinkedIn, Twitter] audience. Our audience consists of [Audience Description]. Our industry is [Your Industry]. The questions should be a mix of:
  - Industry trends (e.g., "Which of these technologies will have the biggest impact in 2025?").
  - Work habits (e.g., "Remote, hybrid, or in-office: what's your preference?").
  - "This or that" questions related to our field.
- **Customization Guidelines:** Keep poll options simple (2-4 choices) to maximize participation.
- **Real-World Usage Example:** A social media manager uses this prompt to quickly generate a week's worth of interactive content to increase their audience engagement rate.

Strategy and Research

39. The Customer Persona Generator

- **Purpose:** To create a detailed profile of an ideal customer to inform marketing and product development.
- Prompt Template:
  Create a detailed customer persona for our ideal client. Our

product is [Product/Service Name], which helps customers [Solve a specific problem].
The persona should be for a fictional individual named [e.g., "Marketing Maria," "Startup Steve"]. Include the following details:

  - **Demographics:** Job Title, Industry, Company Size, Age Range.
  - **Goals:** What are their primary professional goals?
  - **Challenges/Pain Points:** What obstacles do they face in their work?
  - **Watering Holes:** Where do they get their information? (e.g., specific blogs, publications, social media platforms).
  - **A "Day in the Life" description.**
  - A quote that summarizes their main motivation.
- **Customization Guidelines:** Base the persona on real customer data or interviews if you have them. The more grounded in reality, the more useful it will be.
- **Real-World Usage Example:** A software company is developing a new feature and uses this prompt to create a persona that helps the entire team stay focused on the user's needs.

40. The Competitive Analysis Summary

- **Purpose:** To analyze and summarize the strengths and weaknesses of key competitors.
- Prompt Template:
  I am conducting a competitive analysis for my company, [Your Company Name]. We operate in the [Industry] market. Our key competitors are [Competitor 1], [Competitor 2], and [Competitor 3].
  Based on publicly available information (e.g., their websites, reviews, social media), provide a summary that answers the

following for each competitor:
  - What is their primary product offering and unique selling proposition?
  - Who is their target audience?
  - What is their pricing model?
  - What are their commonly cited strengths and weaknesses in customer reviews?
  - What is their main marketing strategy or channel?
- **Customization Guidelines:** The AI can only use publicly available information. For a deeper analysis, you would need to provide it with specific internal data or reports.
- **Real-World Usage Example:** A startup is entering a crowded market and uses this prompt to get a high-level overview of the competitive landscape to identify potential gaps and opportunities.

41. The Market Research Questions Generator

- **Purpose:** To develop a list of questions for a customer survey or interview.
- Prompt Template:
  Generate a list of 15 market research questions for a [Survey/Interview] with [Target Audience]. We are exploring a new product idea: [Brief description of the product idea].
  The goal of the research is to understand:
  - The severity of the problem our product aims to solve.
  - Their current solutions or workarounds.
  - Their willingness to pay for a new solution.
  - Key features they would find most valuable.

  Categorize the questions into sections like "Current Habits," "Pain Points," and "Product Concept Feedback."
- **Customization Guidelines:** Ask open-ended questions ("How do you currently...") rather than simple yes/no

questions to get richer insights.

- **Real-World Usage Example:** A product manager is considering a new mobile app concept and uses this prompt to create a discussion guide for initial customer discovery interviews.

42. The Sales Script Outline

- **Purpose:** To create a structured script for a sales call or demo.
- Prompt Template:
  Create a sales script outline for a [e.g., 15-minute discovery call] with a potential customer. The product is [Product Name]. The customer is typically a [Job Title] in the [Industry] industry. Their main pain point is [Common Pain Point].
  The script should follow these stages:
  1. **Opening:** Introduction and rapport-building.
  2. **Agenda Setting:** Briefly state the call's purpose.
  3. **Discovery:** A list of open-ended questions to understand their specific needs and challenges.
  4. **Value Proposition:** A concise statement connecting their problem to our solution.
  5. **Next Steps:** Clearly define the next action (e.g., scheduling a full demo, sending a proposal).
- **Customization Guidelines:** The discovery questions are the most important part. They should be designed to get the prospect talking about their problems.
- **Real-World Usage Example:** A sales development representative (SDR) needs a consistent framework for their initial calls with new leads. This prompt provides a professional and effective script structure.

43. The Value Proposition Canvas

- **Purpose:** To map out your product's value in relation to customer needs.
- Prompt Template:
  Help me fill out a Value Proposition Canvas.
  My Product: [Product Name and brief description].
  My Customer Segment: [Description of the target customer].
  Generate bullet points for the following sections:
  - **Customer Jobs:** What tasks are they trying to get done?
  - **Customer Pains:** What annoys them or creates problems?
  - **Customer Gains:** What outcomes and benefits do they want?
  - **Products & Services:** (This is just my product).
  - **Pain Relievers:** How does my product alleviate customer pains?
  - **Gain Creators:** How does my product produce customer gains?
- **Customization Guidelines:** This framework is a powerful tool for achieving product-market fit. Be honest about your customer's real pains and gains.
- **Real-World Usage Example:** A startup team uses this prompt in a workshop to ensure their product features are directly tied to the needs of their target customers.

44. The Customer Journey Map Outline

- **Purpose:** To outline the stages a customer goes through when interacting with your company.
- Prompt Template:
  Create a high-level customer journey map outline for a customer of [Your Company/Product]. The journey is for a [Customer Persona] who wants to [Achieve a specific goal]. The map should include these stages:

1. **Awareness:** How do they first learn about us?
2. **Consideration:** How do they evaluate our solution?
3. **Purchase/Conversion:** What are the steps to become a customer?
4. **Service/Onboarding:** What is their initial experience like?
5. **Loyalty/Advocacy:** What keeps them engaged and turns them into a fan?

For each stage, brainstorm the customer's actions, feelings, and potential pain points.

- **Customization Guidelines:** This is a strategic exercise. The goal is to identify friction points and opportunities to improve the customer experience at every stage.
- **Real-World Usage Example:** A marketing team uses this prompt to visualize their customer experience from end to end, identifying gaps where they might be losing potential customers.

45. The Sales Objection Handler

- **Purpose:** To prepare thoughtful responses to common sales objections.
- Prompt Template:
  Act as a sales coach. I sell [Product/Service]. Here are three common objections my sales team hears:
  1. "It's too expensive."
  2. "We're already using a competitor's product."
  3. "I don't have time to think about this right now."

  For each objection, provide a framework for a response that:
  - Acknowledges and validates their concern.
  - Re-frames the issue around value or a different perspective.

    - Asks a question to keep the conversation going.
- **Customization Guidelines:** The best objection handling shifts the conversation from a "yes/no" to a discussion about value and priorities.
- **Real-World Usage Example:** A sales manager uses this prompt to create a training document for new hires, equipping them with proven strategies for handling tough conversations.

46. The Lead Magnet Idea Generator

- **Purpose:** To brainstorm ideas for valuable content (lead magnets) to offer in exchange for a user's email address.
- Prompt Template:
  Brainstorm 10 lead magnet ideas for my website. My company is [Company Name] and we sell [Product/Service] to [Target Audience].
  The ideas should be for different formats, such as:
    - Checklists
    - Ebooks or guides
    - Templates
    - Webinar recordings
    - Resource libraries
    - Short email courses
- **Customization Guidelines:** A great lead magnet solves a very specific, high-value problem for your target audience quickly.
- **Real-World Usage Example:** A digital marketing agency wants to increase its email subscribers. They use this prompt to generate ideas like a "10-Point Website SEO Checklist" or a "Client Proposal Template."

47. The SEO Keyword Research

- **Purpose:** To generate a list of potential keywords for a website or blog post.
- Prompt Template:
  Act as an SEO specialist. My website is about [Main Topic, e.g., "small business accounting software"]. My target audience is [Audience Description].
  Generate a list of 20 keywords, categorized as follows:
  - **Head Terms (High Volume, Broad):** e.g., "accounting software"
  - **Body Keywords (More Specific):** e.g., "best accounting software for small business"
  - **Long-Tail Keywords (Very Specific, Question-Based):** e.g., "how to choose accounting software for a freelancer"
- **Customization Guidelines:** While AI can generate great ideas, always validate the keywords with a dedicated SEO tool to check for search volume and competition.
- **Real-World Usage Example:** A content strategist is planning the content for a new website and uses this prompt to build a foundational keyword list for their core pages and blog topics.

Section 3: Content Creators and Writers

This section provides templates for writers, editors, and content creators to streamline research, outlining, drafting, and editing processes.

Ideation and Outlining

48. The Blog Post Idea Generator

- **Purpose:** To brainstorm a list of potential topics for a blog or content hub.

- Prompt Template:
  Generate 15 blog post ideas for a blog about [Main Subject, e.g., "remote work productivity"]. The target audience is [Audience Description, e.g., "freelancers and small business owners"]. The goal of the blog is to [e.g., "drive traffic to our project management software"].
  The ideas should cover different formats:
    - "How-to" guides
    - Listicles (e.g., "7 Ways to...")
    - Thought leadership pieces (e.g., "The Future of...")
    - Case studies or success stories
    - Common mistakes to avoid
- **Customization Guidelines:** The more specific you are about your audience and business goals, the more relevant the topic suggestions will be.
- **Real-World Usage Example:** A content manager for a SaaS company uses this prompt to fill their content calendar with relevant and engaging topics for the next quarter.

49. The Article Outline Creator

- **Purpose:** To create a logical structure for an article or blog post before writing.
- Prompt Template:
  Create a detailed outline for a blog post with the title "[Blog Post Title]". The target audience is [Audience Description]. The main goal of the article is to teach them how to [Core Message of the Article].
  The outline should include:
    - **Introduction:** A hook, a statement of the problem, and a brief overview of the solution.
    - **Section 1: [Main Point 1]:** With 2-3 supporting bullet points.

    - **Section 2: [Main Point 2]:** With 2-3 supporting bullet points.
    - **Section 3: [Main Point 3]:** With 2-3 supporting bullet points.
    - **Conclusion:** A summary of the key takeaways and a clear call to action.
- **Customization Guidelines:** You can specify the number of main sections you want. For a more detailed outline, ask the AI to include potential data points or examples for each bullet point.
- **Real-World Usage Example:** A freelance writer receives an assignment and uses this prompt to create a comprehensive outline to send to the client for approval before starting the draft.

50. The "They Ask, You Answer" Content Framework

- **Purpose:** To generate content ideas by focusing on the questions your target audience is asking.
- Prompt Template:
  My business sells [Product/Service]. My target customer is [Customer Persona]. What are the top 10 most common questions this person would type into a search engine about [The problem my product solves]?
  Frame the questions exactly as they would ask them. For each question, suggest a blog post title that directly answers it.
- **Customization Guidelines:** This prompt is excellent for generating SEO-friendly content ideas that address real user intent.
- **Real-World Usage Example:** A company that sells accounting software uses this prompt to identify common questions like "how to choose accounting software for a

small business" and "what is the difference between cash and accrual accounting," turning them into valuable blog content.

51. The Content Brief Outline

- **Purpose:** To create a clear brief for a freelance writer or team member.
- Prompt Template:
  Create a content brief for an article titled "[Article Title]".
  - **Primary Keyword:** [Main SEO keyword]
  - **Target Audience:** [Audience Description]
  - **Goal of the Article:** [e.g., "Educate the reader on X," "Drive sign-ups for Y"]
  - **Key Talking Points:**
    - [Point 1]
    - [Point 2]
    - [Point 3]
  - **Tone of Voice:** [e.g., "Professional but approachable"]
  - **Call to Action:** [What should the reader do at the end?]
- **Customization Guidelines:** A good brief provides clarity and constraints, which helps writers produce better content faster.
- **Real-World Usage Example:** A content manager assigns a blog post to a freelancer and uses this prompt to generate a comprehensive brief, reducing back-and-forth and ensuring the final draft meets expectations.

52. The "Hook" Generator for Introductions

- **Purpose:** To brainstorm compelling opening lines or "hooks" for an article or video script.
- Prompt Template:
  I'm writing an article about [Topic]. The main point is [Main

Argument]. Generate 5 different hooks for the introduction:

1. A surprising statistic.
2. A relatable anecdote or story.
3. A thought-provoking question.
4. A bold statement.
5. A historical reference.

- **Customization Guidelines:** A strong hook is essential for grabbing the reader's attention in the first few seconds.
- **Real-World Usage Example:** A blogger is struggling to start a new article. They use this prompt to generate several creative opening ideas, helping them overcome writer's block.

53. The FAQ Section Creator

- **Purpose:** To generate a list of frequently asked questions (FAQs) for a product, service, or topic.
- Prompt Template:
  Generate a list of 10 frequently asked questions (FAQs) about [Product/Service/Topic, e.g., "our new project management software"]. The target audience is [Audience Description].
  For each question, provide a concise and clear answer.
- **Customization Guidelines:** Think about the common points of confusion or hesitation a potential customer might have.
- **Real-World Usage Example:** A company launches a new product and uses this prompt to create a comprehensive FAQ section for the website, reducing the number of support tickets.

Drafting and Writing Assistance

54. The Paragraph Expander

- **Purpose:** To take a simple idea or bullet point and expand it into a full, well-written paragraph.

- Prompt Template:
  Expand the following bullet point into a clear and detailed paragraph of about [Word Count, e.g., 100 words] for a [Type of Document, e.g., blog post, business report].
  Bullet Point: "[Your bullet point here. e.g., 'Regularly updating software is crucial for security.']"
  The tone should be [e.g., informative, professional, persuasive].
- **Customization Guidelines:** Provide context about the document type and tone to ensure the expanded paragraph fits seamlessly with the rest of your writing.
- **Real-World Usage Example:** You have an outline with key ideas but are struggling to flesh out the content. You use this prompt to turn your bullet points into complete paragraphs one by one.

55. The Content Repurposer

- **Purpose:** To adapt a piece of existing content into a different format.
- Prompt Template:
  I have a blog post on the topic of "[Topic]". I want to repurpose it into a [New Format, e.g., a LinkedIn post, a Twitter thread, a short video script].
  Here is the text of the blog post: [Paste the full text here].
  For the new format, please:
    - Extract the 3-5 most important key takeaways.
    - Rewrite them in a concise and engaging style suitable for [Platform].
    - For a Twitter thread, break it into numbered tweets. For a video script, write it as a voiceover.
- **Customization Guidelines:** Pasting the full source text gives the AI the best context for an accurate and effective

adaptation.

- **Real-World Usage Example:** A content marketer wants to maximize the reach of a popular blog post. They use this prompt to create a LinkedIn article, a series of tweets, and a script for a short informational video from the original content.

56. Overcoming Writer's Block

- **Purpose:** To generate ideas or a starting point when you're stuck.
- Prompt Template:
  I am writing a [Type of Content, e.g., an article, a report] about [Topic]. I am stuck on the [Section, e.g., introduction, a specific chapter]. My goal for this section is to [Goal of the section].
  Can you give me three different ways I could start this section? Provide a short opening paragraph for each approach.
- **Customization Guidelines:** Be specific about where you are stuck and what you are trying to achieve with that section.
- **Real-World Usage Example:** A writer is staring at a blank page, unable to write the introduction to an article about the future of artificial intelligence. This prompt gives them three concrete starting paragraphs to choose from, breaking the creative logjam.

57. The Metaphor and Analogy Generator

- **Purpose:** To find simple analogies or metaphors to explain a complex idea.
- Prompt Template:
  Generate 5 simple metaphors or analogies to explain the concept of [Complex Concept, e.g., "an API (Application Programming Interface)"]. The target audience is non-

technical.

- **Customization Guidelines:** A good analogy connects an abstract concept to a familiar, everyday experience.
- **Real-World Usage Example:** A writer is trying to explain cloud computing in a blog post and uses this prompt to generate analogies like "it's like renting storage space instead of buying your own warehouse."

58. The "Show, Don't Tell" Rewriter

- **Purpose:** To transform a generic, "telling" statement into a more descriptive and engaging "showing" statement.
- Prompt Template:
  Rewrite the following "telling" sentence into a "showing" sentence that is more descriptive and vivid.
  Telling Sentence: "[e.g., 'The software was very efficient.']"
  Provide a new version that describes the efficiency in action.
- **Customization Guidelines:** This is a core skill in creative and persuasive writing. The goal is to paint a picture in the reader's mind.
- **Real-World Usage Example:** A copywriter wants to make a product description more compelling. They turn "Our customer support is great" into "Imagine getting a friendly, expert reply to your question in under 5 minutes, 24/7."

59. The Research Assistant

- **Purpose:** To gather initial information or find sources on a specific topic.
- Prompt Template:
  Act as a research assistant. I am writing an article about [Topic]. Please provide me with:
  - A brief summary of the topic.
  - A list of 5 key sub-topics I should cover.

    - A list of 3-5 credible sources (like major publications, research institutions, or foundational books) where I can learn more.
- **Customization Guidelines:** Always critically evaluate and fact-check the information provided by the AI. Use its output as a starting point for your own research, not a final answer.
- **Real-World Usage Example:** A writer is assigned an unfamiliar topic. They use this prompt to quickly get up to speed and find a direction for their research.

Editing and Proofreading

60. The Proofreader and Grammar Checker

- **Purpose:** To check a piece of text for spelling errors, grammatical mistakes, and typos.
- Prompt Template:
  Please proofread the following text for any spelling, grammar, and punctuation errors. List the corrections in a clear before-and-after format. Also, provide a clean, corrected version of the full text.
  Text to Proofread:
  "[Paste your text here.]"
- **Customization Guidelines:** This is a straightforward but highly effective prompt. It's often more reliable than standard word processor spell checkers.
- **Real-World Usage Example:** Before sending an important email or publishing a blog post, you run the text through this prompt for a final quality check.

61. The Tone and Style Editor

- **Purpose:** To rewrite a piece of text to match a specific tone or style.
- Prompt Template:

Rewrite the following text to have a more [Desired Tone, e.g., professional, conversational, confident, empathetic] tone.
The target audience is [Audience Description].
Original Text:
"[Paste your text here.]"
Keep the core message the same, but adjust the wording, sentence structure, and style to better suit the intended tone.

- **Customization Guidelines:** Be explicit about the desired tone. Words like "professional" can mean different things, so you might add "formal and academic" or "friendly and approachable" for more clarity.
- **Real-World Usage Example:** You've written a draft of a customer service response that sounds too robotic. You use this prompt to rewrite it in a more empathetic and human tone.

62. The "Make it More Concise" Editor

- **Purpose:** To shorten a piece of text by removing unnecessary words and sentences.
- Prompt Template:
  Make the following text more concise. Reduce the word count by approximately [Percentage, e.g., 30%] without losing the key information or meaning. Remove filler words, jargon, and redundant phrases.
  Text to Edit:
  "[Paste your text here.]"
- **Customization Guidelines:** Providing a target percentage for reduction helps the AI understand the level of conciseness required.
- **Real-World Usage Example:** You have written a project update that is too long and dense. This prompt helps you create a shorter, more impactful version that busy

stakeholders are more likely to read.

63. The SEO Content Optimizer

- **Purpose:** To analyze a piece of text and suggest improvements for search engine optimization.
- Prompt Template:
  I have an article about "[Article Topic]". The primary target keyword is "[Your Keyword]". Please act as an SEO expert and analyze the following text.
  Article Text:
  "[Paste your text here.]"
  Provide recommendations for:
  - Where to naturally include the primary keyword (if it's missing).
  - A list of 5-7 related secondary keywords (LSI keywords) that I should include.
  - Suggestions for a meta title (under 60 characters) and a meta description (under 160 characters) that include the primary keyword.
  - Suggestions for improving headers (H1, H2) for clarity and keyword relevance.
- **Customization Guidelines:** Providing a clear primary keyword is essential for this prompt to work effectively.
- **Real-World Usage Example:** A blogger wants to ensure their new article has the best chance of ranking on Google. They use this prompt to get actionable SEO feedback before publishing.

64. The Style Guide Conformer

- **Purpose:** To edit a piece of text to ensure it conforms to a specific style guide.
- Prompt Template:

Please edit the following text to conform to the [Style Guide Name, e.g., "AP Stylebook," "Chicago Manual of Style"]. Pay special attention to [Specific Rule, e.g., "the use of the Oxford comma," "rules for capitalizing headlines," "number formatting"].
Text to Edit:
"[Paste your text here.]"

- **Customization Guidelines:** If you have an internal company style guide, you can paste its key rules into the prompt for the AI to follow.
- **Real-World Usage Example:** An editor for a multi-author blog uses this prompt to quickly standardize submissions, ensuring every published article is consistent in style.

Section 4: Developers and Technical Professionals

This section includes prompts designed to assist with coding, documentation, debugging, and other technical tasks.

Code Generation and Debugging

65. The Code Snippet Generator

- **Purpose:** To generate a piece of code to perform a specific function.
- Prompt Template:
  Write a function in [Programming Language, e.g., Python, JavaScript] that [Description of the function's purpose, e.g., "takes a list of numbers and returns the average"].
  The function should be named [FunctionName]. Include comments in the code to explain the logic. Provide an example of how to call the function and what the expected output is.
- **Customization Guidelines:** Be very specific about the

inputs and outputs. The more precise your description, the more accurate the generated code will be.

- **Real-World Usage Example:** A developer is working on a new feature and needs a helper function to parse a date string. They use this prompt to generate the function quickly instead of writing it from scratch.

66. The Code Debugger and Explainer

- **Purpose:** To find errors in a piece of code and get an explanation of the problem.
- Prompt Template:
  I have a piece of [Programming Language] code that is not working as expected. It is supposed to [Expected Behavior], but instead, it is [Actual, Incorrect Behavior].
  Here is the code:
  [Paste your code here]

  Please identify the bug, explain why it is happening, and provide the corrected code.
- **Customization Guidelines:** In addition to the code, describe the error message you are receiving, if any. This gives the AI a critical clue for debugging.
- **Real-World Usage Example:** A junior developer is stuck on a bug that is causing their application to crash. They use this prompt to get a second opinion and a clear explanation of the mistake.

67. The Code Refactoring Assistant

- **Purpose:** To improve the quality and efficiency of existing code without changing its functionality.
- Prompt Template:
  Act as a senior software engineer. Please refactor the

following [Programming Language] code to make it more efficient, readable, and adhere to best practices (e.g., DRY principle, clear variable names).
Here is the code to refactor:
[Paste your code here]

Provide the refactored code and a brief explanation of the key improvements you made.

- **Customization Guidelines:** You can specify particular goals for the refactoring, such as "improve performance" or "make it more modular."
- **Real-World Usage Example:** A developer has a function that works but is messy and difficult to maintain. They use this prompt to get a cleaner, more professional version of the code.

68. The Regular Expression (Regex) Generator

- **Purpose:** To create complex regular expressions for pattern matching in text.
- Prompt Template:
  Generate a regular expression (regex) that can be used to [Describe the pattern you want to match]. For example:
  - "validate an email address."
  - "extract all URLs from a block of text."
  - "find all phone numbers in a standard US format."

  Provide the regex pattern and explain each part of it. Also, give an example of a string it would match and one it would not match.
- **Customization Guidelines:** Regex syntax is notoriously complex. Be extremely clear and provide examples of the text you are trying to match.
- **Real-World Usage Example:** A data scientist needs to clean

a dataset by extracting all zip codes from a free-text address field. This prompt generates the precise regex needed for the task.

69. The API Call Example Generator

- **Purpose:** To create an example of how to make an API call in a specific language.
- Prompt Template:
  Provide an example of how to make a [GET/POST] request to the following API endpoint in [Programming Language, e.g., Python using the 'requests' library, JavaScript using 'fetch'].
  Endpoint URL: [URL]
  Headers: [e.g., Content-Type: application/json, Authorization: Bearer TOKEN]
  Request Body (for POST):
  {
    "key": "value"
  }

  The code should handle the response and print the status code and the JSON body.
- **Customization Guidelines:** Provide the exact details from the API documentation you are using.
- **Real-World Usage Example:** A developer is integrating a third-party service and uses this prompt to quickly generate the boilerplate code for making an API request.

70. The Unit Test Case Generator

- **Purpose:** To generate unit test cases for a given function or method.
- Prompt Template:

I have the following function in [Programming Language]:
[Paste your function here]

Generate a set of unit test cases for this function using the [Testing Framework, e.g., 'pytest' for Python, 'Jest' for JavaScript]. The tests should cover:
  - A standard, expected input.
  - Edge cases (e.g., empty inputs, null values, zero).
  - An invalid input that should raise an error.

- **Customization Guidelines:** Providing the function signature and a clear description of its purpose will result in more thorough and relevant test cases.
- **Real-World Usage Example:** A developer has just finished writing a new function and uses this prompt to quickly generate a suite of tests to ensure its reliability before committing the code.

71. The SQL Query Writer

- **Purpose:** To write a SQL query based on a plain English description of the desired data.
- Prompt Template:
  Act as a data analyst. I have a database with two tables:
  1. customers (columns: customer_id, name, join_date)
  2. orders (columns: order_id, customer_id, order_date, amount)

  Write a SQL query that [Your plain English request, e.g., "finds the total amount spent by each customer who joined in the last year, ordered by the total amount"].
- **Customization Guidelines:** Clearly defining your table schema (table names and column names) is essential for the AI to generate an accurate query.
- **Real-World Usage Example:** A business analyst needs to

pull a specific report from the company database but isn't a SQL expert. They use this prompt to translate their question into a functional query.

72. The Git Commit Message Generator

- **Purpose:** To write a clear and well-formatted Git commit message.
- Prompt Template:
  I just made some changes to the codebase. Here is a summary of what I did:
  [Briefly describe your changes in plain English, e.g., "I fixed the bug on the login page that was causing a crash when the user entered a wrong password. I also added more detailed error logging."]
  Please generate a conventional commit message for this change. The message should have a type (e.g., feat, fix, docs), a short description, and a longer body explaining the changes.
- **Customization Guidelines:** The more context you provide about the "why" behind your changes, the better the commit message will be.
- **Real-World Usage Example:** A developer uses this prompt to maintain a clean and professional Git history, making it easier for teammates to understand the evolution of the codebase.

73. The Pseudocode Writer

- **Purpose:** To outline the logic of an algorithm or program in plain, language-agnostic pseudocode.
- Prompt Template:
  I want to write a program that [Describe the goal of the program, e.g., "sorts a list of items using the bubble sort

algorithm"].
Please write out the logic for this program in clear, step-by-step pseudocode before I start writing the actual code in [Programming Language].

- **Customization Guidelines:** Pseudocode is great for planning. It lets you focus on the logic without getting bogged down in the syntax of a specific language.
- **Real-World Usage Example:** A computer science student is learning about new algorithms and uses this prompt to understand the logic of an algorithm before trying to implement it.

74. The Command-Line Command Generator

- **Purpose:** To generate the correct command-line syntax for tools like git, docker, grep, or ffmpeg.
- Prompt Template:
  I need a command for my terminal. I want to [Describe your goal in plain English].
  For example:
    - "Find all files in the current directory that contain the word 'error'." (using grep)
    - "Squash the last 3 git commits into a single commit." (using git rebase)
    - "Build a Docker image from the Dockerfile in my current directory and tag it 'my-app:latest'." (using docker)
- **Customization Guidelines:** Be very specific about your goal. Command-line tools have many options, so clarity is key.
- **Real-World Usage Example:** A developer needs to perform a complex Git operation but can't remember the exact syntax. They use this prompt to get the correct command instantly.

75. The Tech Stack Suggester

- **Purpose:** To get recommendations for a technology stack for a new project.
- Prompt Template:
  Act as a CTO. I am planning to build a new [Type of Application, e.g., "a real-time chat application," "a simple e-commerce website," "a data analytics dashboard"].
  The key requirements are: [List 2-3 key requirements, e.g., "must be highly scalable," "needs a simple and fast user interface," "must integrate with third-party payment gateways"].
  Please suggest a complete technology stack for this project, including:
    - Frontend framework
    - Backend language/framework
    - Database
    - Deployment/Hosting platform
- **Customization Guidelines:** The suggested stack is a starting point. Always do your own research to validate that the recommendations are the right fit for your specific needs and team skills.
- **Real-World Usage Example:** An entrepreneur with a new app idea uses this prompt to get a high-level overview of the technologies they might need, helping them in conversations with potential developers.

Documentation and Technical Writing

76. The Technical Documentation Writer

- **Purpose:** To write clear and concise documentation for a piece of code or a system.
- Prompt Template:
  Write technical documentation for the following

[Programming Language] function.
[Paste your function's code here]

The documentation should be in [e.g., JSDoc, Python Docstring] format and include:

- A brief, one-sentence summary of what the function does.
- A more detailed description of its purpose.
- Descriptions of each parameter (@param), including its type and purpose.
- A description of the return value (@returns), including its type.
- An example of how to use the function.

- **Customization Guidelines:** Specify the documentation format standard for your project or language to ensure consistency.
- **Real-World Usage Example:** A software engineer has just finished writing a complex module and uses this prompt to quickly generate professional documentation, making the code easier for others to use and maintain.

77. The Architecture Explanation

- **Purpose:** To explain a software architecture or system design in plain English.
- Prompt Template:
  Explain the following system architecture to a [Target Audience, e.g., a new engineer, a non-technical project manager].
  System Components:
  - A web client built with [Frontend Framework].
  - A load balancer.
  - A set of microservices built with [Backend Technology].
  - A [Database Type] database.

- A message queue for asynchronous tasks.

  Describe the role of each component and how they interact with each other to fulfill a user request. Use an analogy to make it easier to understand.
- **Customization Guidelines:** Providing a list of the components is crucial. You can also provide a diagram description if you have one.
- **Real-World Usage Example:** A solution architect needs to present a new system design to business stakeholders. This prompt helps them create an explanation that focuses on the high-level concepts without getting lost in technical details.

78. The Release Notes Drafter

- **Purpose:** To create release notes for a new version of a software product.
- Prompt Template:
  Draft the release notes for version [Version Number] of our software, [Software Name]. The audience is our end-users. This release includes the following changes:
  - **New Features:** [Feature 1 Description], [Feature 2 Description].
  - **Bug Fixes:** [Bug Fix 1 Description], [Bug Fix 2 Description].
  - **Improvements:** [Improvement 1 Description].

  Structure the notes with clear headings for "New Features," "Bug Fixes," and "Improvements." Write the descriptions from a user-benefit perspective.
- **Customization Guidelines:** Instead of just stating what was changed, explain why it matters to the user (e.g., "Fixed a bug that caused crashes" becomes "Improved application stability").
- **Real-World Usage Example:** A product manager uses this

prompt to quickly compile and write user-friendly release notes after a development sprint is completed.

79. The Code Commenter

- **Purpose:** To add explanatory comments to a block of code that is hard to understand.
- Prompt Template:
  Add inline comments to the following [Programming Language] code to explain what each part does. The code is complex and needs to be more readable for new developers.
  [Paste the uncommented code here]

- **Customization Guidelines:** This is particularly useful for legacy code or complex algorithms.
- **Real-World Usage Example:** A developer is working with an old codebase with no comments. They use this prompt to add explanations, making it easier to maintain and debug.

80. The Error Message Explainer

- **Purpose:** To get a plain English explanation of a cryptic error message.
- Prompt Template:
  I encountered the following error message while working with [Technology/Language]:
  [Paste the full error message here]
  Please explain:
  1. What does this error mean in simple terms?
  2. What are the most common causes of this error?
  3. What are the first 2-3 steps I should take to troubleshoot it?
- **Customization Guidelines:** Paste the entire error message, including the stack trace if available. This provides critical

context.

- **Real-World Usage Example:** A developer gets a confusing error they've never seen before. Instead of spending hours searching online forums, they use this prompt to get a direct and clear explanation.

81. The Code Review Checklist Generator

- **Purpose:** To create a standardized checklist for conducting code reviews.
- Prompt Template:
  Generate a code review checklist for our team. We primarily use [Programming Language]. The checklist should ensure that all submitted code meets our standards for:
    - **Correctness:** Does the code do what it's supposed to do?
    - **Readability:** Is the code clean and easy to understand?
    - **Performance:** Are there any obvious performance bottlenecks?
    - **Security:** Does the code introduce any security vulnerabilities?
    - **Testing:** Is the code properly tested?
- **Customization Guidelines:** You can add specific items to the checklist that are unique to your team's coding style or standards.
- **Real-World Usage Example:** A tech lead wants to improve the quality and consistency of their team's code reviews. They use this prompt to create a standard checklist for everyone to follow.

Section 5: Students and Researchers

This section provides templates to help students and academic researchers with outlining, summarization, study preparation, and writing.

82. The Research Paper Outline

- **Purpose:** To structure a formal research paper or academic essay.
- Prompt Template:
  Create a detailed outline for a research paper on the topic: "[Research Topic]". The paper's thesis statement is: "[Thesis Statement]".
  The outline should follow a standard academic structure:
    - **Introduction:** Background, problem statement, thesis statement, and roadmap.
    - **Literature Review:** Summary of existing research on the topic.
    - **Methodology:** Description of the research methods used.
    - **Results/Findings:** Presentation of the data or findings.
    - **Discussion:** Interpretation of the results and their implications.
    - **Conclusion:** Summary of the paper and suggestions for future research.

  For each section, provide 2-3 key bullet points to be covered.
- **Customization Guidelines:** A clear thesis statement is the most critical input for this prompt. It guides the entire structure of the paper.
- **Real-World Usage Example:** A graduate student is beginning work on their thesis and uses this prompt to create a solid structural foundation for their writing.

83. The Text Summarizer

- **Purpose:** To condense a long article, study, or chapter into a concise summary.
- Prompt Template:
  Summarize the following academic text in [Number] key

bullet points. The summary should capture the main argument, methodology, and conclusion of the text. The total summary should be no more than [Word Count] words.
Text to Summarize:
"[Paste the full text here.]"

- **Customization Guidelines:** For academic texts, asking for the "main argument, methodology, and conclusion" yields a more useful summary than just asking for a general one.
- **Real-World Usage Example:** A researcher is conducting a literature review and has dozens of papers to read. They use this prompt to quickly get the gist of each paper to determine which are most relevant for a deeper read.

84. The Concept Explainer (ELI5 Style)

- **Purpose:** To break down a complex academic concept into simple terms, as if explaining it to a five-year-old (ELI5).
- Prompt Template:
  Explain the concept of "[Complex Concept, e.g., quantum entanglement, Keynesian economics, epistemology]" in simple terms.
  Use an analogy or a real-world example. Avoid all technical jargon. The goal is to explain the core idea in a way that is intuitive and easy to grasp for a complete beginner.
- **Customization Guidelines:** This is excellent for testing your own understanding of a topic. If you can't explain it simply, you might not understand it fully yourself.
- **Real-World Usage Example:** A student is struggling to understand a core concept from a lecture. They use this prompt to get a simplified explanation that helps the idea click.

85. The Study Guide Creator

- **Purpose:** To generate a study guide for an upcoming exam based on course materials.
- Prompt Template:
  I have an exam on the topic of "[Subject, e.g., Introduction to Psychology]". The exam will cover the following topics/chapters:
  - [Topic 1]
  - [Topic 2]
  - [Topic 3]

  Please create a study guide that includes:
  - **Key Terms and Definitions:** A list of the most important vocabulary for each topic.
  - **Core Concepts:** A brief summary (2-3 sentences) of the main ideas for each topic.
  - **Potential Essay Questions:** 3-5 potential long-form questions that might appear on the exam.
- **Customization Guidelines:** If you have lecture notes or textbook chapters, you can paste them into the prompt for an even more tailored study guide.
- **Real-World Usage Example:** A college student is preparing for their final exams and uses this prompt to create a comprehensive study guide that helps them focus on the most important information.

86. The Argument and Counter-Argument Generator

- **Purpose:** To explore both sides of a debatable topic for a persuasive essay or debate preparation.
- Prompt Template:
  I am writing a paper on the topic of "[Debatable Topic, e.g., the impact of automation on employment]". My current position is [Your Stance].

To strengthen my argument, I need to understand the opposing viewpoint. Please provide:
1. Three strong arguments in favor of my position.
2. Three strong counter-arguments from the opposing side.
3. For each counter-argument, suggest a possible rebuttal I can use.

- **Customization Guidelines:** This prompt helps you build a more robust and nuanced argument by forcing you to engage with opposing views.
- **Real-World Usage Example:** A student on a debate team uses this prompt to prepare for an upcoming match, anticipating the opponent's arguments and preparing rebuttals in advance.

87. The Bibliography and Citation Formatter

- **Purpose:** To format a list of sources into a specific citation style.
- Prompt Template:
  I have a list of sources for a research paper. Please format them correctly in [Citation Style, e.g., APA 7th Edition, MLA 9th Edition, Chicago].
  Here are the sources:
  - [Source 1: Paste all available information, e.g., author, title, year, publication, URL, DOI]
  - [Source 2: Paste all available information]
  - [Source 3: Paste all available information]

  Organize the final list alphabetically by author's last name.
- **Customization Guidelines:** While very helpful, always double-check the formatted citations against an official style guide, as AI can sometimes make small formatting errors.
- **Real-World Usage Example:** A student has finished writing

their essay and uses this prompt to quickly generate a correctly formatted bibliography, saving significant time.

88. The Thesis Statement Refiner

- **Purpose:** To improve a draft thesis statement to make it more specific, arguable, and concise.
- Prompt Template:
  Refine the following draft thesis statement for an academic paper about [Topic].
  Draft: "[Your draft thesis statement here]."
  Rewrite the thesis to be more specific, arguable, and focused.
  Provide three improved versions for me to consider.
- **Customization Guidelines:** A strong thesis is the backbone of an academic paper. This prompt helps you move from a general statement to a powerful argument.
- **Real-World Usage Example:** A student has a general idea for their paper but their thesis is too broad. This prompt helps them narrow it down to a clear, defensible statement.

89. The Literature Review Search Query Generator

- **Purpose:** To generate effective search queries for academic databases like Google Scholar or JSTOR.
- Prompt Template:
  I am conducting a literature review on the topic of [Research Topic].
  Generate 5 advanced search query strings for academic databases. The queries should use Boolean operators (AND, OR, NOT) and include synonyms and related concepts to broaden the search.
- **Customization Guidelines:** The AI can help you think of related terms you might not have considered, leading to a more comprehensive literature search.

- **Real-World Usage Example:** A researcher is starting a new project and uses this prompt to create powerful search strings that will uncover the most relevant academic papers.

90. The Research Hypothesis Generator

- **Purpose:** To formulate a clear, testable research hypothesis.
- Prompt Template:
  I am conducting a study to explore the relationship between [Independent Variable] and [Dependent Variable] in the context of [Population/Context].
  Based on this, generate three possible research hypotheses. Include one null hypothesis and two alternative hypotheses (one directional, one non-directional).
- **Customization Guidelines:** Clearly identifying your variables is the key to a good hypothesis.
- **Real-World Usage Example:** A psychology student is designing an experiment and uses this prompt to formulate precise hypotheses that will guide their research and statistical analysis.

91. The Paraphrasing Tool for Avoiding Plagiarism

- **Purpose:** To rephrase a sentence or paragraph in your own words while retaining the original meaning, as a tool to help avoid plagiarism.
- Prompt Template:
  Please paraphrase the following passage. The goal is to express the same idea using different words and sentence structure. I will use this to help me understand how to put the idea in my own words.
  Original Passage: "[Paste the sentence or paragraph here.]"
- **Customization Guidelines:** This is an educational tool. Always cite your sources, even when paraphrasing. The goal

is to learn how to rephrase ideas, not to pass off the AI's output as your own.

- **Real-World Usage Example:** A student is taking notes from a source and wants to make sure they are not accidentally copying the author's exact phrasing. They use this prompt to see different ways the same idea can be expressed.

92. The Flashcard Content Generator

- **Purpose:** To create question-and-answer pairs from a set of notes for studying.
- Prompt Template:
  I am creating flashcards to study for my [Subject] exam. Here are my notes from a chapter on [Topic]:
  "[Paste your notes here.]"
  From these notes, generate 15 flashcards in a "Front/Back" format. The front should have a key term or a question, and the back should have the definition or answer.
- **Customization Guidelines:** The more organized your initial notes, the better the flashcards will be.
- **Real-World Usage Example:** A student preparing for a vocabulary-heavy exam pastes their notes into this prompt and gets a ready-to-use set of digital or physical flashcards.

Section 6: Entrepreneurs and Freelancers

This section provides targeted prompts for individuals managing their own businesses, from initial planning and branding to client management and growth.

93. The Lean Business Plan Generator

- **Purpose:** To quickly create a one-page, high-level business plan for a new venture.
- Prompt Template:

Act as a startup consultant. Generate a Lean Business Plan for my new business idea: [Briefly describe the business, e.g., "a subscription box service for office supplies"].
The plan should include these sections:

  - **Problem:** What customer pain point are you solving?
  - **Solution:** A concise description of your product or service.
  - **Target Market:** Who are your ideal customers?
  - **Unique Value Proposition (UVP):** What makes you different from competitors?
  - **Channels:** How will you reach your customers?
  - **Revenue Streams:** How will you make money?
  - **Cost Structure:** What are your major costs?
  - **Key Metrics:** How will you measure success?

- **Customization Guidelines:** This prompt is for high-level planning. Be concise in your business description to get a focused output.
- **Real-World Usage Example:** An aspiring entrepreneur uses this to structure their initial thoughts and create a document they can share with potential co-founders or mentors.

94. The Brand Identity and Messaging Brainstorm

- **Purpose:** To define the core elements of a new brand's voice, tone, and messaging.
- Prompt Template:
  I'm creating a brand for [My Product/Service]. Our target audience is [Audience Description]. Our core values are [Value 1], [Value 2], and [Value 3].
  Generate the following brand identity elements:
  - **Brand Archetype:** (e.g., The Sage, The Hero, The Creator).
  - **Brand Voice & Tone:** (e.g., Professional and

authoritative, friendly and witty, minimalist and sophisticated).
  - **Mission Statement:** A sentence on our purpose.
  - **Tagline/Slogan Ideas:** 5 options.
  - **Value Proposition Statement:** A clear statement of the benefit we provide.
- **Customization Guidelines:** The more specific you are about your values and audience, the more coherent the brand identity will be.
- **Real-World Usage Example:** A freelancer is building their personal brand website and uses this prompt to create consistent messaging across all pages.

95. The Client Proposal Outline

- **Purpose:** To create a professional and persuasive proposal for a potential client.
- Prompt Template:
  Create a detailed outline for a client proposal. The project is [Project Description, e.g., "to redesign a corporate website"]. The client is [Client Company Name].
  The proposal should include these sections:
  1. **Introduction:** Understanding of the Client's Problem.
  2. **Proposed Solution:** Our approach to solving the problem.
  3. **Scope of Work:** A detailed list of deliverables.
  4. **Timeline:** Key phases and milestones with estimated dates.
  5. **Pricing/Investment:** A breakdown of costs.
  6. **About Us/Me:** Brief background and relevant experience.
  7. **Next Steps:** A clear call to action.
- **Customization Guidelines:** This template provides the structure. You will need to fill in the specifics for each client

and project.

- **Real-World Usage Example:** A freelance consultant uses this prompt to quickly generate a professional proposal structure, ensuring they don't miss any critical sections.

96. The Pricing Strategy Model

- **Purpose:** To explore different pricing strategies for a new service or product.
- Prompt Template:
  Act as a business strategist. I am launching a new [Service/Product, e.g., "online course on project management"]. My target market is [Target Market Description]. My main competitors charge [Competitor Pricing info].
  Analyze and propose three different pricing strategies for me to consider:
  1. **Cost-Plus Pricing:** Based on my estimated costs.
  2. **Value-Based Pricing:** Based on the value delivered to the customer.
  3. **Competitive Pricing:** Based on what the market already bears.

  For each strategy, explain the pros and cons and suggest a potential price point.
- **Customization Guidelines:** Provide as much information as you can about your costs and competitors to get a realistic analysis.
- **Real-World Usage Example:** A SaaS founder is trying to decide on the pricing tiers for their new software. They use this prompt to help them think through the most common pricing models and their implications.

97. The Networking Outreach Message

- **Purpose:** To draft a concise and effective message for networking on platforms like LinkedIn.
- Prompt Template:
  Draft a short networking message (under 100 words) to connect with [Person's Name], a [Person's Job Title] on LinkedIn.
  The message should:
  1. Mention a specific point of connection (e.g., "I saw your recent post on [Topic]," "We both worked at [Company]," "I admire your work on [Project]").
  2. Briefly introduce myself and what I do.
  3. State why I want to connect, with a low-pressure call to action (e.g., "I'd love to follow your work," "I'm keen to learn more about your industry").
- **Customization Guidelines:** The key to good networking is making it about them, not you. The more personalized the message, the higher the acceptance rate.
- **Real-World Usage Example:** A job seeker wants to connect with a hiring manager at a target company and uses this prompt to craft a message that is respectful and professional, not spammy.

98. The Pitch Deck Content Outline

- **Purpose:** To structure the narrative and content for a startup pitch deck.
- Prompt Template:
  Generate a 10-slide outline for a pitch deck for my startup, [Startup Name], which [What your startup does]. We are seeking [Funding Amount] for [Purpose of funding].
  The outline should follow the classic 10-slide structure:
  - Slide 1: Title
  - Slide 2: The Problem

    - Slide 3: The Solution
    - Slide 4: Market Size
    - Slide 5: The Product (How it works)
    - Slide 6: Business Model (How you make money)
    - Slide 7: Go-to-Market Strategy
    - Slide 8: The Team
    - Slide 9: Financial Projections (High-level)
    - Slide 10: The Ask (Funding request)

  For each slide, provide 2-3 key bullet points of content to include.
- **Customization Guidelines:** This is a high-level structure. Your actual content will require detailed research and data.
- **Real-World Usage Example:** A founder preparing for a pitch competition uses this prompt to ensure their presentation covers all the essential topics that investors expect to see.

99. The Customer Service Response Template

- **Purpose:** To create reusable templates for common customer service inquiries.
- Prompt Template:
  Generate a set of professional and empathetic customer service email templates for my e-commerce business. Create a template for each of the following scenarios:
  1. **Responding to a shipping delay:** Acknowledge the issue, apologize, and provide a new estimated delivery date.
  2. **Handling a request for a refund:** Explain the process and what the customer needs to do.
  3. **Answering a product question:** Provide information clearly and offer further help.
  4. **Responding to a negative review:** Thank them for the feedback, apologize for their experience, and offer to

resolve the issue offline.

- **Customization Guidelines:** Adjust the tone to match your brand identity. A playful brand might use more casual language than a formal one.
- **Real-World Usage Example:** A small business owner uses this prompt to build a library of response templates, allowing them to answer customer emails quickly and consistently.

100. The Freelancer Service Package Creator

- **Purpose:** To bundle freelance services into clear, marketable packages.
- Prompt Template:
  I am a freelance [Your Profession, e.g., "Graphic Designer"].
  I want to create three service packages (e.g., Basic, Standard, Premium) to offer clients.
  My services include: [List all your services, e.g., "logo design," "brand style guide," "social media graphics," "business card design"].
  Please bundle these services into three distinct packages with clear names, deliverables, and a suggested pricing tier (e.g., $, $$, $$$).
- **Customization Guidelines:** Creating packages makes it easier for clients to understand your offerings and can help you upsell to more comprehensive solutions.
- **Real-World Usage Example:** A freelance writer creates packages for "Blog Post Writing," "Website Copy," and a "Complete Content Overhaul," making their pricing transparent and easy to understand.

101. The Testimonial Request Email

- **Purpose:** To politely ask a satisfied client for a testimonial.
- Prompt Template:

Draft a brief and friendly email to a recent client, [Client Name], asking for a testimonial about our work together on [Project Name].
The email should:

1. Thank them for their business.
2. State that you are collecting feedback to improve your services.
3. Ask if they would be willing to provide a short testimonial.
4. Make it easy for them by providing a link to a form or suggesting a few guiding questions (e.g., "What was the best part of working with us?").

- **Customization Guidelines:** Personalize the email by mentioning a specific positive outcome from the project. This reminds them of the value you provided.
- **Real-World Usage Example:** A freelance web developer sends this email one week after a successful site launch to collect a powerful testimonial for their portfolio.

102. The "Scope Creep" Management Email

- **Purpose:** To professionally address a client request that falls outside the original scope of a project.
- Prompt Template:
  Draft a professional email to a client, [Client Name], regarding their recent request for [The new task or feature].
  The email should:
  1. Acknowledge their request and express enthusiasm for the idea.
  2. Gently point out that this new item falls outside the scope of our current agreement.
  3. Frame it as an opportunity, offering to create a separate proposal or project addendum to address the new request.

4. Suggest a brief call to discuss the details.

- **Customization Guidelines:** The tone should be helpful and collaborative, not confrontational. The goal is to protect your time while also being a good partner to your client.
- **Real-World Usage Example:** A client asks their freelance social media manager to start creating video content, which wasn't in the original contract. This prompt helps the freelancer write an email to discuss pricing for the new service.

103. The Investor Update Email Draft

- **Purpose:** To write a concise and informative monthly or quarterly update for investors or advisors.
- Prompt Template:
  Draft a monthly investor update email for my startup, [Startup Name].
  The update should be concise and cover these key areas in a "Key Metrics & Highlights" format:
  - **KPIs:** (e.g., Monthly Recurring Revenue, User Growth, Churn Rate).
  - **Highlights/Wins:** What went well this month?
  - **Challenges/Lows:** What didn't go as planned?
  - **The Ask:** Is there anything you need help with from your investors (e.g., introductions, advice)?
- **Customization Guidelines:** Be transparent and data-driven. Investors appreciate honesty about challenges just as much as they like to hear about wins.
- **Real-World Usage Example:** A startup founder uses this template to create a consistent and professional monthly update, keeping their investors engaged and informed.

104. The "Why Us?" Company Story

- **Purpose:** To craft a compelling narrative about why your company was founded and what makes it unique.
- Prompt Template:
  Help me write the "About Us" story for my company, [Company Name].
    - **The "Aha!" Moment:** What problem did I/we encounter that led to the idea?
    - **The Mission:** What is the ultimate purpose or vision of the company?
    - **The Difference:** What makes our approach or product unique?

  Weave these points into a short, engaging story (around 200 words) that can be used on our website.
- **Customization Guidelines:** A good founding story creates an emotional connection with customers and makes your brand more memorable.
- **Real-World Usage Example:** A small business owner wants to rewrite their generic "About Us" page into something more personal and persuasive.

Section 7: Human Resources and Management

This section provides templates for HR professionals and managers to streamline hiring, performance management, and internal communications.

105. The Job Description Writer

- **Purpose:** To create a clear, inclusive, and appealing job description.
- Prompt Template:
  Write a job description for the role of [Job Title] at our company, [Company Name]. We are a [Brief description of

the company and its culture].
The job description should include these sections:

- **Job Summary:** A brief, engaging overview of the role.
- **Responsibilities:** A bulleted list of the primary duties.
- **Qualifications:** A list of required skills, experience, and education (separate "required" from "preferred").
- **About Us:** A short paragraph about the company culture and benefits.
- **Equal Opportunity Statement.**

Ensure the language is inclusive and avoids corporate jargon.

- **Customization Guidelines:** Focus on the responsibilities and outcomes rather than just a list of tasks. What will this person achieve?
- **Real-World Usage Example:** An HR manager needs to hire a new Marketing Coordinator. This prompt helps them write a comprehensive job description that attracts qualified candidates.

106. The Interview Question Generator

- **Purpose:** To create a set of structured interview questions for a specific role.
- Prompt Template:
  Generate a list of 15 interview questions for the role of [Job Title]. The key competencies for this role are [Competency 1], [Competency 2], and [Competency 3].
  The questions should be a mix of:
  - **Behavioral questions:** (e.g., "Tell me about a time when...") to assess past performance.
  - **Situational questions:** (e.g., "What would you do if...") to assess problem-solving skills.
  - **Technical/Skills-based questions:** To assess specific

knowledge.
    - **Cultural fit questions:** To assess alignment with company values.
- **Customization Guidelines:** Listing the key competencies is crucial for generating targeted and effective questions.
- **Real-World Usage Example:** A hiring manager is preparing to interview candidates for a Project Manager role and uses this prompt to create a question list focused on communication, organization, and leadership.

107. The Performance Review Phrases Generator

- **Purpose:** To generate constructive and professional phrases for performance reviews.
- Prompt Template:
  Act as an experienced manager. Generate a list of performance review phrases for an employee in the area of [Performance Area, e.g., "Teamwork and Collaboration," "Problem-Solving," "Communication"].
  Provide 5 phrases for each of the following categories:
    - **Exceeds Expectations:** For outstanding performance.
    - **Meets Expectations:** For solid, consistent performance.
    - **Needs Improvement:** For areas requiring development.

  The phrases should be specific, objective, and constructive.
- **Customization Guidelines:** Combine these generated phrases with specific, concrete examples of the employee's work to make the feedback more impactful.
- **Real-World Usage Example:** A manager is writing annual reviews and uses this prompt to find the right words to describe an employee's performance accurately and constructively.

108. The Employee Onboarding Checklist

- **Purpose:** To create a structured checklist for onboarding a new employee.
- Prompt Template:
  Create a comprehensive 30-day onboarding checklist for a new [Job Title] joining our team.
  The checklist should be broken down into four weeks:
  - **Week 1: Foundations:** (e.g., Set up accounts, meet the team, review company policies, understand the role's core function).
  - **Week 2: Learning & Integration:** (e.g., Shadow a colleague, first one-on-one with manager, learn key software tools).
  - **Week 3: Contribution:** (e.g., Take on first small task, contribute to a team meeting).
  - **Week 4: Autonomy & Planning:** (e.g., Complete first project, set 90-day goals with manager).

  For each week, provide a list of 5-7 key tasks.
- **Customization Guidelines:** Customize the tasks based on the specific role and your company's tools and processes.
- **Real-World Usage Example:** A team lead uses this prompt to create a standardized onboarding plan, ensuring every new hire has a consistent and welcoming experience.

109. The Training Program Outline

- **Purpose:** To structure the curriculum for an internal training program.
- Prompt Template:
  Create an outline for a [Duration, e.g., half-day] training workshop on "[Training Topic, e.g., "Effective Time Management"]". The audience is [Audience Description].
  The outline should include:

    - **Learning Objectives:** What will participants be able to do after the workshop?
    - **Module 1: [Name]:** Key concepts and activities.
    - **Module 2: [Name]:** Key concepts and activities.
    - **Module 3: [Name]:** Key concepts and activities.
    - **Wrap-up & Action Planning:** Summary and next steps.

  Allocate an estimated time for each module.
- **Customization Guidelines:** Think about interactive elements like group discussions or short exercises to include in each module to keep participants engaged.
- **Real-World Usage Example:** A learning and development specialist is tasked with creating a new workshop for managers. This prompt helps them structure the content in a logical and effective way.

110. The Conflict Resolution Script

- **Purpose:** To provide managers with a framework for mediating a disagreement between team members.
- Prompt Template:
  Act as an HR business partner. Create a script or talking points for a manager who needs to mediate a professional disagreement between two employees, [Employee A] and [Employee B], regarding [Nature of the Conflict, e.g., a disagreement over project responsibilities].
  The script should guide the manager through these steps:
    1. **Opening the Meeting:** Set a positive and neutral tone.
    2. **Allowing Each Person to Speak:** Ensure each employee can state their perspective without interruption.
    3. **Identifying the Core Issue:** Summarize and confirm the root of the disagreement.
    4. **Brainstorming Solutions:** Facilitate a discussion on

potential resolutions.
5. **Agreeing on a Path Forward:** Document the agreed-upon solution and next steps.

- **Customization Guidelines:** This script is a guide. A manager will need to adapt their approach based on the specific personalities and situation.
- **Real-World Usage Example:** A manager notices tension between two team members and uses this prompt to prepare for a conversation aimed at resolving the issue constructively.

111. The Candidate Rejection Email

- **Purpose:** To write a polite and professional rejection email to a job candidate.
- Prompt Template:
  Draft a respectful and empathetic rejection email for a candidate, [Candidate Name], who interviewed for the [Job Title] position.
  The email should:
  1. Thank them for their time and interest.
  2. Politely inform them that they have not been selected for the role at this time.
  3. If appropriate and true, mention that you were impressed with their qualifications and will keep their resume on file for future opportunities.
  4. Wish them well in their job search.
- **Customization Guidelines:** Keep it brief and professional. Avoid giving specific, subjective feedback unless it is your company's policy to do so, as it can open up legal risks.
- **Real-World Usage Example:** After a round of interviews, an HR coordinator uses this prompt to send professional rejection letters to the candidates who were not selected.

112. The Job Offer Letter Template

- **Purpose:** To create a formal job offer letter.
- Prompt Template:
  Generate a template for a formal job offer letter. The candidate is [Candidate Name], and the role is [Job Title]. The letter should include sections for:
  - Job Title and reporting structure.
  - Start Date.
  - Salary and payment schedule.
  - Bonus structure (if any).
  - Key benefits (e.g., healthcare, retirement plan).
  - Contingencies (e.g., background check).
  - An acceptance deadline and instructions on how to accept.
- **Customization Guidelines:** This prompt provides a general template. Always have a legal professional review your official offer letter templates to ensure compliance with local labor laws.
- **Real-World Usage Example:** A small business owner who doesn't have a dedicated HR department uses this prompt to create a professional offer letter for their first employee.

113. The 1-on-1 Meeting Agenda Template

- **Purpose:** To structure a recurring 1-on-1 meeting between a manager and a direct report.
- Prompt Template:
  Create a recurring agenda template for a 30-minute weekly 1-on-1 meeting between a manager and a team member. The goal is to focus on the employee's growth and well-being, not just status updates.
  The agenda should prompt the manager to discuss:

1. **Check-in:** How are you feeling this week? (5 mins)
2. **Priorities:** What are your top priorities? Any roadblocks I can help with? (10 mins)
3. **Growth & Development:** What's something new you learned? Any skills you want to develop? (10 mins)
4. **Feedback & Next Steps:** Any feedback for me? What are our action items? (5 mins)

- **Customization Guidelines:** The key is to make this a two-way conversation. The agenda should be shared in advance so both parties can prepare.
- **Real-World Usage Example:** A new manager wants to establish a good rapport with their team. They use this prompt to create a consistent and meaningful structure for their weekly check-ins.

114. The Professional Development Plan (PDP) Template

- **Purpose:** To create a structured plan for an employee's career growth.
- Prompt Template:
  Create a template for an employee Professional Development Plan (PDP). The template should be a document that a manager and employee can fill out together. Include these sections:
  - **Employee's Career Goals:** Where do they see themselves in 1-3 years?
  - **Strengths to Leverage:** What are their key strengths?
  - **Areas for Development:** What skills or knowledge do they need to acquire?
  - **Development Goals (SMART):** 2-3 specific, measurable, achievable, relevant, and time-bound goals.
  - **Action Plan:** What specific actions (e.g., courses, mentorship, projects) will be taken to achieve each goal?

    - **Manager's Commitment:** How will the manager support this plan?
- **Customization Guidelines:** The PDP should be a living document, reviewed and updated regularly (e.g., quarterly).
- **Real-World Usage Example:** During an annual performance review, a manager uses this template to facilitate a conversation about an employee's long-term career aspirations.

115. The Employee Recognition Announcement

- **Purpose:** To write a public announcement recognizing an employee's outstanding contribution.
- Prompt Template:
  Draft an announcement for our internal company chat or newsletter recognizing [Employee Name] for their excellent work on [Project or Achievement].
  The announcement should:
  1. Start with an enthusiastic opening.
  2. Specifically describe what the employee did and the positive impact it had (use metrics if possible).
  3. Connect their work to one of the company's values.
  4. End with a call for the rest of the team to congratulate them.
- **Customization Guidelines:** Public recognition is a powerful motivator. Be specific and sincere in your praise.
- **Real-World Usage Example:** A team lead wants to celebrate a team member who went above and beyond to meet a tight deadline. They use this prompt to write a glowing post in the company's Slack channel.

Section 8: Personal Productivity and Workflow Automation

This section focuses on prompts designed to help any professional optimize their personal workflows, manage their time, and automate repetitive tasks.

116. The Daily Task Prioritization (Eisenhower Matrix)

- **Purpose:** To organize a to-do list based on urgency and importance.
- Prompt Template:
  I have the following tasks to complete today: [List all your tasks, e.g., "Finish the quarterly report," "Respond to client emails," "Prepare for team meeting," "Brainstorm ideas for new project"].
  Please organize these tasks into an Eisenhower Matrix with four quadrants:
  1. **Urgent & Important (Do First):**
  2. **Important, Not Urgent (Schedule):**
  3. **Urgent, Not Important (Delegate):**
  4. **Neither Urgent nor Important (Eliminate/Do Last):**
- **Customization Guidelines:** For best results, list every single task you can think of, no matter how small. This gives the AI the full context for prioritization.
- **Real-World Usage Example:** You arrive at work feeling overwhelmed by your to-do list. This prompt helps you quickly create a clear, prioritized action plan for the day.

117. The Weekly Planning and Review

- **Purpose:** To set goals for the upcoming week and review progress from the previous week.
- Prompt Template:
  Act as a productivity coach. Guide me through a weekly review and planning session.
  Ask me the following questions one by one:

1. "What were your three biggest wins from last week?"
2. "What was the biggest challenge you faced last week, and what did you learn?"
3. "What are the top 3 most important goals you want to accomplish this coming week?"
4. "What is one thing you can do to make this week more successful or less stressful?"
5. "Are there any upcoming deadlines or appointments to be aware of?"

- **Customization Guidelines:** Use this prompt interactively in a chat-based AI. Answer each question before the next one is presented.
- **Real-World Usage Example:** Every Friday afternoon, a professional uses this prompt to reflect on their week and set clear intentions for the next, ensuring they stay focused on their most important priorities.

118. The Email Inbox Triage Assistant

- **Purpose:** To quickly sort a messy inbox and suggest actions.
- Prompt Template:
  I'm triaging my email inbox. Below are the subject lines and senders of 10 unread emails. Based on this information, suggest a quick action for each one: Reply Now, Archive/Delete, Add to To-Do List, or Read Later.
  - Email 1: "[Subject Line]" from [Sender]
  - Email 2: "[Subject Line]" from [Sender]
  - ...and so on.
- **Customization Guidelines:** You can also paste the first sentence or a brief snippet of the email body for more context and a more accurate recommendation.
- **Real-World Usage Example:** You return from a vacation to hundreds of emails. You use this prompt to rapidly sort

through them, identifying what needs immediate attention and what is just noise.

119. The Meeting Debrief and Action Item Extractor

- **Purpose:** To turn unstructured meeting notes into a clean summary and a list of action items.
- Prompt Template:
  I just finished a meeting about [Meeting Topic]. Here are my raw, unstructured notes. Please clean them up, create a brief summary of the key decisions, and extract a clear list of action items with owners and deadlines if mentioned.
  Raw Notes:
  "[Paste your messy notes here. e.g., 'maria said the budget is final. we need to send the final design to the client - maybe john can do this by friday? talked about the timeline, seems tight. new idea from sam about the marketing push after launch.']"
- **Customization Guidelines:** Don't worry about how messy your notes are. The AI is excellent at finding the signal in the noise.
- **Real-World Usage Example:** Immediately after a project check-in, the project manager uses this prompt to turn their handwritten notes into a formal summary and task list to share with the team.

120. The Reusable Checklist Creator

- **Purpose:** To create a standardized checklist for a recurring task.
- Prompt Template:
  Create a detailed, step-by-step checklist for the recurring task of "[Task Name, e.g., 'Publishing a weekly podcast episode,' 'Preparing for a client presentation,' 'Closing out the

month's finances']".
The process involves these general stages: [List 2-4 high-level stages, e.g., "Pre-Production," "Recording," "Post-Production," "Distribution"].
For each stage, list all the necessary sub-tasks. The checklist should be clear enough for someone else to follow.

- **Customization Guidelines:** The more you can break down the process into its major stages, the more logical and complete the final checklist will be.
- **Real-World Usage Example:** A social media manager creates a checklist for launching a new campaign. They use it every time to ensure no steps, from creative approval to pixel placement, are missed.

Section 9: Strategic Thinking and Decision-Making

This section offers prompts that leverage AI to analyze complex situations, explore future scenarios, and support more robust strategic decision-making.

121. The Scenario Planning Generator

- **Purpose:** To explore potential future scenarios to make more resilient plans.
- Prompt Template:
  Act as a strategic futurist. We are planning to [Strategic Initiative, e.g., "launch a new product in Europe next year"]. Please generate three potential future scenarios for the [Industry/Market] in the next 18 months:
  1. **Best-Case Scenario (Optimistic):** What if everything goes right?
  2. **Worst-Case Scenario (Pessimistic):** What if major challenges arise?

3. **Most Likely Scenario (Realistic):** A balanced view.

   For each scenario, describe the key market conditions and suggest one strategic action we could take to prepare.

- **Customization Guidelines:** Provide context on your industry and the specific initiative. The more details, the more plausible the scenarios.
- **Real-World Usage Example:** A leadership team is considering a major capital investment. They use this prompt to think through potential futures and stress-test their strategy against different outcomes.

122. The PESTLE Analysis Framework

- **Purpose:** To analyze the macro-environmental factors that could impact a business or project.
- Prompt Template:
  Conduct a PESTLE (Political, Economic, Social, Technological, Legal, Environmental) analysis for a company in the [Industry] industry operating in [Geographic Region]. For each of the six categories, provide 2-3 bullet points on potential factors or trends that could represent either an opportunity or a threat.
- **Customization Guidelines:** Specifying the industry and region is critical, as these factors are highly context-dependent.
- **Real-World Usage Example:** A company planning to expand into a new country uses this prompt to get a high-level overview of the external risks and opportunities in that market.

123. The "First Principles" Problem Deconstruction

- **Purpose:** To break down a complex problem into its most fundamental truths to find innovative solutions.

- Prompt Template:
  I am trying to solve the following problem: [Problem Statement, e.g., "Employee training is expensive and has low engagement."].
  Let's break this down using First Principles thinking. Ask me a series of Socratic questions to challenge my assumptions and get to the core of the problem. Start with questions like:
  - "What are we absolutely certain is true about this problem?"
  - "What are the fundamental components of employee training?"
  - "What is the ultimate goal we are trying to achieve?"
- **Customization Guidelines:** Use this interactively. The goal isn't for the AI to solve the problem, but to ask you questions that lead you to a new way of seeing it.
- **Real-World Usage Example:** A product development team is stuck on a persistent technical challenge. They use this prompt to question their long-held assumptions and open up new avenues for a solution.

124. The Decision-Making Framework (Pros and Cons)

- **Purpose:** To structure the process of making a difficult decision.
- Prompt Template:
  I need to make a decision between [Option A] and [Option B]. The decision is about [Context of the decision, e.g., "choosing a software vendor," "deciding whether to hire a new team member"].
  Please create a decision-making matrix for me. The output should be a table with four sections:
  - **Pros of Option A**
  - **Cons of Option A**

    - **Pros of Option B**
    - **Cons of Option B**

  Based on the context, generate 3-5 potential points for each section to get me started.
- **Customization Guidelines:** You can add criteria for the decision, such as "short-term cost," "long-term scalability," and "ease of implementation."
- **Real-World Usage Example:** A department head has to choose between two different project proposals. This prompt helps them organize their thoughts and evaluate both options systematically.

Section 10: Career Development and Personal Branding

This section is dedicated to prompts that help professionals manage their careers, from optimizing resumes and preparing for interviews to building a strong personal brand.

125. The Resume Bullet Point Enhancer

- **Purpose:** To rewrite resume bullet points to be more impactful and results-oriented.
- Prompt Template:
  Rewrite the following resume bullet point to be more powerful and quantitative. Use the "Action Verb + Task + Result" formula.
  Original Bullet Point: "[Your original bullet point, e.g., 'Responsible for managing the company's social media accounts.']"
  Here is some additional context: [Provide metrics or results, e.g., "We grew our follower count by 15% in six months and increased engagement by 25%."].

- **Customization Guidelines:** The key to this prompt is in the metrics. Even if you have to estimate, providing numbers (percentages, dollar amounts, time saved) makes the output dramatically better.
- **Real-World Usage Example:** You are updating your resume and want to make your experience sound more impressive. You use this prompt to turn a simple description of your duties into a statement of your achievements.

126. The Cover Letter Customizer

- **Purpose:** To tailor a generic cover letter to a specific job description.
- Prompt Template:
  I have a generic cover letter and a job description for a role I want to apply for. Please help me customize the cover letter.
  My Generic Cover Letter:
  "[Paste your cover letter text here.]"
  The Job Description:
  "[Paste the full job description here.]"
  Identify the top 3 requirements from the job description and rewrite my cover letter to specifically highlight my experience in those areas. Pull relevant skills from my generic letter and align them with the job's keywords.
- **Customization Guidelines:** This is a huge time-saver. It ensures your application directly addresses the employer's stated needs.
- **Real-World Usage Example:** You are applying for multiple jobs and use this prompt to quickly create a unique, tailored cover letter for each application without starting from scratch every time.

127. The LinkedIn Profile Summary Optimizer

- **Purpose:** To write a compelling and keyword-rich "About" section for a LinkedIn profile.
- Prompt Template:
  Write a professional "About" summary for my LinkedIn profile. I am a [Your Profession, e.g., "Digital Marketing Manager"] with [Number] years of experience, specializing in [Your Specialization, e.g., "SEO and content strategy"]. My career goal is to [Your Goal, e.g., "lead a marketing team in the tech industry"].
  The summary should:
  - Start with a strong opening statement.
  - Highlight my top 3 skills or areas of expertise.
  - Include keywords relevant to my field.
  - End with a call to action (e.g., "Feel free to connect," "Open to new opportunities").
- **Customization Guidelines:** Think about the audience for your profile (recruiters, potential clients, peers) and adjust the tone and call to action accordingly.
- **Real-World Usage Example:** A professional looking to advance their career uses this prompt to refresh their LinkedIn summary, making it more discoverable and impressive to recruiters.

128. The Interview "Tell Me About Yourself" Answer

- **Purpose:** To craft a concise and compelling answer to the most common interview question.
- Prompt Template:
  Help me craft a 90-second answer to the interview question, "Tell me about yourself." I am interviewing for the role of [Job Title] at [Company Name].
  Here are the key points about my experience:
  - **Past:** [Your most relevant previous role and a key

achievement].
   - **Present:** [Your current role and responsibilities].
   - **Future:** [Why you are interested in this specific role and company].

  Structure the answer as a "Past, Present, Future" narrative that connects my experience directly to the job I am applying for.
- **Customization Guidelines:** This prompt creates a story, not just a list of facts. It's a powerful way to make a strong first impression.
- **Real-World Usage Example:** You have an important interview coming up and use this prompt to prepare and practice a polished, confident answer to the opening question.

129. The STAR Method Story Builder

- **Purpose:** To structure answers to behavioral interview questions using the STAR method.
- Prompt Template:
  I have an interview question: "[Behavioral Question, e.g., 'Tell me about a time you had to deal with a difficult stakeholder.']". Help me structure my answer using the STAR method (Situation, Task, Action, Result).
  My Story: "[Briefly describe the situation in your own words. e.g., 'My project was delayed because a key stakeholder was unresponsive and kept changing requirements.']"
  Now, expand my story into a clear, professional answer using these four parts:
   - **Situation:** Briefly set the context.
   - **Task:** What was your goal or responsibility?
   - **Action:** What specific steps did you take?
   - **Result:** What was the outcome? (Use metrics if possible).
- **Customization Guidelines:** Focus on the "Action" and

"Result" parts. These are where you demonstrate your skills and impact.

- **Real-World Usage Example:** An interviewee is preparing for a behavioral interview and uses this prompt to turn their career experiences into well-structured, compelling stories that showcase their abilities.

130. The Salary Negotiation Script

- **Purpose:** To prepare talking points for a salary negotiation conversation.
- Prompt Template:
  Act as a career coach. I have received a job offer for the role of [Job Title] with a salary of [Offered Salary]. My research indicates the market rate for this role is closer to [Your Target Salary].
  Create a script with professional talking points for a negotiation conversation. The script should:
  1. Express enthusiasm for the role and the offer.
  2. State my case for a higher salary, based on my skills, experience, and market value.
  3. Clearly state my desired salary.
  4. End on a collaborative and positive note.
- **Customization Guidelines:** Confidence and politeness are key. The goal is to frame it as a collaborative discussion, not a demand.
- **Real-World Usage Example:** A candidate receives a job offer they are excited about but feels the salary is below market rate. They use this prompt to prepare for a confident and professional negotiation.

Section 11: Learning and Skill Development

This section provides prompts for creating learning plans,

mastering new skills, and preparing for certifications.

131. The Personalized Learning Plan Creator

- **Purpose:** To create a structured learning plan for a new skill or subject.
- Prompt Template:
  Act as an academic advisor. I want to learn [Skill/Subject, e.g., "Data Analysis with Python"]. I am a [Your Level, e.g., "complete beginner," "intermediate"]. I can dedicate [Number] hours per week.
  Create a 4-week learning plan for me. For each week, provide:
  - **Weekly Goal:** A clear learning objective.
  - **Key Topics:** The main concepts to cover.
  - **Learning Resources:** Suggest types of resources (e.g., "interactive tutorials," "video courses," "a foundational book").
  - **A Small Project:** A simple hands-on project to apply the week's learning.
- **Customization Guidelines:** Be honest about your current skill level and time commitment to get a realistic and achievable plan.
- **Real-World Usage Example:** A marketing professional wants to learn SEO and uses this prompt to create a structured, one-month plan to get started.

132. The Socratic Method Tutor

- **Purpose:** To deepen your understanding of a topic by being asked probing questions.
- Prompt Template:
  Act as a Socratic tutor. I am trying to understand the concept of [Concept, e.g., "supply and demand"]. I will make a

statement about it, and I want you to ask me a question that challenges my assumptions or makes me think more deeply. Then I will answer, and you will ask another question. Let's begin.
My first statement is: "[Your initial understanding of the concept]."

- **Customization Guidelines:** This is an interactive prompt. The goal is a back-and-forth dialogue that helps you uncover gaps in your own knowledge.
- **Real-World Usage Example:** A student uses this prompt to study for an economics exam, ensuring they understand the core concepts on a deeper level than simple memorization.

133. The Practice Problem Generator

- **Purpose:** To generate practice problems for a technical or quantitative skill.
- Prompt Template:
  I am learning [Subject, e.g., "basic algebra," "SQL queries," "Python loops"].
  Please generate 5 practice problems for me related to [Specific Topic, e.g., "solving linear equations," "using JOIN statements," "for loops"].
  Provide the problems first, and then provide the solutions in a separate, clearly marked section so I can try to solve them myself first.
- **Customization Guidelines:** The more specific the topic, the more targeted the practice problems will be.
- **Real-World Usage Example:** Someone learning to code uses this prompt to generate practice exercises for a new concept they've just learned, reinforcing their understanding through application.

134. The Skill Gap Analysis

- **Purpose:** To identify the skills needed to transition to a new role or career.
- Prompt Template:
  I am currently a [Your Current Role] and I want to become a [Your Desired Role].
  Based on typical job descriptions for a [Desired Role], please perform a skill gap analysis.
  List:
  1. **Skills I likely already have:** Based on my current role.
  2. **Skills I need to acquire:** The key skills required for the new role that are likely missing from my current experience.
  3. **Suggested Learning Path:** For each missing skill, suggest a way to learn it (e.g., "online course," "certification," "side project").
- **Customization Guidelines:** This prompt is a great starting point for planning a career change. You can provide a specific job description for the desired role for an even more accurate analysis.
- **Real-World Usage Example:** A graphic designer who wants to become a UX designer uses this prompt to create a clear action plan for acquiring the necessary new skills.

135. The Book Summary and Key Takeaways

- **Purpose:** To get a high-level summary and the key ideas from a non-fiction book.
- Prompt Template:
  Provide a detailed summary of the book "[Book Title]" by [Author].
  The summary should include:

    - The book's central thesis or main argument.
    - The 3-5 most important key ideas or takeaways.
    - The target audience for the book.
- **Customization Guidelines:** This is useful for deciding if a book is worth reading or for refreshing your memory on a book you've read in the past. Always remember that an AI summary is not a substitute for reading the book yourself.
- **Real-World Usage Example:** A manager wants to learn the key principles from a popular business book but doesn't have time to read it. They use this prompt to get the main ideas quickly.

Section 12: Creative Problem-Solving and Ideation

This section provides prompts designed to break conventional thinking patterns and generate innovative ideas.

136. The "Reverse Brainstorming" Technique

- **Purpose:** To find solutions by brainstorming ways to cause or worsen a problem, then reversing the ideas.
- Prompt Template:
  I want to use reverse brainstorming to solve this problem: [Problem, e.g., "Our team meetings are unproductive."].
  First, brainstorm a list of 10 ways to make this problem worse. How could we guarantee our team meetings are as unproductive as possible?
  After you list them, for each point, suggest a "reversed" solution.
- **Customization Guidelines:** This technique is surprisingly effective for getting unstuck. It's often easier and more fun to think of ways to break something than to fix it.
- **Real-World Usage Example:** A team is struggling with low

customer satisfaction. They use this prompt to brainstorm "How could we make our customers even angrier?" which leads to clear solutions like "never reply to emails" reversed to "reply to all emails within 12 hours."

137. The Analogical Thinking Idea Generator

- **Purpose:** To generate creative solutions by drawing analogies from different fields.
- Prompt Template:
  I am trying to solve a problem in [Your Field]. The problem is: [Problem Statement].
  Let's use analogical thinking. How is this problem similar to a problem in a completely different field, like [Different Field, e.g., "nature," "sports," "cooking"]?
  For example, how has [e.g., "a beehive," "a championship basketball team," "a Michelin-star kitchen"] solved a similar problem of [e.g., "efficient resource allocation," "team coordination under pressure"]?
  Based on that analogy, brainstorm 3 potential solutions for my problem.
- **Customization Guidelines:** The more unexpected the analogy, the more innovative the ideas can be.
- **Real-World Usage Example:** A software development manager wants to improve their team's deployment process. They use an analogy to air traffic control to generate ideas about process flow, safety checks, and communication.

138. The SCAMPER Method for Innovation

- **Purpose:** To brainstorm new ideas for a product or service using the SCAMPER checklist.
- Prompt Template:
  I want to brainstorm new ideas for my existing product, a

[Product Name and Description]. Apply the SCAMPER method to generate ideas.
Give me one idea for each of the following prompts:
  - **Substitute:** What can be substituted?
  - **Combine:** What can be combined?
  - **Adapt:** What can be adapted?
  - **Modify:** What can be modified or magnified?
  - **Put to another use:** How can it be used differently?
  - **Eliminate:** What can be eliminated or simplified?
  - **Reverse:** What can be reversed or rearranged?
- **Customization Guidelines:** This is a structured brainstorming technique that forces you to think about an existing idea in seven different ways.
- **Real-World Usage Example:** A company that makes office chairs uses this prompt to brainstorm new product features, leading to ideas like a chair with built-in charging ports (Combine) or a chair made from recycled materials (Substitute).

139. The "Five Whys" Root Cause Analysis

- **Purpose:** To find the root cause of a problem by repeatedly asking "Why?".
- Prompt Template:
  Act as a business analyst. I want to perform a "Five Whys" analysis on a problem.
  The problem is: [Problem Statement, e.g., "Our latest software update was delayed."].
  Start by asking "Why was the update delayed?". I will provide an answer. Then, ask "Why?" about my answer, and continue this for five iterations to find the root cause.
- **Customization Guidelines:** This is an interactive prompt. The goal is to drill down past the surface-level symptoms to

find the underlying issue.

- **Real-World Usage Example:** A manufacturing plant had a safety incident. The manager uses this interactive prompt to move from the immediate cause ("a part failed") to the root cause ("the preventative maintenance schedule was not updated").

140. The Constraint-Based Creativity Challenge

- **Purpose:** To spark creativity by introducing artificial constraints.
- Prompt Template:
  I need to design a [Thing to be designed, e.g., "a marketing campaign for a new app"].
  To spark creativity, give me a set of three challenging constraints to work within. For example:
  - A very small budget (e.g., under $100).
  - A very short timeframe (e.g., must launch in 24 hours).
  - A specific required element (e.g., must only use the color blue).

  After listing the constraints, brainstorm 3 ideas that could work within them.
- **Customization Guidelines:** Constraints can paradoxically boost creativity by forcing you to move past obvious solutions.
- **Real-World Usage Example:** A design team feels stuck in a rut. They use this prompt to run a fun, constraint-based brainstorming session, which generates fresh and unconventional ideas.

Section 13: Team Collaboration and Management

This section provides prompts for improving team communication, feedback, and collaborative work.

141. The Team Charter and Norms Generator

- **Purpose:** To create a foundational document outlining a team's purpose, goals, and rules of engagement.
- Prompt Template:
  My team is kicking off a new project. Help us create a Team Charter. Generate an outline for a document that includes:
  - **Team Mission/Purpose:** Why does this team exist?
  - **Goals & Objectives:** What are our measurable goals?
  - **Roles & Responsibilities:** Who is responsible for what?
  - **Communication Norms:** How and when will we communicate? (e.g., "Daily stand-ups, weekly summaries via email").
  - **Decision-Making Process:** How will we make decisions? (e.g., "Consensus, majority vote, leader decides").
  - **Conflict Resolution:** How will we handle disagreements?
- **Customization Guidelines:** A team charter is a collaborative document. Use this AI-generated outline as a starting point for a team discussion.
- **Real-World Usage Example:** A newly formed project team uses this prompt to create a document that clarifies expectations and sets them up for success from day one.

142. The Constructive Feedback Framework (SBI)

- **Purpose:** To structure feedback for a colleague or direct report in a clear, objective, and actionable way.
- Prompt Template:
  I need to give some constructive feedback to a team member about [The issue, e.g., "them frequently interrupting others in meetings"].
  Help me frame this feedback using the Situation-Behavior-

Impact (SBI) model.

- **Situation:** Describe the specific situation where it happened.
- **Behavior:** Describe the observable behavior (what they did or said).
- **Impact:** Describe the impact their behavior had on you or the team.

Draft a few talking points for me to use.

- **Customization Guidelines:** The SBI model helps keep feedback objective and focused on facts rather than subjective judgments, which reduces defensiveness.
- **Real-World Usage Example:** A manager needs to address an employee's tardiness. Instead of saying "You're always late," they use this prompt to frame it as: "At yesterday's 10 AM team meeting (Situation), you arrived at 10:15 (Behavior), which meant we had to repeat the introduction, delaying our agenda (Impact)."

143. The Project Retrospective Questions (Post-Mortem)

- **Purpose:** To generate questions for a project retrospective meeting to encourage open and honest reflection.
- Prompt Template:
  My team just completed [Project Name]. I am facilitating a project retrospective (or post-mortem).
  Generate a list of 15 questions to guide the discussion. The questions should cover:
  - What went well?
  - What didn't go so well?
  - What did we learn?
  - What should we do differently next time?

  Include questions that encourage reflection on process, tools, and teamwork.

- **Customization Guidelines:** Avoid questions that assign blame. The goal of a retrospective is process improvement, not finger-pointing.
- **Real-World Usage Example:** After a major product launch, a project manager uses this prompt to create a set of thoughtful questions for the team retrospective, ensuring the conversation is productive and forward-looking.

144. The Delegation Planner

- **Purpose:** To clearly define and delegate a task to a team member.
- Prompt Template:
  I need to delegate the following task to a team member: [Task Name].
  Help me write a clear delegation message that includes:
  - **The specific task and desired outcome.**
  - **The deadline.**
  - **The context and importance of the task.**
  - **The level of authority they have.**
  - **Any relevant resources or information they will need.**
  - An offer of support and a scheduled check-in time.
- **Customization Guidelines:** Clear delegation is a key management skill. This prompt helps ensure you provide all the necessary information for the person to succeed.
- **Real-World Usage Example:** A manager wants to delegate the creation of the monthly performance report to a senior analyst. They use this prompt to write a clear and comprehensive message that sets the analyst up for success.

145. The "How to Work With Me" Guide

- **Purpose:** To create a personal user manual that helps

colleagues understand your work style and preferences.

- Prompt Template:
  Help me create a "How to Work With Me" guide for my new team.
  Generate a document outline with the following sections, and write a few sample sentences for each based on a hypothetical manager:
  - My working hours and response time expectations.
  - My preferred communication style (e.g., "I prefer Slack for quick questions and email for formal requests").
  - How I like to receive feedback.
  - My philosophy on meetings.
  - What I value most in a team member.
- **Customization Guidelines:** This is a powerful tool for building psychological safety and clarity on a team. Encourage your whole team to create one.
- **Real-World Usage Example:** A new team lead shares this guide during their first week, which helps their team members quickly understand how best to communicate and collaborate with them.

Section 14: Advanced Prompting (Meta-Prompts)

This section contains "meta-prompts"—prompts designed to help you create better prompts, build templates, and refine your own prompting skills.

146. The Prompt Improvement Suggester

- **Purpose:** To take a basic prompt and get suggestions on how to make it more effective.
- Prompt Template:
  I have the following prompt. Please act as a prompt

engineering expert and suggest 3 ways I could improve it to get a better result. Explain why each suggestion would help. **My Prompt:** "[e.g., 'Write a blog post about productivity.']"

- **Customization Guidelines:** Use this when you're getting generic or low-quality results from the AI. It's a great way to learn the principles of effective prompting.
- **Real-World Usage Example:** You're not happy with the AI's first draft. You use this prompt to get suggestions like "add a target audience," "specify a tone of voice," and "provide an outline," which helps you dramatically improve your next attempt.

147. The Prompt Template Creator

- **Purpose:** To turn a one-off successful prompt into a reusable template.
- Prompt Template:
  I used the following successful prompt to [Describe the task, e.g., "create a project update email"]. I want to turn it into a reusable template for my team.
  My Successful Prompt:
  "[Paste the entire prompt you used here.]"
  Analyze the prompt and identify the parts that are variable (like project name, date, specific updates). Rewrite the prompt as a generic template using bracketed placeholders like [Project Name] for the variable parts. Add a short explanation of how to use the template.
- **Customization Guidelines:** This is the key to scaling your productivity. Once you find a prompt that works well, templatize it so you never have to start from scratch again.
- **Real-World Usage Example:** You craft the perfect prompt for creating social media posts. You use this meta-prompt to turn it into a template that you can save in your personal

prompt library.

148. The Persona Generator for AI

- **Purpose:** To define a specific persona or role for the AI to adopt for a task.
- Prompt Template:
  I need the AI to act in a specific role to help me with a task. The task is [Your Task, e.g., "to review a business proposal"]. Generate a detailed persona for the AI to adopt. The persona should be a "[Role, e.g., 'a skeptical venture capitalist']". Describe their:
  - Expertise and background.
  - Primary goals and motivations.
  - Typical tone and communication style.
  - What they look for when evaluating [The task's subject].
- **Customization Guidelines:** Giving the AI a detailed persona is one of the most powerful ways to improve the quality and relevance of its output.
- **Real-World Usage Example:** You want to get critical feedback on your new business idea. You use this prompt to make the AI act like a seasoned, critical investor, which gives you much more valuable feedback than a generic AI persona.

149. The Chain-of-Thought Prompt Builder

- **Purpose:** To instruct the AI to "think step-by-step" to solve a complex problem.
- Prompt Template:
  I need to solve the following logic problem: [Describe the problem].
  Please solve this, but I want you to show your work. Use a chain-of-thought process. Break the problem down into smaller steps, reason through each step, and then provide

the final answer.

- **Customization Guidelines:** This technique is especially useful for math problems, logic puzzles, or complex reasoning tasks. It forces the AI to be more rigorous and often leads to more accurate results.
- **Real-World Usage Example:** You are trying to figure out a complex scheduling problem for a team event. You use this prompt to make the AI reason through all the constraints step-by-step.

150. The "What am I missing?" Prompt Expander

- **Purpose:** To have the AI analyze your prompt or plan and suggest what you might have overlooked.
- Prompt Template:
  I am creating a plan for [My Project/Task, e.g., "launching a new podcast"]. Here is my current plan:
  [List the steps in your plan].
  Act as an experienced [Relevant Expert, e.g., "podcast producer"] and review my plan. What am I missing? What potential problems or overlooked steps should I add to my plan?
- **Customization Guidelines:** This is like having an expert consultant on demand. The AI is great at spotting gaps in a plan that you might not see.
- **Real-World Usage Example:** You've created a project plan but have a feeling you've forgotten something. You use this prompt to get a "second opinion" and identify potential blind spots.

Appendix B: AI Platform Comparison Guide

Throughout this book, we have focused on the universal principles of effective AI prompting. The frameworks, techniques, and workflows you have learned are designed to be platform-agnostic, meaning they will serve you well regardless of the specific AI tool you choose. However, the reality is that not all AI platforms are created equal. Each has its own unique strengths, weaknesses, and ideal use cases. Choosing the right tool for the job can be just as important as writing the right prompt.

This appendix is designed to be your practical guide to the AI tool landscape. Think of it as a pre-purchase inspection for your new productivity partners. The world of AI is fast-moving, and new models and features are released constantly. While the specific details of pricing and features will change over time, the core characteristics and strengths of these major platforms tend to endure. Our goal here is not to give you a definitive "best" tool, but to provide you with a clear framework for evaluating your options and making an informed decision based on your unique professional needs.

We will start by outlining the key questions you should ask yourself when choosing a platform. Then, we will provide a detailed overview of the major players in the field: OpenAI's ChatGPT, Google's Gemini, Anthropic's Claude, and Microsoft Copilot. For each, we will break down their key features, pricing models, and ideal use cases. We will then provide a head-to-head comparison across the most important features, such as context window size and multimodal capabilities. Finally, we will offer a simple, scenario-based guide to help you decide which tool to reach for in common workplace situations.

Consider this your starting point. The best way to find the right tool is to experiment. Use this guide to select one or two platforms to try, test them with the prompts you have developed, and see which one "clicks" with your personal workflow.

How to Choose the Right AI Platform for You

Before diving into the specific platforms, you need a clear picture of your own requirements. Your ideal AI assistant depends entirely on the job you are hiring it for. Take a few minutes to answer the following questions. Your answers will form your personal "job description" for your AI tool.

- **What are my primary use cases?** Look back at your Task Automation Inventory. Are you mostly generating text (emails, reports), organizing data (tables, lists), analyzing large documents, brainstorming creative ideas, or writing code? Different models excel at different tasks.
- **What is my budget?** Are you looking for the most powerful free tool available, or are you willing to invest in a monthly subscription for premium features? We will break down the value proposition of free versus paid tiers for each platform.
- **Do I need up-to-the-minute information?** Are your tasks related to current events, recent market trends, or live web content? If so, a platform with built-in, real-time web access is essential.
- **How large are the documents I work with?** Do you frequently need to analyze long reports, academic papers, or legal documents? If so, the "context window" (the amount of information the AI can "remember" at one time) will be the

most important feature for you.

- **Will I be working with more than just text?** Do you want to be able to analyze images, charts, or data visualizations? If your work is highly visual, you will need a platform with strong "multimodal" capabilities.
- **How important is integration with my existing software?** Are you deeply embedded in a specific ecosystem, like Microsoft 365 or Google Workspace? An integrated AI might offer a more seamless workflow than a standalone tool.

Keep your answers to these questions in mind as we explore the major platforms.

Overview of Major AI Platforms

Here is a detailed look at four of the leading AI platforms as of late 2025.

1. OpenAI's ChatGPT (Powered by GPT Models)

Overall Summary:
ChatGPT is the tool that brought generative AI into the mainstream. It is an excellent all-rounder, known for its strong conversational abilities, creative text generation, and powerful reasoning skills. It is often considered the benchmark against which other models are measured. It is an ideal starting point for anyone new to AI and a powerful workhorse for a wide variety of professional tasks.
Key Strengths:

- **Strong Creativity and Writing:** ChatGPT excels at brainstorming, writing in different styles, and generating high-quality first drafts of everything from emails to articles.
- **Conversational Fluency:** Its ability to understand and

remember context within a single conversation makes it ideal for iterative prompting and refining ideas.

- **Robust Ecosystem:** With a massive user base, a marketplace for custom GPTs, and extensive third-party support, there is a wealth of community knowledge and resources available.

Potential Limitations:

- **Context Window:** While improving, the context window on the standard paid tier can be smaller than some competitors, making it less ideal for analyzing very long documents in a single prompt.
- **Fact-Checking:** Like all AIs, it can hallucinate, and its web-browsing feature, while powerful, still requires diligent verification of sources.

Pricing and Plans:

- **Free Tier:** Provides access to a very capable, though slightly older, model. It is an excellent way to learn the ropes and handle many basic tasks. It may have usage limits during peak times.
- **Plus/Pro Tier:** This subscription tier has a list price of approximately $20 per month (about ₹1600 INR). It provides access to the latest, most powerful models (like GPT-4 and beyond), faster response times, and advanced features like web browsing, data analysis, and image generation.

Platform-Specific Tips:

- **Use Custom Instructions:** In the settings, you can add "Custom Instructions" to tell ChatGPT about your role, company, and preferred response format. This acts as a pre-loaded "Context" for every new chat, saving you from having to type it out each time.

- **Explore the GPT Store:** The paid version offers access to custom-built GPTs that are pre-prompted for specific tasks, such as creating presentations or analyzing academic papers.

Ideal Use Cases:

- Drafting emails, reports, and articles.
- Brainstorming and creative ideation.
- Summarizing articles and meeting transcripts.
- Learning and explaining complex topics.
- Iterative problem-solving through conversation.

2. Google's Gemini

Overall Summary:
Gemini is Google's flagship AI model, designed from the ground up to be natively multimodal. Its biggest competitive advantage is its deep integration with Google's vast ecosystem of products, including Search, Workspace (Docs, Sheets, Gmail), and the Android operating system. It is a powerful tool for tasks that involve real-time information and a mix of text and visual data.
Key Strengths:

- **Natively Multimodal:** Gemini excels at understanding and analyzing images, charts, and even videos. You can upload a screenshot of a dashboard and ask for an analysis, a capability that is core to its design.
- **Real-Time Information:** With its direct connection to Google Search, it is one of the best tools for tasks that require the most up-to-date information from the web.
- **Workspace Integration:** For users of Google Docs, Sheets, and Gmail, the integrated version of Gemini can be a massive productivity booster, allowing you to generate text and formulas directly within the documents you are already

working in.

Potential Limitations:

- **Long-Form Writing:** While excellent at quick summaries and data-driven responses, some users find its long-form creative writing to be slightly less fluid than competitors like ChatGPT or Claude.
- **Privacy Considerations:** As with any Google product, users should be mindful of the data privacy implications, though Google provides clear settings to manage your activity.

Pricing and Plans:

- **Free Tier:** The standard version of Gemini is free and highly capable, offering many of the core features, including web access.
- **Gemini Advanced:** This subscription has a list price of approximately $20 per month (about ₹1600 INR). It provides access to Google's most advanced models, a larger context window, and deeper integration features within the Google Workspace ecosystem.

Platform-Specific Tips:

- **Use "Extensions":** In the settings, you can connect Gemini to your Google Maps, Flights, and Workspace. This allows you to ask prompts like, "Check my emails from this morning and summarize the key action items," a uniquely powerful integration.
- **Leverage Image Input:** Get in the habit of using screenshots. If you see a confusing chart in an article, screenshot it and ask Gemini to explain it to you in simple terms.

Ideal Use Cases:

- Researching topics with real-time web information.
- Analyzing charts, graphs, and other visual data.
- Summarizing web pages and online articles.
- Drafting content directly within Google Docs and Gmail.
- Managing your schedule and inbox through Workspace integrations.

3. Anthropic's Claude

Overall Summary:
Claude is an AI assistant developed by Anthropic, a company founded by former OpenAI researchers with a strong focus on AI safety and ethics. Its defining feature has consistently been its massive context window, making it the undisputed champion for tasks that involve processing and analyzing extremely large documents.

Key Strengths:

- **Massive Context Window:** Claude's ability to handle hundreds of thousands of words in a single prompt is its killer feature. You can upload entire books, lengthy technical manuals, or extensive financial reports and ask complex analytical questions about the full document.
- **Strong Analytical and Summarization Skills:** It is highly adept at reading dense material and extracting key themes, summarizing complex arguments, and answering specific questions based on the provided text.
- **Focus on Safety:** It is designed to be less likely to produce harmful or inappropriate content, making it a reliable choice for professional environments.

Potential Limitations:

- **Web Access:** Some versions of Claude have more limited or no direct web browsing capabilities compared to Gemini or

ChatGPT's paid tier, meaning it relies more heavily on the information you provide it.

- **Creative Generation:** While a very capable writer, it is often seen as more of an "analyst" than a "creative." For pure brainstorming or highly stylized writing, other models might be a better fit.

Pricing and Plans:

- **Free Tier:** A generous free tier is often available, though it may have daily message limits and use a slightly less powerful model than the paid version.
- **Pro Tier:** The subscription, which has a list price of around $20 per month (about ₹1600 INR), removes message limits, provides access to the most advanced models, and ensures priority access during peak times.

Platform-Specific Tips:

- **"Feed it the Document":** Whenever you have a question about a report, a proposal, or any long document, your default workflow should be to upload the entire file to Claude. Don't waste time summarizing it yourself.
- **Use it for Comparison:** You can upload multiple documents (e.g., two different legal contracts or three vendor proposals) and ask Claude to compare them, a task that is nearly impossible with smaller context window models.

Ideal Use Cases:

- Analyzing and summarizing long documents (reports, books, legal contracts).
- Answering detailed questions about a specific body of text.
- Comparing and contrasting multiple documents at once.
- Drafting technical documentation based on large source files.

- Editing and refining lengthy manuscripts.

4. Microsoft Copilot

Overall Summary:
Microsoft Copilot is less a single destination and more an AI layer that is being integrated across the entire Microsoft ecosystem. Its primary strength is its deep, contextual integration into the tools that millions of professionals use every day: Windows, Office (Word, Excel, PowerPoint), Teams, and Outlook.

Key Strengths:

- **Deep Integration:** Copilot's ability to work across your applications is its superpower. It can create a PowerPoint presentation from a Word document, summarize a Teams meeting you missed, or draft an email in Outlook based on your calendar and notes.
- **Enterprise Focus:** It is built with enterprise security and data privacy in mind, making it a trusted choice for organizations that handle sensitive information.
- **Contextual Awareness:** Because it is connected to your work data (your emails, your files, your meetings), it can provide highly personalized and contextually relevant assistance.

Potential Limitations:

- **Cost:** The full power of Copilot is unlocked through a Microsoft 365 Copilot subscription, which is a premium-priced add-on to a standard Microsoft 365 plan. The list price is approximately $30 per user per month (about ₹2500 INR).
- **Dependence on Microsoft Ecosystem:** To get the most value from Copilot, you need to be heavily invested in using Microsoft 365 for your daily work.

Pricing and Plans:

- **Standard Copilot (Free):** A free version is integrated into Windows and the Edge browser, offering capabilities similar to the free tiers of ChatGPT and Gemini, including web access.
- **Copilot for Microsoft 365:** This is the paid, enterprise-grade subscription that unlocks the powerful cross-app integration features.

Platform-Specific Tips:

- **Prompt with Document References:** Instead of pasting text, you can refer to documents by name. For example, in a blank Word document, you could prompt Copilot, "Write a summary of the '/Q3 Sales Report.docx' document."
- **Use it in Teams:** After a meeting, you can ask Copilot in the meeting chat, "What were the key action items from this meeting and who is assigned to them?"

Ideal Use Cases:

- Creating PowerPoint presentations from Word documents.
- Summarizing long email threads in Outlook.
- Generating formulas and analyzing data in Excel.
- Drafting documents in Word based on other files.
- Getting summaries and action items from Teams meetings.

Feature-by-Feature Comparison

Here is a quick-reference guide comparing the platforms across key features. (Note: "High," "Medium," and "Low" are relative and based on the state of the technology in late 2025).

Core Reasoning and Writing Quality

- **ChatGPT:** High (Excellent for creative and conversational writing).

- **Gemini:** High (Very strong at data-driven and factual responses).
- **Claude:** High (Excels at formal, analytical, and summary writing).
- **Copilot:** High (Leverages underlying OpenAI models, so quality is comparable to ChatGPT).

Context Window Size (Ability to handle large documents)

- **ChatGPT (Plus):** Medium to High.
- **Gemini (Advanced):** High.
- **Claude (Pro):** Very High (The market leader in this category).
- **Copilot:** High (Can reference documents on your OneDrive, effectively giving it a very large context).

Web Access / Real-Time Information

- **ChatGPT (Plus):** High.
- **Gemini:** Very High (Natively integrated with Google Search).
- **Claude:** Low to Medium (Varies by version, generally less of a focus).
- **Copilot:** High (Integrated with Bing search).

Multimodality (Image/Chart Analysis)

- **ChatGPT (Plus):** High.
- **Gemini:** Very High (A core design feature).
- **Claude:** Medium (Capabilities are being added).
- **Copilot:** High.

Integration with Other Software

- **ChatGPT:** Medium (Relies on APIs and third-party tools).
- **Gemini:** High (Excellent integration with Google Workspace).
- **Claude:** Low (Primarily a standalone tool).

- **Copilot:** Very High (Its defining feature is integration with Microsoft 365).

When to Use Which Tool: A Scenario-Based Guide

To bring it all together, here is a simple guide based on common professional tasks.

If your task is... "I need to analyze a 150-page PDF report and extract the key financial data."

- **Your Best Bet: Claude.** Its massive context window is purpose-built for this. You can upload the entire document and be confident the AI will see all of it.

If your task is... "I have a Word document with the script for my presentation. I need to turn it into a 10-slide PowerPoint deck, complete with speaker notes."

- **Your Best Bet: Microsoft Copilot.** Its ability to work across Office applications is unmatched. This is its most compelling use case.

If your task is... "I need to brainstorm 20 creative and unconventional names for a new software product."

- **Your Best Bet: ChatGPT.** Its strength in creative text generation and its conversational nature make it a fantastic brainstorming partner.

If your task is... "I'm watching a live news event and I need a real-time summary of the key developments and an analysis of a chart that was just shown on screen."

- **Your Best Bet: Gemini.** Its combination of real-time web access and strong image analysis makes it the perfect tool for this mix of needs.

If your task is... "I'm a freelance consultant and I need a powerful, free all-rounder to help with drafting client emails, summarizing articles, and creating project outlines."

- **Your Best Bet:** Start with the **free tiers of ChatGPT and Gemini.** Try the same prompt in both and see which output style you prefer. Both are excellent starting points.

Ultimately, you may find that you don't need to choose just one. Many professionals develop a small toolkit, reaching for Claude when they have a long document, Copilot when they are working in Office, and ChatGPT or Gemini for their day-to-day writing and research tasks.

Your journey of AI-powered productivity is a personal one. Use this guide to make an informed first choice, and then let your own experience be your guide. Experiment, explore, and find the AI partner that best fits your unique professional workflow.

Appendix C: Prompt Troubleshooting Guide

Even with the best frameworks and the most carefully crafted prompts, there will be times when your AI assistant does not give you the output you expected. The response might be generic, ignore a key instruction, or just feel "off." This is a normal and expected part of the process. It is not a sign of failure on your part or a sign that the AI is "broken." It is simply a signal that your instructions need to be clarified.

Think of this appendix as your prompt first-aid kit. It is a practical, quick-reference guide for diagnosing and fixing the most common issues you will encounter on your AI productivity journey. We designed this guide to help you get unstuck quickly, turn frustration into a learning opportunity, and get back to producing high-quality work. Every troubleshooting step you take is an act of learning that deepens your prompt intuition.

We will begin with a systematic breakdown of the most common problems, such as getting vague outputs or having your instructions ignored. For each issue, we will explain why it happens and provide a series of quick, actionable fixes you can apply immediately. Next, we will demystify some of the common error messages you might see, explaining what they mean in plain English and what you should do about them.

We will then touch on a few platform-specific quirks, offering simple tips for navigating the unique personalities of the major AI tools. We will close with a Frequently Asked Questions (FAQ) section that addresses some of the broader questions that often come up as you move from a beginner to an advanced AI user.

Keep this appendix handy. When a prompt does not work, do not get discouraged. Refer to this guide, identify the symptom, and apply the remedy. With this toolkit, you will be able to solve nearly any prompt-related problem you encounter.

Common Issues and Quick Fixes

This section is organized by symptom. Find the problem that best describes your situation and then try the recommended solutions.

Symptom 1: The Output is Too Generic or Vague

This is the most common problem of all. You ask for a marketing plan, and you get a textbook definition of what a marketing plan is. You ask for a project update email, and you get a bland template that could be about any project.

Why It Happens:
The AI has not been given enough specific information to work with. Faced with a vague prompt, it defaults to the most generic, statistically probable patterns from its training data. It is missing the Context and Constraints from our CTFC framework.
Quick Fixes:

- **Add a Persona.** The fastest way to add context is to tell the AI who to be. Start your prompt with "Act as a..."
    - **Before:** "Write an email about our new software."
    - **After:** "Act as a marketing manager for a software company. Write an email announcing our new productivity app..."
- **Define Your Audience.** The AI writes differently for different audiences. Be explicit.

    - **Before:** "Explain our new sales strategy."
    - **After:** "Explain our new sales strategy. The audience is our team of senior account executives who are already familiar with our current process."
- **State Your Goal.** Why are you asking for this output? What do you want to achieve with it?
    - **Before:** "Summarize this article."
    - **After:** "Summarize this article. The goal is to extract three actionable tips that our sales team can use to improve their cold calling technique."
- **Provide Key Details.** Give the AI the 3-5 specific names, numbers, or facts that must be included.
    - **Before:** "Create a project plan."
    - **After:** "Create a project plan for 'Project Phoenix.' The key milestones are the UI design completion on October 15th, beta testing on November 1st, and the final launch on December 1st."

Symptom 2: The AI Ignored One of My Instructions

You wrote a detailed prompt asking for a bulleted list of exactly five points, and the AI gave you a three-paragraph essay. Or you asked for a response under 100 words, and it gave you 500.

Why It Happens:
This usually happens for one of three reasons: your instructions were not clear enough, they were buried in the middle of a long paragraph, or you gave the AI conflicting commands.
Quick Fixes:

- **Use Delimiters and Formatting.** Make your instructions stand out. Use headings, bullet points, or numbered lists within your prompt to clearly separate your instructions from your source text.

    - **Before:** "Act as a recruiter and write a job description for a software engineer. It should have a section for responsibilities and a section for qualifications and the tone should be professional."
    - After:
      "Act as a recruiter.
      TASK: Write a job description for a software engineer.
      FORMAT:
      The output must have two sections with these exact headings:
      ## Key Responsibilities
      ## Qualifications
      CONSTRAINTS:
      The tone must be professional."
- **Put Key Instructions at the End.** Some AI models pay closer attention to the instructions given at the very end of the prompt. Try moving your most important command, like the formatting instruction, to the last line.
- **Simplify Your Language.** Your prompt is not an essay. Use clear, direct commands.
    - **Instead of:** "I was hoping you could structure the output as a table."
    - **Use:** "Format the output as a table."
- **Check for Contradictions.** Read through your prompt. Did you ask for a "brief summary" but also ask it to "include all the details"? Did you ask for a "formal tone" but also tell it to be "fun and engaging"? These conflicting constraints can confuse the AI.

Symptom 3: The Output is Factually Incorrect (A "Hallucination")

The AI confidently states a statistic, cites a non-existent study, or mentions a company that you cannot find on the web. As discussed in Chapter 23, these are called hallucinations.

Why It Happens:
The AI is a pattern-matching engine, not a fact database. When it does not have a high-confidence answer in its training data, it may "invent" a plausible-sounding detail to complete the pattern. This is one of the most significant risks of using AI without proper oversight.
Quick Fixes:

- **Ground the Prompt with Source Material.** The single best way to prevent hallucinations is to provide the facts yourself. Instead of asking the AI to find information, give it the information and ask it to perform a task.
    - **Risky Prompt:** "What are the key features of the new 'Innovate 3000' industrial printer?"
    - **Safer Prompt:** "I am providing you with the technical specification sheet for the new 'Innovate 3000' industrial printer. Based on this text, summarize the top five features that would be most important to a small manufacturing business. Here is the text: [Paste the spec sheet]"
- **Ask for Sources.** If you do need the AI to find information on the web, demand accountability.
    - **Add this constraint:** "For every factual claim or statistic you provide, you must include the URL of the source."
- **Lower the "Temperature" (If Available).** Some AI platforms have advanced settings where you can adjust a parameter called "temperature." A high temperature encourages more creative, diverse, and sometimes random outputs. A low temperature (closer to 0) makes the AI more focused,

deterministic, and less likely to stray from the most probable (and often more factual) information. If you have this option, turn it down for analytical or fact-based tasks.

- **Always Verify.** This is not a prompt fix, but a workflow fix. Never trust, always verify. Any statistic, date, or proper noun generated by an AI must be cross-referenced with a reliable external source before you use it in your work.

Symptom 4: The Tone is Wrong

You asked for a professional email, and it sounds too casual. You asked for an upbeat social media post, and it sounds like a dry press release.

Why It Happens:
"Tone" can be subjective. The AI's interpretation of a word like "professional" might be different from yours. It needs more specific guidance.

Quick Fixes:

- **Use a Spectrum of Words.** Instead of one word, use a few to triangulate the tone you want.
    - **Instead of:** "The tone should be professional."
    - **Try:** "The tone should be professional, but also warm, supportive, and encouraging."
- **Provide an Example (Few-Shot Prompting).** The most effective way to teach the AI a specific tone is to show it.
    - Prompt: "Analyze the tone of the following writing sample. It is confident, uses clear and direct language, and is focused on business outcomes.
      [Paste a short sample of writing in the desired tone]
      Now, using that exact same tone, rewrite the following paragraph:
      [Paste the paragraph you want rewritten]"

- **Use Negative Constraints.** Sometimes it's easier to tell the AI what to avoid.
    - **Constraint:** "The tone should be upbeat and exciting. Do not use corporate jargon or overly formal language. Avoid exclamation points."

Symptom 5: The AI Stops Generating Mid-Sentence or Gives an Incomplete Answer

You ask for a list of 10 ideas, and it stops after the seventh. Or it writes half a paragraph and then just stops.

Why It Happens:
This is usually due to the model hitting a built-in length limit for its output. It is not an error, but a technical constraint. It can also happen due to a temporary server or network issue.
Quick Fixes:

- **The "Continue" Command.** The simplest solution is often the best. In most chat-based interfaces, you can simply type "continue," "go on," or "keep going" as your next prompt, and the AI will usually pick up right where it left off.
- **Be More Specific in Your Request.** If you are asking for a long piece of text, break it down. Instead of "Write a 5,000-word report," which will almost certainly fail, use a multi-step approach.
    - **Prompt 1:** "Write the introduction for a report on..."
    - **Prompt 2:** "Now, write the 'Key Findings' section for that report."
- **Check the Platform's Limits.** Be aware of the output limits of the tool you are using. If you consistently need very long outputs, you may need a different platform or a paid plan that offers a higher limit.

Symptom 6: The Formatting is a Mess

You asked for a table, but you got a comma-separated list. You asked for a JSON object, but you got a bulleted list that looks like JSON.

Why It Happens:
Complex formatting requires extreme precision in your instructions. The AI may be getting confused by other parts of your prompt or may not fully understand the structure you want from a simple description.

Quick Fixes:

- **Provide a Perfect Example.** This is the number one fix for formatting issues. Show, do not just tell.
  - Prompt: "Please organize the following data into a Markdown table. The table must have exactly these three columns: 'Product ID,' 'Product Name,' and 'Inventory Count.' The output should look exactly like this example:
Product ID	Product Name	Inventory Count
123	Widget A	450
    Now, apply that format to the following data:
    [Paste your raw data]"
- **Specify the Formatting Language.** Be explicit. Use terms like "Format this as a Markdown table," "Provide the output in a JSON code block," or "Use HTML formatting for the lists."
- **Combine with an Iterative Approach.** If the format is still wrong, correct it in a follow-up prompt.
  - **Follow-up Prompt:** "That's a good start, but you used bullet points. Please reformat that exact same information as a numbered list."

Understanding Error Messages

Sometimes, the AI will not give you a bad output; it will give you an error message instead. Here is what some of the most common ones mean.

- **"I cannot fulfill this request." / "I'm unable to assist with that."**
  - **What it usually means:** You have likely run into the AI's safety filter. Your request might have inadvertently touched on a topic that the platform is designed to avoid, or it might have been misinterpreted as a request for harmful, unethical, or otherwise restricted content.
  - **What to do:** Do not try to argue with it. Rephrase your prompt. Identify any words that could be misinterpreted and find a more neutral way to ask. If you are asking to summarize an article, for example, make sure the article itself does not contain sensitive content.
- **"Network Error" / "Error in generating response."**
  - **What it usually means:** This is usually a technical issue on the provider's end. Their servers might be overloaded, or there was a temporary glitch in communication.
  - **What to do:** The simplest fix is to wait 30 seconds and try submitting the exact same prompt again. If the problem persists, try a shorter or simpler prompt to see if it works. If it does, your original prompt might be too long or complex for the server to handle at that moment.
- **Content Length Errors (e.g., "Prompt is too long")**
  - **What it usually means:** You have pasted more text into the prompt than the AI's context window can handle.
  - **What to do:** You need to shorten your input. If you are trying to summarize a long document, you will need to break it into smaller chunks and process them one at a

time. This is the primary reason for choosing a platform with a large context window, like Claude, for document analysis tasks.

Platform-Specific Quirks and Solutions

While the core principles are universal, each platform has its own "personality." Being aware of these can help you fine-tune your prompts.

- **ChatGPT:**
  - **Quirk:** Can sometimes be overly "chatty" or start its response with conversational filler ("Certainly, here is the email you requested...").
  - **Solution:** Add a constraint to be more direct. "Do not include any introductory or concluding conversational phrases. Provide only the requested output."
- **Gemini:**
  - **Quirk:** Because of its deep integration with Search, it can sometimes rely too heavily on web results, providing a list of links rather than synthesizing the information into a direct answer.
  - **Solution:** Be more explicit in your task. "Do not just provide links. Read the information from your search results and synthesize it into a three-paragraph summary."
- **Claude:**
  - **Quirk:** Its strong safety alignment can sometimes cause it to be overly cautious. It might refuse to answer a seemingly harmless prompt if it misinterprets a word as being related to a restricted topic.
  - **Solution:** Rephrase using the most neutral and professional language possible. If you ask it to "attack the

weaknesses" in a business plan, it might refuse. Rephrasing to "critically evaluate the weaknesses" will likely work.

- **Microsoft Copilot:**
    - **Quirk:** Its power comes from its connection to your Microsoft 365 files. If it cannot find a document you are referencing, or does not have the right permissions, it will fail.
    - **Solution:** Be precise with your file names and paths. Ensure that the files you are referencing are stored in your OneDrive or SharePoint and that Copilot has the necessary permissions to access them.

Prompt Troubleshooting FAQ Section

Q: Why did the same prompt give me a different answer today than it did yesterday?
A: This is due to the "stochastic" (random) nature of AI models. Unless the "temperature" is set to 0, there is always a degree of randomness in the word choices the AI makes. For creative tasks, this is a feature, not a bug. For analytical tasks, if you need the exact same output every time, you should create a highly constrained prompt with very specific formatting instructions and, if possible, lower the temperature setting.
Q: How do I get the AI to "remember" things from our conversations a week ago?
A: You can't, not directly. The AI's "memory" is limited to the current conversation thread (the context window). It does not remember past conversations. The solution is to create your own external memory. This is what your Prompt Hub and Task Automation Inventory are for. When you have a great prompt chain or a useful piece of information, save it in your notes. Then, you can provide that context again in a future conversation.

Q: What is the very first thing I should do when a prompt is not working?
A: Start over in a new chat and make your prompt more specific. Do not get stuck in a long, confusing conversation thread where you are trying to "correct" the AI. It is often faster and more effective to open a new chat (giving the AI a blank slate) and try a revised, more detailed prompt based on the CTFC framework.
Q: I feel like my prompts are getting too long and complicated. Is that a problem?
A: Not necessarily. A long prompt is not a problem if it is well-structured. A 500-word prompt that is clearly organized with headings, bullet points, and examples is far more effective than a 50-word prompt that is vague. The goal is clarity, not brevity. If your prompt is getting results, its length is fine.
Q: Is there a "perfect" prompt that works every time for a given task?
A: The "perfect" prompt is a moving target. As AI models evolve, the best way to prompt them will also change. A highly detailed prompt that is necessary today might be overkill in a year with a more advanced model. This is why the habit of continuous learning (Chapter 24) and periodic prompt refinement (Chapter 29) is so crucial. The goal is not to find a single perfect prompt, but to master the process of creating a great prompt for any situation.

Appendix D: Glossary of AI and Prompting Terms

Welcome to the language of AI. Like any specialized field, the world of artificial intelligence has its own vocabulary. The terms can sound technical, complex, and even intimidating at first. The purpose of this glossary is to demystify that language. You do not need a degree in computer science to be a highly effective AI user, but understanding these key terms will give you a deeper appreciation for how the technology works, why your prompts succeed or fail, and how to speak confidently about AI in a professional context.

Think of this glossary as your personal translator. We have defined each term in plain, simple English, avoiding technical jargon wherever possible. More importantly, for each entry, we have explained "Why It Matters for You" and provided a "Workplace Example," connecting these abstract concepts to the real-world productivity tasks you perform every day.

Our goal is not for you to memorize these definitions, but for you to use this appendix as a quick-reference guide whenever you encounter an unfamiliar term in an article, a podcast, or a conversation with a colleague. A clear understanding of these concepts will empower you to troubleshoot your prompts more effectively, choose the right tool for the right job, and continue your learning journey with confidence.

Algorithm

- **Plain-English Definition:** An algorithm is simply a set of step-by-step instructions or rules that a computer follows to complete a task or solve a problem. Think of it as a recipe for a computer.

- **Why It Matters for You:** AI models are powered by extremely complex algorithms. While you do not need to know how they are written, understanding that AI operates on rules helps you appreciate why your own instructions (your prompts) need to be so clear, logical, and step-by-step.
- **Workplace Example:** When you write a prompt with a Chain-of-Thought process, you are essentially creating a mini-algorithm for the AI to follow to arrive at the correct answer for your analysis.

API (Application Programming Interface)

- **Plain-English Definition:** An API is a way for different software applications to talk to each other. It is like a waiter in a restaurant. You (one application) give your order to the waiter (the API), who then takes it to the kitchen (the other application), and brings the food (the data or result) back to you.
- **Why It Matters for You:** APIs are what allow your favorite productivity tools (like Notion, Slack, or your company's internal software) to integrate with powerful AI models. This is the technology that enables AI to work "inside" the apps you already use.
- **Workplace Example:** A company uses an API to connect its customer service software to an AI model. When a new customer support ticket arrives, the software uses the API to send the ticket to the AI, which then drafts a suggested reply and sends it back to the software for the human agent to review.

Artificial Intelligence (AI)

- **Plain-English Definition:** AI is a broad field of computer science focused on creating machines that can perform tasks that typically require human intelligence, such as learning, reasoning, problem-solving, and understanding language.
- **Why It Matters for You:** The generative AI language models we focus on in this book are just one type of AI. Understanding this helps you see the bigger picture. The skills you are learning are your entry point into a much larger technological transformation.
- **Workplace Example:** The AI model that helps you draft an email is one form of AI. The software that predicts your company's quarterly sales based on historical data is another.

Augmented Intelligence

- **Plain-English Definition:** This term is often used as an alternative to "Artificial Intelligence." It emphasizes the role of AI as a tool to assist and enhance human capabilities, not to replace them. The focus is on human-AI collaboration.
- **Why It Matters for You:** This is the core philosophy of this entire book. We are not training you to be replaced by AI; we are training you to become an "augmented professional" who uses AI as a partner to achieve more than you could alone.
- **Workplace Example:** Instead of spending three hours writing a report from scratch, you use an AI to generate a first draft in ten minutes. You then spend the next hour using your human expertise to refine, fact-check, and add strategic insights. Your intelligence has been augmented.

Bias (in AI)

- **Plain-English Definition:** AI bias occurs when an AI model produces outputs that are systematically prejudiced due to flawed assumptions in the machine learning process. This is most often caused by the training data reflecting existing human biases.

- **Why It Matters for You:** You must be aware that AI-generated content can reflect biases present in its training data. When using AI for tasks like writing job descriptions or performance reviews, it is your responsibility as the human reviewer to identify and remove any potentially biased language.
- **Workplace Example:** You ask an AI to write a job description for a "lead software architect." The AI, having been trained on decades of existing text from the internet, might produce a description that uses predominantly masculine-coded language. Your job is to edit it to be inclusive and neutral.

Chain-of-Thought (CoT) Prompting

- **Plain-English Definition:** A prompting technique where you instruct the AI to "think step-by-step" or break down its reasoning process before giving a final answer.
- **Why It Matters for You:** This is a powerful strategy for improving the accuracy and reliability of AI outputs for complex analytical or problem-solving tasks. It forces the AI to follow a logical path, making it less likely to jump to an incorrect conclusion.
- **Workplace Example:** Instead of just asking, "Is this a good marketing strategy?", you would prompt, "Critically evaluate this marketing strategy. First, analyze its strengths. Second, analyze its weaknesses. Third, based on that analysis, give a final recommendation."

Constraint

- **Plain-English Definition:** A rule, boundary, or limitation that you include in your prompt to guide the AI's output.
- **Why It Matters for You:** Constraints are one of the four core elements of the CTFC framework. They are essential for controlling the tone, length, style, and content of the AI's response, ensuring it meets your specific requirements.
- **Workplace Example:** In the prompt, "Write an email to the client," the phrase "Keep it under 150 words and do not mention pricing" is a constraint.

Context

- **Plain-English Definition:** The background information, setting, and purpose that you provide in a prompt.
- **Why It Matters for You:** Context is the most critical element for getting a relevant, non-generic response from an AI. Since the AI knows nothing about your specific situation, you must provide the "who, what, where, when, and why."
- **Workplace Example:** In the prompt, "Act as a project manager for a software company that is two weeks behind schedule on Project Phoenix...," all of that background information is the context.

Context Window

- **Plain-English Definition:** The amount of information, measured in tokens (or roughly, words), that an AI model can "remember" at any given time within a single conversation. Once information scrolls past the context window, the AI effectively "forgets" it.
- **Why It Matters for You:** This is arguably the most important technical specification to be aware of when choosing an AI tool. A platform with a large context window (like Claude) is ideal for analyzing long documents, while a smaller context

window is fine for shorter, task-based prompts.

- **Workplace Example:** You try to paste a 100-page report into an AI with a small context window, but it gives you an error or only summarizes the last few pages. This is because the beginning of the report exceeded the model's "memory."

CTFC Framework

- **Plain-English Definition:** The core prompting framework taught in this book, standing for Context, Task, Format, and Constraints. It is a simple checklist to ensure every prompt you write is clear, specific, and effective.
- **Why It Matters for You:** This is your fundamental blueprint for success in prompting. By mentally checking for all four elements before you send a prompt, you will dramatically increase the quality of your results.
- **Workplace Example:** Before asking an AI to write a meeting agenda, you check the CTFC elements: You have provided the meeting's purpose (Context), asked it to create an agenda (Task), specified a timed, bulleted list (Format), and stated it must be for a 60-minute meeting (Constraint).

Delimiter

- **Plain-English Definition:** A character or set of characters used to clearly separate different parts of your prompt. Common delimiters include triple backticks (```), triple quotes ("""), or XML tags (<example></example>).
- **Why It Matters for You:** Using delimiters is an advanced technique that makes your prompts easier for the AI to understand, especially when you are providing a block of source text that you want it to work with. It creates a clear boundary between your instructions and the data.
- **Workplace Example:** "Please summarize the following

article, which I have placed inside triple backticks. ```[Paste article text here]```"

Few-Shot Learning

- **Plain-English Definition:** A prompting technique where you provide the AI with a few examples ("shots") of the kind of output you want. This helps the AI understand the desired format, tone, and structure.
- **Why It Matters for You:** This is the most effective way to get the AI to produce outputs in a very specific or unusual format. It is a powerful way to "teach" the AI your exact requirements.
- **Workplace Example:** To get the AI to write product descriptions in your company's unique style, you would provide two or three examples of existing product descriptions before asking it to write a new one.

Format (in prompting)

- **Plain-English Definition:** The part of your prompt that specifies the structure and layout of the desired output.
- **Why It Matters for You:** This is a huge time-saver. By telling the AI exactly how to format the response (as a table, a list, an email, etc.), you get a result that is immediately ready to use, with no manual reformatting required.
- **Workplace Example:** In the prompt, "Organize these ideas into a three-column Markdown table," the instruction for a "three-column Markdown table" is the format.

Foundation Model

- **Plain-English Definition:** A very large, powerful AI model (like the ones that power ChatGPT, Gemini, or Claude) that has been trained on a massive amount of general data. It is called a "foundation" because it can be adapted or fine-tuned for many different, more specific tasks.

- **Why It Matters for You:** The tools you use are all based on these foundation models. Understanding this helps you realize that while the "brand name" of the tool may differ, the underlying technology is often similar.
- **Workplace Example:** A hospital might take a general foundation model and fine-tune it on its own internal medical documentation to create a specialized AI assistant for its doctors.

Generative AI

- **Plain-English Definition:** A category of artificial intelligence that can generate new, original content, including text, images, code, and more. It is different from older forms of AI that could only analyze or categorize existing data.
- **Why It Matters for You:** This is the technology that makes everything in this book possible. The tools you are using are all forms of generative AI.
- **Workplace Example:** When you use an AI to write a new email, you are using generative AI. When you use it to create a new project plan, you are using generative AI.

GPT (Generative Pre-trained Transformer)

- **Plain-English Definition:** The acronym for the type of neural network architecture that powers ChatGPT and many other leading AI models. "Generative" means it creates new content, "Pre-trained" means it has already been trained on a vast amount of data, and "Transformer" is the name of the specific technical architecture.
- **Why It Matters for You:** While you do not need to know the technical details, seeing "GPT" in the name of a model (like GPT-4) is a signal that it is a powerful, modern language

model.

- **Workplace Example:** When you use the paid version of ChatGPT, you are likely interacting with a model called "GPT-4" or an even newer version.

Grounding

- **Plain-English Definition:** The process of connecting an AI model's response to a specific, verifiable source of information, such as a document you provide or a live web page.
- **Why It Matters for You:** Grounding is the single most effective technique for preventing factual errors and hallucinations. By forcing the AI to base its answers on a source of truth, you dramatically increase the reliability of its output.
- **Workplace Example:** Pasting a company's internal policy document into a prompt and asking the AI, "Based only on the text I have provided, what is our policy on travel expenses?" is an act of grounding.

Hallucination

- **Plain-English Definition:** An AI hallucination is when a model generates information that is factually incorrect, nonsensical, or completely fabricated, but presents it with confidence as if it were a real fact.
- **Why It Matters for You:** This is the single most important risk to be aware of when using AI for any fact-based work. Recognizing the potential for hallucinations is the reason why the "Trust but Verify" principle is non-negotiable. Your professional credibility depends on your ability to catch these errors before they make it into your final work.
- **Workplace Example:** You ask an AI to summarize a report

and it includes a statistic: "According to a 2023 study by the Global Commerce Institute, 78% of businesses saw an increase in efficiency." You later discover that the "Global Commerce Institute" does not exist. The AI has hallucinated the source to make its answer sound more authoritative.

Iterative Prompting

- **Plain-English Definition:** The process of refining your AI output through a conversation. Instead of trying to get the perfect result with one prompt, you use a series of follow-up prompts to tweak, correct, and improve the initial draft.
- **Why It Matters for You:** This is the most natural and effective way to work with an AI. It turns the interaction from a simple command into a collaborative dialogue, allowing you to shape the final output with much greater precision.
- **Workplace Example:** After the AI generates a first draft of an email, you follow up with, "That's good, but make the tone more formal," and then, "Okay, now add a sentence about the new deadline."

Large Language Model (LLM)

- **Plain-English Definition:** The technical term for the type of AI at the heart of tools like ChatGPT, Gemini, and Claude. It is a very large, deep learning model that has been trained on a massive corpus of text and can generate human-like language.
- **Why It Matters for You:** This is the engine that drives your productivity tools. When you hear this term, just think "the AI brain that understands and writes text."
- **Workplace Example:** The entire system you are interacting with when you type a prompt into a chat window is powered by an LLM.

Machine Learning (ML)

- **Plain-English Definition:** A subfield of Artificial Intelligence where computers learn to find patterns and make predictions from data without being explicitly programmed for that specific task. The "learning" happens when the machine adjusts its own internal algorithm based on the data it processes.
- **Why It Matters for You:** LLMs are a type of machine learning. Understanding this concept helps you remember that the AI is not "intelligent" in a human way, but is a highly sophisticated pattern-finding machine.
- **Workplace Example:** You provide an AI with 1,000 positive customer reviews and 1,000 negative customer reviews. The machine learns the patterns in the language and can then predict whether a new, unseen review is positive or negative.

Meta-Prompting

- **Plain-English Definition:** The technique of asking an AI to act as a prompt engineering expert and help you improve your own prompts.
- **Why It Matters for You:** This is a powerful learning and refinement tool. When you are stuck or your prompt is not working, you can ask the AI itself to diagnose the problem and suggest a better version of your prompt.
- **Workplace Example:** "Act as a prompt engineering expert. Here is a prompt I wrote. The output was too generic. How could I improve this prompt to get a more specific result? [Paste your prompt]"

Model

- **Plain-English Definition:** In AI, a "model" is the specific digital brain that has been created through a machine learning training process. Different companies create different models (e.g., OpenAI's GPT-4, Google's Gemini, Anthropic's Claude 3).

- **Why It Matters for You:** Different models have different strengths. A newer, more advanced model will generally be more capable than an older one. Knowing which model powers your tool helps you understand its capabilities.
- **Workplace Example:** The free version of an AI tool might use an older, less powerful model, while the paid subscription gives you access to the company's latest and greatest model.

Multimodality / Multimodal AI

- **Plain-English Definition:** The ability of an AI model to understand, process, and generate information across different types of media, not just text. This includes images, audio, and video.
- **Why It Matters for You:** This is the next frontier of AI productivity. It opens up a huge range of new use cases, allowing you to "prompt" the AI with more than just words.
- **Workplace Example:** You upload a screenshot of a complex financial chart and prompt the AI, "Explain the main trend shown in this chart as if I were a new intern."

Natural Language Processing (NLP)

- **Plain-English Definition:** A field of AI that focuses on enabling computers to understand, interpret, and generate human language.
- **Why It Matters for You:** NLP is the foundational technology that allows you to communicate with an AI in plain English, rather than needing to write code. Everything you do with an LLM is a form of NLP.

- **Workplace Example:** When you speak a command to your phone's digital assistant, NLP is what allows the device to understand your words and execute the task.

Negative Prompting

- **Plain-English Definition:** A technique where you tell the AI what you *do not* want to see in the output.
- **Why It Matters for You:** This can be a very effective way to constrain the AI and avoid common pitfalls. It is often easier to specify what to exclude than to list everything to include.
- **Workplace Example:** "Write a project update. Do not use corporate jargon. Avoid overly optimistic language."

Parameters

- **Plain-English Definition:** In an AI model, parameters are the internal variables or "knobs" that the model learns and adjusts during its training. The number of parameters (measured in billions or trillions) is a rough indicator of a model's complexity and power.
- **Why It Matters for You:** You do not need to understand the math, but when you hear that a new model has more parameters than the last one, you can generally assume it will be more capable at handling complex reasoning and nuance.
- **Workplace Example:** A model with 1 trillion parameters is generally expected to produce a more coherent and well-written report than a much older model with only 100 billion parameters.

Persona (in prompting)

- **Plain-English Definition:** Assigning a specific role, job title, or character to the AI at the beginning of your prompt.

- **Why It Matters for You:** This is one of the easiest and most powerful ways to add Context to your prompt. It instantly focuses the AI's response, drawing on the vast patterns of language associated with that role from its training data.
- **Workplace Example:** Starting your prompt with "Act as a skeptical financial auditor..." will produce a much more critical and detailed analysis than starting with "Act as a supportive business coach..."

Prompt

- **Plain-English Definition:** The instruction, question, or input that you provide to a generative AI model to get it to perform a task.
- **Why It Matters for You:** The prompt is the steering wheel for the AI. The quality of your input directly determines the quality of your output. This entire book is about mastering the art and science of the prompt.
- **Workplace Example:** The entire block of text you type into an AI chat window before hitting "Enter" is your prompt.

Prompt Chaining / Prompt Sequence

- **Plain-English Definition:** An advanced technique where you connect a series of prompts together, using the output of the first prompt as the input for the second, and so on. This allows you to automate a complex, multi-step workflow.
- **Why It Matters for You:** This skill moves you from automating single tasks to automating entire processes. It is a hallmark of an advanced AI user and a massive productivity multiplier.
- **Workplace Example:** A three-step chain: 1) A prompt that summarizes a long report. 2) A prompt that takes the summary and rewrites it as a client-facing email. 3) A prompt

that takes the email and creates a list of follow-up questions.

Prompt Engineering

- **Plain-English Definition:** The practice of designing, refining, and optimizing prompts to get the most accurate, efficient, and useful results from AI models.
- **Why It Matters for You:** This is the formal name for the skill you are learning throughout this book. It is a blend of clear communication, logical thinking, and creative problem-solving.
- **Workplace Example:** When you spend time refining a prompt, adding a better persona, clarifying the format, and testing different constraints, you are practicing prompt engineering.

Task (in prompting)

- **Plain-English Definition:** The part of your prompt that contains the specific, actionable command you want the AI to perform.
- **Why It Matters for You:** A clear task is essential for getting a useful result. Vague tasks lead to vague outputs. Your task instruction should always start with a strong action verb.
- **Workplace Example:** In the prompt, "Act as a project manager and create a project plan," the phrase "create a project plan" is the task.

Temperature

- **Plain-English Definition:** A setting in some AI models that controls the randomness of the output. A high temperature (e.g., 0.9) produces more creative, diverse, and unpredictable results. A low temperature (e.g., 0.1) produces more focused, predictable, and deterministic results.

- **Why It Matters for You:** If your AI tool gives you access to this setting, it is a powerful way to control the output style. Use a high temperature for brainstorming and a low temperature for fact-based or analytical tasks where you want reliability.
- **Workplace Example:** You would use a high temperature when asking for creative product names, but a low temperature when asking the AI to extract specific data from a report.

Token

- **Plain-English Definition:** The basic unit of text that an AI model processes. A token can be a single word, part of a word, or a punctuation mark. A rough rule of thumb is that 100 tokens is about 75 words.
- **Why It Matters for You:** Context windows, model pricing, and other technical limits are all measured in tokens. Understanding this concept helps you appreciate the technical constraints the AI is working under.
- **Workplace Example:** If a model has a 100,000-token context window, it means it can process a document that is roughly 75,000 words long.

Training Data

- **Plain-English Definition:** The massive dataset of text, images, and other information that an AI model is "fed" during its development. The model learns by identifying and internalizing the patterns within this data.
- **Why It Matters for You:** The quality and diversity of the training data determine the model's capabilities and its inherent biases. An AI cannot know something that was not present in some form in its training data.

- **Workplace Example:** The reason an AI can write a professional-sounding email is that its training data included billions of examples of emails from the public internet and other sources.

Zero-Shot Learning

- **Plain-English Definition:** A situation where you ask an AI to perform a task without giving it any prior examples of how to do it.
- **Why It Matters for You:** This is how you will write most of your prompts. Modern AI is so powerful that it can often perform a task correctly on the first try (the "zero-th shot") if your instructions are clear enough.
- **Workplace Example:** Simply prompting, "Summarize this article in three bullet points," is a zero-shot prompt. You have not provided any examples of a summary; you are relying on the AI's pre-trained ability to do so.

Appendix E: Additional Resources

Your journey with this book is a significant and powerful step toward mastering AI for professional productivity. You have built a solid foundation, developed a robust skill set, and created a personal action plan for continuous growth. But the learning does not stop here. The world of artificial intelligence is dynamic and ever-evolving, and staying engaged is the key to long-term success.

This appendix is your curated library, a collection of pathways to continue your education and deepen your expertise. The resources listed here are designed to complement the knowledge you have gained from this book, providing you with ongoing insights, new techniques, and a connection to a broader community of fellow professionals who are also on this journey.

We have organized this guide into four key areas. First, we will explore the best online communities and learning platforms where you can ask questions, see real-world examples, and take your skills to the next level with more formal training. Second, we will recommend several (fictional) foundational books that explore different facets of the AI revolution, from strategic implementation to the ethical considerations that all modern professionals must understand.

Third, we will share a list of curated newsletters and podcasts. These are invaluable tools for the busy professional, designed to distill the most important AI news and insights into a format you can consume during your commute or coffee break. Finally, we will introduce the concept of "practice platforms" and "sandboxes," online spaces designed specifically for honing your prompting skills through challenges and experimentation.

This appendix is your map to the wider world of AI knowledge. Use it to build your personal learning network, stay on the cutting edge of this technology, and ensure that your skills as an AI-augmented professional continue to grow and evolve for years to come.

Recommended Websites, Communities, and Courses

Active learning is a powerful accelerator. Engaging with communities and structured courses can provide insights that are difficult to gain on your own. Here is a guide to the types of online resources that offer the most value.

Online Communities: Your Collaborative Learning Space

AI communities are virtual water coolers where practitioners of all levels share successes, troubleshoot failures, and showcase innovative new prompts. They are one of the best ways to see how the techniques from this book are being applied in the real world.

- **Platform-Specific Subreddits:**
    - **What they are:** On the website Reddit, there are dedicated forums (called subreddits) for nearly every major AI platform. These are highly active communities where users share their most creative prompts, ask for help troubleshooting, and discuss new features.
    - **Why they are valuable:** This is where you can see raw,

unfiltered examples from a massive user base. It is an incredible source of inspiration for new use cases and a great place to get a quick answer to a specific technical question.
    - **How to find them:** Search Reddit for the name of the AI tool you use most frequently (e.g., "ChatGPT," "Claude," etc.). Look for the largest and most active communities.
- **Professional Networking Groups:**
    - **What they are:** On platforms like LinkedIn, there are professional groups dedicated to "AI in Business," "Prompt Engineering for Professionals," or "The Future of Work."
    - **Why they are valuable:** These groups tend to be more focused on business applications and strategic discussions than the more technical subreddits. They are excellent for networking with other professionals in your industry who are also integrating AI into their workflows.
    - **How to find them:** Use the search function on LinkedIn to look for groups related to your industry plus "AI" (e.g., "AI in Marketing," "AI for Financial Analysts").
- **The "AI for Good" Community:**
    - **What it is:** The "AI for Good" community is a global, multi-stakeholder movement that is dedicated to identifying and promoting the use of AI to address the world's greatest social, humanitarian, and environmental challenges.
    - **Why it is valuable:** The community holds a series of webinars, talks, and project-based activities all year round. It is a fantastic opportunity to see how AI is being used in a broader context and to connect with experts in the field.
    - **How to find it:** "AI for Good" is a United Nations-led

initiative that is easy to find online.

Online Courses: For Structured, Deep-Dive Learning

While communities are great for informal learning, sometimes you need a more structured approach. Online courses can provide a curated path to mastering a specific aspect of AI.

- **Prompt Engineering Deep Dives:**
    - **What they are:** These are courses, often a few hours long, that focus exclusively on the art and science of prompt engineering. They build upon the foundations in this book, often with video tutorials and hands-on exercises.
    - **What to look for:** A good course will go beyond basic prompting and cover advanced techniques like prompt chaining, context management, and strategies for different AI models. Look for courses created by reputable instructors with strong reviews.
- **AI for Your Profession Courses:**
    - **What they are:** As AI becomes more integrated into every industry, specialized courses are emerging for different professions (e.g., "AI for Marketers," "AI for HR Professionals," "AI for Data Analysts").
    - **Why they are valuable:** These courses provide highly relevant, domain-specific examples and use cases that you can immediately apply to your job.
    - **What to look for:** Search major online learning platforms for your job title plus "AI." A high-quality course will not just show you prompts; it will show you how to build entire workflows that solve problems specific to your role.
- **"No-Code" AI and Automation Courses:**
    - **What they are:** These courses focus on using tools like

Zapier or Make to connect different applications and automate processes, often with an AI component.
  - **Why they are valuable:** This is the next step after mastering prompting. It teaches you how to build systems where the AI can be triggered automatically, moving you from manual prompting to true automation.

Books for Further Reading

This book is your practical guide to implementation. The following (fictional) books are recommended to provide broader context, strategic insight, and a deeper understanding of the world you are stepping into.

- **"The Augmented Professional: Thriving in the Age of AI" by Dr. Evelyn Reed**
  - **What it is:** A strategic look at the future of work. Dr. Reed's book is not a technical manual but a career guide. It explores which human skills will become more valuable in a world where AI handles the routine work.
  - **Why you should read it:** It provides a powerful mental model for your career development, helping you to focus on developing the uniquely human skills of strategic thinking, creative problem-solving, and emotional intelligence that AI cannot replicate. It is the perfect complement to the practical skills you have learned here.
- **"The Alignment Problem: Building Ethical AI That Works for Us" by Jonathan Chen**
  - **What it is:** An accessible, non-technical exploration of the ethical challenges in AI, including bias, transparency, and accountability.
  - **Why you should read it:** As an AI-augmented professional, you are also an ethical actor. This book will

give you a robust framework for thinking through the ethical implications of how you and your company use AI. It is essential reading for any aspiring leader in this new landscape.

- **"System Overload: Designing Intelligent Workflows in the Digital Age" by Maria Flores**
  - **What it is:** A practical guide to workflow design and business process optimization, with a heavy focus on automation.
  - **Why you should read it:** This book picks up where our chapters on workflow design leave off. It provides advanced frameworks for analyzing your team's and your company's processes and identifying opportunities for large-scale automation, moving you from personal productivity to organizational transformation.

Newsletters and Podcasts About AI

Staying current does not have to be a chore. By subscribing to a few high-quality newsletters and podcasts, you can have the most important news and insights delivered to you in an easily digestible format. Here are some archetypes of resources to look for.

Newsletters: Your Daily or Weekly Briefing

- **"The AI Edge" (Fictional Newsletter)**
  - **What it is:** A daily newsletter that curates the top 3-5 most important AI news stories of the day. Each story is summarized in a single paragraph, with links to the original source.
  - **Why it is valuable:** It cuts through the noise. In five minutes, you can get a high-level overview of the entire

AI landscape, ensuring you never miss a major development.

- **"Prompt of the Week" (Fictional Newsletter)**
    - **What it is:** A weekly newsletter that features a single, powerful, and practical prompt for a common business task. It breaks down why the prompt works and how to adapt it for your own use.
    - **Why it is valuable:** This is a fantastic source of continuous inspiration and learning, providing you with a steady stream of new techniques and ideas to add to your prompt library.
- **"The Synthesist" (Fictional Newsletter)**
    - **What it is:** A weekly, long-form essay that explores a single AI-related topic from a strategic business perspective.
    - **Why it is valuable:** While daily newsletters keep you updated, this type of resource helps you understand the deeper implications of the technology. It is for those who want to move from being an AI user to an AI strategist.

Podcasts: Learning on the Go

- **"Productivity Prompted" (Fictional Podcast)**
    - **What it is:** A weekly 30-minute podcast that interviews professionals from different industries about how they are using AI in their daily work.
    - **Why it is valuable:** It is a treasure trove of real-world case studies. Hearing how a marketing manager at another company automated their reporting or how a consultant streamlined their research process can spark ideas for your own workflows.
- **"The AI Breakdown" (Fictional Podcast)**
    - **What it is:** A daily 15-minute podcast that explains a

single piece of AI news in simple, easy-to-understand terms.

    - **Why it is valuable:** It is perfect for your commute. It is a highly efficient way to stay on top of the news and understand the context behind the headlines.

- **"In Conversation with AI" (Fictional Podcast)**
    - **What it is:** A long-form interview podcast where the host talks to the researchers, engineers, and CEOs who are building the next generation of AI tools.
    - **Why it is valuable:** This gives you a look "behind the curtain." It helps you understand the trajectory of the technology, allowing you to anticipate what capabilities might be coming in the next one to two years.

Practice Platforms and Sandboxes

Reading and listening are important, but prompting is a hands-on skill. Just as a writer hones words through repetition, a prompt engineer hones their skill through practice. These platforms provide a space for focused practice and experimentation.

- **Prompting Challenge Websites:**
    - **What they are:** Websites that present you with a daily or weekly "prompting challenge." They give you a specific goal (e.g., "Write a one-paragraph email to a dissatisfied client that turns their negative experience into a positive one") and a set of constraints. Users submit their prompts, and the community votes on the most effective ones.
    - **Why they are valuable:** They force you to think creatively and critically about your prompt construction. Seeing how ten other people approached the same problem is an incredibly fast way to learn new techniques.

- **AI Sandboxes:**
  - **What they are:** Some platforms offer a "sandbox" or "playground" environment, which is a more technical interface where you can experiment with advanced settings like "temperature" and other parameters that are not always available in the standard chat interface.
  - **Why they are valuable:** For those who want to go deeper, this is where you can develop a more intuitive feel for how the AI model behaves under different conditions. It is the equivalent of a chef getting to experiment in a test kitchen.
- **Your Personal "Sandbox Time":**
  - **What it is:** The most accessible practice platform is the one you create for yourself. As we discussed in Chapter 24, dedicating just 30 minutes a week to "structured play" with AI is a powerful habit.
  - **How to do it:** Each week, pick one new technique from this book or a resource you have discovered. It could be trying a meta-prompt, experimenting with a new persona, or attempting a three-step prompt chain. The goal is not to complete a work task, but simply to experiment and learn. This low-pressure practice is where true mastery is forged.

Your education in AI is a marathon, not a sprint. This book has given you a powerful start, and the resources in this appendix are your companions for the journey ahead. By staying curious, engaging with the community, and making learning a consistent habit, you will not only keep your skills sharp; you will position yourself as a leader in the AI-powered workplace of the future.

www.ingramcontent.com/pod-product-compliance
Ingram Content Group UK Ltd.
Pitfield, Milton Keynes, MK11 3LW, UK
UKHW021403190726
13845UKWH00028B/856

9 788199 415164